CALAMITY JANE AND SAM BASS
YVONNE De CARLO
HOWARD DUFF
COLOR BY TECHNICOLOR
Ann BLYTH
Howard DUFF
George BRENT
Zane Grey's RED CANYON
COLOR BY TECHNICOLOR
EDGAR BUCHANAN
THE GREATEST STORY EVER TOLD
ZANE GREY'S
The Lion and the Horse
FIGHTING STALLION vs WESTERN KILLERS...
Savage to those he did not trust... the untamed stallion of the purple canyon feared no one!
STALLION CANYON
STAGECOACH TO FURY
TUCKER BLANCHARD FORD
WILLIAM FOX PRESENTS
Tom Mix AND TONY THE WONDER HORSE
"THE ORPHAN"
THE DEADWOOD COACH
A LYNN REYNOLDS PRODUCTION
WAYNE
FONDA
TEMPLE
FORT APACHE
TROOPER HOOK
McCREA
STANWYCK
THE GIRL IN BLACK STOCKINGS
ROBERT REDFORD
"JEREMIAH JOHNSON"
"THE ELECTRIC HORSEMAN"
The BATTLE AT APACHE PASS
John LUND
Jeff CHANDLER
Susan CABOT
SIERRA
color by Technicolor
A UNIVERSAL INTERNATIONAL Picture
JOHN WAYNE
JOANNE DRU
JOHN AGAR
BEN JOHNSON
HARRY CAREY, JR.
"SHE WORE A YELLOW RIBBON"
JOHN FORD
AL LANE PICTURES, INC. presents
LURE of the WASTELAND
The BIG CAT
COLOR BY TECHNICOLOR
GARY COOPER · RITA HAYWORTH
VAN HEFLIN · TAB HUNTER
THEY CAME TO CORDURA
BRIGHAM YOUNG

A Thousand Miles Of Roaring EXCITEMENT!
SOUTHWEST PASSAGE
CAMERON DRU IRELAND
GARY COOPER RITA HAYWORTH
VAN HEFLIN TAB HUNTER
THEY CAME TO CORDURA
STAGECOACH
IN TELCO COLOR
LURE OF THE WASTELAND
Grant WITHERS Leroy MASON Marion ARNOLD
SNUB POLLARD · KARL HACKETT
JOHN WAYNE in "THE SEARCHERS"
JEFFREY HUNTER · VERA MILES · WARD BOND · NATALIE WOOD
VISTAVISION
GREEN GRASS OF WYOMING
JAMES GARNER SIDNEY POITIER
DUEL AT DIABLO
TONY MARTIN
FRONTIER SCOUT
THE DALTON GIRLS
JOEL McCREA
VERONICA LAKE
DONALD CRISP
DON DeFORE
"RAMROD"
PRESTON FOSTER
ARLEEN WHELAN
CHARLIE RUGGLES
TOMAHAWK TRAIL
THE NIGHT OF THE GRIZZLY
CLINT WALKER
FRANK SINATRA DEAN MARTIN
PETER LAWFORD SAMMY DAVIS JR. JOEY BISHOP
SERGEANTS 3
CLINT "CHEYENNE" WALKER
FORT DOBBS
CANYON CROSSROADS
RICHARD BASEHART · PHYLLIS KIRK
M-G-M Presents
ROBERT TAYLOR
AVA GARDNER
HOW
KE
RIDE, VAQUERO!
Print by TECHNICOLOR
Photographed in ANSCO COLOR
ANTHONY QUINN · KURT KASZNAR
Tim HOLT
in
WAGON TRAIN
with
RAY WHITLEY
EMMETT LYNN
MARTHA O'DRISCOLL
TEX RITTER
"ROLL WAGONS ROLL"
A MONOGRAM PICTURE
VAN JOHNSON · JOANNE DRU
THE SIEGE AT RED RIVER
TECHNICOLOR
RICHARD BOONE
LEONARD GOLDSTEIN
RUDOLPH MATE
SYDNEY BOEHM
ZANE GREY'S first ALL TALKIN
GEORGE O'BRIEN
SUE CAROL
WARREN HYMER
ELIZABETH PATTERSON
Photographed in RAINBOW ARCH UTAH
Directed by A. F. ERICKSON
THE LONE STAR RANC

WHEN HOLLYWOOD CAME TO UTAH

CENTENNIAL EDITION

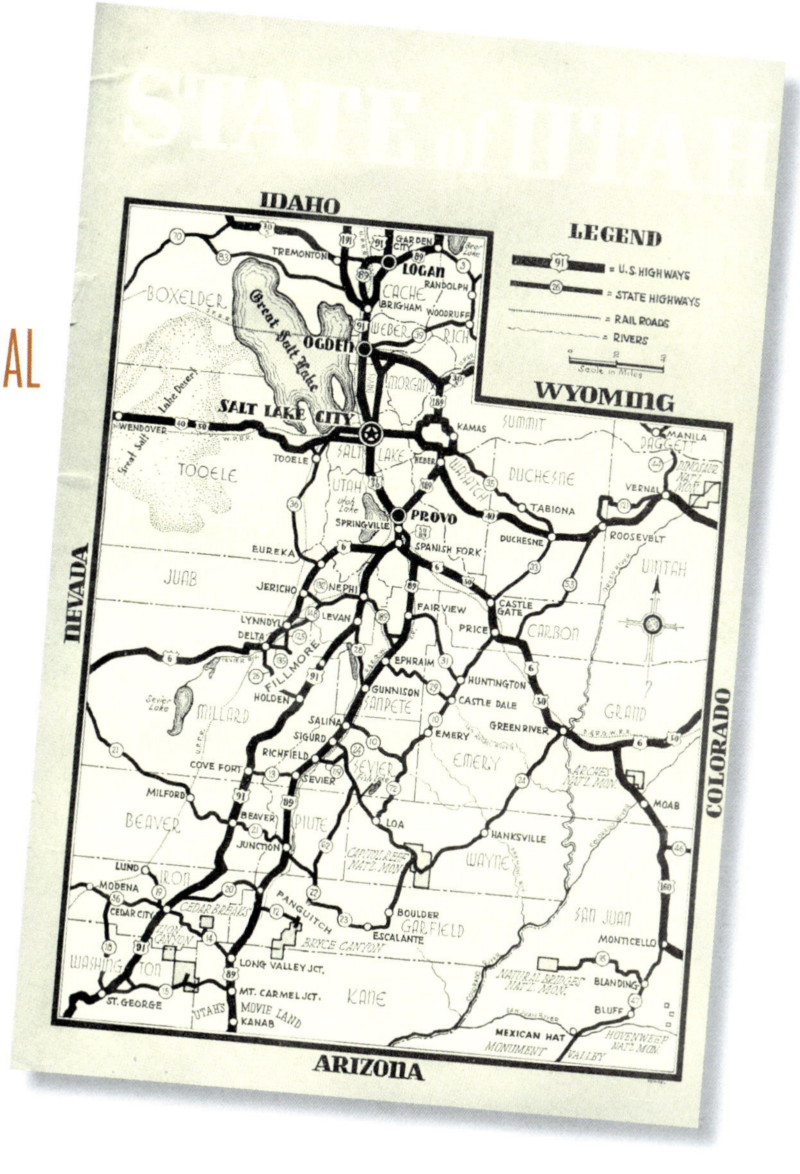

CENTENNIAL EDITION

WHEN HOLLYWOOD CAME TO UTAH

JAMES V. D'ARC

Gibbs Smith

28 27 26 25 24 5 4 3 2

This book was originally published in 2010 under the title *When Hollywood Came to Town: A History of Moviemaking in Utah.*

Published by
Gibbs Smith
P.O. Box 667
Layton, Utah 84041

1.800.835.4993 orders
www.gibbs-smith.com

Designed by Kurt Wahlner and Virginia Snow
Printed and bound in China
Gibbs Smith books are printed on either recycled, 100% post-consumer waste, FSC-certified papers or on paper produced from sustainable PEFC-certified forest/controlled wood source.
Learn more at www.pefc.org

Library of Congress Control Number: 2019936915
ISBN: 978-1-4236-6580-9

Page 1: Vintage map of Utah published in *Utah: Land of Endless Scenic Discovery*, a pamphlet published by the Utah Publicity & Industrial Development (1948). Note Kanab's identification as "Utah's Movie Land." The road cited as "91" is now Interstate 15. Pages 2–3: A box canyon coursed by the river at Paria serves as a gorgeous setting for rustled cattle in *Western Union*. Left: Extras have lunch on the set of *Wagon Master*. Right: Warner Baxter, as the Arizona Kid, serenades Mona Maris amid the splendor of Zion National Park. Page 6: Deanna Durbin and crew on the set of *Can't Help Singing* at Cedar Breaks National Monument.

In loving memory of

Patricia M. D'Arc

the woman of my dreams

CONTENTS

FOREWORDS

I don't know that I chose Utah. What I do believe is that Utah had been speaking to me for a long time, since I was a little boy, really. Whispering. Showing off its quiet beauty. Confident that I would someday come here. That I would one day come, and that it would work its magic so deeply into my soul that it would mark me forever. I honestly believe that.

I have always responded to the unsettling truth of how the great westward movement sorted itself out, with the clash of cultures that would take place repeatedly across the country. It was never pretty, and the outcome was never in doubt. But the land, from sea to shining sea, would stand in silent testament as to what really happened here.

It's a mistake to set yourself up as an authority as to what happened. It would be arrogant to think that I could set history right. All I know is that I have a desire in storytelling to lift the curtain on what must have happened a thousand times. A million times.

A steady wind has been pushing me my whole life to this point. To Utah. To *Horizon*. But it wouldn't be just one story I would tell. It would, in fact, be four. So where would I put it? Where could I film this story that has been speaking so loudly to me for over thirty-five years that would do it justice?

I simply thank God that the scales came off my eyes, and in front of me stood Utah. Its sheer beauty has served this story like a faithful friend. Every morning, and throughout the day, I stop while directing and look around in gratitude at what the majesty of these mountains and these rivers have afforded me.

Utah is a miracle on earth, and it came to be the largest character of this saga. Don't be surprised when you watch *Horizon* if it speaks to you.

Come here. It will fill you up, and you will never be the same.

Kevin Costner

One hundred years ago, millions of moviegoers saw Utah on the screen for the first time. They saw the wind-swept, wide-open spaces of northern Utah in *The Covered Wagon* and the towering rocks and mountains of Cedar City and Zion National Park in *The Deadwood Coach.* While both were silent films, they spoke volumes about Utah's authentic western landscapes, and viewers took advantage of the new railroad to come see Utah for themselves.

Having grown up here, I know the small towns, slot canyons, and vistas by heart that I see on screen in *Butch Cassidy and the Sundance Kid, Thelma & Louise, Footloose,* and *Yellowstone.* Knowing these places, it makes perfect sense to me that Utah has come to represent "The West" and that rugged, independent spirit that itself is so American.

James D'Arc's passion for movies and Utah has created a fascinating tribute to the people and places that appear in a century of film and television. Those films and their Utah locations have the power to inspire a whole new generation of filmmakers and film lovers to discover Utah.

Virginia Pearce, Director
Utah Film Commission

ACKNOWLEDGMENTS

The scope of this book is broad, covering many years, cities and towns, locations, and people. While bearing responsibility for the material presented herein, I am honestly indebted to a large number of dedicated people and institutions who have generously cooperated in order to make possible this historical study. The over thirty years that I have spent on this project always involved my home institution, the L. Tom Perry Special Collections at Brigham Young University's Harold B. Lee Library where, for forty-one years, I was the Curator of the Arts & Communications Archive and the BYU Motion Picture Archive. It was there that E. Dennis Rowley, Curator of Archives & Manuscripts, was a steady supporter of this endeavor beginning in the mid-1970s. He was a mentor without a peer. I am also indebted to the following institutions and individuals:

Academy of Motion Picture Arts and Sciences, Center for Motion Picture Study: Linda Mehr.

Angel Studios: Neal Harmon, Chief Executive Officer; Jeff Harmon, Chief of Content; Judy Day, Executive Assistant; and Kathleen Wilson.

Bison Archives: Marc Wanamaker.

Cedar Breaks National Monument: Nina Fitzgerald, Teri Saa.

The Chosen, Inc.: Brad Pelo, President.

Brigham Young University, Harold B. Lee Library: Randy Olsen, University Librarian. Scott Duvall, Russell Taylor, and P. Bradford Westwood of the L. Tom Perry Special Collections.

Kanab Heritage Museum: Deanna Glover.

Loaves & Fishes Productions: Dallas Jenkins, President.

Moab to Monument Valley Film Commission: Bega Metzner, Film Commissioner.

MoonWater Productions: Martha Williamson, President; Angie Horejsi, Assistant.

Cast and crew prepare to shoot a scene for *Taza, Son of Cochise*, with Dead Horse Point as the stunning backdrop.

1743-P19

John Ford discusses a scene in Monument Valley with Henry Fonda during the production of *Fort Apache*.

Southern Utah University, Gerald Sherratt Library: Janet B. Seegmiller.

Territory Pictures Inc.: A very special thanks to Kevin Costner, Director, Producer, Co-writer, and Star; for penning the foreword and for his gracious hospitality in allowing me on set during the making of *Horizon 2* in Moab; Philip A. Patterson, First Assistant Director; Mark Gillard, Producer; Glenn Kleczkowski, Producer; Howard Kaplan, Producer; Diane Slattery, Unit Publicist.

Twentieth Century Fox Film Corporation: Schawn Belston, Rob Easterla, and Jeffrey Thompson.

University of Southern California, Cinematic Arts Library: Ned Comstock.

University of California at Los Angeles, Arts Special Collections: Lauren Buisson.

Utah Film Commission: Directors Leigh von der Esch and Virginia Pearce. Marie Brockman, Isabel Horton, Melissa Jackson, Carli Mahas, Christina Martin, Derek Mellus, McKay Olsen, Syd Smoot, Trevor Snarr, and Tammy Villa-Humphreys.

Utah Film Studios: Marshall Moore, Vice President Operations, for extraordinary generosity and assistance with memories, photographs, and invaluable counsel, all amidst challenging circumstances.

Utah State Archives: Tony Castro, Doug Misner, Greg Walz.

Walt Disney Archives: Rebecca Cline, Michael Buckhoff, Nicole M. Carroll, Kevin M. Kern.

Walt Disney Company: Susette Hsiung, Executive Vice President, Network Production Management and Operations, Disney Channels Worldwide; Megan Lax, Director, Corporate Communications, Disney Branded Television.

Zebra Stills Photography: Ellen Schiess.

Zion National Park Archives/Human History Museum: Leslie Courtright, Jock F. Whitworth.

Jack Adams, Marvin Adams, Terry Alderman, Karen Alvey, Ralph Beckett, Rudy Behlmer, Stacey Endres Behlmer, Gordon Bench, Robert S. Birchard, Scott Boyter, Kevin Brownlow, Steve Browning, Barbara Burck Cathey, Lex Chamberlain, Anthony Chatterly, Courtney & Cathy Cobb, Linda Adams Crosby, J.L. Crawford, Jean Adams Crosby, Lisa Davis, Lyman Dayton, Vilo DeMille, Andre de Toth, Mary Gay Evans, Morris Everett, Jr. (The Everett Collection), Scott Eyman, Patrick Ford, Billie Frei, Ina Faye Frost, Colin Fryer, Carlo Gaberscek, Kay Giles, John N. Gillespie, Jack Goodspeed, Michael Gordon, Peter Graves, Harvard Heath, Monte Hellman, Charlton Heston, Chris Hicks, Don Holyoak, Norm Jackson, Marjorie Johannes, Calvin Johnson, Eric Johnson, Sylvan Johnson, Dennis Judd, Hawk Koch, Howard W. Koch, Dan & Darlene Longacre, Andrew V. McLaglen, Scott MacQueen, Elizabeth Miller, John W. Morgan, Merle Morris, Betty Motter, Dale Parry, Grayce Beckett Pike, Calvin L. Rampton, Bonnie Riding, Jackie Rife, Shae Robins, Flora & Rupert Ruesch, George Schenck, Packy Smith, Bette Larsen Stanton, Phyllis Stewart, Sam Taylor, Karl Tangren. Louise Parry Thomas, Sterling Van Wagenen, Clint Walker, Tom Weaver, George White, Stuart Whitman, Jeanne Wickan, Paul Wurtzel, Bailey Young, and Melanie Young.

Donna Poulton, my former graduate student who went on to be a successful published author and art curator, was the angel who informed the late Gibbs Smith of my ongoing project to document moviemaking in Utah. He subsequently tracked me down and was persistent in getting me to sign a contract for this book, sight unseen. There was minted only one Gibbs Smith, an innovative, passionate publisher. Suzanne Taylor, publisher and CCO of the company, suggested this updated edition. Warm thanks to a fine editorial and marketing team who functioned with precision and speed: Michelle Branson, Michelle F. Bayuk, Kim Eddy, and Sarah Gorecki.

Finally, I am grateful for the sacrifices made from the very beginning of this project by my late wife, Patricia, who thankfully made certain that our children, Sam, Jon, Melanie, Jennifer, and Laura, were not too seriously damaged by her husband's obsession with the Utah movie saga for so many, many years. At last, they—and their children—can read for themselves what all the fuss was about.

INTRODUCTION

A spacecraft descends on a landscape dotted with strange orange shapes. They have the appearance of the fragile drizzles of piled wet sand that one creates on the beach, their existence as fleeting as the next wave that comes in to obliterate them. On landing, the leader of the American crew breaks the seal and opens the door. Cautiously, he pokes out his head, confirms that there is oxygen in this new environment, and quickly asks of the new habitat, "Is this an alien planet?"

This is not an account of a NASA journey into space, nor is it Jules Verne updated; rather, it is a scene from the 1999 Universal film *Galaxy Quest*, a parody of the phenomenally popular 1960s television series *Star Trek* and its dedicated followers, starring Tim Allen, Sigourney Weaver, and Alan Rickman. The answer to Allen's query, as he peers out onto the landscape of Goblin Valley State Park in Utah's Emery County, is yes, it is an alien planet—and no, it isn't much like any other of America's fifty states. Since the early twentieth century, Utah has been the setting for more than a thousand feature motion pictures, television movies, television series episodes, as well as hundreds of documentaries and television commercials. The varied landscapes of alpine tree-covered splendor, desert canyons, prairie, and watershed has represented Egypt, Germany, Iraq, Ireland, Israel, Italy, Mexico, Scotland, Timbuktu, and Beijing, as well as the states of Massachusetts, Oklahoma, Nevada, Wyoming, New York, Missouri, Arizona, Colorado, South Dakota, California, Iowa, Nebraska, North Carolina, Illinois, and Texas.

This digest of disguises used for a century by Hollywood (and indigenous) moviemakers might suggest that Utah has an identity crisis. However, to promoters and residents of the state, its versatility, attested to by hundreds of productions successfully filmed in Utah, has forged an identity uniquely its own. There have even been a number of television movies filmed in Utah on locations where these Utah stories actually occurred that garnered nationwide attention. These movies include *Child Bride at Short Creek* (1981), which looked back at the 1953 raid of a polygamous community on the Utah-Arizona border, and gave early starring roles to later top-tier actresses Diane Lane and Helen Hunt; *The Executioner's Song* (1982), starring Tommy Lee Jones as murderer Gary Gilmore—with the screenplay by Norman Mailer from his bestselling book—who was the first man to be executed in the US following the reinstatement of the death penalty in 1976; *The Deliberate Stranger* (1986), with Mark Harmon starring as the notorious serial killer Ted Bundy; *In the Line of Duty: The Siege at Marion* (1992), about separatist bombers Adam and Jonathan Swapp; and, *Deliver Them From Evil: The Taking of Alta View* (1992), which dramatized a hostage situation at a Salt Lake Valley hospital, starring Harry Hamblin and Teri Garr.

The coming of Hollywood to Utah, beginning in the 1920s, documents what I consider to be the fourth

Tim Allen has a run-in with a space creature in Goblin Valley in Universal's *Galaxy Quest*.

"invasion" by outside forces into a state that was founded in 1847 by religious pioneers as a place of isolation and refuge from the very outside influences that eventually caught up to them in their intermountain settlements. Members of The Church of Jesus Christ of Latter-day Saints—under their founding prophet, Joseph Smith—began their organization in upstate New York in 1830. Church membership swelled with new converts in the American Northeast as well as thousands of new adherents from England and other countries. Their practice of "gathering" in Ohio, Missouri, and Illinois resulted in a degree of prosperity and voting power on the American frontier that quickly made them aliens in their own country, even as they pointed to protections under the Constitution of the United States for their existence. Driven first from the western frontier of Missouri, where the governor issued an order for their extermination, and finally from their Mississippi River town of Nauvoo, Illinois, in the winter of 1846 following the murder of Joseph Smith by a mob, nearly twenty thousand Latter-day Saints began the largest migration in US history. The first wave of this migration ended on July 24, 1847, more than 1,300 miles to the west in the valley of the Great Salt Lake. The area known as the Great Basin, then a tenuously held Mexican possession, took a historic turn when their prophet Brigham Young uttered the now-famous words, "This is the right place." Their object was to settle in a land that no one else wanted so that they could practice their religion in peace.

For Young and his people, the goals of isolation, home industry, and spiritual regeneration were well underway when three important invasions into their Rocky Mountain home took place. The first occurred not long after their arrival when, beginning in 1849, a stream of travelers passed through Salt Lake City on their way to the California gold fields, trading with the Mormons for much-needed supplies. The second invasion, more predatory in nature, was in the form of the United States Army, sent by President James Buchanan in 1857 to quell what had been rumored by a hostile press and disgruntled federal officials as rebellion by Utahns against the US government. The army came, saw no rebellion, and established an army post just east of Salt Lake City. A third, less-intimidating incursion from the outside world happened a decade later, in 1869, when the Union Pacific and Central Pacific railroads were joined by a golden spike at Promontory Point on the north end of the Great Salt Lake, ushering in a new era of transcontinental transportation, commerce, and exposure to outside influences. Statehood for what was nicknamed the Beehive State (representing enterprise and industry) eventually came in 1896, six years after Church leaders issued a public pronouncement to abandon the controversial practice of plural marriage. Utah began its entry into the American mainstream. Ironically, while each of these incursions created some problems, they also provided much-needed hard currency to the struggling settlement through commerce with outsiders. The fourth invasion, occurring much later in Utah's history, would be no different.

The story of Hollywood moviemaking in Utah began in the early 1900s, but more earnestly in the mid-1920s, thanks to the three enterprising Parry brothers in Cedar City. Politics, social culture, economics, mining, the cattle industry, and tourism are commonly understood to comprise legitimate forms of history for a city, county, or state. However, the history of movie production has for decades been treated as ephemeral, as if impervious to any influence on the inhabitants of a region. This history seeks to address that void in Utah's story. *When Hollywood Came to Utah* is not only the story of places—movie locations within Utah—but of people who worked with Hollywood executives and crews, who plowed new roads in order to get to pristine sites often not seen even by local residents, and who labored as wranglers or as extras on location. Whether residents of Kanab and Moab—each community well under two thousand residents during the time described in this book—or of the more urban Salt Lake City, these were the people who were conversely affected socially and economically by the arrival of movie stars, trucks full of equipment, and what amounted over time to millions of dollars infused into their local economies. The movies made in Utah helped to write various chapters of Hollywood movie history as well, from potboilers on lean budgets to some of the most memorable films ever made.

Why is a history of this kind important? Like Mt. Everest, it is there, but unlike Everest, it has not been explored until now. Among the histories of tourism, mining, industrial manufacturing, military bases, ranching, wars with the indigenous people, education, exploration, and peoples and their movements, the chronicle of moviemaking in Utah is conspicuously absent, quite a surprise for an industry that in 2023 brought in $140 million to the Utah economy from production of films under the state's incentive program. This figure does not include the influx of money into the economy generated by the production of the many commercials and smaller film projects. In addition, there are historical reasons for the preservation and study of commercial Hollywood motion pictures made in Utah. While movies and television programs are usually made for entertainment purposes, they also serve an environmental purpose. The land surrounding many of the filming sites for *The Greatest Story Ever Told*—shot near a quickly rising Lake Powell in 1963—is no longer visible. Footage from the *Flicka* series of features made by Twentieth Century Fox reveals watershed and ground cover that has changed significantly since the 1940s when they were filmed. These films also show, in dazzling Technicolor, the expanse of pastureland and watershed areas that made up the Duck Creek area on Cedar Mountain in southwestern Utah before the appearance of the dozens of vacation homes that now crowd the landscape. Footage from these films and many others is, in most instances, the only motion-picture evidence that exists of the topography, landfall, and water drainage in many rural Utah areas from as early as the 1920s.

I have chosen to tell the story of Hollywood moviemaking in Utah chronologically and by region, focusing on the origins and heyday of filmmaking, generally from the 1920s through 2023. (But for a few exceptions that are noted in relevant chapters, I have not dealt with movies made by Utah film companies.) During these years, the Hollywood studios, major and minor, developed close relationships with the various regions of Utah and their people. It was during these years that the tradition that is still active in the first decade of the twenty-first century began. Work on this history has occupied more than thirty years of combing newspapers, interviewing locals as well as filmmakers, scouring studio archival records, viewing many of the films themselves, and visiting the sites where these movies were filmed. On occasion, layers of local oral and printed mythology about moviemaking had to be peeled back to get at the often-surprising truth about where a film was actually made.

Obviously, not every important Utah-based film can be treated extensively within the limits of one volume. A survey history of this type represented in this book is, by its very nature, selective. Films have been chosen for extended treatment due to their overall importance as well as the information available to accurately tell the story of their making. I have also selected films that reveal a representative process of the interaction between studio crews and townspeople. The film activity generated by Utah and its people is most impressive, even in the years of economic fluctuation, growing restrictions on the use of public lands from the Bureau of Land Management and the National Park Service, and growing competition from other states and countries, that have seen the economic benefits of attracting filmmaking to their locales.

As Utah celebrates its centennial of moviemaking, it is important to remember what a Moab rancher said about the benefits of moviemaking in Utah. Referring to the motion picture companies with whom he often worked: "They don't take anything but pictures and don't leave anything except money." The movie industry has also left a lasting legacy, one that constitutes the dramatic, comedic, and sometimes harrowing story that unfolds in the following pages.

—James V. D'Arc
Orem, Utah

SCENE 1

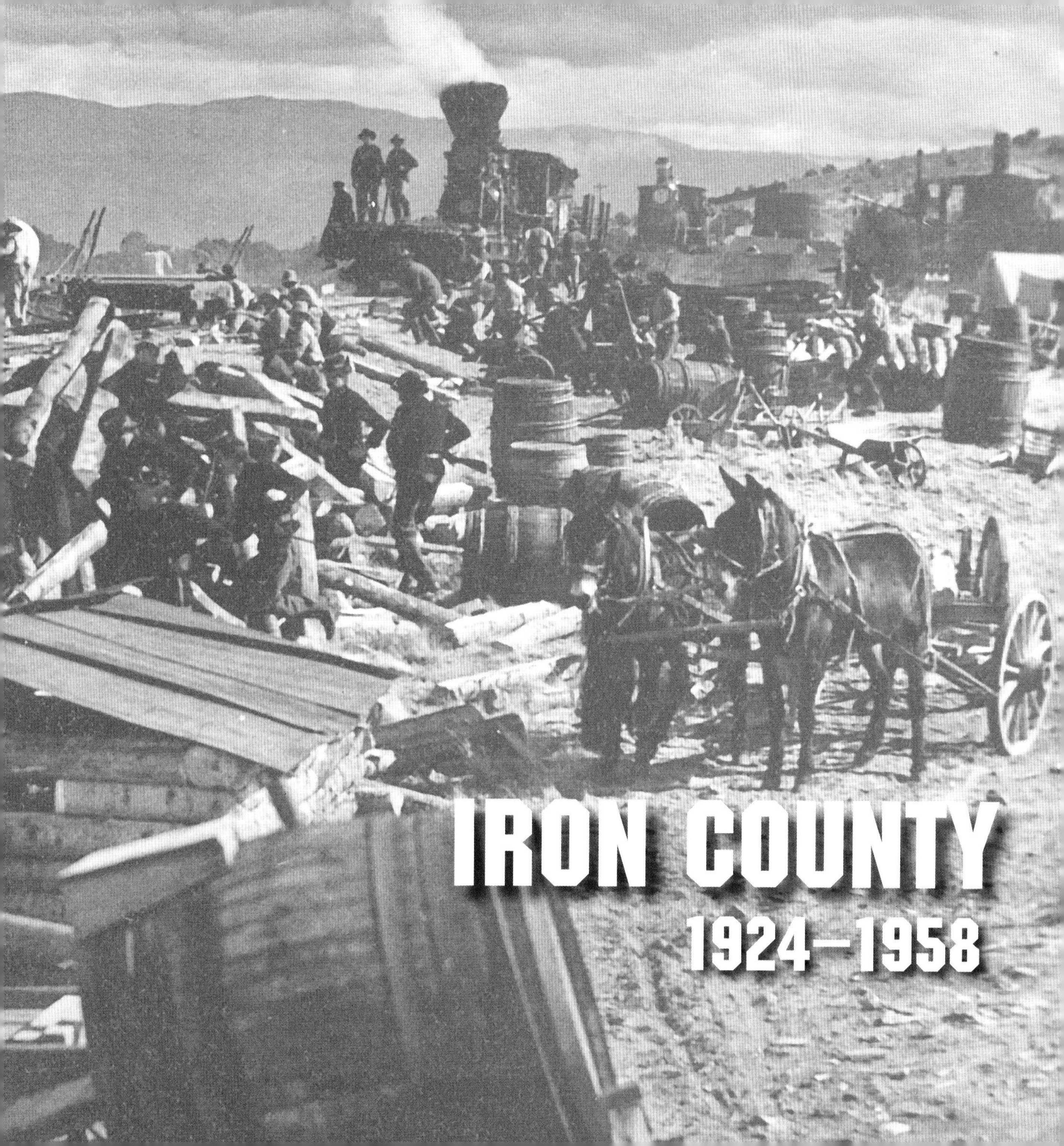

IRON COUNTY

1924–1958

CEDAR CITY AND THE PARRY BROTHERS

This 1929 photo of Zion Lodge dude wrangler Walt Beatty could easily have been Chauncey Parry at Observation Point surveying this natural movie set wonder for Hollywood movie companies.

The story of Hollywood moviemaking in Utah is inseparable from that of the Parry brothers—Gronway, Chauncey, and Caleb Whitney—and their business ventures in Cedar City and nearby Zion National Park. The brothers did not have stars in their eyes, but they were looking to make their mark in the world. They ended up ushering in a new industry to their native state and establishing a corporate template for how Hollywood moviemaking companies might thrive away from home, even in the Depression economy. Without Gronway, Chauncey, and Whitney Parry, the Hollywood movie studio crews might never have come to Utah, or at least not as early—nor as often—as they did at such an important time in Utah's history.

Cedar City was founded in 1851 when Brigham Young sent Welsh, Scottish, and English Mormon immigrants there to mine iron. Situated on the main travel route from Salt Lake City to Las Vegas and then to San Bernardino, Los Angeles, and port cities in California, the city grew rapidly, becoming one of the

Dapper Chauncey Parry, the pioneer of Hollywood moviemaking in Utah.

largest cities in Utah outside of Salt Lake City. Cedar City is surrounded by natural wonders not fully recognized at the time of its founding. Cedar Breaks National Monument covers more than six thousand acres high on the Markagunt Plateau and is distinguished by lush forests and sudden outcroppings of colorful weathered rock, an area aptly named by Indians the "circle of painted cliffs." Northeast of Cedar City, just off Interstate 15, lies the small agricultural community of Parowan, the seat of Iron County, and another access point to Cedar Breaks National Monument as well as Brian Head peak, the highest mountain in southwestern Utah. From the lofty elevation of Cedar Breaks, some four thousand feet above Cedar City and Parowan, there are stunning views of nearby Zion and Bryce canyons and the picturesque system of plateaus and red rock canyons of the Kolob region of Zion National Park.

It was the eldest brother, Gronway Jr., who led his brother Chauncey, and later Whit, from Salt Lake to Cedar City. After graduating from high school, Gronway entered the University of Utah in 1908 and worked on a road survey crew in southwestern Utah during the summer of 1913. In 1914, he transferred from the University of Utah to the Utah

State Agricultural College (now Utah State University) in Logan to get a degree in animal husbandry, as well as veterinary training. It was said that "he loved horses more than people; if this were true, it was because he knew more about them."[1] In the summer of 1915, he became the Iron County agricultural agent in Cedar City and taught animal husbandry at the Branch Agricultural College (now Southern Utah University). He also opened the first steam laundry in Cedar City and sold cars through an automobile dealership. Clearly, Gronway may have been rambunctious but not idle in making his way in the world.

Chauncey, meanwhile, was attending the University of Utah, but was persuaded by his brother to come down and help manage Gronway's other growing commercial enterprises, the Cedars Hotel and a transportation company that shuttled passengers from the Los Angeles & Salt Lake Railroad (soon to be bought out by Union Pacific) at Lund, Utah, to St. George. With whatever time they had left over, the brothers explored the mountains, canyons, and plains of their surroundings, including what was then known as "Little Zion" canyon, not yet a national monument or park.

Shortly thereafter, some government surveyors stayed at the Cedars Hotel. They were there to build a road into Zion Canyon, or Mukuntuweap National Monument, as it was then known. Only a wagon road used by a few farmers to access the area existed at the time. The possibility of roads into this scenic area

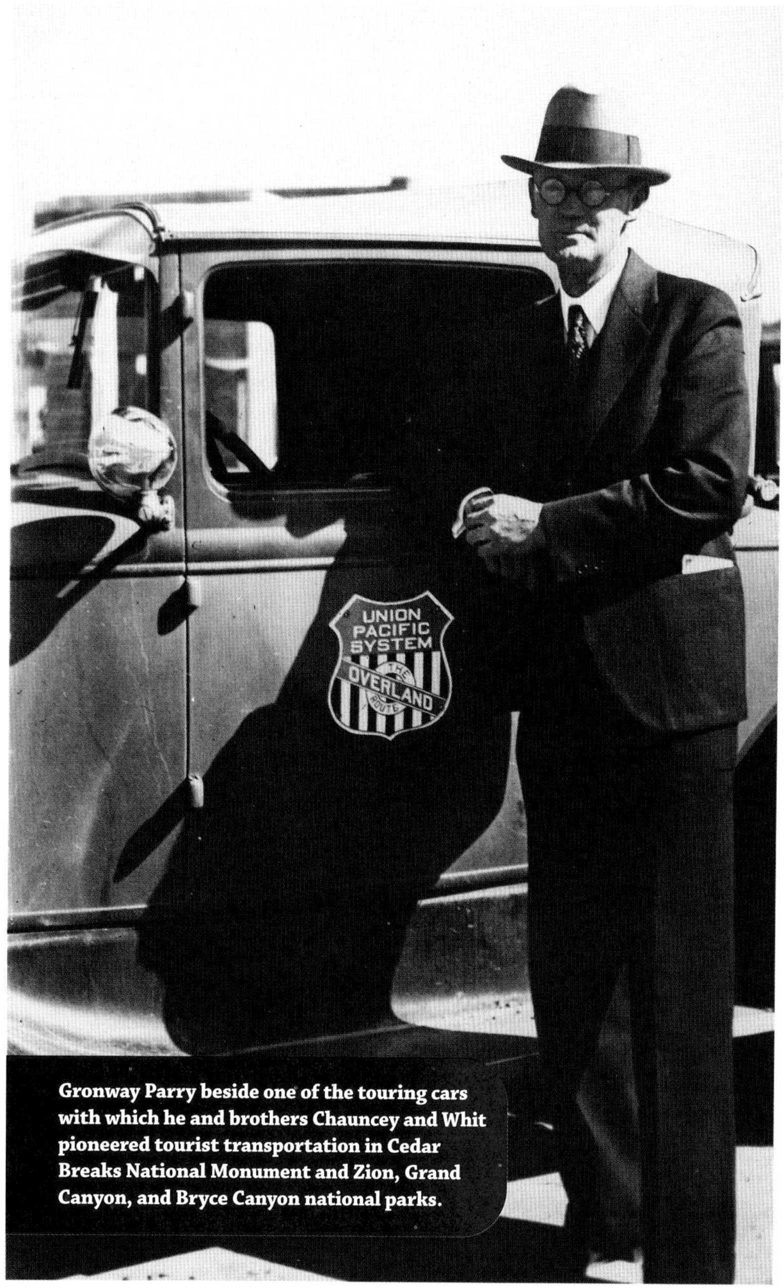

Gronway Parry beside one of the touring cars with which he and brothers Chauncey and Whit pioneered tourist transportation in Cedar Breaks National Monument and Zion, Grand Canyon, and Bryce Canyon national parks.

gave the restless Chauncey an idea: If the surveyors saw interest in access to the canyons, why not others as well? This led the brothers to apply to the Department of the Interior in 1917 for the transportation concession in Zion. William O. Tufts, the engineer who led the earlier road surveying party, endorsed the Parrys as "active business men" who were "well known and well liked throughout the whole territory." He concluded, "They give their whole time and personal supervision to their business."[2]

The brothers next presented a joint proposal with William W. Wylie, owner of the popular Wylie Camps of large tent cottages in Yellowstone National Park, to be the concessioners for lodging as well as transportation at Zion. Tufts once again came to their support. In a letter to Horace Albright, Acting Director of the Department of the Interior, he wrote, "They are enthusiastic about the development of southwestern Utah and are popular with the residents of that region. I should say that possibly their greatest failing might be in a tendency to be over enthusiastic and optimistic and trying to swing more than they could carry." What to Tufts was a failing turned out to be prophetic about the brothers' innate hubris: seldom did they reach out for something they did not eventually achieve. Citing the brothers' many business enterprises, their hotel "full of guests all the time," and their brisk sales of automobiles, Tufts expressed confidence in their ability to handle the concession successfully.[3] The National Park Transportation and Camping Company was incorporated in April 1917. The brothers liquidated their other interests and invested $4,900 in the partnership with Wylie, holding 49 percent of the stock. Wylie served as president, Gronway as vice president, and Chauncey as treasurer. Wylie's brother, Clinton, was secretary.[4]

The new company began with a secondhand seven-passenger Hudson sedan, a Model-T Ford, and three used Cadillacs. "These were big sedans," remembered Dale Parry, Gronway's son, who later drove for the company. "They could probably get four or five paying passengers in each one and they started out with just a handful. They were so poor in those days they would have to get their people there, get the money ahead of time and go get gasoline. They were just a couple of guys starting up a business."[5] Since gas stations were few and far between in those days, gas was carried in metal cans strapped to the vehicles.

Younger brother Whit was brought in to help the fledgling business as a driver. Gronway remembered that the youthfulness of the teenager occasionally surprised Whit's passengers: "We couldn't always afford drivers either, as one of us had to stay and make contacts while the other would drive a car. We didn't hire anyone regularly at first, so we decided to let our younger brother, Whitney, help us out. Because he was so small, we'd have him sit up on pillows to appear larger—it was before the days of drivers' licenses. Often when Whit would get between Cedar City and his destination, he'd have a flat tire, and would get out to fix it. To the amazement of the passengers, he was but a mere boy, so they'd become worried about their safety. We instructed Whit to tell them it was no further to go on than it was to go back, so they would decide to go on. By the end of the trip they'd always vote Whit one of the best drivers they'd ever traveled with."[6]

World War I interrupted the Parrys' growing transportation business as patronage in the parks ebbed. The older brothers enlisted in the Army Air Service in June 1917, but for some reason they did not leave for duty until after the September 1917 visit of Interior Secretary Horace Albright to tour Zion for the first time. Chauncey received flight training at Berkeley Field in California in January 1918, but Gronway was mustered out after a tainted vaccine affected his eyes. He spent the duration of the war managing ranches in Mexico and Nevada. The war over, Chauncey returned to Salt Lake City in early 1920, where he taught high school before the spring tourist season began in the park.

Prior to their departure for military service, both brothers had given their proxies to Wylie. On their return, they discovered that they had been put out of the company. A court battle followed and Chauncey applied for his own franchise in 1921, with the judge ordering the two parties to "set arrangements straight."[7] The company was renamed Utah–Grand Canyon Transportation Company, expanding the scope of service to include the North Rim of the Grand Canyon. Soon, however, Wylie, in debt to the railroad, got out of the company and hired out for wages for the summer to run the Wylie Camp lodging operation within the park. Chauncey invited Gronway, still in Nevada, to join the growing transportation company as the number of tourists increased.

As if running several businesses in the region were not enough activity, Chauncey reveled in traveling—in the saddle or in the cockpit—throughout southwestern Utah and northern Arizona, armed with a camera. He maintained his active interest in flying and is reputed to be the first to fly an airplane into the Grand Canyon. Camera in hand, he was always interested in showing off the scenic splendor of Zion Canyon, Bryce Canyon, the Kolob Canyons, Cedar Mountain, and the area down to the Grand Canyon. When President Warren G. Harding made his western tour in the spring of 1923, he included a visit to Cedar City and to Zion National Park. Chauncey, who wrangled the horses and acted as guide to Zion Canyon, can be seen among the distinguished visitors who, in addition to President Harding, included Utah senator Reed Smoot, Secretary of Commerce Herbert Hoover, Vice President Calvin Coolidge, and LDS church president Heber J. Grant, as well a member of Harding's secret service detail and his chief of staff.

Recognized by the state for his knowledge of southern Utah's seldom-seen regions, in April 1926 Chauncey was chosen by Utah governor George H. Dern to be part of a select group of five travelers that undertook a week-long journey down the Colorado River, from the confluence with

Chauncey Parry in the cockpit of his Curtiss JN-4, which he flew over Zion National Park and the Grand Canyon, taking pictures for area promotion for movie companies.

President Warren Harding visits Zion National Park on June 27, 1923, along with other mounted dignitaries.
United States Secretary of Commerce Herbert Hoover
United States Vice President Calvin Coolidge
United States Senator from Utah Reed Smoot
Cedar City Businessman Chauncey Parry
United States President Warren G. Harding
United States Secret Service Agent Walter Ferguson
The Church of Jesus Christ of Latter-day Saints President Heber J. Grant

the Dirty Devil to Lee's Ferry, a distance of about 170 miles. The group consisted of Governor Dern, his secretary, Oliver Grimes, geologist Glen Ruby of Colorado, Utah guide David Rust, and Chauncey.[8] Scheduled congressional hearings in Washington on the utilization of the Colorado River motivated the trip. Dern was studying the problem of dam building and bridge construction along the river. Two years later, Chauncey was invited to join Governor Dern's horse-mounted expedition into the southeastern part of the state to see Arch Canyon, to fact-find for future roads, and to measure the navigability of the San Juan River.

Meanwhile, the Union Pacific Railroad purchase of the Los Angeles & Salt Lake Railroad had a direct impact on the Parrys' transportation company. In 1923, the Union Pacific built a spur line from Lund to Cedar City, and, with its newly created Utah Parks Company subsidiary, began to expand its activities, building lodges in Bryce Canyon, Grand Canyon, and Zion National Park. The creation of the Utah Parks Company also created competition for the Parry brothers' transportation company. Ultimately, there was no choice for Chauncey and Gronway but to sell out in 1926. They were retained, however, as superintendents of the business for another seventeen years.

The two brothers, filled with the enthusiasm of opportunity, seemed to thrive during the boom years of the 1920s, when Zion National Park and Bryce Canyon National Park (designated in 1928 and enlarged in 1931) became better known to outsiders and transportation and lodging facilities made extended stays practical. They also created what is now the "loop" tour of Zion, Bryce, and the North Rim of the Grand Canyon.

United as they were in the transportation business, the Parry brothers differed in temperament. Gronway seemed to set the tone for the others. He was always on the go, from being the first to establish thriving businesses in Cedar City that led the way for his brothers to follow, to learning to fly at age sixty. His love of horses convinced him to take up polo, and, on trips he made with Chauncey to Los Angeles to drum up movie business for the area, he struck up a friendship with Will Rogers, on whose estate he learned to play polo, then fashionable among the Hollywood set. "Go, Cedar, go!" was Rogers's chant when Gronway took to the polo grounds. However, when he was hospitalized following an accident while playing against a Brazilian team, Gronway gave up the game. He rebuilt vintage covered wagons, carriages, and other rolling stock all through the years, much of it used by motion-picture companies when filming on location. Many of these vehicles formed the core of what later became the Iron Mission Museum in Cedar City. Gronway served as mayor of Cedar City for one term and later built an eighty-five-house subdivision. At Christmastime, locals remember him playing Santa Claus, driving a sleigh with wheels attached to the runners and horses with "antlers" strapped on their heads. When Gronway Parry reached age sixty-seven, his daughter Carol Ann described her father as "the personality he is. A persistent square chin is the most notable feature about his face. Glasses somewhat camouflage his sharp blue eyes and his forehead extends further back than it did thirty years ago. The typical suntan pants and shirt, the worn and calloused hands, and the usual head-in-front-of-the-body walk classify him as a man with his mind on too many things. He should have ten bodies to go with his one overactive mind."[9]

Chauncey was gregarious, friendly, and evidenced great affection for both the locals and the Hollywood elite. Many fall seasons, Spencer Tracy and Clark Gable took Chauncey along cougar hunting because he knew the landscape like no one else. "My dad didn't hunt," remembers Chauncey's daughter Louise. "He didn't like to kill things. So, he used his camera. . . . Those movie stars really appreciated his sincerity, his genuineness. He knew how to treat them, and how to talk to them."[10]

Apparently, Chauncey also knew how to talk to

horses, and that knowledge would also drive him to other forms of speech. Jack Thomas, Chauncey's son-in-law, observed, "If Chauncey had a fault, it would have been his ability to swear. This is often a habit developed by many men who spend most of their lives with horses. Cantankerous horses have been known for bringing out the very worst in a man, particularly his language. Chauncey was no exception. Although a highly religious man, he could blister the paint on buses and melt a camera lens while expressing his displeasure at the performance of a horse."[11]

Chauncey's grace, knowledge, and attention to every detail in caring for those who came to visit the parks was formally recognized in 1926 when Crown Prince Gustav of Sweden and Princess Louise visited southern Utah. Chauncey was their guide through the canyons. The treatment they received from him on their trip was so memorable that the royals conferred the Royal Order of Vasa on the thirty-year-old Chauncey, the fifth person in the United States to enjoy that knighted distinction. Chauncey's *savoir faire* with virtually anyone also led him to the woman he eventually married. Utah governor Dern asked the expert horseman to take his place in the governor's box during a horse show in Salt Lake City, probably in 1927. One of the riders, Helen Daynes, rode up to the box during her performance. Her spirited horse shot a ball of mud straight into Chauncey's face. Chauncey was not only hit, he was smitten. A friend arranged a date with the Salt Lake City beauty. Soon thereafter he invited her to Cedar City to be introduced to the family. He then took her to the Temple

Chauncey Parry being greeted at the San Bernardino, California, train station in January 1922, on his way to meet with movie company executives in Hollywood.

Whit Parry and first wife Grayce "Becky" Beckett in a publicity shot taken in the summer of 1944, during the production of *Thunderhead, Son of Flicka*.

of Sinawava, far into Zion Canyon, and they hiked up far enough to see the canyon spread below them. "I want to tell you that I love you and want to marry you just as soon as you'll let me," goes the family story. They were married in the Salt Lake Temple on June 19, 1928.

Whit, the youngest of the three, went in a different direction than his older brothers. While Chauncey and Gronway were away during World War I, Whit was in high school in Salt Lake City, excelling in history and psychology. The Parry pedigree carried with it a restlessness to get ahead that probably explained his ongoing involvement in school publications, basketball, swimming, and boxing. During the school year he had a paper route for the *Salt Lake Tribune*, and during summer vacations he worked as a service-station attendant. While he claimed that he was an average student, Whit's grades and extracurricular activities were sufficient to get him accepted at Stanford University law school in the fall of 1922. The death of his father that year brought Whit home and, now at the University of Utah, he changed his focus from law to business administration. The openness that characterized his later role as the proprietor of the Parry Lodge was evidenced by his activity in fraternities and sports, and in his senior year he was president of the Alpha Kappa Psi fraternity and the Commerce Club.

During the summer of 1923, Whit drove buses for his brothers' transportation company, and in 1924 he was made a partner in the business. He continued as transportation manager for the company during 1925 and 1926, the year he graduated from the University of Utah. His missionary service to Germany and Switzerland for The Church of Jesus Christ of Latter-day Saints, from December 1926 to mid-1929, occurred during the time that the transportation company was sold to the Utah Parks Company. Whit returned to be transportation manager for the new company at the North Rim of the Grand Canyon, where his interest in the hotel and restaurant business grew. He took that knowledge to Salt Lake City and opened a restaurant on Main Street, but the effects of the Great Depression put it out of business, and he joined the Anderson Boarding and Supply Company, which received a government contract to feed and house the workers building the massive Boulder (later Hoover) Dam. "I had the privilege of working in every department of the kitchen and dining room, waiter, pantryman, fry cook, vegetable man and food checker," Whit reflected in 1941.[12]

The seven-month tutorial with the Anderson Company in Boulder City, Nevada, was enough to persuade Whit to return to Kanab, a remote southern Utah town only a few miles north of the Arizona border, to join his brother Chauncey, who had earlier purchased and converted a modest farmhouse on Center Street into a restaurant and a small "tourist home," as he called it. Chauncey continued to make trips to Hollywood with dozens of photographs of the area to entice studios to make films in the region, and it fell to Whit to manage what was soon known as the Parry Lodge. However, it could only be profitably run during the tourist season that generally ran from March or April to November. During the winters, Whit got various jobs in Salt Lake City. The tourist home would soon become a southern Utah fixture and Whit would gain fame nationwide as the hotelier to the stars in this rugged part of the country.

Whit's features were rougher than those of his older brothers, his "pug" face probably the result of boxing in his college years, but it did nothing to daunt his apparently boundless confidence. "The super salesman type," is how Whit's first wife, Grayce Beckett, to whom he was married from 1940 to 1947, remembered her former husband in the late 1970s. "He was very good at it. He was always a welcome guest no matter where or when he had the door open for him. It was very easy for him. He was just an amazing personality. He had the props knocked from under him two or three times and started again from scratch." In regard to Whit's manner of dealing with requests from the movie companies that came to Kanab, she remembered, "They knew that whatever they

Chauncey and Gronway Parry relaxing in front of the Parry Lodge, early 1940s.

asked, how impossible it might seem, he'd find a way to provide it. Whatever it was, Whitney came through. That is for certain."[13]

His hunger for knowledge, his desire to be up on current events, impressed Whit's brother-in-law, Ralph Beckett, who remembered a time in the late 1940s when Whit took the budding screenwriter with him on a studio visit. "I saw how he operated and it was an absolute gas to me. I was not a salesman. I recognized salesmanship qualities in my father and then I saw the same qualities in Whit. He was a very thoroughly warm, concerned person who could relate easily to anybody. He was relaxed. He was open. He was very verbal. He was alert and up on things. He also brought photographs of the lodge in a professionally polished folder."[14] At other times, Beckett saw him in another mood, such as when they were having lunch together at the Ambassador Hotel in Hollywood. "He was in the middle of a deal and he was thinking. He was literally thinking. He made a couple of phone calls. When things were frustrating him, and they were this day, he was just utterly quiet. He was working it out. He was planning. In no way did he ever blow or show temperament. He really impressed me as a guy that they call today as being cool. A cool guy that was tuned in. Whit apparently sat on feelings and took them internally. He did not blow so he took it out on his ulcer."[15]

The man whom Ralph Beckett called "the hub" of Kanab's largely successful efforts to attract the lucrative Hollywood studios each season earned both praise and criticism in the small town. "There were those whom Whit rubbed the wrong way," said Shirley Ricks, who worked as a waitress in the Parry Lodge in 1947, "but there are those who still remember him with genuine affection and knew him bone deep." Remembering in the late 1970s, Ricks wrote to Whit's ex-wife Grayce, "I am sure he was difficult to be married to because he was TOTALLY devoted to the Lodge and the motion picture element of it—and money. Whatever he was, he was kind, good and a total man, loved by all who really knew him and all who knew him were and are loyal to him."[16]

"He was a good boss," remembered Kanab resident Calvin Johnson. "They'd cuss him and he'd cuss them, but he was a good boss. His friend and business partner Fay Hamblin called him moose face. You know he broke his nose a time or two probably because of his boxing in college, but he had a taster that was out of this world. He would go all over the world in between shoots and when he came back he would get a bunch of Kanab housewives together for his cooks and have them make dishes just like he tasted them, or he'd throw it out. That's what made his food so good."[17]

Tom Mix in Zion National Park during filming of *The Deadwood Coach*.

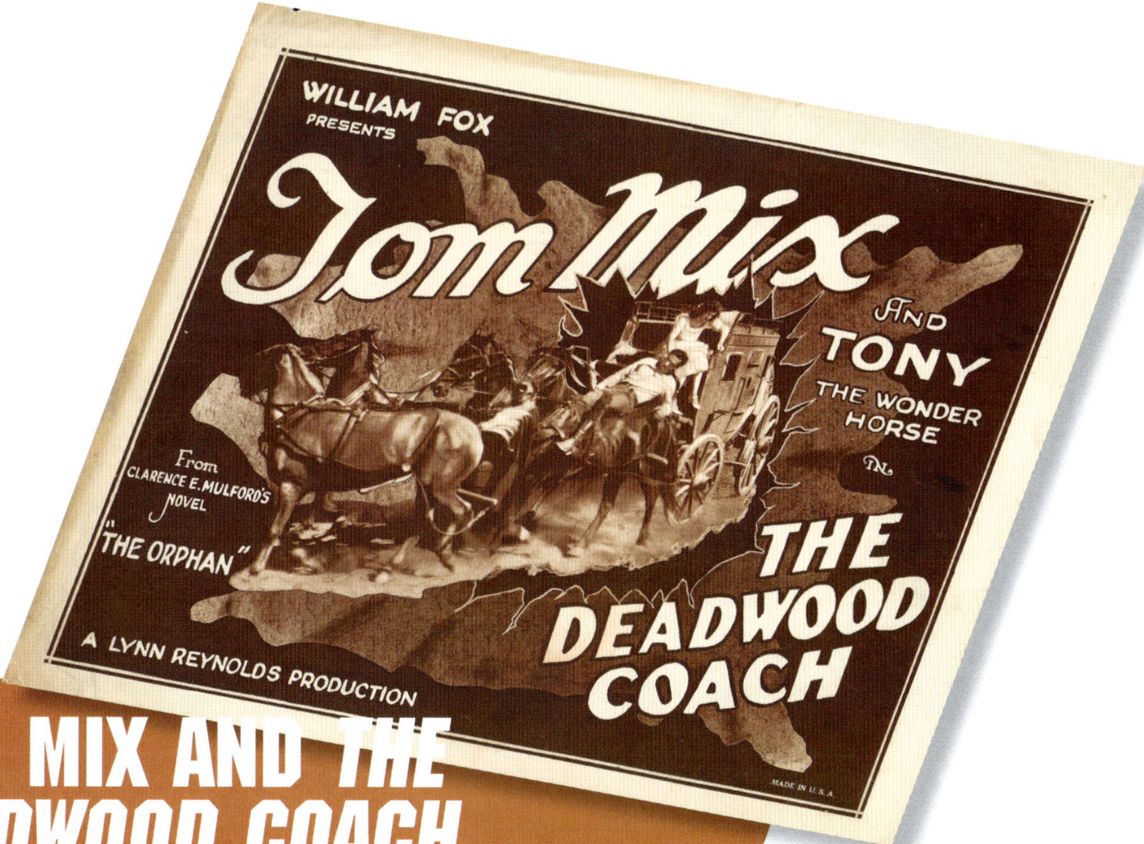

TOM MIX AND THE DEADWOOD COACH

In 1924, Cedar City had a population of approximately 4,500 people and served as the gateway to what is now Bryce Canyon National Park, Cedar Breaks National Monument, and Zion National Park. Gronway Parry had settled in to teaching at the Branch Agricultural College, along with his many other activities. Cattle and sheep ranching were thriving industries in the growing community contiguous to both the broad plains to the west and the lushly timbered highlands of the mountain ranges to the east.

It is probably not surprising that the motion picture that opened up the area to Hollywood moviemaking was a Western. *The Deadwood Coach* starred Tom Mix, the greatest cowboy star of his time, and the box-office champ of the 1920s. His fan club is said to have numbered more than two million members. Solidly built, with a smile to span the Grand Canyon, Mix exuded a carefully constructed studio image of the virile man of the West who was nevertheless simple and fiercely courageous in defending American values. His many Westerns for the Fox Film Corporation were the bread and butter of box-office revenues during this time.

Snagging Mix was a major victory for Chauncey and Gronway Parry, although there is an indication that popular Western novelist Zane Grey recommended the Utah location. "Because Zane Grey had written his first successful novels in Kanab, Tom Mix . . . had asked the Parry brothers to arrange a few location trips," wrote one journalist in the mid-1940s.[1] At the time, Grey was heavily involved in the early motion-picture adaptations of his best-selling novels, having at one time even formed his own motion-picture production company.[2] Lynn Reynolds, the young director of many of Mix's films, traveled to Utah in late July 1924 and was guided by Chauncey to various locations centering on Zion and Bryce canyons. From early reports, some filming was to have occurred in Cedar City as well.

The first public indication of Mix's trip to Cedar City was a report in the local weekly newspaper, the *Iron County Record,* on August 15, 1924. A studio publicity photograph of Mix rearing up on Tony, "The Wonder Horse," announced his arrival by train in Cedar City the following Sunday, August 17.[3] What might have been of greater interest to local residents, however, was the advertisement inside the newspaper, taking up nearly one-third of a page, announcing that Tom Mix would appear at the Cedar City Rodeo for its entire four-day run during the first week of September. "Let's see how our prize winners from Arizona and Utah compare in competition for prizes against the twenty outlaw horses from Colorado and Wyoming and how our riders compare with Tom Mix's men," read the ad copy. Any doubt that to Utahns rodeos were the Mountain West's Olympic games was erased by oversize type at the bottom of the advertisement: "If business interferes—cut out business and COME!"[4] Rumors circulated that Mix might accept an invitation from the Salt Lake City Chamber of Commerce to open the larger Salt Lake City Round-Up. Bill Wildcat, who identified himself as an "Indian," placed an "open letter to Tom Mix" in the form of a display advertisement published in the paper's next issue. He acknowledged the rumors but urged that "You open Cedar City Rodeo SURE!"[5] A full-page newspaper advertisement for the rodeo, published in the last edition before the rodeo was to begin, used the first letters of Tom Mix's name to highlight the events to be featured during the festivities.

When the Union Pacific train arrived at the Cedar City depot "a few minutes late" on Sunday, August 17, the star received "the greatest reception since the coming of President Harding," reported the *Iron County Record*. "A loud cheer went up as Tom Mix appeared on the platform of his car. His smile radiated his appreciation of the huge throng that was there to greet him."[6] Gronway Parry, leading Post 47 of the American Legion—consisting of thirty mounted riders "dressed in rodeo togs"—escorted Mix and his wife in a parade that ended at the recently completed El Escalante Hotel, the pride of Cedar City. Of course, the Parrys' company provided the transportation for the troupe that totaled fifty, including twenty-five "honest-to-goodness cowpunchers."

Right: Sid Jordan and Tom Mix. Facing: Tom Mix poses at Bryce Canyon during production of *The Deadwood Coach*. This collector's card was included with popular chewing gum of the day.

Later that day, Mix sat down with a reporter to make a point about the importance of motion pictures that build better human values. "When he was a youngster attending moving picture shows," the story began, "their influence was such that he went home and tried to rope his sister, and played stagecoach robber and horse thief. It was this that impressed upon his mind the necessity of making pictures that would impress the proper ideas upon the fertile minds of boys and girls." Mix then moralized, "There are many young people in high schools and colleges who refuse to listen to teachers and parents, but who are quick to learn lessons of either good or bad from the movies. In order to help out my young friends I have made it a point never to smoke, drink nor gamble in my pictures."[7]

Mix was perhaps reacting to Prohibition more than offering his personal beliefs, but he was talking to the right audience in predominantly Latter-day Saint Cedar City. He even brought up the 1918 film version of Zane Grey's *Riders of the Purple Sage*, made by the Fox studio, which drew protests from the church's officials and was subsequently "suppressed because of its radical attack on Mormonism." He announced to readers of the *Iron County Record* that he would be starring in a remake of that Western classic, "but every bit of the religious influence has been taken out."[8]

Shooting on *The Deadwood Coach* began in Zion National Park with a principal cast that included Doris May, De Witt Jennings (billed as "character lead"), and George Bancroft (the "heavy"), who made quite a career for himself into the

1940s, including a featured role in John Ford's *Stagecoach*. Unfortunately, *The Deadwood Coach* is among many films made during the silent movie era that, as of this writing, no longer exist. Only a handful of still photographs are left to document the locations used in the filming. These are augmented by the recollections of a few residents of the area who were youngsters then but later shared their memories about Mix's visit. J. L. Crawford remembered that the company stayed in the Wylie tent camps because the Zion Lodge had not yet been built. He also remembered going about a mile up the east fork of the canyon and across the Virgin River "several times." Crawford wrote that his brother Lloyd and his friends, Victor Ruesch, Lawrence Gifford, and Emil Justet, also "got to watch Tom Mix jump off a cliff into the river and stay under water while a whole bunch of Indians rode past."[9]

Another location was between the small communities of Springdale and Rockville, memorable to Crawford because that is where the thirteen-year-old had his picture taken, along with his friends, with the Western movie icon. "The star graciously posed for two shots," Crawford wrote later on. "One standing beside his horse and one in the saddle. He turned out to be very friendly, answering questions freely. He volunteered that the horse he had with him wasn't the famous Tony but this was 'Buster,' with a white blaze painted down his face to make him look like Tony, as he would become 'Tony' in the picture. Tony had been trained to do tricks and was almost as famous as his master. Buster was a little larger and more robust than Tony, who was getting old and too valuable to bring out into this rough country." Crawford also recalled a scene in which "Tom Mix was riding his horse down a real steep hill, and that was taken just off that big slide up in the canyon. I felt real sorry for that horse."[10]

"Oh, yes, I remember him," said ninety-three-year-old Rockville resident Vilo DeMille of Tom Mix. "They made it up by Shunesburg, up where all the apple tree orchards are, up the highway toward the park entrance. On up further, they made a scene or two. My husband was in that movie, and was always talking about Tom Mix."[11] Rupert Ruesch, whose father, Walter, was the acting superintendent of Zion National Park at the time, was in school when the movie was made. His brother Victor told him that Tom Mix wanted to buy his horse. "I was too bullheaded," Rupert recalled, "and didn't sell it to him."[12]

Filming in Zion went smoothly. "Sunshine is always the factor in any production," Mix wrote. "In the case of the Zion Park pictures the management estimated we would encounter four or five days of cloudy interruption. In all the time at that place everybody had to work while not a cloud appeared on the horizon. Working was good, everybody in the company felt like working hard and the result was we finished there four full days ahead of anticipated schedule."[13]

The company had planned filming four days in the vicinity of Cedar City, which would then bring them to Mix's participation, and that of his "cowpunchers," in the rodeo. However, for reasons unexplained, and to the dismay of Cedar City residents, Fox decided that the company would return and film those sequences at another time, which they never did. The next location was in Bryce Canyon. "At Bryce sunshine again pushed us forward two days," Mix's report continued. "We had but two hours of cloud interruption while on that location."[14] This put them ten days ahead of their schedule and four days before the opening of the rodeo. They left Cedar City by train to Los Angeles, Sunday, August 31.

Some wondered if Mix's early departure from Cedar City indicated any displeasure at coming to Utah in the first place. In a lengthy letter to the *Iron County Record*, Mix was effusively apologetic. "It is the first time in my life that circumstances have compelled me to side step anything like

Facing: One of the few surviving photographs from the film. Below: The coach of the film's title seen in the Grotto in Zion National Park, with Angels Landing in the background.

a promise," Mix wrote. "There is nothing I regret more than my inability to be present at the opening of your rodeo." He hastened to assure the paper's readers of his affection for the people he met. "All the way. . . . we found the same wholesome open hearted welcome. That which impressed us most of all was the good old time manners of the people, young and old. Manners which, many times during the past ten years, I had thought had perished from the face of the earth."

In his lengthy remarks written to placate disappointed readers, Mix revealed, in stark language, the confines of an otherwise colorful and lucrative movie career.

> [I]n my work, I am controlled altogether by luck and circumstances. My time is not mine. When I sign a contract I am obliged to be governed by its terms. I am handled like a race horse and like a race horse I have no voice even in the colors I may have to wear, nor the weight of the saddle I have to carry. I do not know what clothes to wear nor how to wear my hat, whether to carry my hat in my hand or to wear it on my head. Time or date has no place in my life, action is demanded and action supersedes time or any other consideration.[15]

Mix concluded on a brighter, if not prophetic, note. "We have pioneered the picture production business in your section much to our satisfaction and that of the director, and we feel that our reports on the possibilities of your country will induce many other companies to follow."[16] Mix assured his Cedar City readers that the Tom Mix company would be back "frequently" making movies, but *The Deadwood Coach* was the only feature he made on Utah locations. Nevertheless, Utah would not wait long for other films to be made there by the Fox Film Corporation and its successor, Twentieth Century-Fox.

To reinforce Mix's explanation and his apparent helplessness in changing his schedule, Sol M. Wurtzel, the general superintendent at Fox, wrote to the *Iron County Record* that "it is impossible for us to have Mr. Mix return because he is in the midst of a production and any delay in the production would be [at] tremendous cost to us."[17] Four months later, when the editing and titling of *The Deadwood Coach* was completed, Mix telegraphed the Cedar City Chamber of Commerce to announce that "to show my appreciation, sub-titles in *The Deadwood Coach* will tell theatre patrons throughout the world that the scenes were shot in Utah. Without question of doubt your state is a mecca of picturesque atmosphere."[18]

J. L. Crawford, who later in life was a ranger at Zion and at Bryce, remembered getting a photograph of Mix from Hollywood "several months" after the completion of filming of *The Deadwood Coach*. It was much longer after that when the film finally came to the little village of Springdale, probably sometime in 1925. It was shown using a portable projector that Alma Flanigan took to many southern Utah towns, "furnishing his own electric power by means of a dynamo attached to the engine of his Model T Ford," Crawford wrote. "It would be two or three years before commercial electricity came to Springdale."[19] Rupert Ruesch recalled seeing the movie, most likely in Hurricane, some twenty miles away. It was the nearest town with a movie theater. "Movies had quite an effect on us when we were growing up. We'd get all dolled up with chaps and six shooters."[20] However, a search of the 1925 and 1926 issues of the *Iron County Record* does not indicate a showing of *The Deadwood Coach* in Cedar City.

Documentation of any kind is important for this particular film because of its "lost" status, specifically in light of subsequent claims by some in Kanab that parts of *The Deadwood Coach* had been filmed in Johnson Canyon, some fifteen miles east of the small southern Utah town. According to Sylvan Johnson, who lived in Johnson Canyon, "I remember Tom Mix filming right at the mouth of Johnson Canyon."[21] Neither press reports nor statements by Mix have cited anywhere other than Zion and Bryce canyons as production locations for the film. Available photographs confirm those claims.

Heaven on earth to Springdale boys Emil Justet, Victor Ruesch, Lloyd Crawford, and Lawrence Gifford, being photographed with Tom Mix at Shunesburg, just outside the entrance to Zion National Park, in 1924.

Above: "What a treat for you," read the publicity card for *The Shepherd of the Hills*. "The *finest* story of your best liked author, *plus* the peerless beauty spot of the west." Facing: Lobby card for *Ramona*. Background: Molly O'Day and John Boles in Cedar Breaks.

THE SHEPHERD OF THE HILLS, RAMONA, AND THE "BATTLE" OF CEDAR BREAKS

The Ozark Mountains in Missouri provide the setting for Harold Bell Wright's novel *The Shepherd of the Hills,* published in 1907. The book is reputed to be the first million-copy seller, and it was a natural for the movies. The film version was co-directed in 1919 by Wright on location in Missouri. Eight years later, in September 1927, director Albert S. Rogell worked out locations for a second film version of *The Shepherd of the Hills.* Having been sold on Utah locations by Chauncey Parry, Rogell brought his crew from First National Pictures in Hollywood, along with lead actors Alec B. Francis (as "David Howitt," the shepherd), Molly O'Day (as "Sammy Lane"), and John Boles (as "Young Matt").

When Wright assembled the notes for what eventually became his novel, he lived at a place in Missouri called Inspiration Point, which has since been enshrined by visitors. A 230-foot "Inspiration Tower" now invites tourists to see panoramic views of the Missouri countryside. That there is also an Inspiration Point at Cedar Breaks National Monument in southern Utah might have added to Rogell's choice of the location, but no one knows for certain.

Nevertheless, it appears that he held his ground when another film company arrived to shoot on the same spot.

Enter a crew from Inspiration Pictures in Hollywood, led by Edwin Carewe, who had recently finished a prestigious feature film called *Resurrection*, which served as the first starring vehicle for the beautiful Mexican-born actress Dolores del Rio. Apparently, Carewe had also been sold on Utah's scenery, and planned to shoot large portions of his new feature, *Ramona*—based on the popular Helen Hunt Jackson saga of early California—at Zion National Park and then at Cedar Breaks. In fact, Inspiration Point was his choice for key scenes for his film, and his crew apparently arrived at the same time that Rogell and his group from First National were filming their picture.

Above: Delores del Rio shares a moment with forbidden love Warner Baxter in a scene from *Ramona*. Right: Taking a break on location in Zion National Park.

According to the *Iron County Record*, First National had arrived at Inspiration Point first, but Carewe and his company, including Miss del Rio, costar Warner Baxter, Carlos Amor, and a production crew of thirty, insisted on their rights to film at the site. The standoff occurred on Saturday, September 9. "The company filming *Ramona* claimed that their advance man had staked off the Inspiration Point some weeks ago," read the newspaper story, "while *The Shepherd of the Hills* company claimed the point because of the fact that it had been at work there for a couple of weeks." The unnamed reporter then exercised some chamber of commerce-type boosterism when he claimed that "both companies characterized this spot and surrounding locations as being the last virgin spot for this purpose in the United States, and as a consequence were desirous of using the scenery for their respective pictures."[1]

In what would appear to be stereotypical Missouri mountain fashion, the crew of *The Shepherd of the Hills* held the *Ramona* crew at bay with "sawed off shot guns loaded with salt." First National gave in and the managers of both companies sat down to a "peace banquet" at the El Escalante Hotel in Cedar City on Sunday night. It was said that reporters from major newspapers, including the *Los Angeles Times*, *Chicago Tribune*, and *Salt Lake Telegram*, were on hand to cover the dispute. The first two papers were even supposed to publish special afternoon editions highlighting the controversy. However, Cedar City's local newspaper reporter was not taken in by what was apparently just Hollywood ballyhoo: "The people here are divided as to whether to believe the affair was staged for purely publicity purposes or whether it was a real, honest to goodness controversy." Nevertheless, the silver lining was there: "Cedar City certainly got publication in every part of the United States because of it. No doubt hereafter Cedar City will be known as the 'Battle Ground of Movie Companies.'"[2] Unfortunately, as with *The Deadwood Coach* and numerous other films made during the silent film era, *The Shepherd of the Hills* is a lost film.

Nevada (1927)

Often associated with Cedar Breaks as a filming location is Bryce Canyon, located in Garfield County but accessible from Cedar City. The earliest feature film shot there was the 1927 version of Zane Grey's *Nevada*, released by Paramount Pictures. Director John Waters, who returned to Utah locations for Paramount more than any other director during the 1920s, shot his third Zane Grey adaptation in Bryce Canyon before it was officially declared a national park. In 1923, the Utah Parks Company had purchased the buildings and homestead of Reuben C. Syrett, who had lived there since 1916. The film starred a very young Gary Cooper and blonde beauty Thelma Todd, who usually appeared in light comedic roles. William Powell, who would be remembered by movie fans less than a decade later when he costarred with Myrna Loy in the "Thin Man" detective series, was also featured in *Nevada*.

Gary Cooper and Thelma Todd with the hoodoos of Bryce Canyon in the background.

GLORY DAYS FOR CEDAR CITY

The fields north of Parowan masquerade as China as an invasion of locusts goes up in flames in the M-G-M dramatization of Pearl S. Buck's novel *The Good Earth*.

When Chauncey and Gronway Parry established in 1931 what would be known as the Parry Lodge in Kanab, it would be only a few years before most film production moved to Kane County locations, but not before a major studio production and parts of a few others closed out the 1930s in Iron County.

In the summer of 1936, the fields north of the little farming community of Parowan were selected by location scouts from Metro-Goldwyn-Mayer studios for a dramatic scene in their feature film *The Good Earth,* from Pearl S. Buck's best-selling novel. Parowan would become the rice fields of China invaded by a plague of locusts.

The agricultural agent for Iron County reported in 1936 that farmers were facing massive grasshopper invasions in the region because of the large number of eggs laid the previous fall. Residents were "warned early regarding the danger." To combat it, the farmers built what they called "hopper dozers" to catch the little critters. Hollywood also came to the rescue at the suggestion of a highly unlikely source.

An official of the Grasshopper Fish Bait Co. of Los Angeles had been brought in by the county the previous year to combat a major grasshopper infestation. With the impending difficulties in 1936, a "Mr. Jones" from the company suggested to M-G-M that they accompany him to Parowan. They could get their footage of a "locust" plague and the company could do its job as well. Hundreds of locals were hired by M-G-M for more than two months for the building of sets and to assist in the rounding up of 18,000 pounds of live grasshoppers used for these sequences. "These were destroyed and buried by the company as fast as they were used," states the report. "The company spent $8,000 in the county for materials, local labor and other expenses."[1]

The most highly publicized filming event of the decade, however, took place when Iron Springs, a broad plain to the west of Cedar City, was chosen by location scouts from Paramount Pictures to represent Cheyenne, Wyoming, for scenes in Cecil B. DeMille's *Union Pacific.* Headquarters for the second-unit film crew that came to Cedar City on October 27, 1938, were at the Parry Building on Main Street in Cedar City, where second-unit director Arthur Rosson arrived on September 8 to negotiate the studio's many requirements with the Parrys. Rosson had surveyed three other states before deciding on southern Utah. "The great diversification of scenery within such a small area is particularly appealing to picture people," he said. "Within ten miles

of Cedar City one can find perfect duplications for the plains states, desert, or any kind of mountain imaginable."[2]

Typically, a second-unit crew on any film shoot does not involve principal cast members, who on this film were Joel McCrea, Barbara Stanwyck, Robert Preston, and Brian Donlevy. Rather, scenes of laying track, Indian attacks on the railroad crews, a train wreck, run-by shots of the vintage Union Pacific train, and activities in Cheyenne were filmed at the abandoned railroad station at Iron Springs. The railroad spur to the iron mines was also used to depict other geographical areas along the route. The *Union Pacific* shoot was the first major test of the Parrys' ability to coordinate with a major film company to provide crew transportation, historic rolling stock (covered wagons, carriages, etc.), local talent (for extras in the cast), labor, teamsters, wranglers, and lodging at the El Escalante Hotel for the one-month shoot.

Nearly one hundred locals were signed as extras and dozens more were hired as laborers for set construction. One of those hired was Helen Parry, Chauncey's wife, who, according to her daughter Louise, played the role of an "old washer woman, made up to look old and poor." In a particular scene where Helen is scrubbing away using a vintage washtub, director Rosson noticed that she was wearing the beautiful diamond ring that her husband had given her at their marriage. "Mrs. Parry, will you please take off that ring? It's inappropriate," he said. "So, in our family," recalls her daughter, "that ring has a history all its own."[3] Rosson went away happy when the production company left Cedar City for Los Angeles on November 20.

Iron Springs, west of Cedar City, stood in for Cheyenne, Wyoming, for rail-laying scenes in DeMille's *Union Pacific*.

Drums Along the Mohawk (1939)

Southern Utah's long-term success in hosting movie studios would only be assured by snagging a major studio production, the entirety of which would be filmed on location. This would not only raise the area's profile among the big studios, but would also result in considerably more money for county businesses and residents as well. As if to fill a custom-made order for Iron, Kane, and Garfield counties, Twentieth Century-Fox announced in the summer of 1939 that it would film *Drums Along the Mohawk* in the Dixie National Forest on Cedar Mountain, to be directed by John Ford, one of the studio's finest directors, and filmed in the seldom-used Technicolor process. Based on the best-selling novel of the Revolutionary War by Walter Edmonds, *Drums* was planned as a major studio release. The hills of Utah would double for the Mohawk Valley of upstate New York in the story of a young married couple (played by Henry Fonda and Claudette Colbert) whose attempt to establish a home in the wilderness with other families is met with continual Indian attacks that end only with the British surrender at Yorktown. Ford had scored big with *The Iron Horse* (1925) as well as *Young Mr. Lincoln* (1939), with Henry Fonda in the title role.

The studio cast and crew arrived in Cedar City by train on July 6, 1939, and were bused to the primary filming location in Sidney Valley, high up on the plateau of the Dixie National Forest, approximately thirty miles from Cedar City, seventy miles from Kanab, and only a few miles from Cedar Breaks National Monument. Ford chose the location because of the "never-failing blue skies, cloudless days, the absence of mist, and all-around ideal picture-making conditions. . . . I decided it was perfect on my first inspection of the Cedar mountain region."[4] Near the shooting location at over ten thousand feet elevation, the weary Hollywood travelers found a sprawling tent city furnished by the Anderson Boarding and Supply Company of Los Angeles—the same outfit with which Whit Parry honed his culinary expertise in Arizona prior to his return to Utah. It was called "Camp Drums" and was the hub of the company's filming at the nearby Kane County locations of Duck Creek and Navajo Lake.

There were accommodations for at least 250 people, consisting of deluxe tent cabins with hot and cold running water, electric lights, and oil heaters. The contract with the Anderson company specified "janitor and/or maid service to furnish and change all towels and linens not less than twice per week" and that the sleeping quarters consist of "coil spring beds, clean mattresses of first-class quality, sheets, pillow cases and an adequate number of blankets."[5] A camp newspaper was published and entertainment was provided each evening, including the projection of movies. A strict regimen was established—up at five o'clock for makeup and wardrobe and lights out by eleven o'clock. "It was indeed a democratic camp," wrote one reporter who visited the location, "fashioned in the good American way of 'free and equal.'"[6] It was estimated that approximately two thousand people from the surrounding counties were hired at one time or another as extras, construction laborers, transportation workers, wranglers, and for the rental of livestock.

John Ford, Henry Fonda, Claudette Colbert, Ward Bond, and others were housed with the rest of the cast and crew at the mountaintop encampment. Merle Morris, a driver for Gronway Parry's transportation company, remembered how

Thrilling! Stirring! Spectacular!
DARRYL F. ZANUCK'S
production of
DRUMS ALONG THE MOHAWK
STARRING
Claudette COLBERT
Henry FONDA
WITH
Edna May OLIVER · Eddie COLLINS · John CARRADINE · Dorris BOWDON
Jessie RALPH · Arthur SHIELDS · Robert LOWERY · Roger IMHOF
A 20th CENTURY-FOX PICTURE
Photographed in
TECHNICOLOR
DIRECTED BY
JOHN FORD
ASSOCIATE PRODUCER
Raymond Griffith
Screen play by LAMAR TROTTI AND SONYA LEVIEN ~ BASED UPON THE NOVEL BY WALTER D. EDMONDS

kind Colbert was in attending the frequent evening dances that were held in Kanab during the production. Morris, who was a good dancer, enjoyed taking a few spins himself with the star on the dance floor.[7] Kanab resident Jackie Hamblin Rife—later a noted extra and stuntwoman—was a youngster at the time *Drums* was in production. She was an extra in a scene that never made it into the finished film. "The one scene that I do remember was when an Indian scalped me," Rife recalled. "He came at me with a tomahawk and I was truly terrified."[8]

Mary Gae Evans of Parowan had family connections that provided what she described as a "wonderful summer." The then-seven-year-old remembered that "It was the most wonderful summer! I just loved it. The [movie] Indians were so good to us children. They made cradles and dolls out of the wood from the quaking aspen trees." Evans appears in a scene where the frontier farm of Henry Fonda and Claudette Colbert is set afire by raiders, and she, along with other children, are hurried onto wagons to escape the blaze. "I can see myself in the movie, wearing a long skirt that was a kind of gray plaid and I was wearing a bonnet. I'm not in the scene long, but I'm there," she said, adding that there was only one take of the fire scene. "There was also a lot of sitting around and waiting, but it was fun. And, oh, how I loved the lunches they served."[9]

In a climactic scene in *Drums,* Evans was among the children inside the fort, which was under attack. "I could hear the gunshots from inside the fort, but I knew that it was play acting. It was more exciting than scary, because I was in the fort with a lot of our good friends and neighbors who were hired as extras." The fort, she remembered with emphasis after sixty-nine years, "wasn't just a front. It was built like a real fort."[10] Evans also remembered that, when the sets were dismantled that summer, her father used

Left: "Camp Drums" was a complete living facility with electricity and running water, built a short distance from the filming site of *Drums Along the Mohawk* in Sidney Valley. Background: British troops lay siege to the fort in *Drums Along the Mohawk*. The massive structure was built a few miles from Cedar Breaks. Facing, left: Parowan resident Mary Gae Evans (third from left) in front of the fort set in Sidney Valley for *Drums Along the Mohawk*. Facing, right: Henry Fonda (standing at far right) participating in evening entertainment at Camp Drums.

the salvaged lumber to build barns and repair cabins, as did many other local residents. After leaving an estimated $300,000 in the local Depression-era economy, the *Drums* company packed up and left on the train from Cedar City for Hollywood at the end of July. "They have enjoyed their stay in the mountains of Southern Utah," noted the *Kane County Standard,* "but they are somewhat disappointed in the citizenry here. They feel that more should be done to advertise to the world the wonderful recreation grounds, scenic attractions and fishing streams and lakes in this section. Several also voiced the fact that they felt they had met some of the most hospitable, open-minded and fun-loving people of the nation in their visit to this section of the state." The unnamed writer encouraged Kane County residents to see the movie on its release later in the year, "if for no other reason than to show that they appreciate the interest these people have shown in this section and the advantages their visit has afforded." The writer even speculated on the viewing experience when that time arrived. "There is no doubt that these things together with the fact that many local people have taken part in this production, will be completely forgotten. They will be overshadowed by the acting, the story, the color and the fact that theatre goers, even many local people, will be seeing the wonderful scenery of this section of the state for the first time."[11]

For Henry Fonda, it was apparently the experience of a lifetime. "There's something in the air up here that makes for good fellowship, and we make the most of it," he observed during the film's production. "I don't believe that any of us ever enjoyed a location more than this. It's a real health resort and, as for the scenery—there's nothing like this country in all the world."[12]

Brigham Young (1940)

In 1938, Darryl F. Zanuck, legendary production chief at Twentieth Century-Fox, chose the plight of the persecuted Latter-day Saints and their trek to Utah as the subject of one of the studio's most ambitious epics. Since Salt Lake City was too populated to serve as the backdrop to the story, most of *Brigham Young* was filmed at Lone Pine, California, the site of dozens of Western films since 1920. However, many scenes depicting a long line of wagons crossing the plains of Nebraska and Wyoming had to be depicted for this epic film, and southern Utah fit the bill. During the summer of 1939, dozens of covered wagons that had been built for the movie in Hollywood joined those that had been restored by Gronway Parry in Cedar City for second-unit shooting on the desert west of the Parowan Gap. The effort it took to assemble the wagons and costume the characters, the weeks of preparation and filming, got only seconds of screen time, but these scenes are deemed invaluable in conveying the size and scope of the film's story. Second-unit shooting brought thousands of dollars to Cedar City and surrounding communities.

A climactic scene in *Brigham Young* was made at Utah Lake, near the college town of Provo in Utah County. One

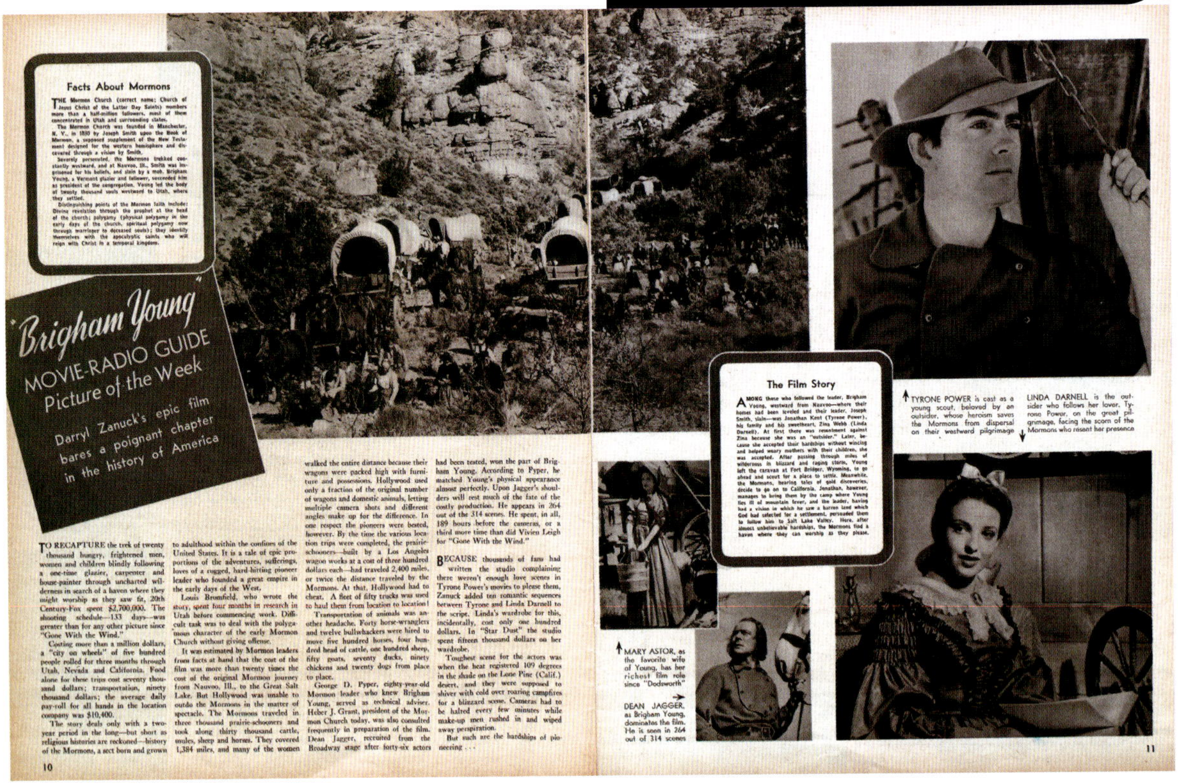

A contemporary movie magazine, summarizing the plot of *Brigham Young*, shows wagons winding through a mountain pass in Iron County.

Facts About Mormons

THE Mormon Church (correct name: Church of Jesus Christ of the Latter Day Saints) numbers more than a half-million followers, most of them concentrated in Utah and surrounding states.

The Mormon Church was founded in Manchester, N. Y., in 1830 by Joseph Smith upon the Book of Mormon, a supposed supplement of the New Testament designed for the western hemisphere and discovered through a vision by Smith.

Severely persecuted, the Mormons trekked constantly westward, and at Nauvoo, Ill., Smith was imprisoned for his beliefs, and slain by a mob. Brigham Young, a Vermont glazier and follower, succeeded him as president of the congregation. Young led the body of twenty thousand souls westward to Utah, where they settled.

Distinguishing points of the Mormon faith include: Divine revelation through the prophet at the head of the church; polygamy (physical polygamy in the early days of the church, spiritual polygamy now through marriage to deceased souls); they identify themselves with the apocalyptic saints who will reign with Christ in a temporal kingdom.

"Brigham Young"

MOVIE-RADIO GUIDE Picture of the Week

Darryl Zanuck's epic film bares a poignant chapter in the history of America

TO RECAPTURE the trek of twenty thousand hungry, frightened men, women and children blindly following a one-time glazier, carpenter and house-painter through uncharted wilderness in search of a haven where they might worship as they saw fit, 20th Century-Fox spent $2,700,000. The shooting schedule—133 days—was greater than for any other picture since "Gone With the Wind."

Costing more than a million dollars, a "city on wheels" of five hundred people rolled for three months through Utah, Nevada and California. Food alone for these trips cost seventy thousand dollars; transportation, ninety thousand dollars; the average daily pay-roll for all hands in the location company was $10,400.

The story deals only with a two-year period in the long—but short as religious histories are reckoned—history of the Mormons, a sect born and grown to adulthood within the confines of the United States. It is a tale of epic proportions of the adventures, sufferings, loves of a rugged, hard-hitting pioneer leader who founded a great empire in the early days of the West.

Louis Bromfield, who wrote the story, spent four months in research in Utah before commencing work. Difficult task was to deal with the polygamous character of the early Mormon Church without giving offense.

It was estimated by Mormon leaders from facts at hand that the cost of the film was more than twenty times the cost of the original Mormon journey from Nauvoo, Ill., to the Great Salt Lake. But Hollywood was unable to outdo the Mormons in the matter of spectacle. The Mormons traveled in three thousand prairie-schooners and took along thirty thousand cattle, mules, sheep and horses. They covered 1,384 miles, and many of the women walked the entire distance because their wagons were packed high with furniture and possessions. Hollywood used only a fraction of the original number of wagons and domestic animals, letting multiple camera shots and different angles make up for the difference. In one respect the pioneers were bested, however. By the time the various location trips were completed, the prairie-schooners—built by a Los Angeles wagon works at a cost of three hundred dollars each—had traveled 2,400 miles, or twice the distance traveled by the Mormons. At that, Hollywood had to cheat. A fleet of fifty trucks was used to haul them from location to location!

Transportation of animals was another headache. Forty horse-wranglers and twelve bullwhackers were hired to move five hundred horses, four hundred head of cattle, one hundred sheep, fifty goats, seventy ducks, ninety chickens and twenty dogs from place to place.

George D. Pyper, eighty-year-old Mormon leader who knew Brigham Young, served as technical adviser. Heber J. Grant, president of the Mormon Church today, was also consulted frequently in preparation of the film. Dean Jagger, recruited from the Broadway stage after forty-six actors had been tested, won the part of Brigham Young. According to Pyper, he matched Young's physical appearance almost perfectly. Upon Jagger's shoulders will rest much of the fate of the costly production. He appears in 264 out of the 314 scenes. He spent, in all, 189 hours before the cameras, or a third more time than did Vivien Leigh for "Gone With the Wind."

BECAUSE thousands of fans had written the studio complaining there weren't enough love scenes in Tyrone Power's movies to please them, Zanuck added ten romantic sequences between Tyrone and Linda Darnell to the script. Linda's wardrobe for this, incidentally, cost only one hundred dollars. In "Star Dust" the studio spent fifteen thousand dollars on her wardrobe.

Toughest scene for the actors was when the heat registered 109 degrees in the shade on the Lone Pine (Calif.) desert, and they were supposed to shiver with cold over roaring campfires for a blizzard scene. Cameras had to be halted every few minutes while make-up men rushed in and wiped away perspiration.

But such are the hardships of pioneering . . .

10

The Film Story

AMONG those who followed the leader, Brigham Young, westward from Nauvoo—where their homes had been leveled and their leader, Joseph Smith, slain—was Jonathan Kent (Tyrone Power), his family and his sweetheart, Zina Webb (Linda Darnell). At first there was resentment against Zina because she was an "outsider." Later, because she accepted their hardships without wincing and helped weary mothers with their children, she was accepted. After passing through miles of wilderness in blizzard and raging storm, Young left the caravan at Fort Bridger, Wyoming, to go ahead and scout for a place to settle. Meanwhile, the Mormons, hearing tales of gold discoveries, decide to go on to California. Jonathan, however, manages to bring them by the camp where Young lies ill of mountain fever, and the leader, having had a vision in which he saw a barren land which God had selected for a settlement, persuaded them to follow him to Salt Lake Valley. Here, after almost unbelievable hardships, the Mormons find a haven where they can worship as they please.

↑ TYRONE POWER is cast as a young scout, beloved by an outsider, whose heroism saves the Mormons from dispersal on their westward pilgrimage

LINDA DARNELL is the outsider who follows her lover, Tyrone Power, on the great pilgrimage, facing the scorn of the Mormons who resent her presence ↓

↑ MARY ASTOR, as the favorite wife of Young, has her richest film role since "Dodsworth"

→ DEAN JAGGER, as Brigham Young, dominates the film. He is seen in 264 out of 314 scenes

11

RIGHAM YOUNG
... revealing the story behind the heroic Mormon trek to freedom ... and the virile, fighting giant of a man who led it! Spectacularly produced ... unforgettable for ...
COURAGE! 20,000 people braving torrents..freezing cold..fever..across endless miles of trackless waste!
THE LEADER! Brigham Young .. colorful, dominant, steel-willed! A man who was to have 27 wives, build one of the world's famous cities, found a great state!
YOUNG LOVERS!.. facing untold dangers for the day they could belong to each other!
MASSACRE AT NAUVOO! Masked raiders riding by night .. burning, pillaging, murdering!
FLIGHT! Men, women, children, babes in arms..driven before guns across the cracking ice of the Mississippi!
STAMPEDE! 5,000 maddened buffalo charging across the plains!
DISASTER! The sky black with devouring insects, ravaging the crops of a starving people!
THE MIRACLE! A million gulls, sweeping in five hundred miles from the sea to save them!

of the most oft-told accounts in Latter-day Saint history has to do with the threat posed by thousands of crickets (later called the Mormon Cricket) to the first harvest of the early settlers in 1848. As the wave of crickets began destroying the valued grain that would carry the pioneers through the following winter, the Church members prayed to God for deliverance from this scourge. Contemporary diary accounts record that seagulls swooped down from the sky to devour and then disgorge the multilegged invaders. The "miracle of the gulls" was a manifestation of hope to the advance contingent of these hardy pioneers and saved their new settlement from destruction. To visualize this episode, a Fox camera crew and director traveled to Provo in the summer of 1939. The goal was to get shots from various angles of large flocks of seagulls coming out of the sky and lighting on the ground. The crew was having difficulty in attracting the birds. Neither meat nor fish thrown out near the shore of the lake enticed them. John A. Widtsoe, one of the church's twelve apostles, who served as the liaison between the studio and the church, drove down to Provo from Salt Lake City. As cameraman Charles G. Clarke later recounted the episode, a minor miracle of its own occurred on that day. "He kindly led the prayer of our re-enactment of the crickets-devouring-the-crops-scene and the seagulls came!"[13]

A color-tinted lobby card shows off the wide prairie expanse west of Parowan.

Can't Help Singing (1944)

Wartime conditions actually increased movie production in Utah, and major singing star Deanna Durbin came to Cedar City in mid-August 1944 to make *Can't Help Singing.* Durbin's films, beginning with *Three Smart Girls* in 1936, had saved Universal Pictures from bankruptcy, and subsequent films confirmed her enormous popularity. The party, consisting of Durbin, her costar Robert Paige, director Frank Ryan, and selected members of the principal cast, were met at Cedar City by Frank E. O'Brien of Utah's Department of Publicity and Industrial Development (PID), created in 1941 by Governor Herbert Maw to help coordinate contacts between the Hollywood movie studios and local Utah municipalities. The department worked well with the Parry brothers in providing the roadwork that was necessary to access movie locations. For some reason, the El Escalante Hotel required $3,000 worth of renovations, paid for by Universal, before the studio entourage arrived.

Why would the story of *Can't Help Singing,* set in California in 1849, be filmed in Utah? The answer came from a reporter who talked with the film's producer, Felix Jackson, associate producer Frank Shaw, and director Frank Ryan, who listed three reasons: "California's green hills are brown and this movie is Technicolor. Utah doesn't have so many high tension lines to get into the scenery. Cloud effects in Utah are prettier than cloud effects in California."[14] Technicolor, used for barely five percent of all movies made at the time, made news. "For the last eight years Deanna has been a black and white shadow on the screen before them," read a Universal Pictures publicity brochure. "Now she is being brought to them in all the beauty of her own natural coloring. . . . The coloring has been captured by the camera in her first Technicolor production, *Can't Help Singing*."

Right: Popular singer Deanna Durbin's only Technicolor film, *Can't Help Singing* was filmed substantially in Iron County, with forays into Kane County. Facing: Recipe for success: Technicolor, cumulus clouds, and the smile of Deanna Durbin.

Deanna Durbin's singing is augmented by the breathtaking beauty of Cedar Breaks.

Left: Pioneers cross near Navajo Lake on Cedar Mountain. Above: The prairie landmark known as Parowan Gap served as dramatic framing for the wagon train that carried Deanna Durbin west to meet her fiancé in *Can't Help Singing*.

The desert west of Parowan was used for wagon train sequences, as was Navajo Lake in Kane County, high in the mountains above Cedar City. The Kane County location of Johnson Canyon, east of Kanab, was the site of the military post of Durbin's fiancé in the film, used only months earlier for William Wellman's *Buffalo Bill* by Twentieth Century-Fox. A highlight of *Can't Help Singing* was set in pine-forested Cedar Breaks. As Durbin begins singing Jerome Kern's tune "Any Moment Now," she walks through the trees, and then the orange limestone formations of Cedar Breaks open up as the finale of the song is performed. Onscreen, it is a breathtaking moment. A color photograph captured by the studio's photographer went nationwide for the Sunday editions in many of America's newspapers.

Variety, the movie industry's trade paper, noted that Durbin "is beautifully displayed in the excellent Technicolor photography provided. In addition, the scenic backgrounds of Utah locations that comprise a major portion of the footage, give fine mounting to the general setting. . . . Exterior locations in Utah are tops for scenic values, with the color photography accentuating the overall eye appeal." The reviewer commended the efforts taken to shoot "the expensive production numbers, and many vistas of the long wagon train threading through the plains and mountains of the western country."[15] The *Salt Lake Tribune,* concluding its coverage of the production, noted with expectation that "this concentration on Utah's national parks as backgrounds of full-length pictures is expected to reap a tremendous tourist trade after the war."[16]

Proud Rebel (1958)

Even though the glory days of Cedar City film production passed with the making of *Can't Help Singing,* there was one more feature to come to the area more than a decade later. By the late 1950s, movie studios were letting go of their contract talent of actors and directors and, in a calculated move to stay solvent, selling their classic-era feature films to television. Samuel Goldwyn Jr. was the thirty-year-old son of one of the few independent producers left in the business. For his third project, he chose a post–Civil War story. The plateaus above Cedar City became southern Illinois in the late 1860s. Up that high there were no towering mountains to betray the mountainous Western location. The normally urbane Olivia de Havilland, distinguished by roles in big-budget films that included *Gone With the Wind,* looked for challenging roles later in her career. In *Proud Rebel,* she plays a farmer who occupies a house situated in Rush Lake, west of Cedar City. Alan Ladd, the "proud rebel" of the film's title, is an ex-Confederate soldier who travels to Illinois in search of medical care for his deaf-mute son, played by David Ladd, the actor's real-life eleven-year-old son.

The pace of *Proud Rebel* is leisurely and the photography by veteran cameraman Ted McCord emphasizes the warm reds and yellows of Utah in the fall, from the quaking aspens near Cedar Breaks to the yellow-brown hues of Rush Valley. Character actor Dean Jagger plays a nasty old rancher trying to get widow de Havilland's land. The film was directed by the venerable Michael Curtiz, who had previously directed de Havilland and Errol Flynn in *The Adventures of Robin Hood* and other films at Warner Bros. during Hollywood's Golden Age. "How did you ever find this place?" a *New York Times* reporter asked Goldwyn. "Looked," he replied. "No high mountains in our camera. We're above them. This is Illinois right after the Civil War. That and the fact they've got sheep here is why we came."[17]

J. L. Crawford was a naturalist at Bryce Canyon at the time *Proud Rebel* was in production. He remembered three people, dressed in hiking attire, who came into the park museum that he managed. One of them, a female, was dressed "in old, faded dungarees, and a sloppy felt hat with the brim turned down." For at least thirty minutes, he answered her questions about the different kinds of trees and sold her a number of publications before the trio left to hit the trails. Later, Crawford met his wife at the cafeteria and met the same group, back from their hike. Their earlier discussion continued until the party left. "When we got home that night, a friend asked us, with some excitement, 'Oh, have you seen Olivia de Havilland

Deaf-mute David Ladd is nearly run over by Olivia de Havilland in *Proud Rebel*.

in the park?' Here I was hobnobbing with her and didn't even recognize her!"[18]

Thanks to Chauncey and Gronway Parry, Cedar City will always remain the city of record that first brought Hollywood to southern Utah with *The Deadwood Coach*. Many films based later on at Kanab would film seconds here, minutes there in the beautiful wilds of Cedar Breaks, Cedar Canyon, and at various locations on Cedar Mountain. By the early 1940s, Cedar City had lost its status as a movie-production hub, but it will never lose its historical importance as the birthplace of the Hollywood movie industry in Utah. The arrival of the *Drums Along the Mohawk* company was, in reality, the end of Iron County's glory days as the center of movie production. Over the next decade, the city of Kanab would establish premiere status as the most-often-used filming location outside of California, and would earn the titles "Utah's Hollywood" and "Little Hollywood."

SCENE 2

WASHINGTON COUNTY 1927–1979

FROM SILENTS TO SOUND

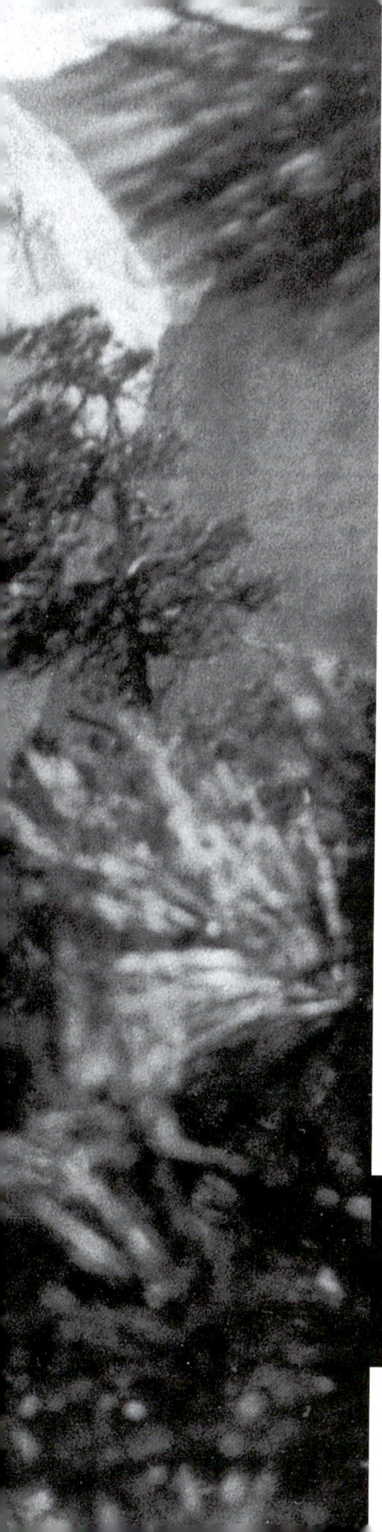

One of the first films to take advantage of Zion National Park's canyons and riverbeds, *Ramona* is not a Western in the traditional sense, but a story of old California. It was the last silent movie filmed substantially within Zion National Park. By the time the crew from Inspiration Pictures arrived in Utah in September 1927, Mexican-born actress Dolores del Rio had become quite a sensation. She came to the United States with her husband to get into the movie business after having become friends with *Ramona*'s future director, Edwin Carewe. Her marriage to Jaime del Rio broke up just months before she arrived in Utah for *Ramona,* but by that time she had appeared in a handful of small films and also in Raoul Walsh's *What Price Glory?* She also had a lead role in M-G-M's epic silent feature *Trail of '98*, directed by Clarence Brown, and released only a month after *Ramona*. In a contemporary publication, del Rio referred to *Ramona* as "my first recognized starring vehicle, and, of course, I am very enthusiastic over it. It is a beautiful love story—the romance of a girl, a half-Indian, who finds happiness in marriage with two men, an Indian and a Spaniard."[1] Her lead role in *Ramona* made Dolores del Rio a star.

Carewe's traveling to Utah to film a California story might perhaps be explained by his fresh approach to making movies: finding locations that conveyed a sense of the story, whether filmed on the locale of the story or not. "There are no time-honored precedents, rules and regulations governing the making of motion pictures to damper the enthusiasm of a pioneering spirit or a man with new ideas," he wrote. "In no other business are new ideas so welcome as in this amazing and fast-growing film art. A director may do a thing one

Left: An ethereally beautiful location for *Ramona*, with Zion Canyon's East Rim in the background. Right: Warner Baxter and Dolores del Rio in Zion National Park.

A lavish hacienda constructed at the Temple of Sinawava in Zion National Park for *Ramona*.

way today and do it entirely differently tomorrow. He need not follow a beaten path and do something this or that way because it was done this or that way by someone before."[2]

Considerable time was spent on *Ramona* in Springdale and in the park. J. L. Crawford recalled a particular scene near the Springdale ditch where del Rio was filming "where there were willows just like a jungle growing. They built a little bridge across the canal and Dolores del Rio walked across this. My father happened to be watching that and he counted the number of takes. He counted 25 walks across the bridge. I can understand why so many actors prefer stage acting to movies."[3]

Crawford was impressed with the equipment needed to film a motion picture. "It seemed that trucks were rolling in for more than a week, bringing equipment and props including palm trees." Most of all, he remembered the construction of a magnificent hacienda "at the end of the canyon road, in the Temple of Sinawava." A cabin was also built on the West Rim Trail that, Crawford claimed, "was burned as part of the story." Crawford also had access to park superintendent Eivend T. Scoyen, who, as Crawford's cousin related to him years later, "almost got fired when Director [Stephen] Mather [of the Department of the Interior] heard about the two buildings he allowed

Several stories by popular Western author Zane Grey were filmed on location in Zion National Park, including the now-lost *The Vanishing Pioneer.* Here, a grateful pioneer expresses thanks at arriving at his destination.

the movie company to erect. He reminded the director that his position gave him that authority, to which Mather agreed, but with the verbal slap-on-the-wrist that he could have said something to his boss."[4] The matter of permissions for movie companies to shoot within the park would become a weightier issue within the next decade.

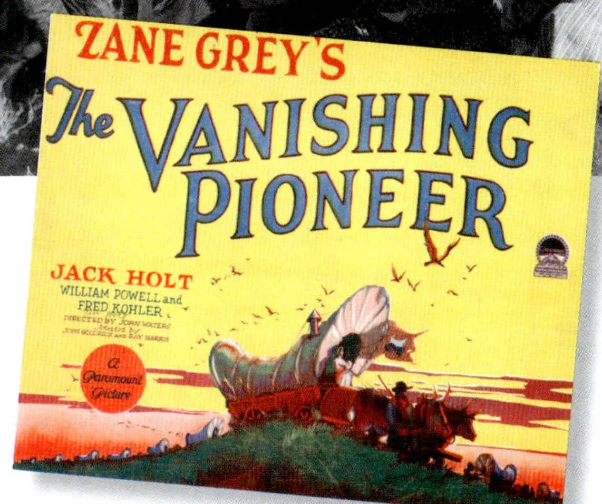

In Old Arizona (1929)

With the Warner Bros. release of *The Jazz Singer* with Al Jolson in 1927, the future of sound films was assured. The Vitaphone process put the dialogue and music recordings on a lacquer disc that was synchronized during projection with the film. By the close of 1929, most of the movie theaters in America were wired for sound reproduction, and studios had switched to all-sound production. Movietone, a sound-on-film process developed by Fox Film Corporation, was eventually adopted by all studios.

"For the first time, William Fox brings to the screen not only the realistic settings but also the *natural sounds* of the great outdoors!" declared a full-page advertisement for Fox's *In Old Arizona,* the first all-talking Western drama.[5] The Western movie would talk first in Utah, utilizing the virtually abandoned pioneer town of Grafton, near the entrance to Zion National Park, for filming. A brief announcement in the *Washington County News* in April 1928 was the first suggestion that Fox was looking for locations for its next film. Toquerville and Hurricane were mentioned as considerations by the unnamed "advance agent" for Fox.[6]

The little town of Grafton was an ideal spot for filming. It already had a combination church and schoolhouse, built in 1888, as well as several vintage homes that were built during the same era. There was also enough room to construct a saloon set and other buildings needed to complete a burgeoning 1880s Arizona town. Grafton had been settled by Latter-day Saint pioneers in 1861, close to the banks of the Virgin River, which flowed out of Zion Canyon and past the villages of Springdale and Rockville. Life was hard in Grafton; the sandy soil resisted attempts by the pioneers to establish an agricultural base—although further up the river near Springdale a large apple orchard thrived—but these were hardy people. Difficulty in getting water and scarce employment in the surrounding area eventually caused the last remaining family to abandon the struggling town in 1944.

Director Raoul Walsh was no stranger to rough-hewn Western environments. Although born and raised in upper-class settings in New York City and educated at Seton Hall, he went to sea following the death of his mother and then punched cattle in Texas and Montana. Following this itinerant lifestyle, he got into acting. D. W. Griffith engaged him as both an actor and an assistant director in his landmark film *The Birth of A Nation*, in which Walsh appeared as John Wilkes Booth. Walsh had a successful career at Fox, directing and acting in the box-office hits *What Price Glory?* and *Miss Sadie Thompson*. Having lived the life of a rough-and-tumble westerner, he was well suited to the story of the Cisco Kid, taken from O. Henry's story "The Caballero Way," which forms the basis of *In Old Arizona.*

Walsh had seen an early "talkie," and he had not been impressed by its claustrophobic sets and stilted dialogue. He was determined to make the first sound feature outdoors on location, telling Fox production chief Winfield Sheehan, "I want a good newsreel truck and a Western script. Let me have the sound truck and I'll give you sound *and* the old action. We'll knock the public dead." This was on a Thursday, according to Walsh. By Sunday, he had written the basis for a script and was ready to leave town. "We traveled light," he recounted in his autobiography. "The only cast I took was our female star, myself, and three cowboys. . . . If I needed any more extras, I would hire them locally. We left Hollywood like thieves in the night; two automobiles, the Movietone truck, and the property van bringing up the rear, not a very impressive mobilization to shoot sound in the desert."[7] Walsh served as both director and star of *In Old Arizona.*

Walsh's story of sudden decisions and rushed departure schedules has an attractive, even romantic, tone to it, but it fails to take into

consideration even the minimal time necessary to build sets and to obtain the permissions to film on private land. Nevertheless, production began with the intention of making the film a two-reeler, approximately twenty minutes long in screen time. Rushes—the daily footage shot by the company—were sent back to Sheehan at Fox studios, and the boss was elated by the results. A scene where bacon is fried mesmerized him: "The sizzling was so real it made me hungry." Sheehan then approved making the film feature length.[8] The script was expanded on location. A shootout where three cowboys fire shots at the Cisco Kid from a high cliff above the Rockville Road area was also filmed.

Next, chase scenes were filmed on the Rockville Road south of Grafton, with the massive formations of Zion National Park towering in the background. Not accustomed to sound recording, the driver of the stagecoach and team, brought hastily from Los Angeles, barked profanities to get townspeople out of the way during the filming of the high-speed chase sequences. "Many of the locals left, shocked because their womenfolk had been exposed to such vigorous language," Walsh wrote.[9]

During the filming of a scene where the Cisco Kid robs the stagecoach, Walsh received bad news: the sound truck had broken down. Calls were made to Los Angeles, and the decision was made to return to the studio and film the remaining sequences in a frontier village on the Fox backlot, with a reconstructed adobe hacienda and saloon. Frustrated, the company packed up and was headed to Cedar City, where they would board a Union Pacific train at Lund for Los Angeles. Walsh was sitting next to the driver in the front seat of the car, which was packed with gear. It was nighttime and his driver was traveling fast. "We missed outcrops and cattle and once scattered a herd of deer," Walsh remembered. "The only thing we did not miss was a big jack rabbit."[10] Apparently, the headlights startled the animal, which then jumped through the car's windshield on the passenger side, sending glass splinters into Walsh's face. Blood flowed from his right eye. With an old rag to staunch the bleeding, Walsh was taken into Cedar City, where a doctor quickly stitched up his eyelid, cheek, and nose. The badly damaged eye was removed at Holy Cross Hospital in Salt Lake City, and Walsh sported a fashionable eye patch for the rest of his life, courtesy of a Utah jackrabbit.

Warner Baxter chortles at a wanted poster for the Cisco Kid in *In Old Arizona*.

As for *In Old Arizona,* enough of the usable long shots had been filmed in Utah to blend in with footage that would be shot on the backlot and on location in Southern California by director Irving Cummings, who took over the project. The popular Warner Baxter, who had been involved with *Ramona* the previous year, was signed to replace Walsh as the Cisco Kid and complete the film in Los Angeles. In the finished film, one can see distinctively California desert landscapes in the stagecoach hold-up scene and Joshua trees in many of the shots with Southern California mountains on the horizon. The opening scenes in a Mexican-type village were filmed on the Fox backlot. Hybrid production though it was, the film's most impressive and dramatic landscapes were those shot in the historic town of Grafton, its surrounding cliffs and valleys and the formations of Zion National Park framing the undulating landscape cut by the Virgin River.

In Old Arizona went on to become one of the studio's biggest hits. It cost $304,588 to make and earned well over $1 million, a very handsome sum in 1929. It was released in New York City in January 1929, but Utah residents in Washington County had to wait until late November to see it at the Electric Theatre in St. George. Warner Baxter received the only Academy Award of his career for his flamboyant portrayal of the Cisco Kid.

Left: Warner Baxter, as the title character of *The Arizona Kid*, smiles in repose on the set at Grafton. Facing: While shooting *The Arizona Kid*, the crew camped in "Foxville," where some of the principals pose for a picture, including Warner Baxter (third from left), Mona Maris (fourth from left), Carole Lombard (fifth from left), producer Sol Wurtzel (second from right), and director Alfred Santell (far right).

The Arizona Kid (1930)

The innovative use of sound on location, combined with the tremendous commercial success of *In Old Arizona,* convinced Fox that they had a franchise on their hands, and an additional Western feature, *The Arizona Kid,* was quickly approved. While the story does utilize a character similar to the Cisco Kid, it is more derivative of the O. Henry story from which the character originated. This time, Grafton was chosen as the sole location and Warner Baxter was engaged to once again play the lead. Future star (and wife of Clark Gable) Carole Lombard had a prominent role in the film. Director Alfred Santell and associate producer Sol M. Wurtzel arrived in Grafton on February 12, 1930, for thirty-two days of filming. A tent city was constructed to house the cast and crew.

"My mother took in the set construction workers as boarders and cooked meals for them," remembered Vilo DeMille.[11] Additional buildings, including a saloon, were built for the film, as well as other "facilities." Careful planning for *The Arizona Kid* resulted in a longer filming period than for *In Old Arizona* and provided employment for many of the residents of Grafton, as well as nearby Springdale and Rockville.

"This was new to all of us," said DeMille. "I was just an extra, crossed the street in the background. I got paid $4 a day. They paid everyone who worked there every night. Men they paid $6, women and kids got $4 a day. I felt so good every night when I came home. I used to spread my money out on the floor and count it."[12] The teenager accumulated $48, which she saved for college.

Production in Grafton finished on March 22. Editing and scoring of the film was rushed so that *The Arizona Kid* could be released to theaters by the end of April 1930. In this sequel, the Arizona Kid is a lovable rogue bandit-hero who, because of a $5,000 price on his head, is known as Chico Cabrillo to the residents of Rockville. *The Arizona Kid* did not fare as well at the box office as *In Old Arizona,* but it is the more accomplished sound film of the

two. *The Arizona Kid* also shows off more of Grafton and its surroundings than its predecessor.

In *The Arizona Kid,* the town in which the action takes place is "Rockville." The Fox studio publicity manual used by theater owners and newspaper reviewers also emphasized the real locale in its "theme and treatment" suggestions: "A vivid, dynamic romance of the old West of fifty years ago. The exploits of a reckless and amorous bandit with two of his many loves, painted with sweeping strokes against the brilliant background of Zion Canyon, Utah, and the color of a re-created frontier city of the period. A stirring, adventurous story of the days when men lived and fought and loved, not always wisely, but always well." The manual also described the filming location of Grafton as "An army post in Utah Territory and Rockville, a mining town in Utah Territory, in the period of 1880. Filmed in its entirety in and about a reconstructed 'ghost city,' three miles from Rockville, Utah, on the borders of Zion National Park and along the Rio Virgin. Not a single studio scene was made on the production, every foot of film being taken on the exact location of the story."[13] In fact, a further studio claim that *The Arizona Kid* was the first sound film to be photographed entirely on location may indeed be accurate.

The movie that closed out the decade of filming in Zion National Park was director King Vidor's *Billy the Kid* (1930), which used just one shot taken in the park. A second-unit crew from M-G-M traveled all the way to the park for one day's work to capture the grand panoramic image of Zion Canyon from Angels Landing. It appears as the establishing shot of the Western, starring Johnny Mack Brown in the title role, which was otherwise filmed entirely in Southern California. Such was the recognition by those in Hollywood of the impact of Zion National Park as an iconographic representation of the West.

Warner Baxter shakes hands with director Alfred Santell high on the Rockville Road. Mt. Kinesava in Zion National Park rises behind the dramatic desert bluffs.

Left: George O'Brien and LeRoy Mason between takes on *The Dude Ranger* in Zion Canyon. Right: O'Brien and costar Irene Hervey at the Zion Lodge pool.

The Dude Ranger (1934)

While *In Old Arizona* turned out to be a tremendous financial success for Fox, their big-budgeted screen epic *The Big Trail* was a major box-office disaster. As the Great Depression worsened, Westerns were relegated to B status, both as to budgets and in presentation. In light of these financial difficulties, Fox signed agreements with independent producers, one of whom was Sol Lesser. He contracted with the studio to make four pictures a year for release by Fox, all starring George O'Brien, who had been a major star at Fox during the 1920s. By the early '30s, however, O'Brien's popularity lay in low-budget Westerns. One of these was Zane Grey's *The Dude Ranger,* filmed in 1934 in Zion National Park, as well as in Johnson Canyon, east of Kanab.

The Dude Ranger is a contemporary Western in which O'Brien, an easterner, travels west after inheriting a ranch that is the object of cattle rustlers. He falls in love with a local girl (Irene Hervey), but suspects her father is the leader of the cattle thieves. *Variety* noted the otherwise conventional plot, "but the way this Zane Grey plot has been handled the picture stacks as first-class supporting material." The magazine also pointed out that whereas most Westerns of this type stressed action, *The Dude Ranger* has "some handsome scenic values."[14] J. L. Crawford remembered the "Lodge personnel were pleasantly surprised to find those two stars were just common people who mixed freely with employees at the swimming pool and evening programs. Imagine, a lowly dishwasher getting to dance with Irene Hervey."[15]

Dennis O'Keefe and Wallace Beery share a campfire at Zion National Park in *The Bad Man of Brimstone*. Angels Landing can be seen in the distance.

The Bad Man of Brimstone (1937)

In the summer of 1936, M-G-M, perhaps remembering its encounter with Zion National Park for *Billy the Kid,* traveled there once again for major sequences of *The Bad Man of Brimstone*, starring the crusty but popular actor Wallace Beery, who thereafter made annual hunting trips to the region, guided by Chauncey Parry. Some Western town buildings were built for the film, above the banks of the Virgin River near Springdale. Other parts of the film were photographed at Johnson Canyon near Kanab in Kane County, where the cast and crew stayed at the Parry Lodge. Sylvan Johnson, born and raised in Johnson Canyon, remembered Beery as a good rider, but he had to use a stepladder to mount his steed. Beery also bought a number of pieces of antique furniture from the owner of the house in Johnson Canyon that was used for the film. The fifteen-year-old Johnson was part of a group "who got out of school, dressed up as Indians and rode bareback, riding and shooting arrows."[16]

Zion National Park was a world all its own, an escape from the vicissitudes of modern urban life, to which thousands of tourists flocked yearly. However, where movies were concerned, that world soon had portents of a turbulent world outside of it, a world at war. One of the preparedness features made for American audiences by Twentieth Century-Fox was *20,000 Men A Year*. Randolph Scott starred as an airline pilot who bought a private airport just as the US government was establishing its Civilian Pilot Training Program in order to build up the Army Air Corps for possible entry in the war. Most of the film was made in Southern California, but an important flying scene necessitated high canyon walls and impressive visual qualities. The top pilot for the movies in those days was Paul Mantz, who operated out of the airport adjacent to Lockheed Aircraft in Burbank, California. Mantz came to Zion National Park to film the highly specialized flying for which he was famous throughout the Hollywood film community. "Residents of Zion and Springdale were treated to some great aerobatics," wrote J. L. Crawford. "Paul Mantz did the flying for that film in a Waco biplane with a larger than usual engine. A landing strip was improvised in an abandoned field opposite the present Zion Canyon Visitor Center."[17]

World War II brought shortages of groceries, fuel, and raw materials to Americans, but was a boon to motion-picture production in Utah. By the early 1940s, the Parry Lodge in Kanab drew motion-picture production to that area almost exclusively. Several movies made there, including *My Friend Flicka, Thunderhead, Son of Flicka,* and *Smoky*, would have parts filmed within Zion, but permissions and red tape imposed by the Park Service made it more difficult for movies to be made within the borders of the park.

UTAH'S CENTENNIAL FILM: *RAMROD* OR "HAMROD"?

July 24, 1947, marked the one hundredth anniversary of the entrance of Latter-day Saint pioneers into the Salt Lake Valley under the leadership of Brigham Young. The Utah Centennial Commission, which had operated as a funded organization for many years prior to the centennial year, scheduled symposia, publications, celebrations, contests, and parades of all kinds. It seemed to some that there should also be a centennial motion picture. How *Ramrod,* starring popular actors Joel McCrea and Veronica Lake, became Utah's centennial film was the result of policy changes at the National Park Service, and the pro-Utah position of its producer, Harry Sherman, and director Andre de Toth.

Since the 1930s, movie companies had been concerned about the escalating fees charged by the National Park Service to film in the national parks. Following the making of *The Dude Ranger* and some scenes of *The Bad Man of Brimstone* in Zion National Park, movie productions stopped using park locations, except for brief segments of *My Friend Flicka,* released in 1943. That same year, representatives of Utah's Department of Publicity

Veronica Lake and Joel McCrea in a color-tinted lobby card for *Ramrod*.

& Industrial Development (PID) began annual trips to Hollywood to meet with studio executives. In their report, PID commissioner H. J. Plumhof and publicity head Frank O'Brien stated that representatives from Twentieth Century-Fox, Universal, Metro-Goldwyn-Mayer, and RKO studios all "complained about the restrictions placed on taking pictures in the National Parks by Secretary [of the Interior Harold] Ickes, and stated that this policy prevented many pictures being taken in the National Parks, which otherwise would be taken and which would extend advertising value to the State of Utah, to say nothing of the economic benefit."[1]

Tracy Barham, head of the Intermountain Theatres chain in Utah, accompanied Plumhof and O'Brien to Hollywood. He wrote to Utah governor Maw that "Mr. Plumhof has some idea about trying to get the situation relieved in our National Parks and I think [that] as much pressure as possible should be placed on the issue."[2] In fact, Plumhof had already written to the director of the National Park Service, communicating the "strong feeling of opposition" of the studios to the Park Service's fee policy. He counseled Director Newton B. Drury that "our National Parks should not undertake to make a profit from taking pictures within National parks and that their fee should merely be sufficient to reimburse them for out-of-pocket expenses."[3] Plumhof also authorized A. S. Brown of the PID to bring the matter to the attention of Utah senator Abe Murdock. In his telegram, Brown urged the senator to "see if Secretary Ickes will not relax these restrictions in view of the fact that there is practically no travel, and filming of pictures gives wide publicity to such scenic attractions and will induce travel." Brown then appeared to turn the screws on the senator: "Governor Maw tremendously interested in this revenue producer for Utah. Please see Ickes and advise at earliest possible moment."[4]

No return correspondence survives in the PID archive, but it appears that the appeals from Utah to the National Park Service had their effect on public policy toward motion-picture companies. In a July 1944 letter to the location manager for RKO Radio Pictures, Plumhof wrote that "as a result of the effort we made, we are advised at last, as far as the national parks in the State of Utah are concerned, that a different type of interpretation of the Ickes ruling has been made, which we trust will result in charges acceptable to the moving picture industry."[5] The first major feature film to be made within the boundaries of Zion National Park following this positive development was *Ramrod,* which also utilized the ghost town of Grafton.

Ramrod's producer, Harry Sherman, was Boston-born but a westerner at heart. As an independent producer, he brought the famous Western hero Hopalong Cassidy to the screen in 1935 and produced Westerns for release by the major studios and distributors. In 1943, he produced Twentieth Century-Fox's lavish Technicolor production *Buffalo Bill* in Kanab, which was directed by William Wellman and also starred Joel McCrea. Sherman was apparently quite taken with Utah. He had been one of those visited by the PID committee in 1943 when he announced that he had chosen Utah in which to film *Buffalo Bill*. He visited the state in May and was given a tour by Gronway Parry and PID officials. "You could make pictures indefinitely and never 'shoot' all Utah's beauty," Sherman said.[6] Director Andre de Toth, with his associate producer Gene Strong, cameraman Russell Harlan, and art director Lionel Banks, chose the locations for *Ramrod,* after Colorado, Arizona, Nevada, and California had been considered. "Nothing appealed to us so much as Zion National Park," said Strong. "This park has the very sort of awe-inspiring beauty we sought as a background for our action-packed picture."[7] One account indicates that Sherman first visited Grafton as early as 1941.[8] Two locations in the Kolob area, about forty miles from the Zion Lodge, where the principal cast and crew were housed, were also chosen. It was reported that the studio also paid to have the Virgin River rechanneled to bring it closer to the Grafton town site, since the river had changed its course as the result of a violent storm in 1896. The result is evident in the opening scenes of *Ramrod*, where a wagon crosses the Virgin River and, after coming up its banks, enters the outskirts of Grafton.

"Kanab had been done," de Toth said, when talking about scouting locations for *Ramrod.* "Location for me is as important as the star. What I liked about the area was the harshness, the cliffs, the river. It was real."[9]

Flora and Rupert Ruesch housed one of the set-construction workers in their small home in Springdale, not far from the Virgin River, and only a few miles from Grafton. That gave the couple privileged access to watch some of the filming of *Ramrod,* including the exciting scene when Joel McCrea guns down Preston Foster on Grafton's

Dave Nash (Joel McCrea) and nemesis Frank Ivey (Preston Foster) in a confrontation in Grafton.

main street.[10] They also managed to take some photographs of the sets, which, in addition to the original church and the Russell home to the north of it, included a sheriff's office, saloon, livery stable, blacksmith shop, and a large structure plainly labeled "Grafton Hotel." These structures, for the most part, were not simply Hollywood fronts, but functional buildings, inasmuch as interior scenes were filmed in them as well.

Gordon Bench, newly married and just home from World War II, drove Veronica Lake, with her dressing-room trailer, from Grafton to various locations inside Zion National Park. "I can't remember what they paid me," Bench remembered. "I only got ninety dollars a month in the Army, so anything was an improvement." He remembered Lake as being "very kind, very friendly." Joel McCrea "easily mixed with the people of Springdale and with tourists. One thing that particularly interested me was that these people live two lives. They were very professional when on location before the cameras, but when shooting was done for the day, they would go back to the Zion Park Lodge and either have dinner first or play softball. Then I would see a totally different aspect of these people, like Jekyll and Hyde. They were very personable. It was a real privilege to be with people of this caliber."[11]

Left: Veronica Lake pauses in Zion National Park during her search for Dave Nash in *Ramrod*. Below: Veronica Lake gets some last-minute prompting on the set at Grafton.

Ramrod was the first release of Enterprise Productions, a postwar partnership of former Warner Bros. vice president Charles Einfield and David Loew, who

Director Andre de Toth sets up a scene with his crew on the Virgin River in Zion National Park.

left a vice presidency at Metro-Goldwyn-Mayer. Postwar tastes in more realistic films brought about the gritty, tough-talking detective thriller later known as *film noir.* The more frank depiction of violence and sexuality in such films as *Double Indemnity* and *Out of the Past* even affected the Western genre. At first glance, it would appear that *Ramrod,* taken from a novel by Luke Short, is a typical sheepherders-versus-cattlemen story until Connie (played by blonde beauty Veronica Lake) is introduced into the narrative. After her sheep-droving fiancé is humiliated and driven out of town by powerful cattleman Frank Ivey (Preston Foster), she vows to bring in cattle, even in defiance of her own father, whose large ranch borders her own land. "From now on, I'm going to make a life of my own," Connie tells her father, "and being a woman I won't have to use guns." Consistent with her portrayals of *femmes fatale* in *This Gun for Hire* and *The Blue Dahlia,* Lake uses men to get what she wants—power over the men who would crush her. She arranges a stampede of her own cattle to implicate Ivey, but, in the process, gets good men killed. Her ramrod, Dave Nash (Joel McCrea), belatedly learns of his employer's ruthlessness. After causing the deaths of the sheriff and her gunslinger friend (played by Don DeFore), Connie walks away to an uncertain future after being rejected by a wiser Dave Nash. She is not killed for her sins, as per the requirements of the industry's strict Production Code; rather, she is denied the hero, who instead finds comfort in the affections of *Ramrod's* good woman, Rose, played by Utah actress Arleen Whelan.

The violence and frank sexuality, by 1940s standards, of what has been referred to as the first adult Western is largely due to director Andre de Toth, Lake's Hungarian-born husband. His body of work, according to one critic, contains "bitter undertones of a disillusioned romanticism [that] gives an extra edge to his lyrical treatment of landscape."[12] "My impression of him was that here was a man who had a specific goal in mind and would go after it," remembered Gordon Bench, who watched de Toth direct. "I think he was a taskmaster."[13] De Toth's choice of filming in black-and-white was a conscious artistic decision. "At that time, Technicolor was a never-land," the director recalled. "Technicolor was beautiful, moonlight, roses, and Shirley Temple. This was not a story of Shirley Temple. It was not a story of beauty. It's hard. The beauty lies in its hardness."[14] But even in black-and-white, Zion National Park, the Virgin River, and the leaves on the trees glisten in the morning and afternoon sun courtesy of Russell Harlan's striking cinematography.

The Salt Lake City premiere of *Ramrod* brought more than fifty movie stars and studio executives to Utah's capital city, more than ever before at one time. Two days before the February 22, 1947, opening of *Ramrod,* Joel McCrea arrived in Salt Lake City. He made an appearance before the Utah House of Representatives and was officially proclaimed cogovernor with Herbert Maw. Veronica Lake arrived with her husband the next day. She, too, was the beneficiary of a legal motion. Salt Lake City mayor Earl J. Glade signed a proclamation making his town "Veronica Lake City," and noted that this was the first time a US city had been named for a movie actress.

On February 21, a Union Pacific train named *The Ramrod Special* brought a contingent of stars and studio executives to Salt Lake's Union Station. Celebrities included some of the principal cast members of the film: Donald Crisp, Arleen Whelan, Don DeFore, and Preston Foster. Others whom the studio brought up from Hollywood to familiarize with the viewing public included Richard Conte, Billy De Wolfe, Jane Withers, Martha O'Driscoll, MacDonald Carey, and Sonny Tufts. They went from the train station to a morning organ recital at the Tabernacle on Temple Square. In the afternoon they were taken by bus to Alta ski resort, "where some of the stars skied while others remained at the Alta Lodge or toured the scenery." At 4:45 that afternoon, a parade, including all film and government dignitaries, followed a circular route through downtown Salt Lake City past a crowd estimated at 65,000 onlookers, including The Church of Jesus Christ official David O. McKay, chairman of the Centennial Commission.

Bill Schell (Don DeFore), Connie Dickason (Veronica Lake), and ramrod Dave Nash (Joel McCrea) guard their cattle from Frank Ivey's gang at Cave Valley in the Kolob region of Zion National Park.

More than seventy radio, newspaper, and magazine correspondents were on hand to interview the stars. Powerful syndicated movie columnist Hedda Hopper flew in from Los Angeles for a live broadcast of her "This is Hollywood" radio program, originating that evening from Kingsbury Hall on the University of Utah campus. Popular radio host Art Linkletter was there as well and broadcast his nationwide programs "People Are Funny" and "House Party" from the Utah Theater, and also served as master of ceremonies for the personal appearances of the stars that evening at the Capitol Theatre. The entourage also made an appearance at the Utah Theater.

"*Ramrod* was worth it," wrote the *Salt Lake Tribune*. "The hoopla and the shouting, the stars and the personal appearances, the special train and the coverage of major news services and magazines. By some magic known only to the Merlins of the west coast, the place Salt Lakers know as the Utah Theater was somehow transformed into Hollywood and Vine and the bright arc lights in front of the theater were pale as candles next to the shining personalities of the people inside." A Salt Lake film critic noted that *Ramrod* "is a western with a difference. . . . Veronica Lake, playing an unscrupulous, power-greedy woman, was attractive and scheming—a happy combination for her role." The same writer acknowledged the offbeat nature of this Western and warned potential viewers, "If you think westerns are as alike as peas in a pod, get a good look at *Ramrod*."[15]

Ramrod was the first motion picture made in Utah to carry an onscreen credit: "This picture was photographed entirely within the confines of southern Utah." Before that credit appeared at the end of the screening at the Utah Theatre, *The Ramrod Special* had already departed Union Station, returning to Hollywood with its precious cargo. The reaction in the next day's press was overwhelmingly favorable, even poetic. An editorial in the *Salt Lake Tribune* called the premiere and the star-studded parade "worthy of the occasion." Then the writer reflected on its greater meaning. "It was a march of times and seasons, of a past period, a present dash and a future interrogation point—punctuating the history of a great and growing commonwealth."[16]

However enthusiastic the Utah press and studio officials may

Dave Nash and Bill Schell confront Ivey's men at the Grafton sheriff's office.

have been with the premiere festivities, the state's lawmakers took a more somber view of the proceedings. In Utah Senate meetings on February 22—the day of the premiere—comments were made calling the film a "fourth class, trashy picture." Senator Rue L. Clegg of Salt Lake proposed that the film's title be changed from *Ramrod* to "Hamrod." "If this is an example of what our Centennial is to be, we are in for a sorry year," Clegg said. "It typifies and exemplifies nothing of the pioneer spirit which we observe this year. A much more fitting title for the show would be 'Hamrod' instead of *Ramrod,* and if it weren't so late in the session I would introduce a resolution to make a change in the title, to have the movie connected with the state of Colorado, which has asked for it anyhow, and to impeach our cogovernor (Joel McCrea) for being connected with such a trashy show." Many other senators seconded Clegg's motion. In the Utah House, Rep. Mark Paxton of Millard County declared that "at this point I am perfectly willing to wash my hands of the whole affair and give the picture back to Colorado. However, the only trouble with this is that nobody in our sister state to the East will want the movie once they see it."[17]

Centennial officials were quick to come to the defense of their controversial film. Governor Maw confessed to not having seen it, but expressed gratitude for "Enterprise Pictures coming to the state and spending seven hundred fifty thousand dollars here to produce that picture." He criticized the legislators for making their outcries so harsh and so public and admonished them to have "better manners" in the future. Gus P. Backman, director of the Centennial Commission, placed *Ramrod* at the center of the Centennial celebration. "Presenting Utah and the Centennial to so many public outlets which resulted in favorable publicity never would have been possible except for *Ramrod.*"[18]

Longtime *Deseret News* film critic Howard Pearson joined the chorus of defenders of the film by reminding critics, as did Maw and Backman, of the positive benefits of *Ramrod* to the state, before he bore in directly on the legislators. Pearson cited the money spent in the state and the publicity generated by the national radio programs and press coverage. "Which brings us to a simple point," he concluded. "How long will Utah receive the graciousness of such men as Mr. Sherman if on the floor of the Utah Senate our legislators, in one fell swoop, undo everything that Utah has attempted to build up in decades of work?"[19]

Above: The now-extinct oil fields at Virgin, Utah, were the setting for *In Old Oklahoma,* in which John Wayne, pictured here with Grant Withers, keeps oil speculators from drilling on Indian lands. Facing: Victor Mature and Colleen Gray near the entrance to Zion National Park in *Fury at Furnace Creek.*

During the 1940s, parts of other films also utilized Washington County locations, including Zion National Park and its environs. Among the least-known aspects of the scenic area of Washington County outside the park are the oil fields that existed for a time near the small town of Virgin.[20] It was there that a set-construction crew from Republic Pictures came in June 1943 to film parts of *In Old Oklahoma,* starring John Wayne. Filming in the desert west of Cedar City and at the Cedar City Union Pacific train depot was followed in late June by photography at the Virgin oil fields. "A friend of mine and me just carried pipe and boards back and forth in the background," remembered Gordon Bench, "but we ended up on the cutting room floor. Even though we were at some distance from him, John Wayne had a striking presence."[21] At least in Cedar City and at the Zion National Park location, the feeding of cast and crew was more democratic than the usual practice of contracting with a single provider. "This time," recorded the newspaper report, "the group will eat at the cafes about town, each member given the privilege of eating at the place of his choice."[22] One suspects townspeople were eating out more often than usual for a chance to see John Wayne, Martha Scott, Albert Dekker, Dale Evans, and George "Gabby" Hayes at a nearby table.

Closing out the 1940s, parts of *Green Grass of Wyoming* and *Fury at Furnace Creek,* released in 1948, were filmed within the park. The former was Twentieth Century-Fox's final installment of the Flicka horse trilogy, which was an unqualified box-office success for the studio. The hub of production for both films was in Kanab, with the chase sequences occurring just south of Grafton in the Rockville Road vicinity.

MIGHTY IN SCOPE
...mighty as this man whose conquests changed the face of the world!
When the great motion pictures of 1956 are talked about...this one will be mentioned first!
HOWARD HUGHES presents
JOHN WAYNE · SUSAN HAYWARD
THE CONQUEROR
CINEMASCOPE
TECHNICOLOR
RKO RADIO
2 YEARS IN THE MAKING...AT A COST OF $6,000,000
"THE WORLD? I WILL TAKE IT!"
"THE WOMAN? I WILL TAME HER!"
co-starring PEDRO ARMENDARIZ · with AGNES MOOREHEAD · THOMAS GOMEZ · JOHN HOYT · WILLIAM CONRAD · TED de CORSIA
A DICK POWELL Production · Written by OSCAR MILLARD · Produced and Directed by DICK POWELL

In 1861, Brigham Young called a group of pioneers—who had already crossed more than thirteen hundred miles to reach the Great Basin of the Rocky Mountains—to travel another three hundred miles southwest to the stark desert landscape they would name St. George. Colonizing this desert terrain included the raising of cotton, thus earning the region the nickname of Dixie. "I believe we were close to hell," wrote Orson Huntsman, who visited the area in 1870, when the settlement was only nine years old. "Dixie is the hottest place I ever was in." The red rock that cradles the Virgin River coming out of Zion Canyon was likely as surprising to those hearty settlers as it is today to motorists traveling south on Interstate 15, passing the verdant highlands of Cedar City and then gradually descending the next forty miles into desert country as trees, grass, and most other vegetation vanishes. In spite of poor soil and a scarcity of water, the pioneers made a thriving town out of St. George. Young maintained a winter home there and the town's permanence was assured when the first temple for the Church of Jesus Christ in the Utah Territory was completed in St. George in 1877, the year of Brigham Young's death. St. George has since become one of the fastest-growing cities in the United States, and, because of its proximity to I-15 and an airport, is a popular gateway city to Zion and other national parks in the region.

Unlike Cedar City to the north and Kanab to the east, St. George did not actively pursue the Hollywood movie industry. When the studios did come, beginning with Republic Pictures' filming of *The Painted Stallion* in February 1937, hotel owner Jockey Hale picked up the cast and crew in Moapa, Nevada, for the hour-long drive to St. George. Film editor William Witney took over directorial duties from Ray Taylor, who was "in his cups" on the first day of shooting. Witney was only twenty-one, but, other than codirector Alan James, there was no one else skilled enough to take over. He agreed to do so, on condition that the studio send out another director immediately. The replacement never materialized, and the career of director William Witney began. The company, with some difficulty, hired about one hundred Utes from the nearby

THE CONQUEROR

reservation. St. George locals and the Utes had been experiencing some differences, and the associate producer had to persuade the Utes to work with the extras he had hired in town.

Expert stuntman Yakima Canutt did the horse and wagon stunts, which were the bread and butter of Western films and serials. Neither of the principal actors—veteran Hoot Gibson and Ray Corrigan—were on location in Utah. Stand-ins took their places in the long-shot sequences; close-ups of the real stars would be filmed and inserted into the St. George footage at the studio. Ten days was all it took to photograph the exteriors for this twelve-chapter serial that would keep youngsters on the edge of their seats on Saturday afternoons in theaters around the world.

More prestigious was Howard Hawks's aviation drama for Columbia, *Only Angels Have Wings,* about an air-freight enterprise in South America. Since jungles are scarce near St. George, the only scene to take advantage of the area's special attractions is one in which a plane sent to pick up a critically ill patient on a remote mesa has to land and take off again. An ideal location was found near town and a crew spent three days building shacks to resemble a mining camp. The scene, lasting barely two minutes in the finished film, shows a high-winged propeller plane taking off over the edge of the mesa against the background of a snowy mountain range behind St. George, only to drop and then perilously hug the hillside as it gains altitude. Footage was also shot of the plane against the background of Zion Canyon, which doubled for the Andes Mountains.[1]

Except for the late-1940s local production of *Stallion Canyon,* St. George was not a featured area in movies until 1955, when Republic Pictures returned to film short scenes for its Ray Milland Western, *A Man Alone,* which looks onscreen as if it could have been filmed in any desert. Clearly, St. George was not inundated by Hollywood, nor did it seem as interested in drumming up such business. The St. George Chamber of Commerce held its regular Wednesday lunch meeting at the end of March 1954. Among the items on the agenda was a shirt factory that might be brought to the town, as well as a plant to manufacture duffel bags. It was probably with little fanfare or expectation that W. Brown Hail, secretary of the chamber, reported that a group of eight location scouts from RKO Radio Pictures had been in the area the previous week for what was described as a "religious extravaganza." The only member of the delegation who attracted any attention was its director, actor Dick Powell, who was also the producer. There was no mention that he was representing Howard Hughes, owner of the studio; that this picture was to be about Genghis Khan; that the lead role would be played by John Wayne; or that the plains and canyons near St. George would be transformed into the Gobi Desert of the twelfth century. What Hail and the chamber of commerce could not foresee was that *The Conqueror* would take over the city of St. George, and years later would be the center of lengthy litigation over atomic testing and the impact of radioactive fallout. The movie would become one of the most expensive Hollywood films made up to that time, as well as one of the select few Hollywood movies to become an object of derision and satire. "I'm sure some of you may wonder why there has been neither news items in this paper nor comment in this column concerning the RKO CinemaScope extravaganza to be filmed in this area soon," wrote columnist Nora R. Lyman of the *Washington County News.* "We gave a promise to the secretary of the Chamber of Commerce that we would hold publicity until he gave the 'Go' signal." Because of failed proposals in the past, she explained, local boosters thought the announcement should be made only when plans were certain.[2]

A few years previous, Dick Powell had gone into directing motion pictures as well as producing and acting in television programs. He searched eight western states to find the perfect setting for his six-million-dollar Mongolian epic before deciding on St. George. "We looked over several states without finding what we sought," said location manager Harold Lewis. "Then, by chance, I talked to a Chamber of Commerce man in St. George, who said he had flown the Hump in World War II. He was familiar

with the Gobi, and advised us to look at the canyons around St. George. We looked and settled immediately.”[3] Snow Canyon, near Ivins; Warner Canyon; and the bench near Harrisburg, twelve miles to the north of St. George, were regions that contained a total of ten shooting sites for the film. At that time, Snow Canyon was not yet a state park and was accessible only on foot or horseback. County road crews began building the road into the canyon in late March, while an advance construction team under Harold Lewis built sets and worked out arrangements with local hotels.

The scale of the project was truly massive for the town of 4,300 people. All nine buses from the school district were employed to transport cast and crew to locations. The high school was given over for dressing rooms and the storage of 1,200 costumes. Nearly all twenty-eight motels in town were booked for the more than five hundred cast and crew members. The Boy Scouts gave up enough tables and chairs to accommodate the feeding of up to a thousand people on location at one time. More than seven hundred locals were hired for a variety of jobs, from stand-ins for John Wayne and Susan Hayward, to maintenance, to extras. During the production of battle sequences in mid-July, four laborers were needed and location manager Lewis had to go to Cedar City to hire them, as every available St. George resident was already working on the film.

Four chartered planes from Los Angeles brought Powell, John Wayne, Susan Hayward, and the cast that included Pedro Armendáriz, Agnes Moorehead, Thomas Gomez, William Conrad, and Lee Van Cleef. Wayne secured a private residence from Wendell and Betty Motter for the five weeks that he would be on location. "We had heard around town that the studio was looking for houses to rent," remembered Betty. "My husband was going to be away on National Guard training and I was happy to rent our house. I would live just next door during that time." Motter recalled Wayne's daughter Melinda and sons Michael and Patrick coming to live with their father for a while. "They were so friendly, so down-to-earth," Motter said. "Some evenings I would be invited to sit and visit with them."[4] Susan Hayward, with her twin sons, rented the Howard Schmutz house for the duration. On location, restaurateur and wrangler Dick Hammer, backed by a crew of fifty-five, served lunches from his famous "stainless steel kitchen on wheels" chuck wagon that could serve 320 hot lunches every twenty minutes. "We have been on location in many places and we have been served by the best caterers," said wardrobe department head Henry Webb, "but never have we had food like Dick's."[5] The operation was run out of Hammer's locally famous eatery, Dick's Cafe.

Susan Hayward was then in her most popular period, enjoying success in *With A Song in My Heart* and *Garden of Evil*, and had played opposite Wayne in Cecil B. DeMille's *Reap the Wild Wind* and in *The Fighting Seabees*. The lineup at her St. George residence got so long that autographs were limited to two and a half hours, starting at 3:30 daily. "Won't you parents talk with your teenagers and cooperate with Miss Hayward and other stars who are in our midst?"asked the local paper.[6] Residents of St. George were helpful in making the large-scale production work for RKO. The cast reciprocated by being accessible to the public and even putting on a benefit baseball game on a warm July 6 evening. The St. George Elks Lodge team played against a studio team. John Wayne and Dick Powell were the officials, and also took turns at playing second and third base during the game. In stocking feet, Hayward "stole third—forcing out one of her own team who already inhabited the base. Susan's family batted one thousand for the evening for her twin nine-year-old sons, Timothy and Gregory, each singled and each scored. Their mother scored, too, with the scores of fans who requested and received autographs."[7] Paying fifty cents apiece, the 1,500 who swelled the Dixie Sun Bowl retired the debt on the ball field. "A spirit of cooperative good-fellowship made itself felt from the time Susan threw the first ball until the last clowning ended."[8]

The cast became regulars around town, eating in the city's restaurants. Birthdays for Susan Hayward and director Dick Powell's daughter Ellen were celebrated. Powell, along with his wife, June Allyson, Michael Wayne, and Agnes Moorehead, were seen by the local newspaper's columnist having dinner together at the Dixie Cafe. "If I have ever seen a typical normal, homey family party dining out, this was a perfect example," she wrote. "They seemed completely unaware that they were unusual people or were possibly being stared at by anyone. They were making their own fun around the table and, at times, convulsed with laughter over their zany antics."[9]

The variable summer weather in Washington County made for long and difficult days of filming. During a scene filmed on the ridge above Snow Canyon, Wayne, Hayward,

Director Dick Powell and John Wayne pause while filming in Warner Valley near St. George for *The Conqueror*.

Moorehead, and others of the Mongols were gathered around a studio-produced water hole when the sky began to darken. Within minutes, rain pelted the cast, crew, and thousands of dollars worth of equipment, and everyone scrambled for cover under tents. The red sand turned into a muddy goo. A jeep quickly came to rescue the stranded director and performers. A crewman was heard saying, "Yesterday we build an artificial water hole and today they are a dime a dozen. Let's sue the chamber of commerce!"[10]

The climactic battle between Mongols and Tartars, filmed on the plains of Harrisburg, was quite a sight for summer tourists to the area. What they saw was up to a thousand men and horses, and nearly 250 wranglers and studio technicians, manning reflectors and camera booms for the three CinemaScope cameras as various parts of the battle were filmed over a six-day period.

For the scenes in the Mongol village in Snow Canyon, the studio hired three hundred Native Americans from the Shivwits reservation to double as Mongols and warriors. The vista of oxen pulling wheeled yurts in a caravan across the desert was surreal to those who lived in this tranquil wilderness. "To local residents, all this scenery is as much a part of everyday living as brushing their teeth," wrote an unnamed source. "But it will be fresh and new and, we hope, intriguing to the millions of movie-goers all over the world who see *The Conqueror.*"[11]

By the time the final production units left St. George for Hollywood on August 4, it was estimated that RKO had poured $750,000 into the St. George economy, not counting the tourist trade attracted by the more than twenty representatives of the press who had traveled to St. George to cover the making of *The Conqueror* for dozens of publications, including *Life, Cosmopolitan,* and the *New York Times.* The frenetic business in stores and restaurants subsided to normal levels. "There's a sort of lonesome feeling around the streets like your home is for a time after a house guest has said the last goodbye and departed," wrote Nora Lyman. "This was our first visit by a major picture company, and I'm sure we are unintentionally guilty of many sins of omission and commission. But, as a whole community, it was our greatest desire to be helpful when needed and out of the way at all other times. . . . We sincerely hope they will come back to mingle with us."[12] Praise came from the departing celebrities. "You have two wonderful crops in St. George," said Dick Powell. "Hospitality and healthy, happy, well-mannered children." Pedro Armendáriz called St. George "a wonderful community of very considerate people." Location manager Harold Lewis confessed that the hills and valleys surrounding St. George were "a tough location, but it would have been a lot tougher if the people here hadn't been so helpful." From the Duke came the most expansive statement: "This is the way we like to think of America—people cheerfully helping people simply because that's a good way to live."[13] Reviews by the major trade press were largely positive, praising Powell's "vigorous direction" and "the raw beauty of the outdoor locations in Utah" that had "scope and splendor." The rest of the press was not so generous.

The Conqueror turned out to be a hit with audiences, earning nearly twelve million dollars in its theatrical release. In a year that included *The King and I, Guys and Dolls,* and *Moby Dick, The Conqueror* fared very well at the box office. It was number eleven in revenue, comparable with *Rebel Without a Cause* and outearning *The Man in the Grey Flannel Suit, Bus Stop,* and even Alfred Hitchcock's *The Man Who Knew Too Much.*[14]

John Wayne woos a resentful Susan Hayward on the desert plain near St. George.

Sweeping Technicolor shots of the St. George landscape were achieved by a boom-mounted CinemaScope camera. Here, director Dick Powell is seen on the boom just below the camera while John Wayne readies for his scene.

Wayne's depiction of Genghis Kahn, in the context of his many Westerns, took on comic aspects that were the object of derision. The film had originally been written for Marlon Brando, whose thespian talents might have made the vintage dialogue palatable. However, by the time Wayne saw the script and objected to the dialogue as undeliverable, it was too late to rewrite his lines.[15] In 1980, a book cited *The Conqueror* as one of the "golden turkeys" of all time.[16]

In 1979, Hughes sold *The Conqueror* to television in a package of eight Hughes-produced films that included *Hell's Angels* and his trend-setting gangster film, *Scarface*. The sale came at the same time a number of lawsuits were filed against the US government by cancer victims and their families in Nevada and southwestern Utah, who alleged they had not been warned about the effects of aboveground atomic-bomb testing during the early 1950s. Those filing the suits were dubbed "downwinders," a reference to the radioactivity carried by winds into Utah following such tests, the most severe of which was the 1953 explosion of a bomb known to St. George locals as "Dirty Harry" at Yucca Flats, Nevada, 145 miles from St. George. A grey ash came over the city, clinging to everything—and everyone—it touched. Sheep and pigs died, but the Atomic Energy Commission denied any connection between the nuclear testing and the deaths. In a widely read account published in *People* magazine, attention was focused on the cast and crew of *The Conqueror* who were exposed to the radioactive fallout during this period, a full year after the explosions.[17] Jack Adams, son of union steward Marvin Adams, who worked on *The Conqueror,* remembered in 2008 the stories his father told about the curious sensation of burning skin and itching, even on cloudy days. Ninety of the 220 crew members contracted cancer, according to the *People* study, of which forty-six died from the disease, including John Wayne, Agnes Moorehead, Susan Hayward, and Dick Powell. Pedro Armendáriz died in 1963 from a self-inflicted gunshot after learning of his terminal cancer.

Top-level congressional hearings were conducted throughout the 1980s. A bipartisan effort by Utah congressman Wayne Owens and Senator Orrin Hatch resulted in the Radiation Exposure Compensation Act, signed into law by President George H. W. Bush in 1990. The act provided payments to those cancer victims who were exposed to the atomic testing, as well as to uranium miners. Inasmuch as many of the victims who worked on *The Conqueror* were heavy cigarette smokers, the question remained as to what was the primary contributor to their deaths. Wayne's son Michael said the theory that his father's death was due to radiation exposure on *The Conqueror* "doesn't hold much water. I don't put much credence in the story. Bill Conrad was in the film. Norman Powell and a lot of other people were out there, but none of us have cancer."[18] Even restaurant owner and location caterer Dick Hammer weighed in on the controversy. "We were there more than anyone else," said Hammer, whose crew of fifty-five served hundreds of meals daily at his restaurant and out on location without any of them contracting cancer.[19] Nevertheless, *The Conqueror,* often referred to as "An RKO Radioactive Picture," will forever be linked with this intense period of atomic testing, the government's negligence, and the tragedies that followed in its wake.

Scott Brady, playing a Navajo, confronts Forrest Tucker and Audrey Totter at Snow Canyon State Park in the remake of Zane Grey's *The Vanishing American*.

VANISHED AMERICANS

When *The Conqueror* was finally within days of its nationwide release in mid-January 1956, columnist Nora R. Lyman, of St. George's *Washington County News,* read of the plans for the film's multiple world premieres in Europe, together with appearances by John Wayne in Paris, London, and Rome. She hoped that "This picture will be worth a great deal in advertising the incomparable beauty of this area all over the world, and I am eager to see how faithfully the colors have been reproduced. No one, until he has seen these vivid masses of color, can believe they actually exist."[1] Neither Lyman nor the residents of St. George had long to wait, as *The Conqueror* was released nationwide the following month. Lyman's hopes were soon realized when Republic Pictures moved in the following year to film three pictures: *The Road to Denver,* starring John Payne; *A Man Alone,* starring Ray Milland in his first film as director; and a low-budget remake of Zane Grey's *The Vanishing American,* the original having been filmed in Monument Valley in 1925. The latter two films carried an onscreen credit that read: "Produced in Utah U.S.A." Only a few months following the departure of *The Conqueror* crew, the St. George Chamber of Commerce wisely formulated a plan to deal with the growing number of film companies coming to the community. "The chamber is merely the bargaining agent to bring the motion pictures into St. George," read a report of the mid-November 1954 meeting. "Each business is to make its own contacts with the advance men as they come to make arrangements."[2] Brown Hail unsuccessfully pushed for the building of a Western street, not only to attract movie companies but also to encourage those already on location to spend extra days there rather than returning to California to film town sequences on their backlots.[3] Beginning in June 1956, Hail and motel owner Andrew Pace visited all of the major studios in Hollywood and "several independent companies" to solicit business.[4]

Above: Ray Milland alone in the desert near St. George for *A Man Alone*. The saguaro cactus in the background was a Hollywood prop, as this species does not survive in high-desert Utah locales.

The King and Four Queens (1956)

Following the end of World War II, the commercial success of motion pictures declined due to increased competition from other forms of entertainment. Stars were either released from or chose to get out of confining studio contracts, which not only limited their financial return but also often forced them to appear in movies in which they had no interest. In the early 1950s, after appearances in *Gone With the Wind* and many other commercially successful films, Clark Gable chose to leave M-G-M because of contractual restrictions and formed a production company with actress friend Jane Russell (who costarred with him in *The Tall Men* in 1955) and her husband, Bob Waterfield. Gable signed on to star in a Western called *The King and Four Queens*, and an advance crew was sent to St. George at the end of March 1956 to start building the sets.

The story of *The King and Four Queens* concerns crusty Ma McDade (played by Jo Van Fleet), who lives in the dusty Western village of Wagon Mound with her four spoiled daughters-in-law, waiting for the arrival of the sole surviving bank-robbing husband so that the $100,000 buried by Ma can be split amongst them. Opportunist Dan Kehoe (Gable) hears of the situation and manages to ingratiate himself with the young women, especially Sabrina (Eleanor Parker), the smartest of the daughters, who leaves the compound with Kehoe after he discovers the hidden cache. It is not considered one of Gable's better films, as, according to his biographer, "he did little but pose with arms akimbo with a leer on his face."[5]

Right: Clark Gable wins over Eleanor Parker, one of the several McDade widows, as they flee Wagon Mound, filmed here along the Santa Clara River near St. George.

The southern Utah setting was chosen by Gable because, according to Lyman, "he is almost a native of this area, having hunted here many times. In fact, he hunted lions with friends on Pine Valley mountain around 1936." A longtime resident of the area, even Lyman was impressed with how the familiar landscape was transformed by the many structures comprising the village set, weathered to looked aged and dilapidated. "It looks as if it had been built by the first pioneers who traveled through Snow's canyon a century ago," she wrote. "What a setting!"[6] Publicity for the film was generous, since the awaiting press was eager to have access to Gable, who had been prohibited from interviewing by his M-G-M contract. Ed Sullivan, host of the popular television program *Toast of the Town,* showed up in St. George to interview the legendary star. The St. George Chamber of Commerce acted as a clearinghouse to schedule tours to the film's locations.

The King and Four Queens was not considered a major film by its director, Raoul Walsh, who returned to make a film in Utah for the first time since his harrowing experience filming *In Old Arizona* in 1928. In fact, Walsh confessed to fellow director Samuel Fuller that he loved the actors and the scenery but hated the script. He jokingly suggested "swapping movies" with Fuller, who was shooting his *Run of the Arrow* for RKO at another Snow Canyon site.[7]

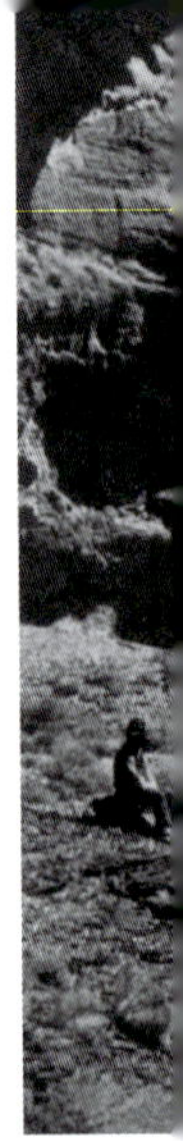

that final bullet at Appomattox.

Themes of race, identity, and adoption permeate *Run of the Arrow,* still one of the director's most highly regarded works. Fuller, writing years later, even linked the landscape to his story:

> I wanted to create the rare western that linked powerful images with emotional turmoil. The bright, clear Utah landscapes are constantly contrasted with O'Meara's dark, brooding nature. Full of hate and confusion, O'Meara is trying to make hard choices between his own self-interest and larger responsibilities to his family, his people, his nation. Every facet of my yarn is full of contrasts, but nowhere more obvious than in the confrontation between races.[8]

The wagon train that takes Confederate veteran O'Meara away from the war-torn Midwest to Indian Country out west was filmed in Snow Canyon State Park.

Run of the Arrow (1957)

New York-born Fuller, known for his tough-talking and often violent war films and urban crime thrillers, produced, wrote, and directed *Run of the Arrow.* The story deals with a Confederate infantryman, O'Meara, who fires the last shot of the Civil War, wounding a Union soldier—whom he carries on his back to a Confederate medic station at Appomattox, Virginia—and witnesses Lee's surrender to General Grant. O'Meara then goes west, refusing to admit defeat. There he befriends an old Sioux army scout, and the pair is caught by a rival tribe and forced to endure the "run of the arrow," wherein the captors give O'Meara a head start as far as his pursuers can shoot an arrow. If O'Meara can outrun them, he's safe, but he is told that no one has yet been successful. Predictably, the old scout does not make it, but Yellow Moccasin, a Sioux woman, takes the exhausted O'Meara to her village before his pursuers discover him. There he joins the Sioux and marries Yellow Moccasin, adopting her mute son. He then becomes the tribe's representative when the US Cavalry chooses the spot to build a fort in the area. The leader of the cavalry detachment turns out to be the man that O'Meara had wounded with

Ignoring the studio's insistence that he hire Gary Cooper for the lead role, Fuller instead pressed for character actor Rod Steiger, who had never before been cast in a lead role. Steiger joined an excellent cast that included Ralph Meeker, Charles Bronson, and Brian Keith. Fifty Navajos from the reservation in Arizona, along with their wives, were also hired, as well as ninety locals from St. George.

The July filming of *Run of the Arrow* went well but for one mishap. In a scene where O'Meara and Yellow Moccasin are in the newly completed fort, renegade Sioux come out of the hills and burn the fort, built by the studio on the "twist" adjacent to the road from Pine Valley to St. George. In order to make sure the conflagration was photogenic, technicians soaked the fort with five hundred gallons of kerosene. During filming, Steiger noticed that the actress playing Yellow Moccasin collapsed before getting out of the burning building. The wind had shifted, enveloping the actress in smoke, and both her costume and Steiger's caught fire as he dragged her from the blaze.

They Came to Cordura (1959)

If Gary Cooper missed his rendezvous with Utah on *Run of the Arrow,* it was more than made up for when, in early October 1959, he, along with Rita Hayworth, Van Heflin, Richard Conte, and Tab Hunter, arrived in St. George to film *They Came to Cordura,* set in Mexico in 1916, when an American corps attacks remnants of Pancho Villa's band. Director Robert Rosson, who wrote, produced, and directed the acclaimed drama *All the King's Men,* loved the Utah landscape's clear, sharp definition. "It is a definite improvement over the smog" of Los Angeles, he said, although there were lines of cars by the motel filled with people desperate to catch a glimpse of the stars, especially teen heartthrob Tab Hunter.[9] For the movie, a large Mexican hacienda, owned by an expatriate American played by Hayworth, was built at Harrisburg, fourteen miles from St. George. Here the US Army's mounted cavalry charged Villa's revolutionaries. Camp scenes were also filmed in Snow Canyon, and more than 350 locals were hired for the film.

Louise Parry Thomas, daughter of Chauncey Parry, was asked by the film's producers to be a stand-in for Hayworth. "I hadn't ridden a horse for a lot of years," she recalled. "I told them that I didn't think I could do it." She and her husband were instead invited to visit the location in Snow Canyon during the shooting of a scene where Cooper is treating wounded cavalryman Richard Conte. "The idea was that Conte's pants were going to fall down," Parry said. "They couldn't figure out how to get his pants to fall down on cue. So, they ended up filling his pants with rocks. We were just in hysterics watching this very serious scene and then pants falling down."[10] Cooper also enjoyed goose hunting after filming on a near-daily basis with local Jack E. Holt. That camaraderie brought Cooper back to St. George after he was diagnosed with inoperable cancer to hunt with Holt for the last time before his death in May 1961.[11]

Brown Hail reported to the St. George Chamber of Commerce that after the troupe from Columbia Pictures left the area on November 21 for their next location at Moapa, Nevada, approximately $500,000 had been pumped into the local economy. This proved to Hail that, more than any other type of industry to bring into the area, "the movie industry is one of the best pay rolls."[12]

Facing: Gary Cooper and Rita Hayworth relax between takes. Left: Richard Conte and Van Heflin flank director Robert Rossen during production of *They Came to Cordura*. Below: A US Army detachment moves against a Mexican hacienda held by Pancho Villa's partisans.

Early on the morning of June 10, 1968, a delegation that included St. George mayor Marion Bowler and Neal Lundberg, president of the chamber of commerce, waited at the St. George hilltop airport for the arrival of a twin-engine executive jet carrying six passengers from Hollywood. This was an important welcome, as director George Roy Hill and five of his studio associates from Twentieth Century-Fox were coming to scout locations for a film that would revolutionize the movie Western and become one of the biggest moneymakers of the decade. After the plane's arrival, Brown Hail joined the group as it toured Rockville, Zion National Park, Snow Canyon, Silver Reef, Pine Valley, and the abandoned town of Grafton for use as locations for filming *Butch Cassidy and the Sundance Kid.*

Robert Redford, who had taken up residence in 1964 at what he initially called Wildwood in Provo Canyon, was a late hire for *Butch Cassidy and the Sundance Kid.* Fresh from his costarring role with Jane Fonda in the enormously successful *Barefoot in the Park*, Redford was a talent of notice. Director Hill championed him over other considerations (when Steve McQueen and Warren Beatty pulled out) and asked Paul Newman to help him convince Fox executives Richard Zanuck and David Brown that Redford was the right choice for the "Kid." Movie history was made with the teaming of Newman and Redford—the "buddy film" was born. (The pair was later cast in *The Sting*, also directed by George Roy Hill.) It was Redford who was "instrumental in attracting the attention of Twentieth Century-Fox to southern Utah."[13] "I've been driving through St. George since the mid-fifties," Redford said years later. "I had always liked the area very much—been drawn to it—and saw early on that it had great potential for film making. They were initially going to film *Butch Cassidy* in New Mexico. I got them to come and look at St. George and, of course, much of it *was* filmed there."[14] This seems fitting,

Butch Cassidy and the Sundance Kid (1969)

Above: Butch and Sundance shoot it out in South America. Facing: A "family portrait" with Etta Place, the Sundance Kid, and Butch Cassidy.

inasmuch as the real Butch Cassidy led his Hole-in-the-Wall Gang from the Parker ranch in nearby Circleville, in Paiute County.

After the train-robbing sequences were filmed on the Durango–Silverton Railroad in Colorado, the Fox film crew arrived in southern Utah in October 1968. Filming began in Cave Valley in the Kolob region of Zion National Park, where the famous confrontation between Harvey Logan (Ted Cassidy) and Butch about the rules of fighting takes place. A frame home was built in Grafton for Etta Place, the Denver schoolteacher played by Katharine Ross, who is in love with the Kid. The home was situated on a corner across from the historic church building, which was partially restored by studio crews.[15] A short distance from the house, in the historic Ballard barn, Etta frolics with Butch, who then takes her for a ride on the handlebars of his bicycle in a montage of shots under the Burt Bacharach tune "Raindrops Keep Falling on My Head." Chase scenes, with a posse in pursuit of the fleeing Butch and Sundance, were filmed in Zion National Park and in Snow Canyon near St. George. Production there was completed at the end of October, when the company traveled to central Mexico for the South American sequences. The Utah locations comprise approximately three-fourths of the finished film. Leigh von der Esch, veteran twenty-year head of the Utah Film Commission, called *Butch Cassidy and the Sundance Kid* "a lark and a romp through the beauty of Utah. Redford showcased the Utah locations with director George Roy Hill in a John Ford way, driving the narrative with the landscape."[16]

The principal cast and creative talent often came in for dinner at Dick's Cafe in St. George. "They came in every night to eat, Paul Newman, Robert Redford, the

Above: Cave Valley in the Kolob region of Zion National Park was the picturesque setting for the famous "rules" confrontation between Butch Cassidy (Paul Newman) and Harvey Logan (Ted Cassidy). Top: Paul Newman as Butch Cassidy. Facing, bottom: Katharine Ross and Paul Newman seen against the historic Russell House in Grafton during the "Raindrops Keep Falling on My Head" sequence.

director and some others," said Billie Frei, a waitress at the restaurant. "Paul Newman would make the salad for everyone. Even then, before Newman's Own, he would have the ingredients brought to him and he'd make the salad dressing. They would all eat in the dining room, right along with everyone else, but would be at a long table over to the side of the room. I knew that Paul Newman was such a big name, but I really liked Robert Redford, who would often be off at another table being interviewed by the press."[17]

Butch's producer, John Foreman, said, "This area of Utah has a remarkable variety of scenic settings for our picture. Within twenty or thirty miles are deserts, high plateaus, heavily wooded timber country, alpine lakes and fantastic mountains."[18] Cinematographer Conrad Hall was so entranced with the area that, sometime after the film's completion, he returned to the Utah locations to "go back, sit around and look at the old spots we shot in, see what was left and think about the passions that it took to get things on film the way that we have."[19] With profits from the film, Redford purchased additional land at his Wildwood property and renamed it Sundance, which he ran as a ski resort, and, later, as the Sundance Institute for independent filmmakers.

Jeremiah Johnson (1972)

Based on Vardis Fisher's 1965 novel, *Mountain Man, Jeremiah Johnson* chronicles the protagonist's disaffection with contemporary society as he strikes out into the wilderness, learning survival skills from a crusty trapper (Will Geer), taking a common-law Flathead Native American wife, and adopting an abandoned white boy as his son. When Johnson reluctantly guides a cavalry detachment through sacred Crow Indian lands to rescue a wagon train, he returns to his cabin to find his wife and son murdered by Crows. He begins a crusade of vengeance against the Crows, and is ultimately honored by them as a valiant warrior. Redford's strident environmentalism was enhanced by lush spring landscapes as well as harsh winter mountain scenes etched against a deep blue sky. With

Robert Redford and Will Geer in a scene for *Jeremiah Johnson*.

the traditional movie Western in decline by the 1970s, the *New York Times* nevertheless saw many things to praise in director Sidney Pollack's film. "To replace the more usual affairs of men, the film concentrates on the power of nature, or the powers that simple men can wrest from nature, and, almost unavoidably, it keeps giving the impression of a literary interpretation of its materials," wrote critic Roger Greenspun. He also noted Pollack's "treatment of landscape, his calculated merging of people and places." Greenspun also speculated that the role of the hardy, anti-societal trapper, as played by Redford, "must be very real to his own mind and feelings."

Robert Redford, as Jeremiah Johnson, with fellow mountain man Will Geer. Mt. Timpanogos rises in the background, overlooking Redford's Sundance Resort.

The Man Who Loved Cat Dancing (1973)

For the first time in nearly a century, teepees were visible along the Virgin River near Grafton and Rockville in Washington County when, in March of 1973, construction crews from Columbia Pictures finished outfitting a Native American village and began filming the offbeat Western *The Man Who Loved Cat Dancing*. After many years in television roles, and after starring in *Deliverance*, Burt Reynolds became noticed in this story, scripted by Eleanor Perry from Marilyn Durham's novel about an ex-con train robber who takes with him the wife (Sarah Miles) of one of the passengers (George Hamilton) and escapes with her into the mountains. On their journey, he learns that she is on the run from a loveless marriage with Hamilton, entered into for money needed by her father. Cat Dancing is the common-law Native American wife of Reynolds, by whom he has a son. As Hamilton and Sheriff Lee J. Cobb pursue the pair to the tribal village and then up into the snowy mountains, Miles falls in love with the conflicted but essentially decent Reynolds, and the sheriff grows weary of Hamilton's desire for vengeance. The harshness of the desert winter, with the leafless trees and light dusting of snow near Virgin, Utah, and the snow-covered mountains to which Reynolds and Miles go for refuge, make *The Man Who Loved Cat Dancing* a convincing case for making all Westerns entirely on location rather than on studio backlots.

Burt Reynolds, with accomplices Bo Hopkins and Jack Warden, on the run from the law in the Washington County desert, near Hurricane.

Clint Eastwood peers down a ravine in *The Eiger Sanction*.

The Eiger Sanction (1975)

Though opportunities were limited in the 1970s, Zion National Park was the site for one week's filming by Universal Pictures and director Clint Eastwood for *The Eiger Sanction*. Eastwood portrays a college professor whose proficiency at mountain climbing comes in handy when he needs to raise funds for special projects. However, for a mountain climb in which he is to participate in Switzerland, he becomes dangerously involved with a counterspy. After filming in Switzerland, the film company came to Zion National Park in late September 1974 to film training sequences, where climbing mentor George Kennedy puts Eastwood through his paces on the cliffs and trails of the park. Many scenes were photographed at the old Zion Lodge and the pool, both of which are now gone. A scene in *The Eiger Sanction* attests to cinema's power to manipulate both time and space. Kennedy is shown meeting Eastwood's chartered flight at a Monument Valley airstrip. The drive to the park, says Kennedy, is only about "twenty minutes" away. Shortly after the characters depart the airstrip, the scene cuts from the vast expanse of the red-tinged soil of Monument Valley to the cliffs and aspen trees of Springdale and the entrance to Zion National Park, a drive that would have taken, in reality, a full day to accomplish.

The Car (1977)

One of the most bizarre motion pictures, not only to be filmed in Utah, but to come out of Hollywood, was the 1977 Universal thriller *The Car*. The vehicle of the film's title is a 5,500-pound Lincoln Mark III that, possessed by the devil, indiscriminately runs down and kills local residents. Director Elliott Silverstein was riding the success of two previous films, *Cat Ballou* and *A Man Called Horse*, when he got approval from Universal to make this unusual movie. Filming in the St. George area began on July 28, 1976. The local sheriff in *The Car*, played by James Brolin, spent the balance of the film chasing the anthropomorphic vehicle around Washington County, including the road through Zion National Park's tunnel, as the car edges two young bicyclists off the road to their deaths. The small town where other homicides occur was represented by the Washington County community of Hurricane. Other scenes were filmed at the Dixie Downs area near St. George. The Kanab High School marching band appeared in these scenes, and sixty St. George locals were also hired—mostly terrorized children whose mothers tried to get them out of the way of the predatory automobile. Billie Frei was the only one with a speaking part, which, she remembered years later, "ended up on the cutting room floor."

Silverstein praised the extras. "They turned out to be true pros," he said. "After only a few rehearsals, they were hitting their marks, not looking into the camera and ignoring the hundreds of spectators we had on the set."[20] One of the unnamed housewives hired as an extra was quoted as finding the movie work boring, but not without its uses: "The excitement and novelty wore off after the first day and I was considering quitting because it was getting boring. But then I remembered that I wanted a new stove and refrigerator."[21] For Frei, it was a matter of having to go back to her day job, "even though I earned $2,000 for two weeks' work because I had a speaking part."[22] At the end of the movie, the vexatious hunk of metal is finally cornered in a box canyon near Kanab, where the crew filmed for ten days after their three-week shoot in the St. George area.[23]

Two unwary teenagers on Highway 9, admiring the Towers of the Virgin at the entrance to Zion National Park, are soon to be run off the road in *The Car*.

The Electric Horseman (1979)

By the late 1970s, Robert Redford was a full-fledged star. *The Electric Horseman* gave him an opportunity to profile his concerns for animal rights and big business in America through the down-and-out character of Norman "Sonny" Steele, once a championship horseman but now handsomely paid to publicize breakfast cereal for a large corporate conglomerate. Frustrated that the corporation has drugged the prize horse used in its promotions, Steele, wearing a light-bedecked costume, rides the horse out of Caesars Palace in Las Vegas and into the desert, holding it hostage before finally releasing it in Silver Reef, Utah. Crusading television reporter Jane Fonda finds Steele in the desert to expose his eccentric behavior, only to fall in love with him and champion his cause. While not critically successful, *The Electric Horseman* was a tremendous moneymaker.

Silver Reef is just one of the references to the actual Utah locations on which *The Electric Horseman* was filmed. At the beginning of the movie, one of Steele's partners tells Sonny, "I always thought you should have gotten that place in Spanish Fork instead of the house in Malibu." Fonda's search for the fugitive pitchman cowboy takes her to Snow Canyon, where Redford is treating the horse for its company-imposed drug ailments. A general store, and, later in the film, an isolated old brick home were located in Silver Reef near Leeds, Utah, about twenty miles northwest of St. George, where filming went on for more than three weeks, beginning in late January 1979. Light snow—not Hollywood flakes—can be seen in the Snow Canyon scenes. A reporter for the *Washington County News* tried in vain to get photographs of Redford and Fonda but "was met with a reaction somewhere between shock, dismay and sorrow" from the Columbia Pictures publicity man. "I tried for the horse. The answer to that was another neigh. . . . I even invited him to come swimming in our swimming pool but he objected to having to break away the ice to get to the water—you can't please some people."[24]

Facing: Robert Redford as a pitchman for a breakfast cereal company in *The Electric Horseman*. Above, left: Has-been cowboy turned corporate pitchman Sonny Steele (Robert Redford) and investigative journalist Hallie Martin (Jane Fonda) meet up at Snow Canyon State Park. Above, right: Hallie Martin, now sympathetic to Sonny Steele's crusade, watches as Steele releases the horse to freedom.

Cast members mixed with the locals on more than one occasion. Willie Nelson, who played Wendell Hickson, Redford's manager, surprised patrons of the 101 Rancho in the little town of Virgin after filming one night and played a few sets. Redford spoke to a group of Latter-day Saint youth at St. George's Dixie College. "He would like to see a sound stage constructed here in St. George," the newspaper reported, "and see a production company based here."[25]

Redford waxed philosophical in his reflections on St. George. "My fondness for St. George almost approaches a sacred degree," he told Lyman Hafen. "So the word 'Saint' really kind of fits. I see incredible variety and space there and I feel something quite spiritually prehistoric about the place. So when you say 'St. George,' I think of a wonderful, God-developed area. The best developer in St. George has been God himself."[26]

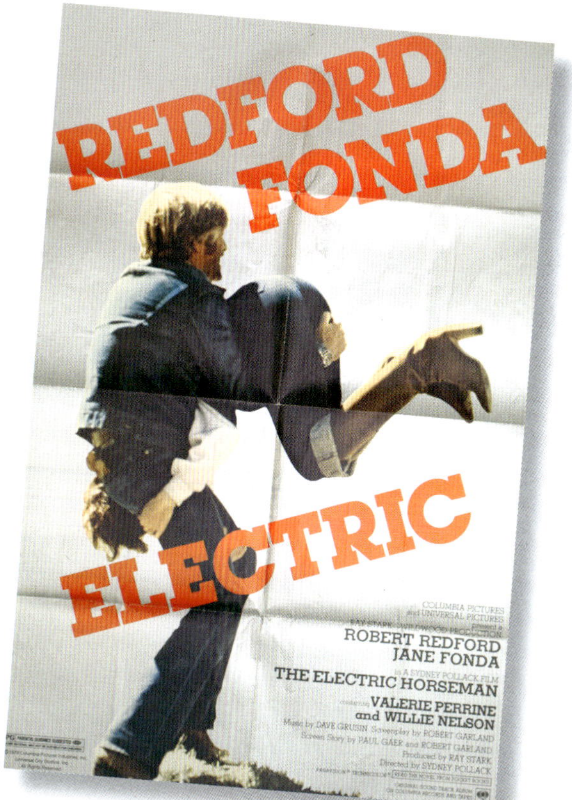

SCENE 3

KANE COUNTY
1928–1978

UTAH'S HOLLYWOOD

"This is the land of the Wizard of Awes." A magazine writer used these words to describe Kanab and Kane County in the 1940s. "It is a land of make-believe and disbelief. It is not of this world, nor is it of any other—yet it is there. The people who live in it do not believe it, even when they see it in the movies, even when they see it all around them. The most uncommon place in the world is to them commonplace, and what happened there never happened at all. Or did it?"[1]

In this remote southwestern Utah town—the furthest from a railroad for a town of its size in the United States—there were, in 1930, less than 1,300 residents. Kanab's unique international renown as a movie location came as a result of the Parry brothers, who cooperated to provide the studios with a full-service arrangement that delivered on transportation, location scouting, lodging, catering, livestock, and even covered wagons and carriages for Western films. To do this, the entire town signed up as extras, wranglers, drivers, laborers, and, when the Parry Lodge and the few other motels in town were full, as landlords renting out rooms in their own homes for stars, crews, and tourists lured to what *Life* magazine called "Utah's Hollywood."[2]

Kanab is a Paiute word meaning "the place of the willows," a reference to the willows that line Kanab Creek as it comes out of the canyon just north of town. Jacob Hamblin, a pioneer frontiersman, visited the area throughout 1860 on assignment from Brigham Young, who came through the area in 1870 and "dedicated" it for settlement. Kanab finally incorporated in 1884. The bare Vermilion Cliffs to the north of Kanab provide a stunning backdrop to this high-desert community nearly six thousand feet above sea level. Approximately sixteen miles east of Kanab is Johnson Canyon, discovered by Nephi Johnson, who is also credited with being the first non-Native American to visit what later became Zion National Park. Kanab also serves as the seat for surrounding Kane County, named for Col. Thomas L. Kane, an attorney and philanthropist who was especially

Street-level view of Kanab in 1956. The Kanab Theater, where studio directors would often view dailies of films being shot, is at right.

Reminiscent of New England more than the American southwest, the Parry Lodge got its start in 1931. The cottages that became a special attraction can be seen at far right.

friendly to the Latter-day Saints during their persecutions and while on their trek west from Illinois.

The Parry Lodge, with its colonial-style, columned structure, together with small cottages, had its start as a small three-bedroom frame house owned by Justin M. Johnson. According to Whit Parry, before he left Utah for Boulder City, Nevada, he "purchased a large house and some property" in Kanab to hold as an investment. Returning to Kanab, he "decided to fix the place up, open a small dining room and convert my house into a 'Tourist Home.'"[3] While this account is consistent with the image of the man who would be inseparable from the Parry Lodge in later years, the facts show that it was Whit's older brother Chauncey who purchased the Johnson home on December 12, 1928, and then acquired a parcel of land directly north of that property in 1938 on which to build additional rooms.[4] Chauncey began work on refurbishing and expanding the home for a hotel and dining room in March 1931. The additions included small "summer cabins" just north and west of the central building. The Parry Lodge opened for its first tourist season in June of that year.[5] Available sources indicate that Whit became involved with the Parry Lodge in 1932, when he and his sister Kathryn were in Kanab running the establishment.[6]

While Chauncey Parry continued to visit Hollywood in order to attract studios to make their movies in southern Utah, business did not immediately come to Kanab. However, 1938 turned out to be a banner year for Kanab and the Parry Lodge, giving the three brothers an opportunity to perfect their integrated system of negotiating with studios for locations (Chauncey), transportation and vintage wagons (Gronway), and food and lodging (Whit).

Working closely with the Parrys was Merle "Cowhide" Adams, a colorful local rancher who handled the wrangling of horses and livestock. Adams's long career as a wrangler began on *The Dude Ranger* in 1934 and continued into the early 1970s. Cowhide's infectious personality also got him onscreen parts in a number of films, some of them

Talkative and full of charm, Kanab rancher Merle "Cowhide" Adams proved a first-class wrangler for movie companies from the early 1930s through the 1970s. He also managed to wrangle many onscreen appearances.

with dialogue. Whether teaching young Roddy McDowall how to rope for the Flicka pictures or working with Fred MacMurray on *Smoky,* Cowhide Adams was a favorite of Hollywood movie crews and executives alike.

Ever the local boosters, Chauncey and Gronway invested their own money in the first Hollywood feature to be filmed completely in the Kanab area, *Feud of the Range* (1939), starring Bob Steele and Gertrude Messenger. The film was directed by Harry S. Webb and made by Metropolitan Pictures, a "poverty row" Hollywood studio, certainly not in the same league of the "big five" studios such as Warner Bros. or Paramount Pictures. Nevertheless, the Parrys and the citizens of Kanab were excited when "27 movie people and big truck loads of equipment from California" arrived in Kanab in September 1938. Press reports referred to this production as *The Kanab Kid,* but apparently the local reference was considered too limited in its appeal, even to its primary investors.[7] Chauncey and Whit's names nevertheless appear in the onscreen credits as "associate producers." During the same time period, *El Diablo Rides* was another Western feature made by the same studio, with the Parry name prominently appearing in the screen credits. As satisfied as they may have been to participate in two completed features, the Parrys had no illusions about the modest returns on movies of this kind, distributed to theaters on a regional and not national distribution basis, but it was a start. Moreover, the making of these two films is an indication of the Parrys' insatiable drive to succeed and get moviemaking going in Kanab. Two more low-budget Westerns finished out the year, *Westbound Stage* and *Lure of the Wasteland*, the first movie in the area filmed in color.

Denver Dixon, who played the bit part of "henchman" in both *Feud of the Range* and *El Diablo Rides*, inaugurated a significant new chapter in Kanab's quest to become a filmmaking center. Previously a minor producer-director at the Monogram studio in Hollywood, Dixon contacted a number of prominent people in Kanab and incorporated Security National Pictures. The December 1938 incorporation had Dixon as president and local businessman Guy Chamberlain as vice president. Fourteen to twenty other Kanab residents completed the roster of investors/stockholders in the new movie company. Coincident to the creation of this enterprise was the construction of a studio complex consisting of a forty-by-sixty-foot covered stage with an adjacent Western street. Construction was completed by the end of January 1939, and the studio was dubbed "Utah's Hollywood." That term, with reference to both the studio and the Kanab/Kane county environs where movies were being filmed, was added to the masthead of the *Kane County Standard* newspaper beginning with the issue of September 1, 1939. A dance and party inside the stage facility celebrated the completion of the stage and the set. "Kanab people are anticipating one of the biggest and best times ever held in the history of the town," read the *Kane County Standard*'s announcement of the January 20 event. "It marks the beginning of a new industry in this section of the country

Above: Bob Steele lassoes bad guy Charles King, who conspires with railroad representatives to cause a range war between the area's most powerful ranchers in *Feud of the Range*. *Feud* was cofinanced by Chauncey and Whit Parry in order to attract more film business to Kanab.

Right: This hand-colored lithograph lobby card suggests the beauty of Johnson Canyon and Kanab's cloud-dotted sky in *Lure of the Wasteland*, the first color feature to be photographed in Kanab environs.

Above: Pioneer settlers deal with the death of a Native American in the now-lost film *The Mormon Conquest*. Inset: Kanab's Bonnie Chamberlain atop her pony.

that will bring more money here. The movie dance will be given in a real Hollywood setting with soft lights and good music." A screen test for the "best impersonation or imitation of any star in filmdom" was promised to contestants.[8] Following the gala event, the newspaper reported that "Local residents feel highly elated over the fact that this section of the country is being looked upon as a potential moving picture production area."[9]

Dixon's first film venture was from his own script about the settlement of Kane County. He hoped to bring popular B-Western stars George O'Brien and Monte Blue to appear in the fledgling production *The Mormon Conquest.* Dixon even journeyed to Salt Lake to film exteriors of the Salt Lake Temple and meet with church authorities "to make his film as authentic as possible." Newspaper reports kept readers in the county apprised of the film's progress as shooting moved from the Western town (with facades torn down and redesigned twice) to the crimson-colored Vermilion Cliffs towering behind the studio. By early February 1939, *The Mormon Conquest* had not been finished and Dixon was on one of his many trips to California "making another film," probably to generate needed revenue for the studio. Apparently, Dixon was successful in negotiating the lease of Utah's Hollywood to Monogram for the making of *Roll Wagons Roll* (also from Dixon's script), starring radio singer Tex Ritter, and *Westbound Stage*. Dixon then resumed production on *The Mormon Conquest.* Unfortunately, no copies of *The Mormon Conquest* are known to exist, but the coverage of the film by the newspaper was very descriptive: "The trek of the pioneers to southern Utah, incidents in the settlement of Kanab, the discovery of Zion Canyon by Nephi Johnson and the incident of Jacob Hamblin at the Navajo Indian lodge will be portrayed in the movie production."[10]

Filming locations for *The Mormon Conquest* included Zion and Bryce canyons, as well as Kanab Canyon, Three Lakes, and the Grand Canyon. Dixon returned to Hollywood, "where sound films were made," for the dubbing of the feature film. While in Hollywood, he got Bonnie Chamberlain, daughter of his Kanab business partner—who had been featured as an orphan girl in *The Mormon Conquest*—a screen test. A short film was made featuring Chamberlain and her pony, and the Shirley Temple look-alike was given a screen name, Penny Lane.

The Kanab premiere of *The Mormon Conquest* on July 11 and 12, 1939, appear to have been the only showings of this film. As it turned out, neither George O'Brien nor

Above: Tex Ritter sings one of his country songs to a friendly gathering stopped for the night in the low-budget Western *Roll Wagons Roll*, with the white cliffs of Johnson Canyon in the background.

Monte Blue could be induced by Dixon to be in the film, but the cast did include five-year-old Bonnie Chamberlain and a host of locals to give it county-wide appeal.[11] The high hopes of Kanab residents for a local production facility apparently were deflated, as there is no record of Dixon's activity in the area following the limited release of *The Mormon Conquest*, and no one surviving today remembers Denver Dixon or the studio that he created, except for the now-grown Bonnie Chamberlain Cutler.

The previous year, Chauncey and Whit Parry drew Columbia Pictures to Kanab to feed and house their crew and stars for *The Great Adventures of Wild Bill Hickok*, a low-budget serial. Columbia returned to begin shooting another serial, *Overland With Kit Carson*, in late May 1939. Both movies starred popular B-Western actor Bill Elliott. Production of the serials went at a lightning pace; both films were made in a total of six weeks. Directors Norman Deming and Mack Wright used locations primarily in Johnson Canyon, but also in Kanab Canyon.

Cowhide Adams handled the wrangling on these serials, but the work also provided for the debut of another star behind the camera, rancher Fay Hamblin. A descendant of Latter-day Saint frontiersman Jacob Hamblin, Fay Hamblin endeared himself to the Hollywood folks with his mild-mannered speech as well as his can-do attitude in making sure that local livestock, personnel, and locations were accessible and made available to movie companies on time. In contrast to Adams, Hamblin's demeanor was neither attention-getting nor eccentric. Rather, his steady reliability distinguished him, by the early 1940s, as Whit Parry's right-hand man in matters ranging from locations and cattle to negotiating with studio representatives in Hollywood and their often anxious moments when dealing with Whit. In *Overland With Kit Carson,* Hamblin also donned a breechcloth and brown makeup, along with other Kanabites, to play a raiding party.

Bill Elliott demonstrates his horse-riding skills in *The Great Adventures of Wild Bill Hickok*, a fifteen-chapter serial made by Columbia Pictures in Johnson and Kanab canyons.

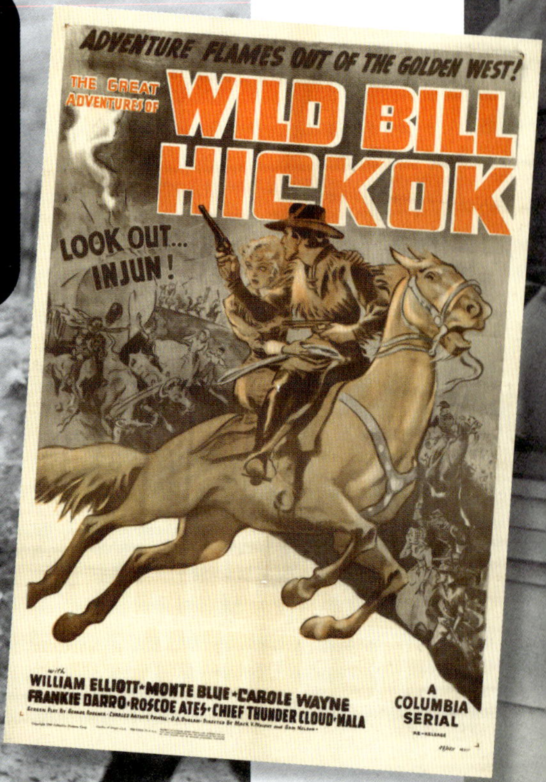

Director George Sherman (right) and his wife meet at Parry Lodge with Kanab rancher and movie contact man Fay Hamblin to discuss locations for Universal's *Black Bart*. Sherman returned to Kanab in 1949 to direct *Red Canyon* and *Calamity Jane and Sam Bass*.

In late September 1940, Salt Lake City hosted the largest movie premiere in the United States, and perhaps the world, which was then embroiled in war. And the story told by Twentieth Century-Fox's lavishly budgeted *Brigham Young* was Utah's own. Seven theaters sold out simultaneously as stars went from venue to venue to speak to the crowds. Heber J. Grant, president of the LDS Church, called *Brigham Young* a friendmaker. Even the Fox Movietone Newsreel recorded the festivities. The big-name stars of the film were Tyrone Power and Linda Darnell, but getting the most screen time was Dean Jagger, who won a seven-year contract at the studio by virtue of his performance in the title role.

IN GLORIOUS TECHNICOLOR!

Below: Randolph Scott (center) and Robert Young (right) look across the prairie outside Kanab in *Western Union*. Right: A Fox camera crew adjusts an 800-pound Technicolor camera.

Western Union (1941)

Barely one week following the premiere of *Brigham Young*, Dean Jagger returned to the Beehive State—this time to Kanab—along with director Fritz Lang and fellow cast members Randolph Scott, Robert Young, Chill Wills, John Carradine, and Virginia Gilmore, for yet another historical epic, *Western Union,* filmed in Technicolor. Jagger plays the part of Edward Creighton, head of the crew stringing the first telegraph line from Omaha to Salt Lake City in 1861. "Here's one on Dean," quipped Robert Young, who was borrowed from M-G-M for the part of the eastern tenderfoot. "We kid him a lot about playing Brigham Young. The people all over Utah have practically elevated him to sainthood. He's the biggest star in Hollywood in the Mormons' eyes. So Mr. Lang told Dean he couldn't smoke any cigarettes in public, nor be seen drinking tea or coffee. Emulating Brigham Young certainly has its drawbacks."[1] Fox's decision to make *Western Union* in Kanab, with headquarters at the Parry Lodge, was the first major test of the Parry brothers' by-then well-oiled machine, and proved to all the major studios that the town was ready to handle any production requirements.

Western Union was adapted from Zane Grey's final novel, published just days before his death in October 1939. In fact, Grey recommended the casting of Randolph Scott, who had appeared in more films based on his stories than any other star. Scott appears in *Western Union* as Vance Shaw, the "man with a past." The $1.3-million film showcased what reviewers nationwide would refer to as "thrilling Technicolor photography of Southern Utah's brilliantly tinted landscapes."[2] From the beginning of production in September 1940 to its conclusion on October 20, Whit Parry lodged the cast and crew and fed them on location while Chauncey coordinated the efforts of crews to build roads into Paria Canyon, forty-five miles east of Kanab. *Western Union* was the first film to display the multicolored parfait-like rock strata in the Paria area, which would appear in Westerns for the next thirty-five years. A few miles southeast of Kanab on the Arizona Strip is an area known as Six Mile, where scenes of Western Union crews stringing wire were filmed from a high knoll with billowing clouds and a dramatic orange sunset on the horizon. Camerawork and scenery of this kind prompted prominent *New York Times* critic Bosley Crowther to praise the film, saying "the shots of plains and Indians have the exciting richness of Frederic Remington's famous paintings."[3]

Ironically, the very quality of the Kane County locations that lent themselves to color—the dazzling red rock—proved to be too much for the properties of the Technicolor film. Lang insisted that the colors would look too garish, so workers spray painted the bright rock walls to tone down the intensity. Deemed not impressive enough were the local Paiutes, who looked forward to working on the film. Lang thought them too "short and rotund" to use, and so "Hollywood Indians" were brought in.[4] Nevertheless, genuine Native Americans—also brought from Hollywood—Chief Thundercloud, Chief Big Tree, and Iron Eyes Cody appear in the film. Of the $80,000 left in Kanab by the studio during its one-month shoot, the daily pay coming to Kanabites, was, in the words of a *New York Times* correspondent, "staggering."[5] In a city where $18 per week was a good wage, Fox was paying cowboys $5 to $15 a day, and bit players could earn from $15 to $100 per day. Production in Kanab went very well, and the Parrys managed to make a success of working with the first big production to film in the area. When the film was released nationwide in February 1941, it was enthusiastically reviewed by critics.

Between the time that Fox left Kanab in late October 1940 and the arrival of Columbia Pictures in the spring of 1942, two events occurred that would significantly affect the fortunes of Utah's Hollywood in Kanab. Franklin Roosevelt's call for a declaration of war against Japan on December 8, 1941, introduced Americans to an array of restrictions on meat, sugar, gasoline, automobile tires, and numerous other items. Movies, however, were viewed by the government as morale boosting, and arrangements were made to accommodate the needs of film companies that had to travel to various locations for production purposes. "The Parry brothers were given special certificates that went along the panels on the side of the door inside each car, a certificate of war necessity," remembered Dale Parry, "and we had all the gasoline we ever wanted."[6]

The second event that affected Utah's Hollywood was the creation of the Department of Publicity & Industrial Development (PID) within the Utah state government, with A. S. Brown as chairman and H. J. Plumhof as commissioner. Up to this time, the Parrys had single-handedly managed all contacts with the motion-picture studios during the winter season, when the lodge was closed and tourism was almost

A box canyon coursed by the river at Paria serves as a gorgeous setting for rustled cattle in *Western Union*. Fox crews experienced a powerful rainstorm that, for a time, stranded them at Paria.

nonexistent. Whit often took his wife, Grayce, on their trips. "Many times, Whit would leave me to make the contacts with the studios," she later recalled, "when he went off to do other business."[7] Cowhide Adams and Fay Hamblin also made trips to Hollywood, as the importance of agreements with local cattlemen and horsemen were vital for Western productions. With the PID established, Kanab could now quickly resolve complicated tax matters involving studio payrolls and purchases, and, more importantly, the city could call on the state department of roads to assist in building routes to remote filming areas.

The PID's report to the governor of Utah in June 1942—covering its first year of operation—specified the benefits of film production in the state:

> It brings cash income and employment into Utah areas that are not naturally favored, due to location and topography, as to either agriculture or industry. It offers perhaps the finest medium in publicizing Utah in all its vivid coloring to many millions of people. It is estimated that about one-third of the cost of a motion picture is spent on location. From this fact alone, it becomes evident that the cultivation of this industry can make it a valuable asset to the state.[8]

Roddy McDowall poses with Frank O'Brien of Utah's Department of Publicity & Industrial Development, a state agency that coordinated services to movie companies.

When location scouts from Universal Pictures arrived in Kanab in May 1942, they were accompanied not only by Whit Parry, but also by PID commissioner H. J. Plumhof, on an airplane tour of Kane County. With Utah having previously stood in for Arizona, Texas, and upstate New York during the Revolutionary War, Universal was now looking for sites that would look like the Middle East, specifically the sand dune regions surrounding ancient Baghdad, for the upcoming film *Arabian Nights*. Universal's scouts found just such a place eleven miles off Highway 89 northwest of Kanab, known to locals as the Coral Pink Sand Dunes, so named because of their distinctive coloration at the right time of day. This was of particular interest to Universal officials because *Arabian Nights* would be the studio's first film made in the perfected three-strip Technicolor process. "In Technicolor the pink sands photograph a rich hue," reported the *Salt Lake Tribune*, "but, according to Hollywood experts this desert is even more valuable for filming in black and white. Ordinary sands photograph a clear white and it is difficult to see the burnoosed figures of Arab riders against it. The Kane County dunes, however, photograph many shades darker and provide a striking contrast. For this reason the dunes are being hailed as a major discovery."[9] However, there was no access road from the highway to the dunes. The PID report noted that the growth of the movie industry in Utah might be limited by "access roads to new scenic locations." Because of the joint scouting trip and a formal appeal by Kanab to the state, a road linking the sand dunes location to the highway was constructed with the express support of Governor Herbert Maw, just in time for the arrival of Universal's production crew in late August. The Salt Lake premiere of *Arabian Nights* on February 11, 1943, was a big affair attended by the governor and a number of legislators at the prestigious Centre Theatre.

The Desperadoes (1943)

The first company to arrive in Kanab during the 1942 production season was from Columbia Pictures, for the studio's first Technicolor film, *The Desperadoes*. Cast and crew arrived on June 18, late because of the "lack of transportation facilities caused by the nation's all-out war effort."[10] Budgeted at $750,000 and directed by Charles Vidor, the film begins with a foreword that identifies the story, in "1863—the newest frontier was Utah. Utah's gold was its wild horses, which the Union Army was seeking to buy. Men rushed to the new frontier—some to break these horses, others to break the law." The law in *The Desperadoes* is Randolph Scott, sheriff of Red Valley, Utah, whose only bank had been robbed with the cooperation of its president and the livery stable owner, Uncle Willie (Edgar Buchanan). Glenn Ford is Cheyenne Rogers, a man with a price on his head who is trying to go straight but is blamed for the robbery after his arrival in Red Valley. Matters become even more complicated when he meets Willie's daughter, played by Evelyn Keyes, who is unaware of her father's knowledge of the bank owner's deception. Claire Trevor is featured as the Countess, a childhood friend of Cheyenne and the proprietor of the local saloon and gambling hall. In addition to scenes filmed in the Paria area, the Gap was used for one of the largest horse stampedes in movie history. Under the direction of Fay Hamblin, fifty cowboys took two weeks to gather over six hundred horses from ranches within "a radius of a hundred miles from Kanab."[11] Hamblin's seventy-five-year-old father, Walt Hamblin—son of legend Jacob Hamblin—had a brief appearance in the film as the head of the posse looking for Cheyenne Rogers. *The Desperadoes* premiered in Salt Lake City in May 1943. Evelyn Keyes had her picture taken with Walt Hamblin at the Utah Theater, where Governor Maw and members of the state legislature attended.

Especially on location shoots far from the studio, a film's director must see the results of the day's work before more of the script can be shot the next day. On most productions in Kanab, the studio would hire a pilot to fly the exposed negative of the day's filming (called "rushes") from the nearest airport, which was about five miles south of Kanab at Fredonia, Arizona, to Las Vegas, where a commercial flight would take it the rest of the way to Los Angeles. The film would then be processed overnight at the studio and flown back to Kanab the next day to be reviewed by the director and his production crew. Pilot Glynn Wolfe had more than his share of problems in making sure the film got to Hollywood safely. Barely a week into production, Wolfe was returning from a film-delivery run to Las Vegas when the engine of his airplane failed. The airplane crashed into Kanab Creek as Wolfe tried to land at Fredonia. Even though the plane was beyond repair, Wolfe escaped with only a scratched hand, but had to drive to Las Vegas for another plane. Two weeks later, this time in Las Vegas, Wolfe left the precious temperature-sensitive Technicolor negative at a creamery, where it was routinely stored to await its placement on an airline flight to Los Angeles. However, the creamery caught fire. Wolfe was a hero, rushing into the conflagration to rescue the footage before the roof caved in.

A group shot at Parry Lodge of the cast and crew of *The Desperadoes*, summer 1942. Whit Parry and wife Grayce stand next to the left porch post. Glenn Ford and Claire Trevor (in white shorts) are on either side of the right post. Bearded Edgar Buchanan, a favorite of Kanabites, is standing to the left of the entrance door. Director Charles Vidor is at center.

COTTAGES

After *The Desperadoes,* the staff at Parry Lodge and the citizens of Kanab had just over a month to prepare before the late August arrival of Jon Hall, Maria Montez, and Indian actor Sabu, starring in Universal's *Arabian Nights.* Only the sand dune scenes were filmed in Kanab, so the stay was relatively brief. The subject of the film was worlds away from the present wartime drama, but the records of studio scouts reflect a glaring reality, a portent of things to come. One of the locations considered in their search of areas in California and Arizona was just outside Alamogordo, New Mexico, at the White Sands National Monument. In communicating with the location manager at Universal Pictures, a contact reported that "I have been told that at the present time Alamogordo is filled up with workmen building some sort of war plant near there, but that job should be finished early in May and that there will be accommodations available in the town for your company."[12] The "war plant" referred to was the Manhattan Project, which produced the atomic bomb.

My Friend Flicka (1943)

Filming at the same time as *The Desperadoes,* but in Dixie National Forest some fifty miles away, were director Harold Schuster and a Twentieth Century-Fox production crew for *My Friend Flicka,* the first of three highly successful Technicolor movies based on the beloved novels by Mary O'Hara. The Fox company making *My Friend Flicka* was based for a time in both Cedar City and Kanab, because Kanab's limited lodgings were fully committed to other studios besides Fox. *Flicka* starred fourteen-year-old Roddy McDowall, who was acclaimed for his portrayal of Huw in John Ford's *How Green Was My Valley,* released the previous year. Preston Foster and Rita Johnson rounded out the McLaughlin family, which was carried through the two sequels written by O'Hara. While Kanab Canyon was used for some scenes, most of *My Friend Flicka* was filmed on the Cedar Mountain locations of Duck Creek, a substantial clearing surrounded by low foothills covered with pine and aspen trees where the McLaughlin Ranch set was built on

land owned by Ward Esplin. Cedar Breaks, Bryce Canyon, Zion National Park, and Navajo Lake were also used to show off the Technicolor-friendly beauty of land, lake, and sky.

Kanab resident Jack Adams, only a few years older than McDowall, was hired as his stand-in and double at the Duck Creek location. According to Adams, McDowall presented considerable difficulty to the filmmakers on location: "He was a very pampered little boy, hated what he was doing, and got pushed into it by his parents. He was absolutely petrified of animals. In the majority of shots where he was supposed to be doing something with animals, he didn't even sit on a real horse. He sat on a barrel and put a saddle on it." Years later, Adams understood the position that the protected McDowall was in. "I don't think that Roddy McDowall had been allowed to play with kids. He didn't know much about life at all. He never mixed with the children in Kanab at all. You never saw him without his parents and his nanny. He had been so sheltered and yet here Norm Swapp and myself could run, jump, climb fences and throw balls without any difficulty. The major problems in the production of that film centered around his inability to act like a western kid."[13] Eventually,

McDowall was able to ride a horse, as surviving stills from the film attest, although this was all new to the British-born youngster. *My Friend Flicka* had its premiere in Salt Lake City on April 7, 1943, with McDowall making an appearance as part of a nationwide tour to teach him about the "institutions and people of the United States."[14]

"I doubled for the little English girl, Diana Hale, who was the bratty little next door neighbor to Roddy MacDowall," remembered Louise Parry Thomas, Chauncey's daughter. "I was her double because they didn't want her to ride horses. The one instance that I can remember the most was in the barn when they were collecting eggs. He's putting them in the basket and she's pestering him. He takes the basket full of eggs and pours it over her head. That was me, the person whose head was doused with eggs!"

Above: Kanab wrangler Cowhide Adams watches as Roddy MacDowall trains with a lasso. Right: Horse trainer Jack Lindell earns a smile from Roddy MacDowall.

A month before the premieres of both *Arabian Nights* and *The Desperadoes,* tragedy struck Kanab, Cedar City, and everyone in surrounding Kane and Iron counties who benefited from the pioneering efforts of Chauncey Parry. On the morning of March 2, 1943, he was driving two of his daughters to school in Cedar City. "I was in the front seat of the car and my sister Sharon was in the back seat," remembered Louise. "A guy ran a stop sign at the intersection and hit us broadside. We flipped and rolled three times, ending up on the lawn of the Mormon church. I bumped into the dashboard and just cut my lip a little bit. However, the steering wheel went right into my father's chest."[15] Four days later, Whit telegraphed Gronway, who was in Washington, DC, on business, that "Chaunce was badly hurt and very sick. Feel sure he [is] past crisis. Much stronger [in] every respect tonight."[16] Chauncey was alert and appeared to have no life-threatening difficulties, except for pains in his stomach. It surprised everyone when he died on March 10 from internal injuries. "In those days," remembered Louise, "we had viewings in our homes. I remember daddy's coffin in the living room. 'Why did daddy have to die?' I asked my mother. I was only six. She said, 'because God needed your daddy.' It was the most perfect thing that she could have said to this little girl, I thought."[17]

News of Chauncey's death was a front-page story in Utah's newspapers. In the *Kane County Standard* it ran alongside the two stories heralding the premieres of *The Desperadoes* and *Arabian Nights*. The funeral in Salt Lake City was generously attended. LDS apostle George Albert Smith eulogized Parry as a modern pioneer.

> The name of Chauncey Parry will be written among the names of the builders of our day. . . . When I think of what he has done down there at the Grand Canyon and Cedar Breaks and Zion Canyon—all those places that are so wonderful to America—it was this man and his family who, in a very large measure, advertised and brought to the attention of the world what the Lord has placed down there, not to be hidden from the eyes of the people, but to be enjoyed by all His sons and daughters who found it possible to go that way. I am sure if we were in Cedar City we would find hundreds of people that looked up to this man and could say, "This man helped me to blessings that I would not otherwise have had." I am sure that many of them will bless his name for his consideration of them, for his kindness to them.[18]

Helen Parry, with three small girls to take care of, deeded the Parry Lodge to Whit Parry and moved to Salt Lake City, where her family lived. Gronway continued his involvement with the movie companies, but primarily as a provider of transportation and vintage wagons and carriages for Westerns.[19]

Above, left: Cowhide Adams holds the head of the horse used as Banner's double to simulate his death in *Thunderhead, Son of Flicka*. Above, right: Preston Foster holding the horse's head, as practiced by Cowhide Adams.

Thunderhead, Son of Flicka (1945)

So successful was *My Friend Flicka,* with Technicolor and its wholesome story of a young boy's transition to manhood, that Fox soon authorized the production of a sequel, *Thunderhead, Son of Flicka*, headquartered at Parry Lodge. The director and cast arrived on July 7, 1944, and redressed the ranch set at Duck Creek. Filming also took place in Bryce Canyon, Zion National Park, and in Red Canyon, sixty-five miles from Kanab. The two years since McDowall had been in Utah evidently improved his skills and his manner. "By the time of *Thunderhead,* he had grown a lot," remembered Jack Adams. "He had matured,

Facing: Roddy McDowall searches for the white stallion at the Narrows in Zion National Park. Below: The lush meadow of Duck Creek, high on Cedar Mountain (left), alternates with the rugged beauty of Kanab Canyon, cut by Kanab Creek (right), in *Thunderhead, Son of Flicka*.

and developed a personality. On *Flicka,* he wouldn't open his mouth except to cry and whine. When he came back, he would say 'I can do that' or "I will do that.' I had such a low enough opinion of him at that time that I was quite surprised that, on his return, he was quite self-sufficient. He had grown."[20] The fights between horses were expertly choreographed by trainer Jack Lindell, who worked with them in California for two months before location filming in Utah. Director Louis King was known to wait until just the right clouds were in the sky before shooting, often upsetting the front office at Twentieth Century-Fox. Time, after all, is money on a movie location. Locals would refer to the billowing white cumulus clouds alternately as a "Louis King Sky" or a "Hollywood Sky."

Green Grass of Wyoming (1948)

King returned to Kanab in the summer of 1947 for the third installment in the Flicka trilogy, *Green Grass of Wyoming*, which seems oddly separate from the other two, perhaps because of the cast changes that were made. Lloyd Nolan replaced twice-used Preston Foster as Ken McLaughlin's father. Robert Arthur was cast in place of Roddy McDowall, and three new characters were introduced to the story: Gus, the kindly ranch hand at the McLaughlins (played by velvet-voiced singer Burl Ives); Carey Greenway (played by English actress Peggy Cummins); and Carey's grandfather, Beaver Greenway (Charles Coburn), who lives near the McLaughlins. In this installment, Thunderhead, the stallion that Ken sets free at the end of *Thunderhead, Son of Flicka,* snatches one of the prized horses from Beaver Greenway's corral, causing friction between the Greenways and the McLaughlins. Many of the same locations used for the two previous Flicka films were shown, once again in Technicolor, to great advantage, but with the addition of two important Utah locations. Downtown Kanab is seen briefly in a scene with Cummins and Coburn inside Harry Ackerman's Kanab Equitable grocery and dry-goods store, and a dance was held at a popular Kanab outdoor dance platform at Three Lakes, just north of town alongside Highway 89. There, with guitar in hand, Burl Ives sang "Where, O Where Is Dear Little Susie" for the dancers. "I danced in that sequence," says Jack Adams. "They picked boys and girls as extras to dance around Peggy Cummins. They would orchestrate where you would dance within camera range and you could not stay in one spot."[21]

Above: Lunch catered by the Parry Lodge at the Duck Creek location for *Green Grass of Wyoming*. Charles Coburn is seated at the left end of the table, facing the camera. To his right are cameraman Charles G. Clarke, Peggy Cummins, director Louis King, and Robert Arthur. Lloyd Nolan, who replaced Preston Foster in the role of Rob McLaughlin, sits across the table with four unidentified crew members. Below, left: A hot summer day brings out locals to pose with Charles Coburn at the historic Kanab Equitable. Below, right: Guinn "Big Boy" Williams (kneeling), Edgar Buchanan, and Glenn Strange relax with Columbia Pictures actors in front of the Kanab Equitable.

Left: The third "Flicka" film continued the same McLaughlin family characters, but featured a completely new cast. The family "lived" in the same Duck Creek ranch house that had been retained from the previous two movies. Below, left: Charles Coburn, Lloyd Nolan, and Robert Arthur confer outside Grafton as they search for the wayward stallion. Below, right: Robert Arthur and his beloved steed at the Kanab Race Track, with Kanab's signature sandstone bluff in the background.

Smoky (1946)

With the success of *My Friend Flicka*, Fox was convinced of the commercial value of horse stories. *Smoky*, starring Fred MacMurray, immediately grabs the viewer's attention. After the main title credits play over scenes of Cedar Breaks, the camera pans to the towering walls of Zion Canyon and a lone rider, played by MacMurray, watching a herd of horses being driven across the canyon floor. He is taking special notice of a striking near-black horse that breaks away from the herd, frustrating the wrangler's attempt to catch him. MacMurray trails the stallion and delivers him to the Rocking R Ranch and its owner, played by Anne Baxter. MacMurray gets a job for his efforts and he becomes attached to the horse,

Bruce Cabot, Burl Ives at the guitar, and Fred MacMurray relax in camp during a round-up scene from *Smoky*. In the background stands Cowboy Butte, just a few miles south of Kanab.

ROCKING R RANCH

as well as to Miss Baxter. After Smoky is stolen by his larcenous brother, MacMurray spends the second half of the film searching for the horse at rodeos throughout the West.

Using the same Duck Creek ranch location as *My Friend Flicka* and *Thunderhead, Son of Flicka* might have seemed tedious, but director Louis King gave *Smoky* a freshness all its own. Whether in Zion National Park, Cedar Breaks, Kanab Canyon, the undulating series of cliffs and knolls south of Grafton on the Rockville Road, or out on the range near Fredonia, Arizona, King gets the most out of Technicolor and the locations. *Smoky* was certainly one of the most traveled of films, using locations that included Ogden, Utah; Flagstaff, Arizona; Klamath, Oregon; and Cheyenne, Wyoming. When two carloads of scouts and other personnel from Twentieth Century-Fox arrived in Kanab in late May 1945 after driving throughout the West, "They stated that in the entire trip they found no place to compare with Kanab and Southern Utah for scenery and facilities for transportation, housing, livestock, and manpower."[22] Whit had remodeled the Parry Lodge, and artist and future state senator L. H. "Dude" Larsen had made recent improvements at the Larson Hotel in anticipation of the *Smoky* company's arrival on July 12 for two weeks of filming. Fay Hamblin, Cowhide Adams, and Kane County sheriff George Swapp served as technical advisers. Adams also appeared briefly onscreen as one of the cattle drovers. Lillie Hayward, author of the screenplay, visited the film's location for a week and consulted with Hamblin and Adams to make sure that dialogue and ranching practices were accurate.

"We had Burl Ives over to our house for dinner on more than one occasion," remembered Jack Adams, whose father, Marvin, was a local union steward. "He was down-to-earth and very friendly." Without being intrusive, Ives's ballads "Blue Tail Fly," "Down in the Valley," and "The Streets of Laredo" come as naturally as talking. Ives even shared a ballad, "The Wooly Boogie Bee," with MacMurray. *Smoky* turned out to be more commercially successful than *My Friend Flicka* when it was released nationwide following its Salt Lake City premiere at the Utah Theater on June 19, 1946, and was the third-highest-moneymaking film produced by Fox for 1946.[23] The press also took note of *Smoky*. "While the pattern of the story is far from new, the picture emerges as an engrossing bit of entertainment," wrote *Film Daily*, "with its Technicolor photography of the wide-open spaces of Utah, where the picture was largely filmed, helping to contribute a refreshing quality to the footage, not to mention a pictorial allure that should advance the picture's fortunes considerably."[24] Even the *New Yorker*, which traditionally looked down on Westerns, favorably suggested that "One of those summer evenings, you might go see *Smoky*. You'll find it as relaxing as a drive in the country."[25]

Facing: A painterly image of Fred MacMurray at the Duck Creek location for *Smoky* offers a look at why Hollywood movie companies returned often to Kane County. Right: Visitors were allowed on movie locations during the 1940s and 1950s, as long as they were quiet during filming. *Smoky* costar Anne Baxter signs autographs at Duck Creek during a break in filming.

America was taking note of Kanab's frequent use as a location in movies. In a story for the *Saturday Evening Post*, Florabel Muir wrote, "There's only one star on the lot. That is Old Mother Nature, with a capital N." The article praised the work ethic of the local talent and the availability of the local Paiutes. "Hollywood's No. 1 branch production center, Kanab, Utah," the magazine observed, "is the only place of its kind in the world."[26] The following year, *Coronet* magazine featured the town in its story "Out Where the Horse-Operas Grow," describing the Kanab of late 1946 as having "nine stores, six service stations, eight hotels and auto courts, three cafes." Whit Parry said that the glamour of the studio presence in Kanab largely left the town unchanged, even though the money left by the movie companies represented about fifty percent of the town's economy. "She's still just a cow town at heart."[27] A cow town perhaps, but not necessarily one that had gone unchanged since Hollywood came to town.

One of the more prevalent concerns in Kanab was the Hollywood lifestyle that lit up after the cameras ceased cranking and the sun went down. Utah was a dry state and hard liquor was sold only in state liquor stores, one of which was in Kanab. In a predominantly Latter-day Saint populace, business was modest, catering mostly to tourists. As early as 1945, when *Smoky* was in production, Whit Parry concluded that the "rowdy element" had to be contained. He refurbished a small log cabin at the back of his property that was reputed to be the earliest such structure in Kanab. Locals knew it as the Black Cat. Stocked with pool tables, a bar, and, for a time, slot machines, the Black Cat was expressly forbidden to locals. "There were perhaps twelve people in the whole town who weren't Mormon," remembered Jack Adams, who worked briefly as bartender of the Black Cat. "You could buy hard liquor in the State Liquor Store in Kanab or you could go across the border to the Buckskin Bar in Fredonia, if you just wanted a drink at a bar." The Black Cat was only in operation when a movie company came to town.

> There was a nice bar, about thirty feet long, and in the front portion was a gambling area, where they played poker and blackjack and had three or four slot machines. We had a total of four, but one didn't work well. Whit would import people from Las Vegas to run the poker games. There was a mutual agreement between the city fathers and Whit Parry and the motion picture companies because they'd had a bit of a problem with people from motion picture companies going down to the local pool hall, drinking beer and causing some commotion and harassing some of the young girls in town. I don't know who proposed it, whether it was the city fathers or Whit Parry, but they let him operate this private club, but only for the motion picture people.[28]

What did Adams's parents think of his stint as a bartender? "My family was a little embarrassed, but I never drank anything stronger than a Coke in my life. In my estimation the Black Cat was a good thing. It contained those people and those elements that previously had caused some trouble around town." While the Black Cat limited the drinking and gambling to one place, occasionally there were problems. "On one occasion, I refused to give any more drinks to one individual because he was getting to be so rowdy," Adams remembered. "He was getting mad about it. A couple of others who were more level-headed took him outside and he kicked in a back window and so one of the guys went out and got in a fight with him and knocked him down. That was the most raucous thing that I can remember." As it turned out, the Black Cat was short lived. After Adams was drafted into the Army for service in Korea in the summer of 1951, a fire burned the Black Cat to the ground, and it was never rebuilt. "When I came back, I was told by my dad and by Whit Parry that after I left, another person was hired to work there and then someone else who didn't work out began to let some of the local people in. Somebody took it upon himself to torch it."[29]

Sierra (1950)

Kanab finished out the 1940s with a twenty-fifth anniversary motion picture starring a decorated war hero and national recognition from a major magazine for its moviemaking legacy. *Sierra* began shooting at Aspen Mirror Lake on Cedar Mountain in mid-September 1949. It is a rather brooding Western, not particularly distinguished. However, what cachet *Sierra* had was the Utah scenery in Technicolor and its young star, Audie Murphy, who, with thirty-three decorations including the Medal of Honor, was the most-decorated hero of World War II. On his return from service, the short, soft-spoken Murphy did not get film roles that suited him, and in 1949, just months before his arrival in Kanab, he married twenty-one-year-old actress Wanda Hendrix. The marriage was troubled from the beginning, Hendrix wanting to advance her movie career and Murphy beset with war trauma. *Sierra* was their first film together. However, for a war hero, Murphy's character in *Sierra* was, to say the least, against type, as he played the antisocial son of a father (played by Dean Jagger) who keeps the pair in the mountains because of accusations of a crime that he didn't commit.

Sierra marked a milestone in Utah moviemaking. On September 23, 1949, while the company was filming in Kanab Canyon, Utah secretary of state Heber Bennion presided at a small ceremony commemorating the twenty-fifth anniversary of moviemaking in Utah. Bennion noted the first film in Utah as being *The Deadwood Coach*, starring Tom Mix. The outdoor ceremony was followed by a banquet that evening at Parry Lodge, where it was reported that Whit Parry "provided an elaborate lay-out."[30]

Sierra stars Wanda Hendrix, Dean Jagger, Burl Ives, and Audie Murphy pose with Utah secretary of state Heber Bennion at a brief celebration held between scenes. The silver anniversary was appropriate in that the Hollywood–Utah connection began with a Western, _The Deadwood Coach_, and was celebrated during the production of another Western in 1949.

Stallion Canyon (1949)

Utahn Hugh R. "Denver" Brandon left his hometown in Emery County to become a stuntman, grip, and electrician in Hollywood. After twenty-five years there, he settled in Kanab, built the Brandon Motel, and got restless. In addition to working as a wrangler on *Sierra,* Brandon decided to get into film production and helped formed Kanab Pictures, Inc., in November 1947. Loren H. "Dude" Larsen, local rancher and artist, was president.[31] Larsen was a major player in Kane County matters, having been for a time manager and publisher of the *Kane County Standard,* attorney for Kane County, hotel owner, and state senator. Kanab Pictures' first—and only—feature film, *Stallion Canyon* began filming in 1947, mostly in the St. George area, including Ivins and Washington City. The movie had its origins in a documentary about wild horses, which evolved into a feature film. Denver and Bob Brandon were the principal production crew for this modest film, budgeted at about $50,000. It premiered in St. George on June 23, 1949. Filmed in color, no prints are known to survive in that form. The story is, to Western watchers, a familiar one. Bad guy and horse rustler Tom Larson (Forrest Taylor) owns the mortgage on the ranch of Aunt Milly Collins (Alice Richey), threatening the livelihood of her niece, Ellen (Carolina Cotton), and hired hand Curt Bensen, played by singer and sometime actor Ken Curtis, who would later distinguish himself in John Ford films and more significantly as "Festus" in the long-running television series *Gunsmoke.* Larson bets Aunt Millie's mortgage on his nag in the local horse race, but Bensen has a local friend, Little Bear (Billy Hammond), ride a wild stallion to victory to save the ranch. *Stallion Canyon* also had parts for Dick Hammer, the restaurateur from St. George, and Kanab residents "Dude" Larsen and Donald C. Swapp.

Ken Curtis (far right) talks to Forrest Taylor (center in black hat) and cast members of *Stallion Canyon*.

Red Canyon (1949)

Ann Blythe gets friendly with outcast Howard Duff at Aspen Mirror Lake in ***Red Canyon*.**

In 1927, George Sherman was an assistant director on *The Shepherd of the Hills*, shot at Cedar Breaks. He returned to the region in mid-June 1949 to direct his own picture in Kanab, *Red Canyon,* taken from the Zane Grey novel *Wildfire*, about a stallion that wins a race and helps to capture a gang of outlaws. The Kanab Race Track was used to good advantage for the climactic race, providing many wide shots of the area now occupied by the Kanab Public Library. "The Race Track was also the location where the Indians camped with their teepees when coming into town for a movie shoot," said Jackie Rife.[32] Howard Duff stars as the man trying to regain his honor by exposing his cattle-rustling brothers, the Corts. In the process, he wins the love of a ranch owner's daughter (Ann Blythe). Duff was only then becoming a film actor, usually in tough urban dramas including *Brute Force* and *The Naked City*, having gained considerable attention in the title role of the popular radio program *Sam Spade, Detective*. In fact, over one weekend, Duff had to fly to back Los Angeles for a broadcast and then return to Kanab the next day to resume filming. *Red Canyon* had its premiere in Salt Lake City on March 19, 1949, with Ann Blythe, Howard Duff, Edgar Buchanan, and Chill Wills making appearances. For the prints of *Red Canyon* distributed to Utah theaters, a special leader was placed at the head of the film thanking the State of Utah for its cooperation, a nod that was sure to have pleased PID commissioner Rulon S. Howells. The film had originally been titled *Black Velvet*, the name given to the stallion in the movie. However, the title was changed to *Red Canyon* shortly before production concluded in Kanab because its producer, Leonard Goldstein, "decided to capitalize on the beautiful red cliffs which surround Kanab."[33]

Below: School was cancelled and workers left their daily labor when Kanab locals were needed to get into costume and become a crowd at the Kanab Race Track for the horse-racing scenes in *Red Canyon*.

Calamity Jane and Sam Bass (1949)

Howard Duff and director George Sherman returned to Kanab in October, along with Yvonne De Carlo, for another Western, *Calamity Jane and Sam Bass*. The arrival of the cast and crew in a giant American Airlines four-engine DC-4 transport from Los Angeles inaugurated the new Kanab airport, created to accommodate the increased movie production in Kanab. Yvonne De Carlo formally dedicated the facility and christened the large plane the *Calamity Jane* as one hundred private planes arrived to mark the occasion.[34] With the creation of the airport, Kanab was now only a short two hours away from the Hollywood studios.

By the late 1940s, Kanab was riding high with income from movie production and from increased attention from the national press. Whit Parry expanded the capacity of the lodge in 1949, and had made enough money during the 1940s to winter in Mexico, the Caribbean, the South Seas, and Cuba. *National Geographic* published a major

pictorial article that included more than thirty-five pages on Kane County. The *Saturday Evening Post* carried a feature article by Utah novelist Maurine Whipple about a possible Montezuma's treasure in Johnson Canyon, east of Kanab.[35] A syndicated newspaper story appeared with the headline "Kanab Runs Hollywood Close Second on Movies,[36] and an M-G-M publicist called Kanab "The Capital of Western Motion Pictures."[37] Even the yearbook for Kanab's sole high school dedicated its 1948 edition to "the motion picture industry," singling out Twentieth Century-Fox, "for it is they who have filmed the most pictures here."[38] A signal recognition, however, came from the ubiquitous *Life* magazine when it named Kanab "Utah's Hollywood."[39]

Popular radio and film star Howard Duff headed the cast in *Calamity Jane and Sam Bass*, with beautiful Yvonne De Carlo as the gunslinger.

WILLIAM WELLMAN'S *BUFFALO BILL*

In early February 1943, PID commissioner H. J. Plumhof and publicity man Frank O'Brien, along with Tracy Barham of Utah's Intermountain Theatre chain, visited with representatives of each major studio in Hollywood to discuss how they might be attracted to Utah for future film production. J. G. Mayer, vice president of Metro-Goldwyn-Mayer, "commended our governor and the State of Utah on its forward-looking policy in creating a State Constituted Organization to look after the motion picture industry" and then shared the "miserable treatment" the studio received when filming its 1940 Technicolor adventure film *Northwest Passage* in the Payette Lakes region of northern Idaho. Mayer claimed that there was "an organized ring of Idaho people who victimized them" with exorbitant fees. "So far as Idaho was concerned, they would never return to that State." M-G-M's shot across Utah's bow was likely meant as a warning to the state about the need for the new state agency to work closely with local communities and their merchants to prevent price gouging. In a meeting with PID representatives, independent producer Harry Sherman talked of a picture then in development about the life of Western legend William F. Cody, more popularly known as Buffalo Bill. If wartime transportation limitations could be

A gag sign erected by the construction crew. It reads: "Fort William Wellman, in memory of Buffalo Bill, founded by a rugged band of pioneers who proceeded from Hollywood under orders from Col. Zanuck of the Fox colony traveling the old Union Pacific Trail to Lund thence by the Parry Waffle Iron landing at Kanab, Utah, June 27, 1943." Studio production chief Darryl F. Zanuck held a colonel's commission in the United States Army (to make training films) and the *Buffalo Bill* company did travel by train to the Lund, Utah, stop just short of Cedar City, where trucks carried equipment to Kanab. Passengers were transported by the Parry limousines (known as "waffle irons") to the Parry Lodge in Kanab, Utah.

JOEL McCREA
MAUREEN O'HARA
LINDA DARNELL
Buffalo Bill
in TECHNICOLOR
A 20th CENTURY FOX PICTURE
WITH Thomas MITCHELL
Edgar BUCHANAN
Anthony QUINN
DIRECTED BY WILLIAM A. WELLMAN
PRODUCED BY HARRY A. SHERMAN

ELECTRICAL
NGK. DEPT.
24" ARC
87
DANGER

overcome, Sherman said, he would be "willing to come to Utah to make this picture."[1] Sherman kept his word and, in May 1943, toured the state with PID representatives to identify locations for *Buffalo Bill* (1944), a motion picture that would be called by the editor of the *Kane County Standard* "the greatest picture to be filmed in Kane County."[2] While it may not stand up to that claim, the big-budgeted Western shows off Kane County locations as few other films have before or since, and proved to be great entertainment.

By 1943 Sherman had made more than fifty commercially successful Westerns, including the enormously popular Hopalong Cassidy series. Some years before, he had purchased the rights to the life of Cody, the legendary frontier fighter, scout, and creator of the internationally famous Buffalo Bill's Wild West. Sherman signed Western star Joel McCrea to play the lead role five years before Twentieth Century-Fox finally gave him the go-ahead to produce his epic film in Technicolor. The script, by Aeneas MacKenzie, Clements Ripley, and Cecile Kramer, freely massaged the historical record. William A. Wellman, whose forte was crime dramas and adventures, was signed to direct. Wellman's acknowledged maverick status with producers (his nickname in the industry was "Wild Bill") did not diminish his value to them, as he turned in solid hits most of the time. In later years, Wellman claimed to have written a factual script on Buffalo Bill with Gene Fowler but, over drinks one evening, burned it page-by-page in Fowler's fireplace because they could not see tarnishing a noble image.[3]

On their arrival in Kanab, nearly two hundred technicians built a large fort costing $75,000 in Johnson Canyon and an Indian village in the Paria area, which housed two hundred Navajos from the reservation on the Arizona strip. The top-tier cast included Maureen O'Hara. A reporter for the local newspaper described her as having "come from Ireland only four years ago, and has never seen anything like the rock formations here."[4] Also cast were Linda Darnell as an Native American maiden, Thomas Mitchell as Ned Buntline—who sensationalized Cody in dime novels— and Anthony Quinn as Cody's friend-turned-nemesis, the Sioux chief Yellow Hand. Utah-born actor Moroni Olsen was cast as O'Hara's father.

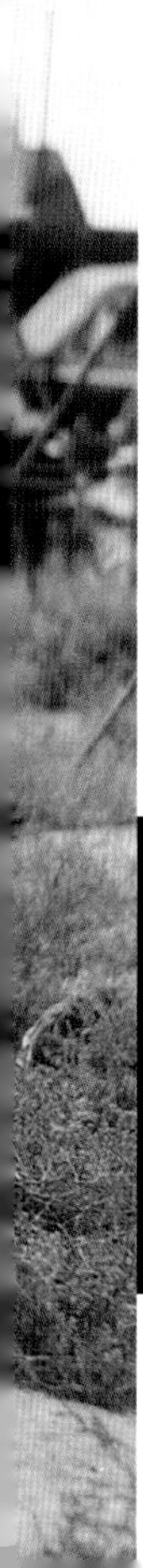

Joel McCrea, still in costume for his title role in *Buffalo Bill*, visits with Kanab old-timer Walt Hamblin, son of Jacob Hamblin, who is himself dressed up as an extra in the film.

The casting offices for the more than two hundred locals hired for *Buffalo Bill* were set up in front of the Parry Lodge and across the street at an abandoned gas station. Wardrobe tents were set up in back of the lodge property for daily fittings and makeup. The days began early and ended late as the haggard performers returned in buses from locations in Johnson Canyon, the Gap, or far out in the Paria area. Fortunately, one unnamed participant wrote a vivid account of his day on location.

> Saturday night I was going down the main drag minding my own business I thought, when I was accosted by Leslie, with the proposition of going to work for the movies the next day as a scout. Next day being Sunday and also being my day off, the proposition seemed OK Sunday morning I was at the wardrobe at seven o'clock, and following the line, I came to the boss who handed out characters and time cards. After thumbing through the cards, he found my name, then looked at me and said, "OK, you'll be an Indian." After being handed a costume I went to the dressing room to dress. The last one who had worn the pants hadn't removed the foxtail, which stuck to the legs of the trousers, and by the time I had removed them I was one of the last three to leave the dressing room. We three came on to the street where the buses were loading, and the last full bus was just pulling away. Another bus backed in and we climbed aboard, took the front seats and waited for the bus to fill up. Along comes Gron[way Parry] and he motions to the Indians standing by, and the bus soon filled with about twenty-five of the dusky ones. I shoved my head out the window, so I would have fresh air, and soon we were on our way to Fort Wellman, where the shooting was to take place. Arriving at the fort we roamed around waiting for the

Left: The script for *Buffalo Bill* required a full-size fort to be built in Johnson Canyon against the picturesque chalk cliffs. Above: The Fox camera crew is all smiles at Paria before the cavalry charge that would, in the finished film, kick up water into the lens of the Technicolor camera, and become one of the most dramatic cavalry encounters in cinema.

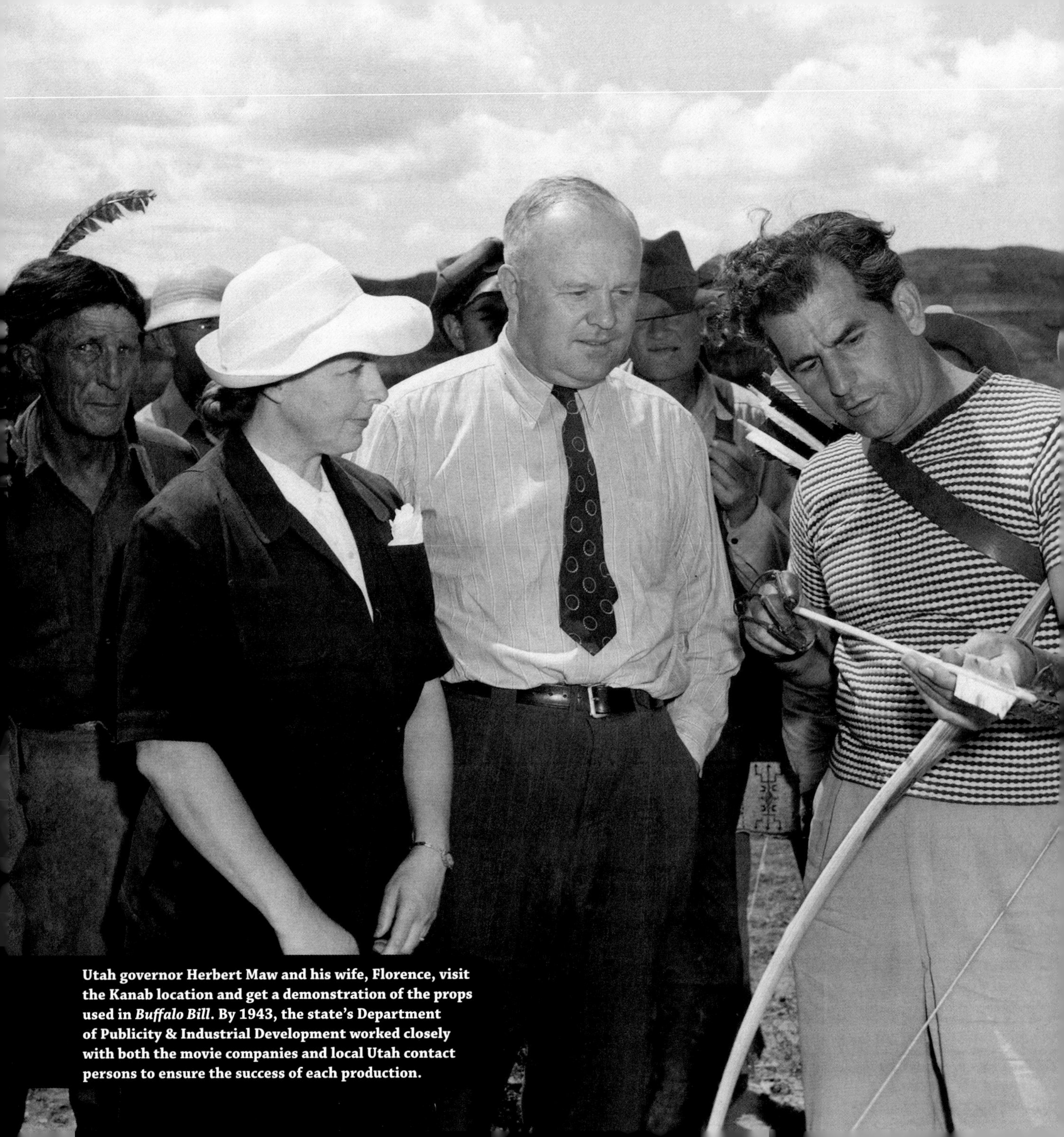

Utah governor Herbert Maw and his wife, Florence, visit the Kanab location and get a demonstration of the props used in *Buffalo Bill*. By 1943, the state's Department of Publicity & Industrial Development worked closely with both the movie companies and local Utah contact persons to ensure the success of each production.

> shooting to begin, and the sun to come out from behind the clouds. Along about eleven o'clock the sun began to peek through in places and Director Wellman decided it was time to start rehearsing for the play. Also about that time a mean-looking little guy, with a misplaced eyebrow, came up to me and glued a small piece of horsetail on my upper lip, and said I looked better. I was not sure what he meant, but I was afraid to look into the glass for fear I would take offense at what he said. But after looking around for a while I saw several more guys with an old-time coffee strainer on so I figured I was not the only one who might resemble a certain part of a horse. When Director Wellman started to give instructions I was sure the moustache was of no value to me or to the pictures, as orders were not to look at the camera, and all they wanted was a picture of our backs. The first excitement was when the General tried to mount his steed to lead the cavalry from the Fort. The horse shied and the General and his blue gold uniform hit the dust. After several rehearsals, Jimmy and "Cowhide" [Adams] would hold the horse and heave the general into the saddle, the director decided the action was good enough, and the sun bright enough to make a "take." We saw the fort gates open and Bill Cody came driving a span of black horses on a covered wagon. The cavalry was lined up and counted off. The General and Bill Cody had a few minutes of conversation. The General ran to his horse and was mounted, a few sharp orders were given, the Indian scouts led out, followed by white scouts, then the color guard was followed by the column of cavalry headed by the general and his staff. It was a pall-mall exit from the fort, and the excitement increased as one of the wheel horses on one of the supply wagons threw one of his feet over a stretcher chain, which threw him to the ground and the wagon rolled over him. After a camera stopped, the wagon was tipped off from the horse and he was released. Chow was then sounded and we formed in line and received a very fine lunch from Parry's Lodge lunch bus. The afternoon was spent in taking close-ups of the scene. After the close-up of the cavalcade's exit from the fort, which was very fast moving, we were all released and were transported back to town, just as a heavy deluge of rain came down in one big sheet.[5]

Navajos from the reservation in Arizona were hired to play Cheyenne. They laughed at some of the things they were asked to do (the method of fighting, the "tortures") by the studio's paymaster. Usually, extras were paid by the week. The Navajos preferred their $6.50 in cash every day, but they were confused and suspicious of all the money withheld from their pay due to Social Security taxes, unemployment, workers compensation, etc. So resolute were their protests that Fox decided to give them their daily allotment—plus $1.50 food allowance—and the studio absorbed the deductions. In addition, they would not eat the "white man's food" served up on location by Whit Parry, preferring instead to eat their own lunch of sheep and goat meat with beans and bread made from cornmeal. A writer for *Collier's* magazine observed that "among themselves, the Navajos are merry and jovial. Their sense of humor is quick and ready and evident. They admitted that they had a very good time making *Buffalo Bill* and would be interested in seeing the finished picture in one of their two motion picture theaters on the reservation, where films, mostly action ones, are shown every Friday night."[6]

So great was the national coverage of the making of *Buffalo Bill* that Kanab residents got more than a little of their civic pride hurt when apparently the PID erroneously referred to Moab and Salt Lake City—not Kanab—as the site for *Buffalo Bill*. A Kanab newspaper editorial advised state bureaucrats, "We should be left alone in this industry. Movie filming in Utah was started in Kane County. Kane County has the scenery, and also has the facilities for taking care of the people. We claim Utah as our state, we demand all our buying in Utah. And what builds Kane County builds Utah. So Utah please give us a break."[7]

All $2 million of *Buffalo Bill's* budget—the second highest for a Fox film that year—showed on the screen. The action highlight was the recreation of the 1876 Battle of War Bonnet Gorge in South Dakota, when Cody killed Yellow Hand, which he claimed was "the first scalp for

***Buffalo Bill* showed off one of the greatest cavalry–Indian battles ever captured on film. It was so dramatic that the footage was used in two subsequent films.**

front, but they had a little metal plate right here [pointing to his chest]. And I thought, 'Are you sure you can hit this little thing?'"[10]

Kanab's Ada McAllister plays a four-year-old whom Joel McCrea greets after emerging from the fort's schoolhouse. "Hello, Ada," he says, taking her up in his arms. She even gets a solo shot as she says good-bye to Buffalo Bill. In the background are two children on a seesaw. The little blonde girl who looks back is nine-year-old Jackie Hamblin Rife, who later became a stuntwoman and frequent extra in movies made in Kanab. "Three hundred people came to Kanab for *Buffalo Bill,*" said Kanab store owner D. K. Ackerman. "Practically everybody in the neighborhood was employed, every available room was rented, and a fortune was spent in the town. And what goes out of it? Half a dozen tins of exposed film."[11]

Custer." The encounter between the Sioux, the Cheyenne, and the cavalry was filmed over five days on the Paria River. The Utah Department of Roads and the Kane County road crews constructed three dams on the Paria River to create a large lake through which the charging horses could kick up water, making a spectacular image for the cameras. However, violent August storms washed out the dams three different times. "The studio called me up and said this is your last time, it's too expensive," Wellman recalled years later. "So I did it once more and this time we just did get it. And the next day they had another flash flood and washed it right out."[8] With gunshots and whoops echoing off the red walls of Paria Canyon, the attack was one that, in the words of the reviewer for *The Hollywood Reporter,* "almost defies adequate description. So well do [cameraman Leon] Shamroy and the Technicolor cameras attain complete reality that an audience feels impelled to dodge the spray of the muddy waters."[9] One of the cavalry troopers shot off his horse was Johnson Canyon resident Sylvan Johnson. A sharpshooter with bow and arrow was "standing on a rock and shoots me in the back. Over I go. They padded me with foam on the back and on the

With Kanab's moviemaking success so evident, Mayor R. C. Lundquist reminded residents of changes that can result from a flurry of national publicity, the continual influx of stars, and the magical luster of the movie business. When, on some location work, jobs were not always available to everyone in town who wanted one, disputes between families erupted. Lundquist chose to air these and other concerns in an editorial that he titled "Kanab's Responsibility." The favorable publicity in the media, he wrote, has given Kanab a "job to do. . . [I]t is up to us to maintain, and develop, the good reputation that has been established for us. It doesn't necessarily mean that we must change our own way of living for the benefit and pleasure of outside visitors, for there is no harm in remaining an honest, plain and happy community." Lundquist urged his neighbors to prepare for an increase of visitors. "Just now we stand at the crossroad, and the kind of town Kanab becomes in the future will be determined by the citizens who live here now," Lundquist wrote. "[W]e spend a lot of time talking, complaining, and demanding. . . . Let's complain less and work more."[12]

In the spring of 1944, Universal Pictures rented the fort built by Twentieth Century-Fox the previous year for a brief scene in Deanna Durbin's Technicolor musical, ***Can't Help Singing***. Director Frank Ryan is seen here with script girl, Deanna Durbin, and Robert Paige.

The 1950s brought significant changes to the motion-picture industry. A US Supreme Court ruling in a long-running antitrust suit forced the major studios to sell off their profitable theater chains, resulting in fewer movies being made and budgets being slashed. Television, introduced in the late 1940s, was making serious inroads into movie audiences. Thousands of theaters closed as viewers stayed home to watch their free television programs. On the other hand, the popularity of Westerns—on both the big and little screens—was never greater. For most of the 1950s, Westerns accounted for between 18 to 34 percent of feature films, and, by the end of the decade, there were forty-eight Western series showing up each week on television.[1]

Kanab enjoyed some regularity in production with television series that included *Death Valley Days, Have Gun–Will Travel, Gunsmoke, Route 66,* and, in the 1960s and '70s, *Daniel Boone* and *How the West Was Won.* Nevertheless, the number of larger feature productions overall was significantly reduced from the high levels seen during the 1940s. During most of the 1950s, an average of less than three features per year were made in Kanab.

THE RUSTLER FROM KANAB

The M-G-M crew readies the scene where a covered wagon breaks loose to crash at the bottom of a hill.

Westward the Women (1951)

In early 1951, director William Wellman arrived with truckloads of equipment from Metro-Goldwyn-Mayer to film *Westward the Women*. The story was developed by producer-director Frank Capra, whose home studio, Columbia Pictures—not known for Westerns—refused its most successful director's request to make a movie in Technicolor. The story intrigued Capra's friend Wellman, who took it to M-G-M. Scriptwriter Charles Schnee (who earlier wrote the successful John Wayne Western *Red River*) worked from Capra's original story "Pioneer Woman," which dealt with a wagon train of mail-order brides brought from Chicago to California in 1851. Popular leading man Robert Taylor was chosen to play Buck, the reluctant trail boss. Print advertisements sized up Taylor's challenge in the film: "He led 200 Husband-Hungry Women Across A Wilderness!" The bevy of women he was to lead west included Paris nightclub actress Denise Darcel, Julie Bishop, Hope Emerson, Lenore Lonergan, and Marilyn Erskine. Wellman insisted on three weeks of rigorous physical training at the studio before the troupe made the journey to Utah. Weight training, horseback riding, wagon driving, working with a six-up team of horses, and lessons in

handling a bullwhip were part of the strenuous daily regimen for the core cast. By the time shooting began in Johnson Canyon, they had been expertly trained.

The physical requirements for the month-long filming of *Westward the Women* were impressive, as thirty covered wagons had to be trucked from Gronway Parry's collection in Cedar City and 174 horses, 98 mules, and truckloads of reflectors, costumes, and lighting equipment came from Hollywood. The insistence on the appropriate location was apparently Wellman's idea, inasmuch as the backgrounds lent a sense of authenticity to the film's story. In an unprecedented move, he sent cinematographer William Mellor to Kanab to finalize the locations for the film, rather than going himself. As Mellor was driving with Fay Hamblin and Calvin Johnson in his Jeep, retracing previously agreed-upon locations at Paria and Johnson Canyon, Hamblin mentioned an area unused by any movie company, about sixty-five miles east of Kanab. Johnson turned the vehicle in that direction, and when Mellor saw Surprise Valley, he knew it would fulfill the requirements of the script. "The valley had every pictorial element we could ask for," Mellor said, "from stark desert wastes to deep walled canyons, plus a stream that grew from a small rivulet far up the canyon to a good size river with many pictorial possibilities. Here in this valley we could shoot the greater part of the exteriors written into the script; do most of the picture here, and save the studio considerable in production costs."[2] Mellor phoned Wellman, who flew out to Kanab to okay the location. "Not only did he approve the site," wrote correspondent Arthur Rowan, "but [he also] began a mental rewrite of the story in order to take further advantage of the unusual pictorial elements he found so abundant there."[3] Mellor used a four-wheel-drive camera car, dubbed the Blue Goose—equipped with a hydraulic lift—in order to get into Surprise Valley, where new roads had to be blasted and graded for the M-G-M buses and trucks. *Challenge in the Wilderness*, a special promotional trailer shown in theaters, elaborated on the unique location and the difficulties encountered in getting into Paria and Surprise Valley.

One of the long-term legacies of *Westward the Women*

The small town built in Johnson Canyon by M-G-M included a shack and saloon. The town appeared in many motion pictures and television Westerns over the years.

The unused Surprise Valley location for *Westward the Women* allowed for scenes such as this, unencumbered by highways, telephone poles, or fences.

was a small Western town built in Johnson Canyon that would remain and be added to for many years by many studios. Redressed and decorated, what became known as the Johnson Canyon Movie Set would be seen in dozens of television episodes and many feature motion pictures. As a change for Kanabites, many more women—150 in all—than men obtained employment on the film. One writer noted that the men of Kanab were transformed from laborers into babysitters for *Westward the Women*.[4]

Hours in the hot sun made production difficult to bear, including for the hot-tempered Wellman, as illustrated by the director's Kanab driver, who saw the following scene play out. In the film's story line, guards are posted around the wagon train, and instructions are given for no one to leave the group. However, Denise Darcel sneaks out to go down by the stream to freshen herself. There was about a five- or six-foot rise from the river to the plateau above where the wagon train was positioned. Darcel was wearing a heavy dress, quite low cut. Robert Taylor was lying on the ground under a tree with his arms folded, his hat down over his eyes. Darcel was to walk up over a little ridge, step across his legs, and tell him that she was there. "As she came up over the ridge, her long old-fashioned dress would slip down over her breasts, and so she would pull it back up," remembered Calvin Johnson. "Wellman didn't want her to touch the dress, so he was having to keep going back to retake her entrance. After several times, she came up to Robert Taylor, stepped across his legs, and said, 'Well, here I am, tits and all. How do you want them, on a platter?' Wellman was so amused by her performance that he had to shut down production for awhile. He raved on and on, as it made him happy about the way she did that."[5]

Jackie Rife, an extra on the film, remembered Wellman's almost sadistic nature: "He'd have us girls standing in a circle out in Paria and he'd had boys gathering up rattlesnakes all morning and turn them loose in the middle of us to see which one scared us the most. Man, you talk about a stampede. Everyone just scattered!"[6] In reality, according to Frank Thompson, Wellman's "admiration and respect for women was steadfast." In most of his films "women are shown the stronger, more intelligent and principled sex. In these films and others, women provide the moral and emotional center of the events and relationships."[7]

Bugles in the Afternoon (1952)

As soon as M-G-M was finished, in came Warner Bros. with the Ray Milland cavalry drama *Bugles in the Afternoon*. Johnson Canyon, Asay Creek, and Kanab Canyon became the Black Hills of South Dakota and southeastern Montana. Milland plays an army officer stripped of his rank for something he didn't do who goes west to join up again to regain his honor. There he meets the commander (Hugh Marlowe) with whom he had differences and who then took out his revenge on Milland. Through all of this runs George Armstrong Custer, as Milland, along with one of his troopers (Forrest Tucker), watches the encounter at the Little Big Horn. Kanab resident Sylvan Johnson got the job as the bugler when Milland's cavalry regiment is attacked. "It was filmed in a side canyon, just a little ways north of where we are sitting," Johnson remembered on his Johnson Canyon ranch.[8] Studio records show that the canyon was rented for $100 a day for filming, $25 per day for construction and striking of sets.

Right: Enemies when the cameras roll, friends when they stop: Kanab extras Charlene Johnson and Diane Morrill take the arms of Ray Milland while shooting *Bugles in the Afternoon*.

The Lion and the Horse (1952)

Making movies in Kanab was not reflexive instinct to Warner Bros., as the surviving location scouting notes for *The Lion and the Horse* attest. Louis King (*Thunderhead, Son of Flicka, Smoky, Green Grass of Wyoming*) traveled with studio location scouts to Flagstaff and Sedona, Arizona, where Oak Creek Canyon was explored. After listing the locations visited, the report simply states, "We were not able to find anything suitable to Mr. King. . . . [H]e felt he could do better in the Kanab area." In early August 1951, a party of four, including King, visited the town. The Mark Hamblin Ranch, eight miles from Kanab, was chosen as the primary location, but the group also visited Rockville, just outside Zion National Park. The writer of the report was greatly impressed with this location: "It would be impossible to get our generators or lights up for this setup, but it is so gorgeous we should definitely use this for the opening sequence in the picture, using reflectors, etc. The very fact that we establish our picture here sets up the premise for the whole picture of high plateaus and beautiful backgrounds."[9] One concern, however, was noted for the few shots within Zion National Park: "Thursday, Friday, Saturday or Sunday are the days on which tourists over-run the park." The report recommended filming in the park on a Monday or Tuesday.[10] Such was the change in the habits of the American tourist from the early 1930s to the early 1950s.

The Lion and the Horse is an unusual Western story, one that does not involve conflicts between cowboys and Indians, but, like *Smoky,* is a contemporary story about a drifter (Steve Cochran) who, with a spirited stallion named Wildfire, takes refuge from the law by hiring out at a ranch where the rancher's little girl takes a liking to him. His new position also places him in the middle of a confrontation between Wildfire and a lion that has escaped from a traveling circus. Strongly influenced by *Smoky*, *The Lion and the Horse* was the first film photographed in WarnerColor, the studio's name for a variant of the Eastman Kodak color film process. The studio generated considerable publicity about the unused nature of the locations chosen for the picture. Display advertisements for newspaper use contained the phrase "A story that echoes through the rugged Utah canyons!" In a promotion manual to be used by theater owners to advertise the film is a studio-generated "plant" article for newspapers entitled "Warner Bros. 'Discover' New Land for Film." In an overly sensationalistic manner, the copy states that "scenic sections of American wilderness included in the film had never previously been explored, mapped or surveyed except by aerial photography," and goes on to state that such areas have opened up because of the uranium boom in America. Barracks Canyon, Robinson Canyon, the Rockville Road area near Grafton, and Kanab Creek were obviously not new discoveries, but King did show off many areas in *The Lion and the Horse* that had not been used in other movies made in the area.[11]

An unusual feature of another kind in the film is what one might refer to as a theme song for Kanab. In one scene, Cochran and his fellow ranch hands are sitting in the bunkhouse when one of them (George O'Hanlon) decides

In a story reminiscent of the earlier *Smoky*, *The Lion and the Horse* features a protagonist who fights to own the stallion that captures his imagination. Here, he keeps the animal at the home of a rancher and his daughter.

to play an instructional record for his ukulele lessons. On the record, the distinctive voice of Harold Peary instructs the cowboy to strum his instrument and sing the following lyrics to "The Rustler From Kanab," which then gives way to yet another tune, "The Widow From Kanab."

> A rustler who came from Kanab,
> He'd steal all the cows he could grab,
> The sheriff he sought him and one night he caught him,
> And he hangs by a rope in Kanab, Kanab, Kanab, Kanab,
> He hangs by a rope in Kanab.
>
> A widow who lived in Kanab,
> Her muscles were turning to flab,
> To make matters worse, she lived in a hearse,
> And cooked all her meals on a slab
> In Kanab, Kanab, Kanab, Kanab,
> She cooked all her meals on a slab.
>
> Maybe you've never been to Kanab,
> And you've never seen a white slab in Kanab,
> But certain as sin when you are done in,
> They'll bury you deep in Kanab, Kanab, Kanab, Kanab,
> They'll bury you deep in Kanab.

This song was actually composed by O'Hanlon, a minor actor featured in a series of short films produced by Warner Bros. Certainly, this is one of the few instances in motion-picture history when a song was inserted into a film about the locations on which it was filmed.

Actor and songwriter George O'Hanlon (with ukulele) leads his bunkhouse mates in "The Rustler from Kanab."

Pony Express (1953)

For *Pony Express*, a pre-Moses Charlton Heston made the first of three moviemaking trips to Utah. He stars in the film as Buffalo Bill Cody, who, along with Wild Bill Hickok (Forrest Tucker), pioneers the Pony Express route from St. Joseph, Missouri, to Sacramento, California, against the double threat of Indians and outlaws. Rhonda Fleming and Jan Sterling provide the necessary female component. The production was filmed in the summer of 1952 in the Kanab area, including the Johnson Canyon movie-town set and the flats south of town. When Heston and Tucker are attacked and Heston yells, “Let’s head for Turkey Crossing,” viewers in Kanab knew just what he was referring to: a familiar spot on Kanab Creek that widens, and the perfect place for these two Western heroes to hold off their attackers.

Charlton Heston, as Buffalo Bill, fends off an attack at Kanab Creek in Paramount’s *Pony Express*.

After World War II, there appeared a number of Westerns geared to their own postwar period, the Civil War. Two of these were made in Kane County, *The Outriders* and *Best of the Badmen*. And in the summer of 1953, Robert Taylor and Anthony Quinn came to Kanab, along with Howard Keel and Ava Gardner, to star in *Ride, Vaquero!* a post–Civil War story set in Brownsville, Texas. Quinn plays a Mexican bandit who burns down the home of the newly married Keel and Gardner. Taylor is Quinn's foster brother, rescued in childhood by Quinn's parents after Taylor's parents were killed. What delighted residents of Kanab was not only the cast, but also the visit of Ava Gardner's then-husband, Frank Sinatra. After the couple landed in Cedar City and signed autographs for the "youngsters who had gathered to see the celebrities," Sinatra announced that he hoped Kanab "would be large enough to have a golf course, for he's here on a vacation and not to do work."[12] On that score, Mr. Sinatra was disappointed.

1954 would see no film production in Kanab, much to the distress of "Little Hollywood," which had grown accustomed to the added income, as well as the change of rhythm in town, when the studio trucks rolled down Highway 89 into the barely four-block-long business district. For the first time in at least fifteen years, the movie business was moribund. This stemmed, in part, from a condition that studios faced in virtually every location they used, close to Los Angeles or around the world: allegations of being overcharged for local services. Howard Pearson, the theater and film columnist for Salt Lake City's *Deseret News,* openly revealed the problem in a front-page story published in the summer of 1950, which quoted a "prominent southern Utah leader" who claimed that his information that one studio would cease production and that another studio had moved a Utah-bound production to Colorado locations came from "rumors, tips, and comments from residents of the Beehive state's moviemaking communities and from leaders in distribution and exhibition branches of the industry in Salt Lake." Pearson's source said that "one company which had made several pictures around Cedar City and Kanab in past years said four years ago they would never return."[13] To readers in Kanab and Cedar City, it was obvious that the "one company" was Twentieth Century-Fox. The studio's last film made in Kane County was *Fury at Furnace Creek*, in 1947. Fox would not return to Kanab until 1956.

Howard Pearson's article also told of another company that would not return "after their accounting department had informed them the charges were 'exorbitant.'" The unnamed producer of that studio's "three top-budget movies in Utah" moved a film shoot from Kanab to Colorado. The studio was Universal, and the producer referred to was Leonard Goldstein, who was responsible for *Black Bart*, *Calamity Jane and Sam Bass*, and *Sierra*. Pearson also observed that RKO, in filming *Best of the Badmen* recently in Kanab, had cut back time spent on location from the normal twenty days to nine because of the high rates charged. "The southern Utah business leader declared that the movie companies which have quit the state do not have any gripe against Utah, but believe they have 'had to pay too much for facilities,'" Pearson wrote.[14] He concluded by noting that Arizona had built soundstages and "comfort facilities" to attract permanent film production and that Colorado was already picking up more film production.

The difficulties in Kanab may be attributed to two factors: first, charging errors—whether by intent or not—may have begun when production dramatically increased in the early 1940s. Dale Parry remembered a simpler time when he accompanied his father, Chauncey, around Kanab in the late 1930s and early '40s to pay off the local merchants following the departure of a film company. "We would leave the Parry Lodge and start on one side of Kanab and he'd take his checkbook and they'd just go down one side and go into all of the businesses he dealt with on the motion picture. He'd walk in, find out what his bill was, write out a check. I followed him along and I always learned from that."[15] However, beginning in 1942, the increase in productions demanded a more centralized method of planning and payment. With Chauncey's death in early 1943, Whit became the primary studio contact for Kanab, with Gronway, based

Charlton Heston and Forrest Tucker try to break up a catfight in *Pony Express*.

in Cedar City, handling transportation concerns, and Fay Hamblin in Kanab dealing with Kane County ranchers to contract for locations and livestock. This centralized system had the benefit of efficiency and speed, key ingredients in a successful location shoot, especially when more than one film was being shot during a given production season. By the late 1940s, however, the allegations of overcharging became more public, and Pearson's article brought them out completely into the open. Calvin Johnson, Kanab resident and union steward for the teamsters, said that not only was there a temporary strike of Kanab extras over pay rates, but after finishing production on *Smoky* in 1945, he heard Fox's head of transportation "tell Gronway Parry that they wouldn't make any more pictures here, and if they did they would bring their own equipment" because of Gronway's inaccurate claim that he had a franchise on all transportation in the southern Utah area .[16]

Facing: Kanab resident Bette Larsen (standing), later of the Moab Film Commission, was a stand-in for Arlene Dahl on *The Outriders*. Above: Fay Hamblin (left) and director William Russell (center) and Kane County Sheriff Mason Meeks (right) during a break on Cedar Mountain while filming RKO's *The Best of the Badmen*.

expense before they take their cut from the amount paid by the production companies." The writer argued for an understanding of the complex financial transactions that are involved when big movie companies come to a small town, and the many tasks done by the Parrys unseen or ignored by studio executives:

The second reason for the heated allegations of overcharging was a failure of both sides—the studios and the Parrys—to come to an understanding about what was involved economically in the enormity of a movie shoot. This was precisely the point made by a Cedar City respondent to Pearson's provocative article, who wrote, "Since the people from whom we [have] heard seemed to consider the article to be about the Parrys, I'm wondering if it were meant to be taken as some people are doing?" The writer even speculated that "For all I know it may have been instigated by the Parrys for they have tremendous

> I think people are prone to forget about knowing that [the] Parrys, who bring movies into this area, do much before a movie is ever brought in. They fine comb the area for likely spots, take pictures, do a lot of correspondence and telephone calling, squire around and dine representatives sent to look the situation over, provide untold properties, some of which, as the oxen, require constant training, grooming and feeding although they may be used seldom. There are many other things which we overlook, and the movie people probably do too.[17]

Short of a state agency to absorb these costs, the writer insightfully observed, someone had to front all of these expenses. Overcharging, the correspondent seemed to say, is in the eye of the beholder. The writer confessed that "we need the movies, and I am concerned about their withdrawing from Southern Utah. They are economically important to the area, particularly Kanab. But they are costly, and whether or not they are being charged too much, I wouldn't be sure, until I'd really considered all angles."[18]

Dale Parry admitted that there was clearly another aspect to the frequent claims of overcharging movie companies:

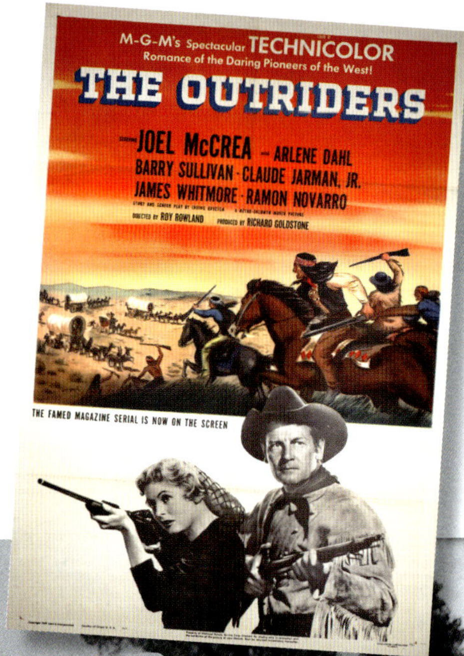

Left to right: Cowhide Adams, Joel McCrea, and Fay Hamblin on the set of *The Outriders*.

> In those days a handshake was as good as a contract. He [Gronway] and Whit and Chaunce had very good relationships with the Hollywood people and some that weren't so good. They [the studios] would order a wagon to be built, literally, to their specifications, and they'd get up here and decide they didn't want that. Well, Gronway had put out a lot of money to get that built and they didn't want to pay him for it. That used to really put him into a fit. Parry brothers and some of the Hollywood producers had a falling out for a while and then they kind of got back. They didn't honor their word and dad always felt that you should.[19]

While these concerns may have prevented Fox from returning to Kanab, it did not inhibit Warner Bros. and Paramount from substantial production activity in Kane County. Perhaps for this reason, Kanabites, hired as extras, were emboldened to strike for higher wages in late 1953, following the six major feature films made there since 1951, not including the more recent *Pony Express* and *Ride, Vaquero!* A small group of Kanab extras met to organize their own union and push for higher pay rates. They chose to confront a newcomer named Howard W. Koch—a man who, in the end, would turn out to be their best friend.

Anthony Quinn leads his Mexican *bandidos* in the post-Civil War film *Ride, Vaquero!*

HOWARD KOCH AND BEL-AIR PRODUCTIONS

While *Westward the Women* was in early production, an advance party was in Kanab scouting for another M-G-M picture, *Lone Star*, featuring Clark Gable and Ava Gardner. The entourage included assistant director Howard W. Koch, an up-and-coming filmmaker who began as a second-assistant director at Twentieth Century-Fox in the mid-1940s. Dining at the Parry Lodge, actor Robert Taylor and director William Wellman overheard Koch discussing the specific needs of his film. Taylor offered Koch the use of his private plane, whereupon Wellman muttered, "Don't lend them anything. They don't need any help." When Koch left the dining room, Taylor caught up with him outside in the parking lot and urged him to "Go ahead, take the plane." This is how Koch first met Fay Hamblin, who accompanied him on the flight, and with whom he began a lifelong friendship. "Kanab didn't look like Texas," Koch remembered, "so it was not used for the film, but it introduced me to Fay Hamblin and I fell in love with Kanab."[1]

Howard Koch had gone into independent production with Aubrey Schenck, a New York City attorney whose uncle Joe Schenck founded United Artists. Aubrey Schenck successfully produced *Shock*, starring Vincent Price, for Twentieth Century-Fox, and then moved to Eagle-Lion, where he brought in his friend Koch. After Eagle-Lion's demise, Koch returned to M-G-M until he and Schenck joined forces in 1953 to found their independent company, Bel-Air Productions, releasing through United Artists. "They were very different guys," remembered Aubrey's son George:

> My father worked with the writers and then handed the script to Howard. I don't think Howard had the patience. He loved working with the cast and the crew. Even though Howard started out that way, he didn't like to be involved in the editing process either. That's where my father came in, putting the story together in the editing room. If Howard and the cast and crew were on location for a couple of weeks, my father would be there for the first few days. They had fun together. They bought a station wagon and my father would wait out in front of our house and Howard would drive up and they'd go to the studio, Eagle-Lion first and then later the ZIV studio where Bel-Air Productions had its offices. Every day they'd come back together. They only needed one car. That station wagon became their camera car, the car that took them to work, and picked people up from the airport.[2]

Bel-Air specialized in low-budget movies, often with sensational titles such as *Big House U.S.A.*, *The Black Sleep*, *Bop Girl Goes Calypso*, and *Pharaoh's Curse*. Schenck crafted

The triumvirate of Bel-Air Productions: (left to right) Edwin Zobel, Howard Koch, and Aubrey Schenck, who saved the movie industry in Kanab. Young George Schenck, on the hood of the car, is concerned about other things.

the deals and Koch either directed the films himself or hired someone else, and then monitored the pictures on-location throughout the production process. "At United Artists, the Mirisches were making the big pictures. Bel-Air was making the little pictures," said George Schenck. "The way that the deals were made was they would just call United Artists head Arthur Krim in New York and say, 'We want to make this *Quincannon* picture.' Krim would ask, 'How much will it cost Aubrey?' $500,000 would be the reply and then a question would come up about the star who would be in it. At that time, Frank Sinatra had just become a big movie star. So, Tony Martin, another singer, came up in the conversation and it was agreed that if Aubrey could get him and still make the picture for $500,000, he got permission to go ahead and do it. Maybe Krim or someone at United Artists read the script, but I don't think it mattered."[3]

The Yellow Tomahawk (1954)

The first Western from Bel-Air was *War Paint*, filmed in Death Valley. Koch steered the company to Kanab for the studio's next picture, *The Yellow Tomahawk*. Peter Graves, who appeared in both *War Paint* and *The Yellow Tomahawk*, remembered being picked up in the Bel-Air station wagon at the airport in Las Vegas for the three-hour drive to Kanab. "I don't think I had heard of Kanab before going there," he said, "although I think it may have been discussed from time to time, as was Monument Valley and John Ford's use of it. I remember going through Zion National Park and seeing those marvelous shapes of rock and stone. It was my first time there. Aubrey, at one point, was gazing around at these wonderful shapes and said, 'I wonder what a psychiatrist would make of all of this?' Howard, who was doing the driving as Bel-Air didn't have a driver, looked over at Aubrey and said, 'If you live in a place like this, you don't need a psychiatrist.'"[4]

Graves remembered the Parry Lodge as a "kind of fairy-tale place." Having grown up in a small town himself, he loved Kanab. "Kanab was a lovely small town and had spectacular scenery around it, set off by beautiful cottonwoods and other foliage that grew there. . . . I never said, 'What am I doing in this hick town?'"[5]

Lesley Selander directed *The Yellow Tomahawk*, with a cast that included Rory Calhoun, Peggie Castle, Rita Moreno, Warner Anderson, and Lee Van Cleef. The production time was a slim sixteen days, certainly not what Kanab was used to, but "Mr. Parry said that it may be the thing that is needed to pave the way for continued movie work in this area, by showing the larger companies that it is still economical to produce movies here." Whit Parry wanted any film business that could be had. During a recent trip to Los Angeles, he had "offered producers the lowest cost in ten years for their contract [for] housing, meals, and transportation."[6]

Bel-Air needed all the financial consideration it could get. Both Schenck and Koch had put their houses up as security for the completion of *The Yellow Tomahawk*, and every additional day of weather delays meant more money fronted for the picture. Fay Hamblin became Koch's right-hand man on all the pictures he made in Kanab. Koch remembered a fateful day on the film.

> This was our biggest day with cowboys and Indians. We were up in Johnson Canyon, and I awoke in the morning and it was snowing. I thought, "This is the end." So I got Fay and I said, "Fay, let's go up on the hill and take a look." So we drove up the hill, got out of the truck, and looked around. You couldn't see the sky. The snow was coming down like mad all over our location, which was a tent city and a kind of primitive fort. I said, "Fay, are you very religious?" "Nah, I'm not," replied Fay. I said, "I'm not very religious, either. Let's both pray that it will stop so we can get our work done." I closed my eyes and said a prayer. When I opened my eyes, the snow had stopped falling. I looked at Fay and he said, "Whose prayer was it, yours or mine?" If we'd blown that day, I'd have been out of business.[7]

(left to right) Peggie Castle, Warner Anderson, Peter Graves, and Rita Moreno kidding around on the set of *The Yellow Tomahawk*.

Peter Graves was amazed at director Selander's lightning speed. "He knew the picture business well. He had been brought up in it and was a mover and a herder the same way that Howard Koch was. You'd come to the end of a scene and he'd say, 'cut, now move it over here.' The cameraman would already have the camera on his shoulder and would move on command."[8] Koch kept things moving along as well. While tolerating good-natured fun between takes, he was a taskmaster for discipline. "Howard would not allow bad language on the set," said Jackie Rife, who was an extra and stuntwoman on many Schenck-Koch films. "He wouldn't allow hanky-panky. If his people did something wrong, they were gone."[9]

Reviews were unusually good for the *The Yellow Tomahawk*, with the *Hollywood Reporter* calling the film "a good, suspense-laden western that neatly combines rugged action and character development for telling effect."[10] Schenck and Koch included an onscreen credit at the end of the film: "Made in Kanab, Utah." Bel-Air donated a showing of *The Yellow Tomahawk* at the Kanab Theatre to raise funds for the landscaping of the new elementary school in town.

Fort Yuma (1955)

Beginning in 1955, Bel-Air produced its modest films back-to-back. One cast would leave town and the other would be in Kanab the same day ready to begin the second feature. "We finished the movie on a Saturday morning," said actress Lisa Davis. "The second crew was there to start another picture Saturday afternoon. We were all sitting on a bus, and Aubrey Schenck was sweating bullets. [Director] Reginald Le Borg was ranting and raving and we were in the middle of a sheep drive lumbering past this bus with Schenck dying because they wouldn't move fast enough for them to start the next movie."[11]

This fort (shown below in *Fort Bowie*) was first built in 1952 for *Pony Express* and augmented by Howard Koch for many movies until 1978, when an explosion for *The Apple Dumpling Gang Rides Again* rendered it unusable.

Quincannon, Frontier Scout (1956)

Popular singer Tony Martin, who starred as an ex-Civil War officer in *Quincannon, Frontier Scout*, was unaccustomed to shooting on a low budget. "Tony Martin would ask me, 'Where's the dressing room?'" remembered Paul Wurtzel, location and unit manager for Bel-Air. "'Well,' I said, 'go behind the bush and change there!' Howard would say, 'Tony, come on, we don't have dressing rooms up here,' and would give him a bottle of Scotch and tell him to calm down. He went along with it."[12]

Not like the large trucks used by the major studios, the Bel-Air Productions equipment van looked good enough to the citizens of Kanab, who had gone for too long without movie work until Howard Koch and Aubrey Schenck arrived in the fall of 1953.

The Dalton Girls (1957)

One of the more unusual films made by Bel-Air was *The Dalton Girls*, a story that begins with the death of the entire notorious Dalton Gang. The four daughters—Holly, Rose, Columbine, and Marigold—are snubbed by the locals because of their notorious heritage. The town undertaker even tries to rape one of them as she visits the remains of her father at the morgue. The girls vow to avenge their father's death by embarking on a life of crime that includes stagecoach robberies and bank holdups. In a remarkable scene, Rose (Lisa Davis), the leader of the female gang, sings a song of male hatred:

> You can't trust a man because a man will lie,
> But a gun stays beside you till the day you die.
> A man is a wanderer and his heart will roam.
> A man is a cheater with his trifling ways,
> But a gun's always faithful 'cause a gun never strays.
> A man is unfaithful, he will lead to strife,
> But a gun is my true love, yes, a gun is my life. [13]

After Rose's vocal solo, her sister observes, "You're so hard, Rose. Were things that tough for you and Holly?" Rose responds, "There are things you can't talk about, not even to your sisters. Bad things you have to do. After a while, you get to like them. It gets easier that way." "Quite the thing for an English girl," remembered Davis, years

The Dalton girls ponder their fate. Facing: The daughters of the notorious Dalton Gang get their revenge on the male of the species.

THEY MADE MEN CRAWL BEFORE THEIR GUNS BY DAY...
...AND SNARED THEM IN THEIR LOVE TRAPS AT NIGHT!
THE DALTON GIRLS
starring MERRY ANDERS · LISA DAVIS · PENNY EDWARDS · SUE GEORGE · JOHN RUSSELL · Screenplay by MAURICE TOMBRAGEL · Music by LES BAXTER · Directed by REGINALD LE BORG · Produced by HOWARD W. KOCH
Executive Producer AUBREY SCHENCK · A BEL-AIR Production · RELEASED THRU UNITED ARTISTS

Rose (Lisa Davis) entertains her sisters around the campfire with a man-hating song.

after her portrayal of Rose. "Here I was rolling cigarettes, shooting guns, and singing this song. The odd thing about the casting in this movie is that I have always been and remain very British. Just about the same time that I was doing *The Dalton Girls* I was doing the lead voice in Disney's *101 Dalmations*. So, I have a very British outlook and here they cast me as this female Jack Palance and always I had to struggle with an American accent."[14]

The Dalton Girls was directed by the eccentric Reginald Le Borg. "I liked him," said Paul Wurtzel, "but he'd drive you nuts, and Reggie was always trying to get the girls to open their blouses to get some cleavage, and would waste a lot of time. Howard would tell him to get on with the filming. Reggie certainly looked the part [of a director], with a dapper moustache and a long cigarette holder."[15] Lisa Davis's recollection of the production reflects what made working with Bel-Air exciting for her.

> You had Howard Koch who was so very elegant, a lovely man. Then there was Aubrey Schenck who was the nervous one. He'd walk around sweating bullets with Reginald Le Borg, who was confusing everybody making statements like he did in one scene where some Indians had to ride down a hill. He shouted at them, "These Indians came down the hill too fast, too slow," meaning that they started too soon and arrived on their marks too soon as well. Le Borg, the wild Hungarian.[16]

In 1955, Kanab extras went on strike during production of a Bel-Air picture. They didn't want to stand by the agreement made earlier to work for less than the standard rate. Jackie Rife remembered being asked by the rest to approach Koch with their grievance. "I went ahead and told him what they were talking about, and what they wanted," she said. "Then Howard stood up and asked, 'Now, is this what you want?' Not one of them said a word in response. I thought that they were foolish to stage a protest. Number one, that was big money in those days. To start getting greedy was not a good thing."[17] "I remember my father being really upset," said Fay Hamblin's daughter Ina Fay Frost, "because they agreed to what they were working for and then after Koch got there they wanted the same price that extras got in Hollywood."[18] Calvin Johnson remembered that Koch did the best he could under the circumstances, but the extras put him in a corner: "Howard Koch came in here as an independent producer and everyone agreed, that where they had their wages up to like $12, they would work for Howard for $7.50 to $10 as walking extras. And that's the only way that Howard could get in here and get these movies going and so the Kanab extras modified their price."[19]

Labor difficulties involving extras continued through the years mainly because the extras were not a part of the Hollywood union. (Drivers, wranglers, and carpenters had worked under union contracts since the early 1940s.) Also, Whit Parry, as the *de facto* concessioner for Kanab movie business, deducted a portion of each extra's pay. They finally decided to create their own Screen Extras Guild Local. "Greed raised its ugly head," wrote Kanab mayor George Aiken. "When the extras in Kanab (although they were making more money than they had ever made in their lives) found out the extras in Hollywood were making more money, they called a strike. They didn't take into consideration the difference in living costs between Kanab and Hollywood, so they killed the goose that laid the golden egg, by joining the Screen Extras Guild."[20]

Mayor Aiken, who also built and operated a motel in Kanab, met with the local extras and pleaded with them, saying that if they persisted in demanding higher wages that "it was not just the screen extras that would be deprived of wages, but the entire town would suffer a loss of revenue if the film industry pulled out. The union let the members withdraw, but the damage had been done. Although some pictures were shot in Kanab after that, it was never the same as it was before the strike."[21] Two years later, in 1957, some extras lobbied to create their own union, which prompted another meeting with Mayor Aiken. The extras backed down.

While Mayor Aiken may have overstated the effect of the protest by the Kanab extras, the city did move to create a chamber of commerce to centralize contacts with the studios and coordinate the services provided by town merchants. In late 1958, Academy Award-winning cinematographer Arthur C. Miller spoke about the importance of having a single contact person in Kanab to work with Hollywood studios. That man, Miller assured them, was Fay Hamblin, who represented "the best chance of being sure of consideration for any future pictures being made here."[22] It was Fay Hamblin who would announce many of the future productions in Kanab, including *Fort Dobbs*, starring Clint Walker, whose tremendously successful television series, *Cheyenne*, was only in its first season.

Utah extra and stuntwoman Jackie Rife and Peggie Castle at Pipe Springs National Monument near Fredonia, Arizona, during filming of *Quincannon, Frontier Scout*.

The Girl in Black Stockings (1957)

Howard Koch made a total of nine motion pictures in Kanab under the Bel-Air banner, from 1953 through 1957. He dealt squarely with people, provided work, and endeared himself to everyone. "Howard would do anything for anybody, always," said Paul Wurtzel. "He wasn't phony. If he told someone he'd do something, he'd do it. He was honest. Howard's word was his bond."[23] Bel-Air's films were successful in theaters and featured much of Hollywood's budding talent, including Peter Graves, Anne Bancroft, Ben Johnson, Lex Barker, Chuck Connors, Rita Moreno, and Stuart Whitman. In his final year of Bel-Air production in Kanab, Koch filmed a murder mystery, *The Girl in Black Stockings*, written around named Kanab locations and filmed at the Parry Lodge. The film stars Anne Bancroft (in her last minor film before briefly returning to Broadway), Lex Barker, Mamie Van Doren, and Utah native Marie Windsor. "That Howard Koch is probably the sweetest man in the world," remembered Windsor years later. "My husband Jack and I were in Utah visiting my family, and Howard tracked me down through my agent because he wanted me for this part in *The Girl in Black Stockings*. They found out I was in Marysvale, Utah, so the agent phoned and they wanted me to start like tomorrow. First Jack and I went down to Kanab and I got wardrobe-fitted in the motel [Parry Lodge] gift shop, and the next day I was to shoot."[24]

One source noted that *The Girl in Black Stockings* "anticipated the plot of Alfred Hitchcock's classic *Psycho* by three years."[25] Lex Barker plays David Hewson, a vacationing Los Angeles attorney who is seen dancing at Three Lakes with Parry Lodge employee Beth Dixon (Anne Bancroft). "Los Angeles, gray flannel suit, court briefs, files, somehow they seem to have all gone out of my life," reflects Hewson, as he looks into Dixon's eyes. "Suddenly they seem five hundred years away instead of five hundred miles. Kanab, Utah." The romance is interrupted by the grisly murders of two women, one of them played by blonde bombshell Mamie Van Doren. The lodge owner, Edmund Parry (Ron Randell), is a bitter, wheelchair-bound man, cared for by his sister Julia (Marie Windsor). Hewson pegs Julia as the culprit, but Dixon is soon revealed as the psychotic murderer whose only desire is to be the single woman remaining at the lodge. Stuart Whitman, playing Dixon's estranged husband, does a brief walk-on, and, along with the Kane County sheriff, he returns Dixon to the mental hospital in the east from which she had earlier escaped.

Filming of *The Girl in Black Stockings* was done primarily at the Parry Lodge. Additional scenes were shot inside Whit Parry's home and at the Buckskin Bar, a few miles away in Fredonia, Arizona. Overt references to Kanab-area businesses such as the Kaibab Lumber Co. and Peaches Beard's Trails End restaurant make the film virtually unique in the annals of Hollywood moviemaking.

Whit Parry would not only appreciate the homage to Kanab and to his lodge in *The Girl in Black Stockings*, but he also likely enjoyed seeing his wife, Barbara, appear in two additional Bel-Air Westerns filmed in Kanab, *War Drums*

Future star Anne Bancroft poses in a publicity shot in the Parry Lodge's Pink Poodle clothing store.

and *Fort Bowie*. Overall, however, his feelings at this time were likely bittersweet, as growing debts led him to sell the lodge.[26] Local sentiment for Parry had apparently worn thin, as indicated by the response to a sharply worded letter he sent to the *Southern Utah News* in which he told of a proposal that he be the agent to rent the gymnasium in the old elementary school to the movie studios, with the proceeds going to the school fund. After two prominent school-board members turned down Parry's proposal, he accused one of them of planning to "over-charge and gouge any studio that might want to use [the gymnasium] and thus reflect adversely against Kanab as a location."[27] The newspaper's editor, Errol G. Brown, issued a front-page apology for having even printed Parry's letter. "To our way of thinking," he wrote, "it shows a very unjust and childlike attitude toward two men who are doing a good job in both private and public service. . . .We believe that Mr. Parry has too long valued the dollar above everything else."[28]

Above: Director Howard Koch lines up a scene with Lex Barker in front of Parry Lodge for *The Girl in Black Stockings*. Below: Barbara Parry (far left) and Whit Parry (far right) relax at Parry Lodge with Lex Barker and his wife, actress Lana Turner.

Above: Anne Bancroft and Utah native Marie Windsor prepare for a scene in the Parry Lodge pool. Below: Ron Randell, playing lodge owner Edmund Parry, readies for a scene with Anne Bancroft.

Sergeants 3 (1962)

Howard Koch produced his final Kanab-based film for Frank Sinatra's production company, Claude-Essex Pictures, in 1961. *Sergeants 3*, starring Sinatra, Dean Martin, Peter Lawford, Joey Bishop, and Sammy Davis Jr., was a thinly veiled adaptation of the 1939 hit film *Gunga Din*. The locale for *Sergeants 3* was transferred from British colonial India to the American Southwest, where the US Cavalry fights renegade Sioux trying to reclaim their ancestral lands. Trapped by the Sioux in a town whose communications have been cut off, the Rat Pack is held hostage and beaten. When the rescue detachment of cavalry is about to enter a trap, Sammy Davis manages to rouse himself and blow the bugle, alerting the army to an impending ambush.

W. R. Burnett's screenplay was so shamelessly lifted from *Gunga Din* that the Rudyard Kipling estate filed a lawsuit against the production company when the time came to distribute the film in the United Kingdom. The suit was subsequently settled out of court.

The reputations of the phenomenally successful members of the Rat Pack preceded them to the already world-wise town of Kanab and resulted in their adjacent rooms at the Parry Lodge being roped off from access by anyone but Koch. The stars were also prohibited from eating with the others in the lodge's dining room, and were instead driven to Whit's home, where Sinatra resided, for meals. "Whit brought in some women, older women, from the Arizona Strip to serve them dinner because of their language," remembered Ina Frost. "One night we were up there at the Parry Lodge and Peter Lawford started to go into the restaurant and Howard just stopped him cold. He talked to Lawford like he was a dog and said, 'You do not go in there.' Sinatra had food flown in from Italy and hired a German chef to cook it for him at Whit's house."[29]

Sinatra remodeled Whit's home extensively to suit his tastes, complete with an elaborate stereo system, cedar-lined closets, and other modifications that cost nearly $60,000.

Frank Sinatra, Peter Lawford, Dean Martin, and Sammy Davis Jr. send Sioux Indian Henry Silva to his death.

Jackie Rife remembered stern warnings about Sinatra and the Rat Pack from area parents to their children. "I remember my parents telling me, 'Don't you go near those people,' but I was working with them and I didn't see a reason for concern. You couldn't have asked for a nicer person than Sammy Davis or Frank Sinatra." On one occasion after a day's filming on *Sergeants 3,* Rife was asked by Whit to help in the kitchen at his home. "Frank came into the kitchen," said Rife. "I had my back turned and he reached into my pocket. Well, hey, you don't do that to me! I just turned around and I was going to hit him and he said, 'Whoa!' So, when I went home and took my uniform off, I reached into my pocket and found that he'd put a hundred dollar bill in there just for helping that night." Sinatra also donated gymnasium equipment to the Kanab High School, as well as football uniforms and a tractor to keep the field maintained. "He was a very generous fellow," said Rife, "and he was very nice. I don't know what he did in Hollywood, but while he was here, I didn't see a thing wrong with Sinatra or any of the Rat Pack."[30]

If Jackie Rife did not see anything one might classify as wrong, Fay Hamblin's daughter did, as she witnessed some of the group's antics at Parry Lodge. "They all had connecting rooms," she recalled. "They got into a water fight one evening and got hoses and sprayed water in their rooms. There was quite a bit of damage done in the rooms, drapes torn down, water everywhere."[31] However, the Rat Pack would not be around long enough to cause much commotion in Kanab, as they would often fly to Las Vegas after a day's shoot to appear in their evening casino show, then reappear the next morning at the Kanab airfield barely ready for the day's filming.

For *Sergeants 3,* a Western town set was built in Paria below the historic ghost town that had been there since the 1860s. The set, used again for *The Outlaw Josey Wales*, fell into disrepair, was partially restored in the early 1980s, and was maintained by the Bureau of Land Management until 1999, when it was torn down. Two of the buildings were rebuilt and moved from their original location. These buildings were destroyed by fire in 2007. A final footnote to *Sergeants 3* involved wardrobes taken home by many of the Kanab extras. "The production company went out of their way to let the users here dress at home," stated an article in the *Southern Utah News*, "and were very accommodating in that respect. A list of missing items can be found in an ad in the Classified section."[32]

In 1990, the town of Kanab invited Koch, now a major independent producer at Paramount Pictures, to attend a celebration in his honor.[33] By this time he was directly responsible for some of the studio's biggest moneymaking films, including *The Odd Couple*, *Airplane*, and *Airplane II—The Sequel*, and he had also received the Jean Hersholt Humanitarian Award from the Academy of Motion Picture Arts & Sciences. When Kanabites greeted him at the airport on October 27, the mayor declared the day "Howard W. Koch Day." Free screenings of his latest blockbuster, *Ghost*, were offered at the Kanab Theater. At a banquet that evening, Koch made a special presentation honoring his friends Fay Hamblin and Whit Parry, who had passed on some years before. Dennis Judd, who worked on many of Koch's films, said, "When we think of Westerns here in Kanab, we think of Howard Koch. Howard spread his enthusiasm about movies and filming to this little town and its people. . . . I hope we never forget that this is the town Howard helped to build."

"I don't know how I'll ever repay you for this moment of my life," Koch said at the local press conference. "Kanab is the same lovely place it always was, with the lovely people that lived here."[34]

Both Howard Koch and Aubrey Schenck made one final trip to Kanab. In February of 2001, the spouses of both men—whom Peter Graves described as being "joined at the hip"—suggested that their ashes be spread over one of their most beloved locations just south of Kanab. On a clear, brisk morning, their widows, grown children, and a few invited guests looked skyward from the banks of Kanab Creek as a lone airplane dispersed the remains of the Bel-Air Brothers above the red Utah soil, never to leave again.

Dean Martin signs autographs for visitors at the Kanab location of *Sergeants 3*.

The Rat Pack—minus Joey Bishop—poses with Whit Parry while filming *Sergeants 3*.

REEL CHANGE IN KANAB

In August 1955, independent producer Jack Wrather brought Clayton Moore and Jay Silverheels to Kanab to shoot part of the film version of the popular television show *The Lone Ranger*. "This is the first major movie company to come to Kanab in

some two years," boasted the *Southern Utah News*.[1] Over a hundred locals were hired as extras, including Peaches Beard, proprietor of the Trails End restaurant; Scott Betenson, owner of Kanab's only movie theater; and Bob Aiken, the mayor's son. For loyal audiences who had been watching on black-and-white television since 1949, color was a major selling point for *The Lone Ranger*. The popular characters had been on radio since 1933, and could be followed in a daily comic strip in three hundred newspapers. The opening credits of the film are shown over a slow camera sweep of the sandstone walls of Kanab Canyon to the familiar signature theme of the William Tell Overture, culminating in the Lone Ranger's famous "Hi-Yo, Silver!" while rearing up on his horse. The masked rider and his "faithful Indian companion" Tonto are then seen overlooking the green floor of Kanab Canyon, cut by the sliver of Kanab Creek. Barracks Canyon and Johnson Canyon are also used to great advantage in this well-made feature. The remainder of the picture was filmed on locations near Los Angeles, including Bronson Canyon in Hollywood and the Iverson Movie Ranch. One reviewer noted that "the rugged range country of Southern Utah . . . is magnificent."[2] A Los Angeles film critic appreciated the film because it "puts the western right back where it was in the galloping flickers, before words like 'psychological' and 'offbeat' came into the screen lexicon."[3]

On the heels of *The Lone Ranger* came Bel-Air Productions to film *Ghost Town* and *Quincannon, Frontier Scout*. Independent producer Albert C. Gannaway came to Kanab in the summer of 1956 to film *The Badge of Marshal Brennan*, starring B-Western favorite Jim Davis and Utah native Arleen Whelan, and *Raiders of Old California*, also starring Davis and Whelan, along with Faron Young and Marty Robbins. In 1957, Howard Koch returned to make *The Girl in Black Stockings* and *War Drums*, Bel-Air's final productions. Following the sale of the Parry Lodge, movies and television programs still came to Kanab, but only an occasional major feature that typified the halcyon days of the 1940s. An additional impediment to film production statewide was Utah's refusal to exempt out-of-state motion-picture companies from a withholding tax.[4]

Facing: Clayton Moore and Jay Silverheels in Kanab Canyon during production of *The Lone Ranger*.

Good luck always
The Lone Ranger
& TONTO

Fort Dobbs (1958)

Even more popular than *The Lone Ranger* television show was the new series *Cheyenne,* starring tall, broad-shouldered, deep-voiced Clint Walker. It was the highest-rated one-hour Western program on television, seen by forty to fifty million viewers each week. *Fort Dobbs* was Walker's first feature-length film. Gordon Douglas directed the black-and-white feature after an extensive tour of Kane County locations. The scouting report noted the presence in Kanab of a community "Service Committee," composed of the local union stewards, for "cooperation with picture companies," which also served as a "grievance committee and clearing for any complaints, and hopes to settle any complaints without bothering the picture company." The report added that "they claim success for this and refer to the recent operations there by Howard Koch and by Filmaster, who just finished." A "Supreme Committee" that included Mayor Aiken, *Southern Utah News* editor and publisher Errol Brown, and others in the community not directly connected with motion-picture revenues would handle matters that could not be resolved by the other committee. In addition to the presence of NBC Television production crews in town, "Kanab is pretty full, with tourists and government building projects, roads, and a Colorado River Dam [later designated as the Glen Canyon Dam]."[5]

As a ten-year-old Cedar City resident, Scott Boyter had the thrill of his life when he met Clint Walker on location making *Fort Dobbs.*

> Television was new in our community. Clint Walker was a hero to me. He was tall and he always won in whatever he did. I was intrigued by it because we had a cowboy background in our family. My mother first heard that he was on Cedar Mountain filming. I was quite surprised that she would take me up for something like that, but I remember going up to Cedar Mountain in our car and I took my little Brownie camera along with me. What is

you." He turned around and, in a deep voice, said, "Yes, son?" I was scared to death and managed to nervously ask, "Mr. Walker, may I have your autograph, please?" "Where do you want it, son?" "Oh, anyplace is fine," I replied. So, he opened up the comic book and signed his name in pencil, since I did not have a pen with me. "Is that all right?" he asked. "Yes," I said, "that's just fine." He then closed the comic, handed it to me and left. Virginia Mayo gave out a little laugh, as she thought that was pretty cute.[6]

In *Fort Dobbs,* Gar Davis (Walker) is falsely accused of killing the husband of Celia (Virginia Mayo), whom he had earlier rescued, along with her young son, Chad (Richard Eyer), from a Comanche raid. Fleeing the Comanches, they arrive at Fort Dobbs. Brian Keith plays a ne'er-do-well, gun-running acquaintance whom Walker has to dispatch toward the end of the film. "This is not a big western like *The Searchers*," wrote the *Hollywood Reporter,* "but it is better than most you'll see on TV and with a much less hackneyed plot."[7]

particularly interesting at that time, one could drive right up to the set. It was at Aspen Mirror Lake, right off Route 14. We got out of the car and walked a few steps and there they were. No one was yelling at us to get out of the way or to be quiet. I quickly took a few pictures when I recognized Clint Walker. You couldn't miss him, as he stood literally head and shoulders above everyone else. They were filming a scene with Brian Keith and Virginia Mayo by a campfire at the time, followed by a break. Virginia Mayo got up from the campfire set and walked into the meadow where Clint Walker was, and the still photographer began to take pictures of them, after which Clint Walker and Virginia Mayo sat and talked. My mother told me that if I wanted his autograph, I'd have to go over there and ask him. I had also taken with me a *Cheyenne* comic book so I carefully walked across the meadow and when I got there he had his back to me. Virginia Mayo then said, "Clint, there is someone behind

Facing, top left: The scene on Cedar Mountain that greeted youngster Scott Boyter. Above: Virginia Mayo and Clint Walker get to know one another. Below: Between takes on location.

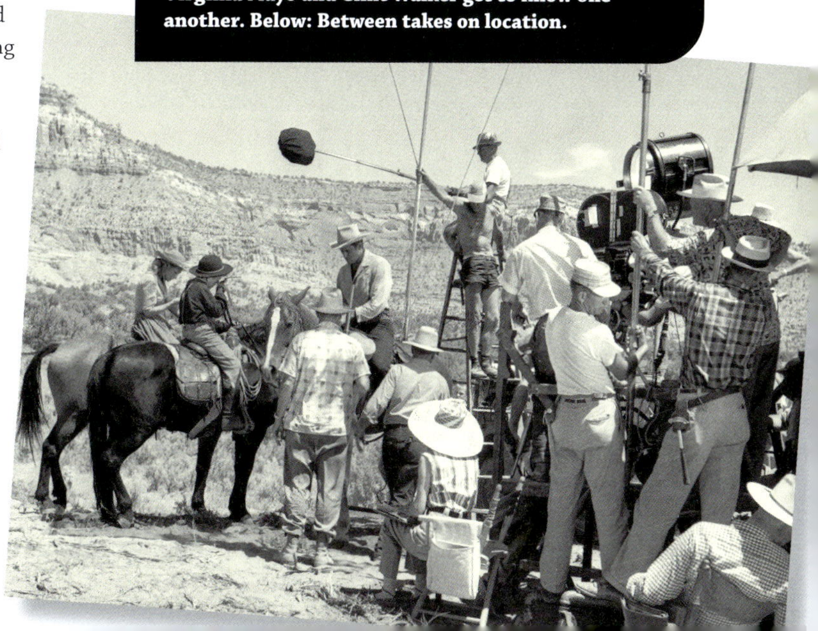

The Greatest Story Ever Told (1965)

Television production of *Death Valley Days* and other programs occupied the late 1950s and the early '60s, with the exception of Howard Koch's return for Frank Sinatra's *Sergeants 3* (1962). It appeared to be a time of reflection for Kanab, as evidenced by an article in the *Salt Lake Tribune* revisiting the decaying sets of many of the movies made in the area during the 1940s and early '50s. Photographs of the collapsed McLaughlin house from the *Flicka* films were painful to see. The writer correctly observed that "The days of the epic western with a cast of thousands seems to be on its way out."[8] Westerns on television would continue, but with a decidedly more personal, offbeat approach befitting the cultural changes of a less authoritarian new era. There were attempts to remake the classics, such as Cecil B. DeMille's *The Plainsman*, starring Don Murray, Guy Stockwell, and Abby Dalton. The remake was judged as "old fashioned" and a "standard western for devotees of the genre."[9]

In the late 1950s and early '60s, another major project occupied the attention of Kane County residents. The Glen Canyon area in Arizona was chosen as the site for a massive seven-hundred-foot dam that would provide hydroelectric power to the growing West and also create a new recreation area, featuring what would be called Lake Powell, after John Wesley Powell, the original surveyor of the Colorado River and the Grand Canyon. This massive public-works project, begun in the late 1950s and not completed until the mid-1960s, provided much-needed employment for those in

Photography began on October 29, 1962, at the Crossing of the Fathers—the site where Father Escalante crossed with his party in 1776 in search of a route to California. The first key scene to be filmed was of John the Baptist (Charlton Heston) baptizing Jesus (Max von Sydow). Prior to filming, Stevens held an interfaith service at the riverbank. Prayers were offered by representatives of Roman Catholics, Community Methodists, and Latter-day Saints. Heston's initial commitment for eight days of filming grew into nearly two weeks. Director-producer Stevens spent mornings "thinking (walking up and down on the bank, unapproachable)," wrote Heston in his diary. "George [Stevens] is a wonder in rehearsal using ideas, improving on them all. I think this'll be a good scene; I'm anxious to get into it, but we lost the light without turning a camera." Writing later about the length of time spent to shoot the baptismal scene, Heston recounted, "The Colorado River that November was no place to linger. . . [I]t got down

Above: While *The Greatest Story Ever Told* was neither a critical nor a commercial success, it was a visually dazzling experience. Right: Director George Stevens (right) talks with Kanab's Dr. George Aiken (center) at the Lake Powell location.

Kane County as well as in northern Arizona.

While the dam was under construction in late August 1962, Fay Hamblin announced that producer-director George Stevens had selected an area along the Colorado River as a principal location for his upcoming biblical epic, *The Greatest Story Ever Told*. The multimillion-dollar film would benefit all of southern Utah. While the logistics of food and other supplies were handled in Page, Arizona, most of the support crew, including extras, came from Kane County. Fay Hamblin handled all of the preparations for roads to access the six major locations in the Glen Canyon area.

Above, left: Workers prepare a Lake Powell location for the scene in *The Greatest Story Ever Told* where John the Baptist baptizes Jesus and many of his followers. Above, right: The same location a short while later, with the waters of Lake Powell rising behind Glen Canyon Dam as Charlton Heston, playing John the Baptist, baptizes Jesus (Max von Sydow). Below: A surprising sight for tourists: a long line of crucified bodies stretches into the distance.

in the forties every morning. At the end of one trying day, George noticed my discomfort and asked me how I felt. 'I'm OK, George,' I said. 'But I'll tell you this: If the River Jordan had been as cold as the Colorado, Christianity would never have got off the ground."[10]

As fall progressed into winter, bad weather necessitated closing down the production before Christmas.

When filming resumed in January, Stevens invited a delegation of Utah lawmakers to tour the sets. Utah representatives from Garfield, Spanish Fork, Panguitch, Moab, Salt Lake City, and Kane County toured the huge Jerusalem set, the city of Nazareth, and the house of Lazarus and its adjoining vineyard, created from one hundred olive trees trucked in from California.[11] The location camp comprised 110 aluminum and canvas cottages encircling a large tent used as a dining hall that served up to two thousand meals a day. Twenty-one buses and twenty station wagons were used to transport principal cast members and extras to the sets. Together with the fuel requirements of the large trucks and other vehicles used during filming, the gas and oil bill for the month of

Left: Kanabite Marvin Adams, who worked on movies made in Kane County for more than two decades, stands by the gate of Jerusalem built for George Stevens's *The Greatest Story Ever Told*. Below: A view of the enormous camp housing personnel for the film. Employment on this film was the longest for a single film within memory of those in Kanab.

November alone was $33,000. By May 1963, production ended in Kane County and casting began in Moab for the remainder of the film.

Typical of the new Westerns being made by independent companies were *Ride in the Whirlwind* and *The Shooting*, filmed mostly at Paria and coproduced by then-struggling actor Jack Nicholson. Millie Perkins, whose fame derived from her title role in George Stevens's film *The Diary of Anne Frank*, appeared in both films, which, for economic reasons, were shot at the same time and on the same locations. The stars and their families arrived in Kanab in early April 1965 and stayed at the Parry Lodge through the early summer. Everyone doubled up on job assignments, from carrying camera equipment to moving reflectors, lights, and sound booms.

The Shooting, costarring Perkins, Warren Oates, Will Hutchins, and Nicholson, concerns the mysterious Perkins hiring Oates to track a man who, it turns out, is his own twin brother. *Ride in the Whirlwind,* written and coproduced by Nicholson, deals with Cameron Mitchell and Nicholson, unjustly pursued by a vigilante posse, who take refuge with a local farmer and his family. Extensive shooting in Paria used the colorful but ultimately barren environment, underscoring the posse's hostility toward the protagonists. Both films were made for $150,000 combined. Their existential plots and tone made them favorites in Europe, but they were rarely seen in the United States until 1971, after Nicholson's star rose with his appearance in *Easy Rider*. "They're darned good westerns," said Nicholson. "I've never felt I had to make excuses. . . . My westerns are better than a lot of big, pretentious ones."[12] Nicholson claimed to have received only $1,400 for his contribution to the two films. Oddly enough, the Kanab location that Nicholson thought was a departure from the usual Monument Valley location was in fact recognized by French movie aficionados who had seen Fritz Lang's *Western Union,* as well as a number of other films.

Duel at Diablo (1966)

Duel at Diablo was the first major studio film to hit Kanab in more than a few years. Producer Martin Rankin had originally planned to film the Western in Durango, Mexico. However, local villagers in Durango had recently destroyed a set left behind for Paramount's *The Sons of Katie Elder*, prompting United Artists to seek another location. Directed by Ralph Nelson (*Lilies of the Field*) and starring Sidney Poitier, James Garner, Dennis Weaver ("Chester" on *Gunsmoke*), and Bibi Andersson, *Duel* is a racially themed, action-packed Western. Poitier plays an ex-cavalry sergeant who trades horses to the army and encounters discrimination along the way. With James Garner, Poitier is involved in saving Bibi Andersson from what they thought was rape, only

Horse trader Sidney Poitier joins Bill Travers (in sling) after they are cornered by Indians in *Duel at Diablo*.

to discover that Andersson wants to return to the Native American father of her child. A black man living in the Old West had not been previously portrayed by a top box-office star, and Poitier was criticized by some for doing little more than "holding James Garner's hat." However, Poitier said, "I agreed to make it solely because I would have a role as a Negro cowboy. . . .[N]o one knows the Negro contribution to the building of the West. . . . I also did the film because it gave me an opportunity to give a hero imagery to Negro children to encourage them to love Westerns."[13]

The premiere of *Duel at Diablo* in Salt Lake City was a progressive tour, originating in Page, Arizona, with fifty members of the world press traveling in buses to Zion National Park and then to Salt Lake City, where principal cast members made personal appearances on May 12, 1966. The beginning of the film showed an onscreen credit that read: "This picture was made in Southern Utah, U.S.A."

Bill Travers leads his cavalry detachment past the picturesque Cockscombs at Paria in *Duel at Diablo*.

Planet of the Apes (1968)

In the barren but starkly beautiful desert crust bordering Lake Powell, Charlton Heston returned to Utah for the filming of *Planet of the Apes*, a modestly budgeted film that would become a commercial phenomenon and lead to sequels and even a remake. The year is 3978, when three astronauts crash-land on what they think is another planet. As their spacecraft sinks, the weary space travelers row away in a raft on the deep blue waters of Lake Powell and go ashore on the Utah side of the lake. Their long walk is shown across the desert expanse that, just three years earlier, had depicted the Holy Land where Heston had baptized Christian converts. "The heat is bad here," he recorded in his journal, even though it was only late May. "One of the other two actors playing astronauts passed out from the heat."[14]

Facing, above: Heston and crew marvel at the strange simian shapes in the desert. Above: Charlton Heston does not yet know what lies before him after he and two other astronauts make it to the shore of Lake Powell.

Even before Whit Parry sold the Parry Lodge in 1966, Fay Hamblin had taken over the principal liaison work between Kanab and the Hollywood studios. With greater competition from surrounding states and cities, including Moab to the east, Kanab began a campaign to build a sound stage, a Western movie set, and a second movie fort. The Kanab Area Motion Picture Association sought pledges to help in funding trips to Hollywood. Local postmaster Claud Glazier headed up the committee and Bureau of Land Management officials showed slides of backcountry areas suitable for production work to studio representatives. Taylor Crosby, head of the Kanab Chamber of Commerce, said that "Of all the things we have been doing and talking about it looks like this project will bring more money into the community faster than anything else."[15] The group incorporated in December 1967 as Kanab Movieland, Inc. Special subcommittees were set up over materials, site locations, sound stages, props, and interiors. Crosby, who was president of the organization for a few years, joined a group of local investors to purchase Kanab Canyon and preserve it as a filming location for visiting production companies, but, during the ten years of their possession, little production was seen. Also, renewed federal restrictions on the use of public lands made filming more complicated.

The meetings that culminated in Kanab Movieland, Inc., were missing two individuals in this ever-growing organization of local movers and shakers. The first was Whit Parry, whose fortunes were frequently described in roller coaster proportions by those who knew him. Whit's second marriage, to Barbara Langer, ended in 1960, and he suffered financially as a result. The Parry Lodge was sold at a sheriff's sale in 1966 to Whit's good friend and business partner Bernell Lewis, who had loaned Whit money over the years and had purchased the lodge's various mortgages. Whit, now a vagabond unconnected to the lodge or to the movie business, went to California for a while and then to Arizona. His recurring problems with ulcers and other ailments ended with cancer that resulted in the amputation of his right arm. For less than a year, Whit's competitive drive manifested itself in starting a restaurant directly across the street from the Parry Lodge. However, it, too, failed. The man who put Kanab in a place of international prominence died there on June 23, 1967. A small granite marker identifies Caleb Whitney Parry's burial spot in the Kanab Cemetery. "Hardly a tribute to a man who helped transform Kanab into 'Little Hollywood,'" wrote Loren Webb, editor of the *Southern Utah News*.[16] "He was one of the best friends I ever had," said Phyllis Stewart, who worked for Whit for nearly a quarter century. "When I started working for him as a waitress, I had no self-confidence whatsoever. He noticed it and went about working to change my attitude. He would get in a crowd of people and I would walk in and he would make a comment such as, 'My, that's a pretty dress you have on.' I would freeze, but gradually I got to where I could accept that. We were very good friends and could talk about anything under the sun. There were a lot of people who hated his guts, but he was always my friend. What I missed the most when he left the Parry Lodge was just the feeling. You knew that he wasn't there."[17] The Parry Lodge was purchased in 1971 by Golden Circle tours, which enlarged the venerable hotel from thirty-seven to eighty-two units. The company was organized by Kanab resident Norm Cram in an effort to include Kanab in, and to capitalize on, the growing popularity of bus tours to the major national parks in southern Utah and northern Arizona.

The other man missing from Kanab Movieland, Inc., was one of Whit Parry's pallbearers, Fay Hamblin. The organization was careful not to drive Hamblin off by its collective bureaucratic efforts. President Taylor Crosby noted that he wanted it "clearly understood" that there is "no intention in any way for this newly formed corporation to interfere with any person or group of individuals to promote movies in or around Kanab." Two months later, in February 1968, Milton Jolley of the Utah Travel Council chose Fay Hamblin to represent the state of Utah at meetings in California between Governor Calvin Rampton and the studios. Whether this was a calculated effort to recognize Hamblin's long service and take advantage of his contacts for the purposes of the state is unclear.

MacKenna's Gold (1969)

In 1968, producer Carl Foreman, director J. Lee Thompson, and an international cast of stars led by Gregory Peck, Omar Sharif, Telly Savalas, Edward G. Robinson, Kennan Wynn, and Lee J. Cobb came to Kanab to film major sequences for a big Western, *Mackenna's Gold*. The team hoped to repeat the success of their earlier film, *The Guns of Navaronne*, with a story about a fabled treasure. The production filmed scenes at Sink Valley (near Alton), Kanab Canyon, and Paria. Julie Newmar, the curvaceous sensation of the day, had a nude swimming sequence with Sharif and Peck, which was filmed at the fish hatchery in Panguitch. The crew had a difficult time with the bluing poured into the water to appropriately prevent Newmar from revealing too much skin to the camera, resulting in numerous retakes. Linda Adams Crosby, granddaughter of Merle "Cowhide" Adams, was Newmar's stand-in and double. "I was on only for a week, doubling for Julie Newmar in a lot of far-away shots riding horses. Then we moved to the fish hatchery. I remember that her character had to sneak up the mountain and bend over a guy there. She has a knife and comes out of the pool. I just walked through it, with my back to the camera, until Miss Newmar was ready to come down and be in the scene. I remember that I was in awe when she did it, so tall and so pretty."[18]

The scene in *Mackenna's Gold* where the canyon walls are laced with gold (sprayed that color by the studio crew) was filmed at Paria. Fay Hamblin came through as he took the company to various sites within the canyon and always met their needs. "Fay Hamblin has a face like an old boot," observed a writer for the *Saturday Evening Post,* "and the mild, shrewd, faintly amused expression of a man who has gone a long time without meeting anything he couldn't handle."[19] Columbia Pictures spent five weeks in Kanab and spent about $400,000 in the area. Hamblin worked to keep pay scales competitive for townspeople so that the movie companies would keep coming back. While the film did not live up to Columbia's expectations, it did make a profit.

Studio painters cover a canyon at Paria with gold spray paint for a scene in *MacKenna's Gold*.

Rough Night in Jericho (1967)

Sharpshooter Dean Martin looks down at a passing stage-coach from the Gap, near Kanab.

In the following years, there was a succession of studio contact men in Kanab, including Merrill MacDonald and Dennis Judd, even though by the late 1970s there was no longer a formal movie committee. More trips to Hollywood were made by delegations from the chamber of commerce and there were a few important films attracted to Kanab. Dean Martin returned to town, without his Rat Pack associates, to appear as a lawman-gone-bad in *Rough Night in Jericho* for Universal Pictures. The Western, set in the 1870s, also features George Peppard, Jean Simmons, and John McIntire. A scene where Martin stands on a vantage point atop a rocky foothill at the Gap, five miles east of Kanab, shows the ideal locations still available in Kanab for Westerns, which were now a dying breed. While praised for "some attractive location filming," the movie was also criticized for "a backlot look and is weighted by an undue amount of breakfast table and sickbed conversation."[20] Roger Corman's Civil War-era drama, *A Time for Killing*, starring Glenn Ford and George Hamilton, was lensed in Zion National Park and the Coral Pink Sand Dunes. It included then little-known actor Harrison Ford, who appears among the Union soldiers at the fort.

James Garner stops to see if he is being trailed by a detachment of cavalry for deserting the US Army.

One Little Indian (1973)

In September 1972, Walt Disney Pictures arrived in Kanab with James Garner, Vera Miles, and a young Jodie Foster—and a camel—for *One Little Indian*. "Usually the first 'greeter' is Fay Hamblin who has made more movie arrangements and lined up more shooting schedules than most Hollywood directors," wrote a newspaper reporter.[21] Hamblin was open about the value of the Disney production in Kanab. "This is a good company to work with, and we are glad to have them. Money for a production this big has been hard to come by the last few years, and we are glad to get it."[22] Garner plays a US Cavalry trooper absent-without-leave who flees with a young Native American boy across the desert (the Coral Pink Sand Dunes), during which time he loses his horse, making the trip instead on a camel that had strayed from a cavalry detachment then experimenting with the Arabian beasts. Much of the filming of *One Little Indian* took place in Kanab Canyon, where, according to Dennis Judd, a wrangler on the film, "Our horses kept getting tangled up in this wire-like stuff. We couldn't figure out what was going on and we got up and looked around. Without knowing it, we were riding around on a big patch of marijuana plants!"[23] The camels used in *One Little Indian* reminded local residents of *Southwest Passage* (1954), also filmed in the area, where Joanne Dru, Rod Cameron, and John Ireland (Dru's spouse at the time) use camels to scout for a trail to California.

The Outlaw Josey Wales (1976)

In Clint Eastwood's *The Outlaw Josey Wales*, partially filmed in Kane County, Fay Hamblin finally got the speaking part that had gone to Merle "Cowhide" Adams in so many other films. Hamblin and his movie wife are rescued at Paria when Josey Wales (Eastwood) and his friend (Chief Dan George) come upon the couple whose wagon and possessions are being ransacked by bandits. Hamblin is staked spread-eagle to the desert floor and left for dead. A short time later, in town, one can finally hear that soothing, peaceful voice that endeared Hamblin to his neighbors and many a studio executive when there were seemingly insurmountable problems to solve. *The Outlaw Josey Wales* would also be the last time that the town set built by Howard Koch for *Sergeants 3* would be seen in a movie.

After filming was completed for *The Outlaw Josey Wales*, the adobe house in the background was moved from Kanab Canyon to downtown Kanab as a reminder of glory days gone by.

In 1972, Fay Hamblin was recognized by Kane County with the first annual Distinguished Service Award, for his nearly forty-year affiliation with visiting movie companies. He accepted it with "very few words." Hamblin was pensive, as he saw a decline in Western films, with more contemporary programming being filmed in Salt Lake City.[24] "Most filming will be done for TV," he said. "This means that if Kanab is going to recapture its place in the sun as a film hub, we'll have to go after the TV series and show 'em all over again that we have country here that's suitable for more than westerns. If the state doesn't want to send someone to solicit [the studios] who knows what he's doing, I'll do it myself, just like I used to. If people are going for cops and robbers now more than westerns, we'll show 'em we have possibilities for that, too. Most people try to nick 'em. I try to save 'em money. They've trusted me in the past. They will again."[25]

On July 29, 1976, the sixty-eight-year-old Hamblin was preparing to speak on movie matters to the Kane County Area Chamber of Commerce when he suddenly passed out. Not knowing what was wrong, his family had him flown from the Kanab hospital to Salt Lake City for treatment. He died of a blood clot before doctors could perform surgery. From his first acting job in *The Dude Ranger* in the summer of 1934, through his subsequent work in arranging for livestock and locations, Hamblin was respected as a man of his word. Howard Koch, now production chief at Paramount Pictures, flew from Hollywood to Kanab to eulogize his friend. "Fay was completely unselfish," remembered Koch years later. "The things he did were for Kanab, one hundred per cent for Kanab, because he could never get rich on what we paid him."[26]

The Apple Dumpling Gang Rides Again (1979)

Following Hamblin's death, others attempted to revive the movie business in Kane County, but the last major feature film to be made in the area was Disney's Western spoof *The Apple Dumpling Gang Rides Again* (1979). Vincent McEveety directed this sequel to the very successful *The Apple Dumpling Gang*. Comedians Tim Conway and Don Knotts bumble their way through this entertaining romp as outlaws who are frustrated in their attempts to go straight. The primary special effect in the film unintentionally provided a sense of finality to major Hollywood moviemaking in Kanab. The scene called for a spectacular explosion at the army fort. The cost of preparing the explosion was $15,000, which paid for 3,500 feet of buried pipeline, wire, and hundreds of gallons of kerosene. When the explosion occurred, it was "a spectacle to behold."[27] As a result, the movie fort first built in 1952 by Paramount was severely damaged and never repaired, symbolizing an end to feature filmmaking in Kanab.

After the summer of 1978, no other major motion pictures, Westerns or otherwise, were made in Kanab. More than a half-century of moviemaking and movie promoting had come to an end. In its stead remains the old movie town in Johnson Canyon: a weathered, crumbling ghost, a fading witness to a time when Buffalo Bill Cody, Kit Carson, Wild Bill Hickok, the Lone Ranger, the Western Union company, George Custer, Matt Dillon, Paladin, Daniel Boone, Black Bart, Calamity Jane, Smoky, our "friend" Flicka—and a camel or two—occupied the same expanse of real estate.

Army cooks Tim Conway and Don Knotts look at one another in amazement after accidentally blowing up an army fort in *The Apple Dumpling Gang Rides Again*.

SCENE 4

SAN JUAN COUNTY
1925–1995

JOHN FORD'S MONUMENT VALLEY

Movies, television, and print advertising have made Monument Valley one of the most recognized expanses of land in the world. For many, it is *the* symbol of the American West. Yet as late as 1956, the area was home to so few people that it was described as "the valley nobody knows."[1] In 1921, Harry Goulding first set eyes on this vista of stone and sand. A native of nearby Durango, Colorado, Goulding joined the army during World War I. Returning from the war, he did what many veterans did—wander. He and a friend, John Stevens, set out to see what lay beyond the Lukachukai Mountains and the San Juan River. What he saw in Monument Valley brought him back, alone, in 1923, in one of the first automobiles ever driven into the area. Two years later he came back to settle with his new wife, Leone, known as "Mike" to everyone they dealt with.[2] The couple built a two-story rock home against the eight-hundred-foot sheer stone face of Rock Door Mesa, a few miles north of the Arizona border, and paid $320 for 640 homesteaded acres, on which Goulding's Trading Post began. A sheep man by profession, Goulding assisted the local Navajos in buying and selling herds, as well as selling the wool to eastern factories. The Navajos called him Tall Sheep. The trading post stocked the staples needed by the tribes, all brought in either from Flagstaff, Arizona, or from Salt Lake City. Mail was picked up intermittently at Kayenta, Arizona, twenty-five miles south of the trading post, where John Wetherill and his wife had established a trading post in 1910.[3]

The story of how Hollywood came to Monument Valley is, as with many such accounts, filled with contradiction. John Ford claimed to have learned about the area from actor Harry Carey, who had explored it in the 1920s.[4] John Wayne claimed to have first come upon the spot himself.

"It's a secret I've kept for many years," he told biographer Maurice Zolotow in 1974. "I was the guy who found Monument Valley. And I told Ford about this place." Wayne claimed that, while working on a George O'Brien Western being filmed in Arizona (probably *The Lone Star Ranger*), he drove out to the Navajo reservation and saw Monument Valley for the first time.

> I never forgot about it, and when Mr. Ford was talkin' about locations for *Stagecoach* I told him about Monument Valley and he looked at me as if I was stupid because he thought he knew the Arizona and Utah country and he never heard of the Valley. I was with him on a party when he was scoutin' locations in Arizona. Well, we were drivin' along and finally came to this reservation and went down the road and came to the Valley and then Mr. Ford pretended to see the buttes and said, 'I have just found the location we are going to use.' It was Monument Valley. And the old buzzard looked me straight in the eye. I said nothing. He wanted to be the one who found it. I don't know why he never wanted to give me credit for tellin' him about Monument Valley.[5]

According to Harry Goulding, in the summer of 1938, "This news came in over the radio that Hollywood was looking for a place away out somewhere, a good spot to make this Indian picture." He gathered photographs of the area taken by noted photographer Josef Meunch, as well as those visitors had sent him, and drove with his wife to Hollywood. They there stayed with his wife's oldest brother, who took them to the United Artists studio.[6] Goulding reported that the reception was cool. A secretary told him that he had to know someone at the studio in order to get an appointment. "Oh," he replied, "that don't worry me a bit. I've got a rig right out here across the street. I've got a bedroll, and I've got a little grub left in there yet." The secretary called a studio official to bounce the intruder off the lot, but when the man, who turned out to be the location manager for

Stagecoach, saw Goulding's pictures, he took him up to see John Ford. Ford then grabbed Walter Wanger, his backer, and showed him the photographs. According to Goulding, the three talked until one o'clock the next morning.

Goulding remained in Hollywood while Ford and five others flew to Flagstaff, where Goulding's friend Lee Doyle drove the group into Monument Valley. There they were met by another Goulding friend, Maurice Knee, who showed them around the area. When Ford and his group returned to Hollywood, Ford cut a check for $5,000 to Goulding. The *Stagecoach* company arrived in Monument Valley in September or October 1938, just days after Harry and Mike's return. Writer Garry Wills largely discounts Goulding's "self-aggrandizing legend" and points to the Wetherills as the people with whom studios worked in movies made prior to *Stagecoach*. It was with the Wetherills, Wills points out, that Ford and the principal cast lodged while making *Stagecoach*. Wills also asserts that the Gouldings made their contact with Walter Wanger Productions at United Artists through the Weatherills.[7]

In truth, it was prolific Western author Zane Grey who first brought the movies to Monument Valley when he insisted that Paramount Pictures make the film version of his novel *The Vanishing American* in the area. Made on a lavish budget, *The Vanishing American* stars Richard Dix as the Native American who falls in love with a Caucasian schoolteacher from the East. Grey, who had first visited Monument Valley in 1920, "believed that the Arizona–Utah settings for his novels were both essential and a slighted resource," wrote biographer Thomas H. Pauly. "For years he had been taking a camera on his trips, and his photographs filled his mind with images of the spectacular backgrounds for film versions of his Westerns. His characters, like Grey himself, were inspired by desert waste, twisted gorges, and eerie rock formations, and his poetic descriptions realized their atmospheric potential."[8]

Novelist Zane Grey (third from right) took Paramount Pictures producer Jesse L. Lasky (at Grey's left) to Rainbow Bridge and Monument Valley in the early 1920s, insisting that his stories be filmed by the studio on location.

In September 1923, the best-selling author took Paramount production executive Jesse L. Lasky on a ten-day horseback expedition to Monument Valley and Rainbow Bridge.[9] The trip convinced Lasky to make *The Vanishing American,* as well as many subsequent Zane Grey-based films owned by Paramount, in the picturesque locale. In a telegram to Lasky on the morning of the first screening of *The Vanishing American,* Grey wrote, "The picture is greater than the story. What more can an author say? Words, no matter how skillfully assembled, could never match the gorgeous beauty of the scenes that unfolded before me this morning. That first sweeping view of Monument Valley made me homesick."[10]

On his trip with Grey to the area, Lasky wrote that "It looked to me like a big new background. In it is the Rainbow Natural Bridge, largest in the world. . . .I remarked to Mr. Grey that it would be a wonderful background for an American picture. . . .We agreed that he should do it."[11] Cameraman Harry Perry remembered filming the prologue in many Utah locations, including Rainbow Bridge, during the crew's trying three weeks in the desert in that summer of 1925: "We slept out in the open on the ground, under blankets."[12]

Above: With the release of Ford's *Stagecoach*, the Mittens became iconic symbols of the American West.

Stagecoach (1939)

The Monument Valley scenes in John Ford's *Stagecoach* amount to ninety seconds, or 1 percent of the film's total screen time. Most of the classic Western was filmed on California locations. Nevertheless, the brief exposure of the Mittens and the undulating valley floor on which they stand became the signature image from the film and, soon thereafter, an iconographic statement of the West. "The landscape is truly part of Ford's technique in translating the Western into legend," noted Ford biographer Andrew Sinclair, referring to Monument Valley's "eroded crimson and scarlet buttes and bluffs, the gigantic sculptures of time and weather which make the efforts of mankind appear irrelevant and vain. By setting the wheels of transport and the uniforms of an official army against these prehistoric masses, Ford reduces the image of human progress to a few insects crawling beneath the indifferent stone faces of the ages."[13]

Fall weather in Monument Valley is ever changing, and Goulding wanted to accommodate the demands of the man who was pumping money into his cash-dry community. "We'd like to have a few nice theatrical clouds hanging around in the sky," Ford told Goulding, who knew just the person to go to for rain, snow, clouds, anything—Navajo medicine man Hosteen Tso. In fact, Ford put Tso on the payroll—at $15 a day, or three times the amount paid to Indian extras—for the entire location shoot. "If you'd see General [John] Ford," said Goulding, "if he was alive, he'd tell you that Hosteen Tso made the weather. And if you would say that couldn't be, you'd be piled on! Mr. Ford would give me the signal coming in, and the medicine man and I would come to his room. He always had some real good whiskey, and he asked me if it would be all right if he'd give the old fellow a drink. 'Yea,' I says, 'one drink, not too big, that'd be fine, because he's a one-drink man.' Mr. Ford talked about what he wanted, and I'd tell Hosteen Tso—Tso means big; Mr. John called him Fatso—I'd give Fatso the message, and sure enough the weather would be there the next day."[14]

Stagecoach became the first of many John Ford Westerns filmed in Monument Valley. In fact, the valley virtually became his private filming preserve, with two exceptions. George B. Seitz (who directed *The Vanishing American*) returned to Monument Valley to make *Kit Carson*, starring Jon Hall, Dana Andrews, and Ward Bond, and M-G-M filmed a brief sequence for *Billy The Kid*, with Robert Taylor in the title role. *Stagecoach* also solidified a relationship between Goulding and the Navajos. "The movie people paid them [Indians] forty-eight thousand dollars in cash wages," remembered Goulding, "and it was like a pass from the skies."[15]

The issue of which state can lay geographical primacy to movies made in Monument Valley is literally one of logistics—or camera angle. Since the Monument Valley Tribal Park sits astride the Utah–Arizona line, a film company utilizing the most picturesque buttes, such as the Mittens, North Window, Three Sisters, and Big Indian, are shooting in both states, depending on the camera position. Provisioning for the most part out of Goulding's lodge may also argue for the Utah claim, especially from the late 1930s onward. But with articles on moviemaking in the valley appearing periodically in *Arizona Highways,* claims to the filming domain are contradictory, to say the least.

The arrival of studio trucks in Monument Valley was manna in the desert to the local Navajo, who were severely affected by the Great Depression.

Crews from Twentieth Century-Fox rebuilt Tombstone, Arizona, in Monument Valley for John Ford's *My Darling Clementine*. Facing: Locals receive dinner on the set.

My Darling Clementine (1946)

The war years brought hardships to the Navajos in Monument Valley, but the situation improved with John Ford's return in May 1946 with crews from Twentieth Century-Fox for *My Darling Clementine*, a romanticized Western about Wyatt Earp and the shootout at the OK Corral. Henry Fonda stars as Earp, with Victor Mature as Doc Holliday, supporting players Walter Brennan, Ward Bond, and Linda Darnell (as a Mexican señorita), and Cathy Downs as Clementine Carter, Earp's love interest. Ford built a $250,000 replica of Tombstone, Arizona, in the valley. By that time some of the Navajos had learned carpentry and the rudiments of electrical work, and were hired on with the crews from Hollywood that built the sets.

The State of Utah recognized the value of motion-picture work in elevating the economic level in Monument Valley and San Juan County when, in 1942, the state's Department of Publicity & Industrial Development transported piping to Monument Valley in order to get water from a well recently dug by Goulding. "One of the most important sources of cash income to Utah's Navajo Indians as well as to the white residents of San Juan County," stated the department's report to the governor, "is their employment in motion pictures that use Monument Valley as a location."[16]

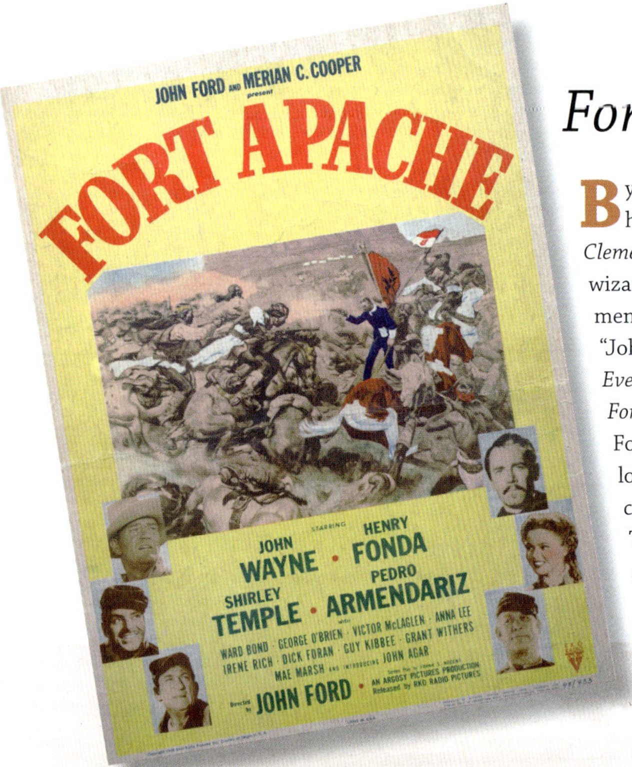

Fort Apache (1948)

By June 1947, much of Hollywood's top talent, including John Ford, had gone independent of the larger studios. Following *My Darling Clementine,* Ford joined forces with director, producer, and financial wizard Merian C. Cooper to form Argosy Pictures. Their first of three memorable Western films, later referred to by film scholars as the "John Ford Cavalry Trilogy," was *Fort Apache*. Taken from the *Saturday Evening Post* story "Massacre" by prolific writer James Warner Bellah, *Fort Apache* is a thinly disguised retelling of the Custer story. Henry Fonda stars as the stern, violent general "Owen Thursday," who has a low opinion of Native Americans. John Wayne, as Kirby York, is the captain who tries to restrain Thursday's emotional behavior. Shirley Temple and her real-life husband John Agar supply the romantic ingredient. A generous budget of $2.5 million was allocated to the film. Once again, Ford chose Monument Valley as the film's location.

Above: Tough-talking Lt. Col. Owen Thursday (Henry Fonda) angers the Apache chief as Capt. Kirby York (John Wayne) restrains himself in *Fort Apache*. Left: The cast of *Fort Apache*, headed by Henry Fonda and John Wayne (center), pose for a portrait in Monument Valley.

She Wore a Yellow Ribbon (1949)

The second installment of the trilogy, *She Wore A Yellow Ribbon*, was adapted by Bellah from two of his own stories, with final polishing by Laurence Stallings. Captain Nathan Brittles (John Wayne) is about to retire from service, but still has one last patrol to make. Fresh from playing an older man for the first time in his career in Howard Hawks's *Red River,* Wayne moved into this part with ease, sporting grey hair and wrinkles on his face. In one scene, Wayne fumbles with a pair of gold-rimmed spectacles to read an inscription on a pocket watch given him by the men of his regiment. More loosely structured than Ford's previous Westerns, *She Wore a Yellow Ribbon* is an elegiac tribute to military duty, the older generation passing the baton, as it were, to the younger folks represented in the film by Harry Carey Jr., John Agar, and Joanne Dru. Wayne's weathered face and the timeworn sandstone of Monument Valley underscore this point. The film is also full of Ford's Irish humor, with stock company veteran Victor McLaglen swilling whiskey and getting into fistfights. With beautiful Technicolor photography by expert cameraman Winton C. Hoch, Ford achieved a texture reminiscent of Frederick Remington's paintings.

The travel to Monument Valley and the accommodations for the movie's entourage were circuitous and somewhat primitive by Hollywood standards. Cast and crew boarded a Santa Fe train at Union Station in Los Angeles and detrained in Flagstaff, Arizona. Buses then took them a full day's ride to Monument Valley. Anderson Camps of Sedona, Arizona, set up a tent city below the bluff occupied by Goulding's Trading Post. Ford, Wayne, and Joanne Dru stayed in rooms above the lodge or in cabins. The rest were billeted in the tents in pairs or threesomes.

Each tent had a kerosene heater and beds with Navajo blankets. Showers were taken beneath a five-gallon drum of water in outdoor shower stalls by the trading post. Principal cast and technical crew ate their meals up at the lodge at a long table, headed by Ford.

Goulding's Trading Post played a prominent role in the film, serving as Captain Brittles's headquarters for close-up shots. The dining hall at Goulding's served as the sutler's store in the film. The company shot for three weeks in October 1948. On the last day, the sky darkened, the wind blew, and the rain fell. The legendary but true story of the production of this film is that as lightning struck, the cavalry was on its way back to the fort. Winton Hoch, according to most accounts, was asked by Ford to get a shot even though the light levels were too low for Technicolor film to record the images properly. Hoch refused. Ford then shot back, demanding that he shoot the scene. Harry Carey Jr., who was there the day it happened, remembered it differently. In contrast to the shouting and threats listed in most popular accounts, Carey recalls that Ford asked Hoch to take a chance with the shot. Hoch responded that he would try, but that it probably would not "take." Ford said that he would take the responsibility for the shot (all time spent on a shoot, not to mention the thousands of feet of expensive Technicolor film, resulted in increased costs of production).[17] The result was a spectacular scene of wet cavalrymen marching in line with dark clouds above them, the wind whipping their protective rain gear, and then a dazzling bolt of lightning. Hoch won the Academy Award for best color cinematography.

Facing: Poised by the Mittens, Capt. Brittles (John Wayne) leads one last mission before retiring from the army. Above: *She Wore a Yellow Ribbon* offers one of John Wayne's most mature and restrained roles. Right: A photo of John Wayne looking out over Monument Valley is indicative of the quality of Winton Hoch's Academy Award-winning cinematography for *She Wore a Yellow Ribbon*.

In *The Searchers,* John Wayne played the darkest character of his career.

The Searchers (1956)

Ford would not return to Monument Valley for seven years, but the result was well worth waiting for. In 1955, the director arrived with John Wayne, Ward Bond, Harry Carey Jr., Wayne's son Patrick, Jeffrey Hunter, and Vera Miles for *The Searchers*, regarded as Ford's most beautiful Western. The story revolves around John Wayne's character, Ethan Edwards, and his overt racial hatred of Native Americans. Edwards, together with Martin Pawley, the quarter-Cherokee adopted son of Ethan's brother Aaron, go in search of Martin's sister, Debbie (Natalie Wood), who has been kidnapped by a Comanche raiding party. So conflicted is Edwards in his five-year search that he eventually wants to find and kill Debbie rather than return her to her family. The racial aspects of the film, as well as the generational differences between Ethan and Martin—not significant factors in the original novel—were written and emphasized in the film by screenwriter Frank C. Nugent. In retrospect, these racial aspects were in harmony with the racial struggles that were evident in America during the 1950s.

The Searchers was photographed in Technicolor and employed a wide-screen process called VistaVision. The results were breathtakingly beautiful. Nearly every major Monument Valley formation is shown towering over John Wayne and his search party as they travel amid the brilliant colors of the valley. The film's beautiful skies and billowing white clouds were achieved in 115-degree heat. Some shooting also took place further north on the San Juan River near Mexican Hat. There were frequent arguments between Hoch, taking his time to get a shot just right, and Ford, who wanted to keep production moving along.

John Ford touches up an extra's makeup.

Monument Valley in the 1950s was, in many respects, no different than the same location Ford had left in the late 1940s, except for the upgraded facilities at Goulding's.[18] The director could now provide motel rooms for his cast and crew as well as himself. *The Searchers* company was the largest Ford had yet brought into the valley. *Warner Bros. Presents,* an early television show broadcasting older Warner Bros. films for television, contained progress reports from week to week on the building of roads, a water system, prop and wardrobe tents, and many other highlights in establishing a location camp in the valley.[19] Life on location with a Ford production fell into its predictable patterns. "Every night the company gathered outside the dining room at Goulding's," wrote Dan Ford, the director's grandson, "and waited for John to enter. Then the dinner bell was rung and everyone obediently filed in. After dinner John and a select group of actors and stuntmen adjourned to his room, where a green felt cover was spread over the table and they had their game of pitch."[20]

During location shooting, Ford was given an honor that had deep meaning for him. The Navajos inducted him as a member of their tribe. The day began with horse races and other activities, including the Old Man's Foot Race, which Ford won. Three large sides of beef were brought in and barbecued, and a truckload of watermelon was unloaded on the plain just below Goulding's Lodge. Later in the afternoon, the Navajos presented the director with a beautifully lettered deerskin bearing his Navajo name, Natani Nez, the "Tall Soldier." The photograph of the presentation shows Ford, dutifully tight-lipped, wearing a white hat and the ever-present dark glasses. The inscription on the deerskin read:

A tent city built near Goulding's in Monument Valley housed the crew of *The Searchers* during the hot summer of 1955.

In your travels may there be
Beauty behind you,
Beauty on both sides of you,
And Beauty ahead of you.

Following the completion of *The Searchers,* the cast and crew felt more than a little melancholy. Producer C. V. Whitney decided to get out of feature films and invest instead in a string of television stations. Merian C. Cooper decided to retire, bringing his long professional association with Ford, which began in the 1930s with *The Lost Patrol*, to an end. Ford started his own production company but came to realize that the movie business was a greater challenge than it once had been.

In 1962, M-G-M, in partnership with Cinerama, filmed the epic Western *How the West Was Won*, a saga composed of five parts. The final segment, "The Outlaws," directed by Henry Hathaway, features George Peppard and Carolyn Jones. Peppard, having rid the county of a menacing outlaw (Eli Wallach), welcomes a visiting aunt (Debbie Reynolds) at the train station and all ride in a buckboard to their ranch, past the sentinels in Monument Valley. The cameras pull back to show the astonishing vastness of this unique and colorful part of America as Reynolds leads the travelers in a rendition of "Greensleeves." A magnificent shot of Monument Valley is the final image of the Old West before a montage of modern, industrial America fills the screen and ends the film.

Cheyenne Autumn (1964)

Shooting for John Ford's final epic Western, *Cheyenne Autumn*, began on October 8, 1963, and continued for a month until the cast and crew moved to Moab. The story was an adaptation of a 1957 novel by Mari Sandoz about the journey of the Northern Cheyenne from Oklahoma to their homeland in the Yellowstone country of Montana. The director and his son Patrick prepared a lengthy treatment that emphasized the Cheyenne as victims of broken promises and bureaucratic bungling on the part of the American government. Warner Bros. was enthusiastic about the film and committed $4.5 million to the project. Difficulties began almost at once. Ford's gruff way with actors offended Ricardo Montalban and Sal Mineo. Ford was uncharacteristically sullen and morose during the Monument Valley shoot, and at one point he confined himself to his motel room for five days. The directorial job was temporarily given to second-unit director Ray Kellogg. Ford said to his old friend George O'Brien, who had a small part in the film, that moviemaking was "just no fun anymore."

The release of *Cheyenne Autumn* in October 1964 hyped the Ford name for all it was worth. The film, however, was not in the Ford tradition. It was beautiful to watch, but with a running time of two hours and thirty-nine minutes, it was long and slow. The last time Ford returned to the land now familiarly known as John Ford Country was in 1971, for Peter Bogdanovich's television documentary *Directed by John Ford,* in which Ford directed John Wayne in a stunt, and for *The American West of John Ford,* a CBS television broadcast with Wayne, James Stewart, and Henry Fonda.[21] Ford's love of Monument Valley stayed with him throughout his final years. "My favorite location is Monument Valley," he said to *Cosmopolitan* in 1964. "It has rivers, mountains, plains,

Cheyenne Autumn **was a wide-screen epic of the bitter march of the Cheyenne.**

desert, everything that land can offer. I feel at peace there. I have been all over the world, but I consider this the most complete, beautiful and peaceful place on earth."[22] Ford died of cancer on August 31, 1973, and was buried in Culver City's Holy Cross Cemetery. Said actor Woody Strode, whom Ford cast in *Sergeant Rutledge* and *The Man Who Shot Liberty Valance*, "He should be buried in Monument Valley."[23]

Italian director Sergio Leone confirmed the valley's international status when he selected it as his main location for *Once Upon A Time in the West*, starring Henry Fonda, Charles Bronson, Claudia Cardinale, and Jason Robards. Parts of many other films were shot in Monument Valley from the 1970s onward, including the countercultural trip *Easy Rider*, with Peter Fonda and Dennis Hopper; the transcontinental trucking drama *White Line Fever*; *The Trial of Billy Jack*; Clint Eastwood's *The Eiger Sanction*; the tongue-in-cheek Western spoof *The Legend of the Lone Ranger*; and *National Lampoon's Vacation*. In 1982, the classic environmental documentary *Koyaanisqatsi* featured stunning shots of the landscape. The third installment of the *Back to the Future* series included a few scenes in the valley, and the Walt Disney Western comedy

Despite restrictions, Monument Valley makes it to the screen on occasion. From the top down: 1969's *Easy Rider* depicted Dennis Hopper and Peter Fonda on a different sort of adventure in the West, while part of *Back to the Future III* was filmed in the park. Nick Stahl hopes that Roger Aaron Brown can hit the spike the first time in the Monument Valley setting for Disney's *Tall Tale*, about a young boy whose dreams of Western heroes give him the courage to fight a land baron attempting to steal his parents' farm.

Tall Tale brought Patrick Swayze to its lonely vastness.

In the 1990s, Gerald and Ronald La Font, who acquired ownership of Goulding's Trading Post, continued receiving calls from Hollywood studios, which wanted them to set up catering, special lodging requirements, and early morning meals. But, for the new lodge owners, Hollywood did not have the allure of an earlier time, when studio money kept the starving Navajos alive from season to season. "If they [Hollywood film studios] want to pay the price, they can come," said the owners, "but there's a lot more profit in tourists than in Hollywood."[24] Curiously, it is largely because of Hollywood that tourists flock to this remote area of the west. The old stone trading post has been restored upstairs the way the Gouldings had it as their living quarters, and the main floor is provisioned as it was during the 1930s and '40s. In the back is a museum devoted to memorabilia associated with films made in the area. A $2 million expansion has increased the number of rooms from 19 to 60. The dining hall, where John Ford once presided, is now a modern restaurant with large picture windows that look out over the rooftop of the motel and down into the valley below.

John Ford makes his last visit to Monument Valley for the documentary *Directed by John Ford.*

SCENE 5

GRAND COUNTY

1949–1997

A view of downtown Moab in the late 1940s.

MOAB MEANS MOVIES

Moab, Utah, lies approximately 230 miles south of Salt Lake City and 150 miles north of Monument Valley. Bounded on the north by the Colorado River, Moab Valley was first visited in 1855 by Latter-day Saint missionaries assigned to what was then referred to as Grand Valley. Indians, explorers, and cattlemen discouraged permanent residents until 1879, when a post office was established. A committee of pioneer settlers decided on the biblical name Moab for their new home. Another group of 230 had been "called" by their church leaders to leave their settlement at Escalante in south-central Utah, make their way south across some of the most challenging topography in the United States, and settle in the San Juan River region. These hardy saints came up against a formidable barrier—a mass of rock—lying directly in their path. For three months, between December 1879 and late February 1880, they blasted and chipped a passage through solid rock, through which their wagons would be lowered over 1,500 feet to the Colorado River below. The now-famous Hole-in-the-Rock remains a symbol of their determination against virtually any obstacle. Aspects of that adventure were fictionalized by John Ford in *Wagon Master*, the first Hollywood film made in the Moab area, which led to the creation of the longest continuously operating film commission in the United States.

The story of how the celebrated director was led to the little Utah community is fraught with varied accounts. Ford's son Patrick, for a time his father's associate producer, claimed in 1985 to have suggested "filming the story where it happened." Patrick said that while on location in Monument Valley for *She Wore A Yellow Ribbon*, he "got to know some of the rough old Mormon pioneer descendants who were riding and supplying horses for us. They fascinated me. They wore leather clothes, and they had a hardness about them, a frontier hardness. They were the real McCoy, not Hollywood extras. . . .We rarely had Sundays [free], but when we did I would listen to stories of how their people got into that country in the 1880s, quite a while after the more illustrious of the Mormons first came to the Salt Lake Valley in the 1840s with Brigham Young." Patrick suggested that a fictionalized version of that story should be told to complete a four-film commitment with RKO. He and screenwriter Frank Nugent crafted a script in the summer of 1949, and it only seemed natural to make it in the region where the story took place. "'These are the people I want,' the Old Man would say as I showed him photographs in Hollywood of the people in the Moab area," Patrick said. "Because he was a perfectionist, he wouldn't get a Hollywood extra if he could do otherwise. He wouldn't use a Hollywood Indian when there was still a real Indian alive. His term was 'I want stone-age faces. I want faces of men and women who have seen people die of snake bite, whose women and babies die in childbirth, and whose men die from being bucked off horses, just the life of primitive people.'"[1]

A later account cites Harry Reed, a professional photographer in Moab, as the one who introduced Ford to the area after showing the director color slides of the formations inside the Arches region.[2] Most likely is the account related by George White—a state highway superintendent on whose ranch a number of important movies would be made—who claimed to have gone down to Monument Valley to visit Ford while he was filming *She Wore A Yellow Ribbon*.[3] This account is corroborated by that of Moab *Times-Independent* editor and publisher Loren "Bish" Taylor, who recounted being informed by his friend Harry Goulding in Monument Valley that the director was coming north to look at what Moab had to offer as a movie location.[4] Other sources indicate that as early as 1941 producer Harry Sherman, who had used Kanab and Zion National Park for *Buffalo Bill* and *Ramrod* respectively, had visited Moab and even talked of establishing production facilities there.[5]

By the fall of 1949, when production began on *Wagon Master,* Moab was behind Kanab in film activity by about twenty-five years. The Moab Movie Committee, started by George White, immediately began to coordinate all aspects of lodging, food, livestock, transportation, and bureaucratic relationships with the state's Department of Publicity & Industrial Development. White took care of maintaining contact with the studios, scouting locations with studio representatives, and supplying the film shoot with local extras, wranglers, and equipment. The chartered airplane bearing John Ford and Argosy Pictures vice president Lowell J. Farrell to Moab was met by J. A. Theobald, chairman of the new Utah Publicity Department. Ab Jenkins, famed Utah auto racer and former mayor of Salt Lake City, also accompanied the delegation from Salt Lake. Both had been assigned by Utah governor J. Bracken Lee to provide whatever assistance was necessary. With allegations of trouble between movie companies and the Parrys in Kanab, state officials wanted to be certain that a John Ford production at a new Utah movie location went well.

In *Wagon Master,* John Ford demonstrated that the landscape around Moab could be as iconic as his beloved Monument Valley.

Ford was taken to a number of locations. George White remembered showing him the Colorado River as it flowed through Professor Valley. "I took him up the river, saw Onion Creek, Ninemile Bottom, Fisher Towers, different places and he said, 'I don't think I can make it here.' I said, 'Would it help any if you used the ranch?' 'Yes,' he said. So they went in and took over my ranch for the filming."[6] White became the driving force of the Moab Film Commission, working to improve normally inaccessible roads so that the movie companies could film on location. Director Gordon Douglas called him "the god of Moab."

Opportunities for community growth provided by the arrival of the movies were outlined in an editorial published more than two weeks before the cast of *Wagon Master* arrived to begin shooting. Moab's *Times-Independent* editor announced that "A new enterprise has been launched at Moab, with the coming of Argosy Productions for the filming of a major western feature in this vicinity. If there is a genuine effort by local people to give one hundred cents in services and chattels for every dollar expended by the picture company, then the success of this first picture will be assured, and the chances will be more than favorable for filming many more pictures in this locale." Perhaps with the idea in mind that some in the small community would take advantage of "big movie money" coming to town, the editor also advised that "Moab has a great opportunity for launching an important new industry here. Let's don't muff this opportunity."[7]

After a quick tour of Moab, Ford returned to Hollywood while Lowell Farrell remained to work out logistical details. A representative from Anderson Camps in Sedona, Arizona, arrived about a week later to arrange for the construction of a tent city for the cast and crew. Only half of the expected 150 people being flown in for *Wagon Master* could be accommodated by the one motel and private homes available for rent. Anderson housed the remainder in his tent city that went up in a vacant lot across the street from Bowen's Auto, complete with running water and bath and toilet facilities hooked up to Moab's sewer system. The Arches Cafe ballroom was secured for all meals in town. The Anderson Boarding and Supply Company, which provided food and lodging to movie location shoots nationwide, handled location catering for lunches.

Landing at Moab's airstrip was a dramatic beginning for Ben Johnson and Harry Carey Jr., two of the principal stars of the film. "We finally landed! *Bumpity-*

This panoramic photograph, taken during a break in filming for *Wagon Master*, looks north across the Colorado River to the massive sandstone bluffs that are the southern border of Arches National Park.

bump-bump-bump—screech and stop," wrote Carey of the experience. "We bolted out of the plane and looked around. We had landed on an immense sort of mesa. The nose of that DC-3 was not more than fifty yards from a huge abyss."[8] News of the company's arrival generated an editorial in Ogden's *Standard-Examiner* that seemed to suggest that a movie audience, on seeing the beautiful area of Moab in the completed film, would not believe that such a country exists. "There is only one thing against Moab as a motion picture setting. Most movie fans will doubt that there is in nature any such place. They will insist that an over-imaginative scene painter was permitted to go to extreme length. Moab, the fans will say, is as fictitious as Shangri-la."[9]

Studio owner Howard Hughes insisted that Mormons depicted in *Wagon Master* be uncharacteristically attired in black. Here, Moab locals, hired as extras, mouth the Latter-day Saint hymn "Come, Come, Ye Saints."

Johnson and Carey, who had previously appeared in Ford's *3 Godfathers* and *She Wore A Yellow Ribbon*, play horse traders who are approached by Elder Wiggs (Ward Bond), head of a pioneer wagon train, to lead the settlers to the San Juan River country. The group encounters a theatrical troupe that has been run out of the same town as the newcomers, and Johnson falls in love with the troupe's showgirl (Joanne Dru). This enlarged band of Latter-day Saints and dramatists is met on the trail by the notorious Clegg Gang, consisting of Uncle Shiloh (Charles Kemper) and his band of wild nephews, including Hank Worden and a very young James Arness. The settlers, with the help of their guides, eventually rid themselves of the Clegg Gang and reach the promised land, to the strains of the Latter-day Saint hymn "Come, Come, Ye Saints."

Ford used locations along the Colorado River near George White's ranch, including Fisher Towers in Professor Valley, about twenty miles north of downtown Moab. Since

his ranch was in the valley bordering the river, and because he ran cattle there, White knew the places to safely cross the river without losing horses and wagons. The black-and-white photography is striking as the long line of wagons rolls in the sharp sunlight. The songs for the film, composed by Stan Jones and played by the Sons of the Pioneers, give *Wagon Master* a flavor that characterizes the westward movement of a people determined to find a home.

On days off and in the evenings, the cast and crew pitched in and contributed entertainment for the Moab locals. On Thanksgiving Day, the film crew played softball against the Moab team. The film crew lost 20 to 18. However, the *Times-Independent* noted that "the scorekeepers were home-town boys."[10] On November 30 and December 1, the film stars also staged two shows at the high school for the Lions Club Christmas Fund. People came from throughout San Juan and Grand counties. Each show drew 600 or more people in a town of barely 1,300. The properly British Alan Mowbray, who plays an alcoholic Shakespeare-quoting thespian in the film, emceed one evening's performance while movie veteran George O'Brien was master of ceremonies the next.

Production of *Wagon Master* was completed in nineteen days—three days under schedule—and without difficulty. Because of inclement weather, the company was bused to Grand Junction, Colorado, and then flown back to Hollywood to complete interior shots at the studio. "The gang are all back safe and sound from Moab," wrote Ford to the Moab Chamber of Commerce a few weeks afterwards, "and the picture is finished. The boys have shaved off their beards and the girls have taken off their heavy underwear (so I have been told on good authority) and we are all homesick for beautiful Castle Valley. I have never known a troupe to enjoy a location so much. In behalf of the troupe I wish to thank you for the pleasant hospitality and welcome we received, the many friendships and the general good feeling enjoyed by all. I hope we are still welcome, we hope to come back in the late spring to do it again."[11]

The release of *Wagon Master* in the spring of 1950 brought good, but not great, box-office returns against the relatively modest $848,000 cost. The reviews, however, were favorable to both the film and the locations displayed in Moab's first feature film. "The 'star' of *Wagon Master*," according to the *New York Times,* "is the vast, colorful Utah locale in which a portion of it was filmed."[12] *Variety* noted that the "site of the story and the filming in Utah, and the rugged locale supplies fresh backgrounds for the action."[13] Harry Carey Jr. observed that "Uncle Jack always said *Wagon Master* was his favorite picture. I think *The Searchers* was his best film, but *Wagon Master* was the most joyful. The entire filming was done in a spirit of friendliness, every member of the company doing their best. One month of total unity and happiness—that was *Wagon Master.*"[14]

Real-life champion roper Ben Johnson stays in the background as local church leader Ward Bond deals with outlaw Uncle Shiloh.

Rio Grande (1950)

John Ford was true to his word. He returned to Moab in the spring of 1950 to scout locations for his next big Western, *Rio Grande*, this time for Republic instead of RKO. Republic president Herbert J. Yates had struck a deal with Ford, assuring him that he would be allowed to make a film that was close to his heart—*The Quiet Man*—with virtually no limitations on budget *if* he first made a surefire box-office hit. Ford

John Wayne leads the cavalry through Professor Valley in *Rio Grande*.

Left: Director John Ford (wearing sunglasses) enjoyed being on location in Moab for *Rio Grande*, if only to temporarily escape the controlling tendencies of Republic Pictures head Herbert J. Yates (far left). Facing, above: John Wayne, as the post commander, is in the difficult position of having his estranged son toe the line with other troops. Facing, below: A cavalry charge distracts the Indians while hostage children are rescued from an adobe church.

chose a story he had purchased in 1948, "Mission With No Record," written by his old friend James Warner Bellah. The story concerns a US Cavalry detachment patrolling the United States–Mexico border in the 1870s. John Wayne plays regimental commander Kirby York, whose job is to keep Chief Natchez from crossing the border and raiding American settlements. To complicate things, Wayne's son (Claude Jarman Jr.) shows up as a recruit and begins an effort to get his father back together with his mother. Ben Johnson and Harry Carey Jr. returned to Moab to play soldiers under Wayne's command. Newcomers to Moab included Chill Wills (in his first film for Ford) and Ford veteran Victor McLaglen.

As with *Wagon Master,* Ford was greeted on his arrival at Moab by J. A. Theobald and Ab Jenkins. National Park Service representatives Bates Wilson and Earl Worthington, along with George White and others, took Ford around Arches National Monument, Dead Horse Point, and other locations not used in *Wagon Master.* Nevertheless, Ford decided on the same area as before—George White's ranch and Professor Valley, along with the addition of Castle Valley. The roads to these areas were widened even more than had been done the previous fall and were covered with fresh oil in order to accommodate the thirty-two cars, trucks, and buses that carried personnel and equipment to and from the location.

The majority of the crew arrived with John Ford, John Wayne, and Maureen O'Hara on June 14, 1950, in a four-engine DC-6 airliner. Since the production of *Wagon Master,* the Moab airport, located just south of town, had been enlarged, and this was the first time large aircraft could be handled. The Anderson Boarding and Supply Company's city of twenty-nine tents housing five men per unit was already in place just off Main Street, and the town's one hotel and three motels were full of crew members. Fifty Navajos, brought from the reservation by Lee Bradley, camped near the county

HERBERT J. YATES presents John Ford's
RIO GRANDE
JOHN WAYNE · MAUREEN O'HARA
BEN JOHNSON · CLAUDE JARMAN, Jr. · HARRY CAREY, Jr. · CHILL WILLS
J. CARROL NAISH · VICTOR McLAGLEN · GRANT WITHERS · SONS OF THE PIONEERS
A REPUBLIC PICTURE

wounded soldiers coming back from battle," recalls Tangren, "and we come through the fort gates built on White's Ranch on a travois. Maureen O'Hara was supposed to come out of this tent and greet John Wayne, who was her husband. She could never say her part right. Never could get her lines right. That was one movie I really remember redoing over and over and over. Man, I thought we were going to choke to death on that hot and dry day dragged behind a horse."[15]

fairground. Eighty cavalrymen were hired locally, in addition to twenty-five wranglers and twenty women as extras.

The next day, extras were dressed, made up, and bused out to the locations. There was great excitement in Moab having John Wayne in town for the first time, although, according to nineteen-year-old Karl Tangren, who would later figure prominently in the Moab Film Commission, there was also the tediousness of retakes. "I was one of the

In that same scene, Sam Taylor's mother was one of the women on whom the camera lingered as the wounded men entered the fort. "John Wayne was such a gentleman," remembered Taylor. "He was a big rough-and-tumble guy, but he had the politeness of a southern gentleman. He didn't like staying in a motel. He would rent a house. He liked walking so when he would walk down to the drugstore and pass people that he knew, he'd tip his hat

and greet them and did the same shopping in the stores. A real gentleman."[16]

The cast and crew of *Rio Grande* put on a special show at Moab High School, which was attended by people who came from as far away as Grand Junction. The audience was treated to "a collection of skits, musical numbers, both humorous and serious; two or three dramatic acts, and a 'ya-ya-chi' dance by twelve Navajo Indians." Gravel-voiced Chill Wills was master of ceremonies, and Maureen O'Hara sang three solos "that brought down the house." John Wayne and Victor McLaglen were in a skit as prizefight promoters with stuntmen taking pratfalls. One of the final acts involved Wayne, McLaglen, Ben Johnson, Harry Carey Jr., Claude Jarman Jr., and others singing an original song written for the occasion. "They made up in volume," opined the *Times-Independent,* "what might have been considered lacking in musical quality." The producer of the show, John Ford, came up to the stage and "drenched the songbirds with a pail full of water."[17]

The three-week shoot for *Rio Grande* was completed on July 7. The next day, the entire company was bused to Grand Junction and flown back to Hollywood. Ninety-five percent of the film had been made on location in Moab. Little work remained to be done except editing and scoring the picture at Republic. *Rio Grande* was released nationally on November 15, 1950. The pace in Moab slowed down once again, but residents still flush from the activity and the money left by Ford heard more good news from the Moab Film Committee. Location scouts from M-G-M, headed by director Richard Thorp, had been in town. Twentieth Century-Fox had telephoned many times for information on locations, and Yates was talking about three more pictures to be filmed in Moab by Republic in the near future. To cap it all, in August 1950, *Deseret News* theater critic Howard Pearson's article on allegations of price gouging of movie companies in Kane County had been reprinted in Moab's *Times-Independent,* in which the growing filmmaking activity in Moab was noted as a bright spot in an otherwise somber article. "We were aware of what had happened in Kanab from the movie companies," remembered Sam Taylor, "and you can credit the very strong people like my dad and George White cautioning merchants, livestock owners and so forth to be square and honest with the movie people."[18]

Facing, above: Director John Ford shares a laugh with Maureen O'Hara and John Wayne during shooting. Facing, below: One of the visually stunning scenes in *Rio Grande* that caused some to mistake Professor Valley for Monument Valley. Right: Maureen O'Hara comforts wounded husband John Wayne as he is brought into the fort in *Rio Grande*. The fort was built on the George White Ranch, today the location of Red Cliffs Lodge.

The Battle at Apache Pass (1952)
Taza, Son of Cochise (1954)

Universal expressed its disappointment with the way the Parrys were doing business in Kanab not by giving up on Utah, but instead crossing the state to film *The Battle at Apache Pass* in Moab. The Technicolor Western, made in the wake of Fox's successful *Broken Arrow,* starred Jeff Chandler, Hugh O'Brian, and Richard Egan, and dramatized the feud between Cochise and Geronimo. Battle sequences were filmed in Arches National Monument. The following year, a sequel, *Taza, Son of Cochise*, was filmed in dazzling 3-D, with Chandler reprising his role as Cochise, who passes the chieftainship of the Apaches to his son, played by Rock Hudson. Hudson dons a cavalry uniform and urges his Apache brothers to make peace as he falls in love with Oona, an Apache maiden played by Barbara Rush. The fort built at White's ranch for *Rio Grande* was utilized for the battles. Dead Horse Point, with its breathtaking two-thousand-foot drop to the Colorado River, is a visual feature of the film. Barbara Burck, daughter of Moab's mayor, began her minor movie career with a small part in this film. Burck's father and director Douglas Sirk approached her together. "There were covered wagons down by the Colorado River," Burck recalled about her scene. "I was coming up from the river bringing some water to the covered wagon and said some things to my husband in the movie and got shot with an arrow. I was quite nervous having to be shot with an arrow on a board underneath my dress. Mr. Sirk was very kind to me, but he would coach me to speak a little louder, because I was so nervous. There were probably eight takes before they got the shot they wanted. I was paid about $1,000, which I saved and bought a car with when I went to college that fall."[19]

Facing, left: The dramatic backdrop of Arches National Monument made for memorable scenes in *The Battle at Apache Pass*. Facing, right: Barbara Burck, daughter of Moab's mayor, gets a cameo in *Taza, Son of Cochise*. Above: The success of *Battle at Apache Pass* provided for a sequel, in the new 3-D format, which became *Taza, Son of Cochise*. The film offered an early starring role to Rock Hudson.

Border River (1954)

When director George Sherman arrived to make *Border River* with Joel McCrea and Yvonne De Carlo, he was surprised by the change that had come over Moab since he made *The Battle at Apache Pass.* The discovery of uranium in the area in 1952 created a boomtown condition. Sherman discovered that Universal now had to compete with prospectors for extras, wranglers, and laborers, as well as for hotel rooms. The town had been selected for filming, according to studio sources, because the setting for the story on the Texas–Mexico border would have required using the Rio Grande river, except that "the once-imposing Rio Grande River has dried up considerably down through the years."[20] The Civil War-era story has McCrea as a Confederate soldier swimming the Rio Grande to escape his Union Army pursuers. He is rescued by De Carlo and together they attempt to foil efforts by Pedro Armendáriz to steal the gold that McCrea had squirreled away to aid the Confederacy. Barbara Burck doubled for De Carlo in scenes in the boat on the Colorado River, and recalled swimming with De Carlo on days off and having lunch together at the Arches Cafe. "We sometimes had to sneak out when we were noticed because the local people were the ones in awe," Burck said. "They would come closer to the table and try and get her autograph."[21]

Joel McCrea enjoys a swim in the Colorado River as co-star Yvonne De Carlo reaches out to help him ashore. McCrea made eight movies in Utah and De Carlo appeared in five.

Smoke Signal (1955)

Smoke Signal brought Universal back to Moab a third time, with Dana Andrews playing a renegade cavalry officer who escapes a Ute attack along with Piper Laurie, a lieutenant (Rex Reason) to whom Laurie is engaged, and an army captain (William Talman). The group braves the San Juan River all the way from Mexican Hat (approximately one hundred miles south of Moab) to Lee's Ferry, nearly two hundred miles down the Colorado River. Local resident Clea Johnson doubled for Piper Laurie in the river-running sequences and spent seven days with the film's cast and crew camping on the riverbanks by night. Those hired for the arduous shoot were advised about "our problem of the necessity of camping out each night on the banks of the river."[22] Two flatboats were used for cinematographer Clifford Stine and his Technicolor cameras. It was the first time the area had been traversed for a feature film, and water, silt, and sun presented frequent obstacles to the movie expedition. Meals came from canned goods after the crew pulled up on shore at nightfall. Breakfast was hastily consumed at the break of dawn before launching the boats to make progress each day. Including the exploratory trips downriver prior to actual production, Universal was in Utah for slightly over one month during June and July 1954.

Left: In *Smoke Signal*, Dana Andrews is branded a deserter, but he wins the love of Piper Laurie. Right: Heat stroke, overturned boats, and damaged film dogged the second unit.

Canyon Crossroads (1955)

Moab's population grew from approximately 1,300 to 6,000 as the uranium boom escalated. While the rush for uranium was on, movie companies were accommodated in private homes as coordinated by the Moab Film Committee. *Canyon Crossroads*, a low-budget film made on location in 1954, was a unique document of Moab's time and place. In this contemporary drama, Richard Basehart is a down-on-his-luck prospector suspicious of a powerful mine owner (Stephen Elliott) who harbors resentment because Basehart will not work for him. However, when a geologist and his daughter (Phyllis Kirk) show up, he accepts their grubstake and leads them to a uranium mother lode, only to be dogged by the mine owner chasing him across the Moab landscape by helicopter. Downtown Moab is ably documented with street scenes in which one of the buildings is labeled "Atomic Energy Commission Regional Office, Moab, Utah." This was actually a local store made over, as there was no such office at the time in Moab. The interior of a local watering hole was also used, and Professor Valley, the Colorado River, and the surrounding cliffs were featured extensively. *Canyon Crossroads* is, unfortunately, a virtual lost film in the twenty-first century. *Variety* openly commented that its producer "didn't see fit to invest in color lensing since the Utah canyon country obviously would have looked much better in tint than in the existing black-and-white print."[23]

A Moab storefront was redressed to appear as the regional office of the Atomic Energy Commission, which was actually located in Grand Junction, Colorado. Above: Richard Basehart (center) and Phyllis Kirk wonder what to do next with their valuable uranium mine.

Warlock (1959)

Due to Moab's uranium fever, residents were less aggressive than they might otherwise have been in attracting film companies to Grand County. However, once the boom subsided, the movie industry was once again courted by the Moab Film Commission. They managed to successfully attract Twentieth Century-Fox, which made *Warlock* there in the summer of 1958. *Warlock* is a major studio film, photographed in CinemaScope and color, with a cast headlined by Henry Fonda, Anthony Quinn, Richard Widmark, and Dorothy Malone. In this complex Western, Fonda and violent sidekick Quinn are hired by the town of Warlock to rid it of the bad guys from a nearby cattle ranch. One of the cattlemen, Widmark, undergoes a change and becomes sheriff of the town. This veiled Wyatt Earp–Doc Holliday story shows off Dead Horse Point and Professor Valley in a splendid manner in the wide-screen format. Directed by Edward Dmytryk, *Warlock* supplies novel twists on old Western formulas.

A top cast and a thoughtful story of law and order made *Warlock* a superb Western.

DOLORES MICHAEL

Facing: Henry Fonda discusses a scene with director Edward Dmytryk at Dead Horse Point, overlooking the Colorado River. Above: Dorothy Malone gets a visit from Marshal Richard Widmark at a graveyard in Professor Valley.

***Ten Who Dared* followed John Wesley Powell's exploration of the Grand Canyon. Copywriters failed to acknowledge that it was the Colorado River at Moab that stood in for the Grand Canyon.**

Ten Who Dared (1960)

In late 1959, the Walt Disney studio came to Moab to film *Ten Who Dared*, a dramatization of John Wesley Powell's 1869 expedition down the Colorado River and the Grand Canyon. Director William Beaudine turned in a film that was spectacular in its location photography, with a cast that includes Brian Keith, James Drury, R. G. Armstrong, L. Q. Jones, and Ben Johnson. George White shows up for a cameo appearance helping to launch the flatboats into the Colorado River. The Disney crew spent nearly a month filming in Moab and along the Colorado River, with weather problems contributing to many delays. The departure point for the original Powell expedition—Green River, Wyoming—was replicated for *Ten Who Dared* at the Dewey Bridge north of Moab. Intended originally as a two-part presentation for Disney's television program, color film and escalating costs caused the studio to steer the movie into theaters in the fall of 1960.

The Comancheros (1961)

John Wayne returned to Moab after an eleven-year absence to star in the Twentieth Century-Fox production *The Comancheros,* with George Sherman as producer. Michael Curtiz, the legendary director of such classic films as *The Adventures of Robin Hood, Casablanca,* and *The Charge of the Light Brigade,* took charge of what turned out to be his final film. Color and CinemaScope would show off the Moab landscape in an impressive way. Construction of twenty-three buildings in Professor Valley, the largest of which was a sprawling stucco-and-tile ranch house built on a flat in the shadow of Fisher Towers, began on June 1, 1961. It would be the home of Nehemiah Persoff, the leader of the Comancheros—white gun-runners to the Indians—who manage to trap a Texas Ranger and his prisoner, Stuart Whitman, who are spying on the settlement. Ina Balin, a rising Fox actress, plays Persoff's daughter, who falls in love with Whitman. Also in the cast are Patrick Wayne, Lee Marvin, and Western old-timers Bob Steele and Guinn "Big Boy" Williams.

By the 1960s, John Wayne had become an icon to moviegoers, and that aura preceded him to Moab. Wayne,

The Comancheros camp, filmed in Professor Valley, burns to the ground in the film's climactic moments.

however, had recently experienced a stormy personal life, and Moabites saw a hint of his less friendly side. "He was hard to get along with," said Don Holyoak, a local wrangler who worked on the film. "He was a grouch. I found out that John Wayne was different working with him than he was on the screen. But, he is still my hero."[24] Director Michael Curtiz was ill with cancer and John Wayne took over the picture's direction, and kept much to himself in the evenings, working on his real estate investments and other production deals. He also made sure that care was taken with twenty-two rare longhorns he rented to Fox from his own Texas herd.

Below: A youngster getting an autograph from the Duke on location in Moab during production of *The Comancheros*. Facing: Director Michael Curtiz and John Wayne confer on the Moab location of *The Comancheros*. Wayne took over directing the picture when cancer made it impossible for Curtiz to continue.

Rio Conchos (1964)

Gordon Douglas, who had been in Moab in 1961 for *Gold of the Seven Saints* with Clint Walker and Roger Moore, came back to town in mid-February 1964 to scout locations for his post–Civil War Western *Rio Conchos*. Five surrounding states were under consideration for this story about gun-runners to the Apaches, led by an expatriate Confederate officer. A week later, George White and the Moab Movie Committee announced that Moab had won the competition. The art director from Twentieth Century-Fox arrived within days to prepare sets against the natural backdrop of Professor Valley, which would be filmed in CinemaScope and color. On March 12, the main construction crew from Fox arrived to build the sets, and a few days after that, Richard Boone, Tony Franciosa, Stuart Whitman, and football star Jim Brown (in his film debut) arrived in Moab.

Barely two weeks into filming, a giant snowstorm swept through southern Utah, dropping more than five inches on Moab and halting production. The inclement weather continued with cloudy skies and rain for nearly two weeks. At an average expense to Fox of $10,000 to $12,000 per day, Douglas considered filming interiors at a renovated warehouse in the Moab area. However, with only half of the picture completed, he announced a suspension in production and took the entire company back to Hollywood for the filming of interior scenes. On April 20, they all returned to Moab, but by then trees and flowers were budding and shots had to be carefully composed to avoid catching the first signs of spring. More bad weather plagued the company, now eight days behind on its shooting schedule. Employment of locals as extras and construction workers went from a high of 425 to 325 while Douglas nervously waited out Mother Nature. Edmond O'Brien developed an eye problem that required his return to Hollywood, threatening to force Douglas to recast the part and reshoot all of O'Brien's footage. Fortunately, O'Brien returned to complete his scenes and the weather finally cleared up. The last scenes of Boone, Franciosa, and Brown being dragged around the hard earth outside O'Brien's mansion and the final explosion of the Apache gunpowder supply were filmed by mid-May. On Sunday, May 17, the Fox company flew back home from Grand Junction.

Manuel "Bud" Lincoln, head of the Grand County Employment Services and cochair of the film commission with George White until the mid-1980s, compiled the favorable figures of the economic impact of *Rio Conchos* on

Right: O'Brien's mansion burns as his plan for an armed uprising ends. Facing: Wende Wagner, Jim Brown, and Stuart Whitman look on as Richard Boone negotiates with Edmond O'Brien for the sale of powder and guns.

the area. Fox spent fifty-three days on location in Moab and hired two hundred locals in addition to one hundred Navajos from the reservation. A total of $400,000 was spent by Fox in the Moab vicinity, in addition to many intangible benefits of goodwill. There was also a note of amusement on the *Rio Conchos* set. Actor Richard Boone's brother was a wealthy oil magnate in Texas. As they were talking by phone one day, Boone happened to mention to his brother where the group was filming the next day. As production was underway the following morning, a plane flew overhead and promptly dropped thousands of rubber ducks into the Colorado River. After the surprised cast and crew recovered from the practical joke, Boone promised he would never again disclose his whereabouts to his brother.

In late fall, John Ford helped make 1963 a banner year for moviemaking in Moab. The month-long shoot for *Cheyenne Autumn* that had been going on in Monument Valley was over, and, on November 9, the company moved to Moab for two weeks of location work. The principal locations were Professor Valley, Onion Creek, George White's ranch, Arches National Monument, and Klondike Flat. At Ninemile Bottom, the Warner Bros. crews laid three miles of railroad track for key scenes. By the 1960s, more and more tourists were discovering this beautiful, arid country for themselves. One tourist was driving near Klondike Flat when he saw a man on the ground with an arrow in his neck. "Did you see the Indian who shot him?" the panicked driver asked another passerby. Only then did he realize that not far away the film crew was setting up another scene.

On Friday, November 22, 1963, everyone in town was affected by the assassination of President John F. Kennedy. Ford was filming at the George White Ranch when the news reached him. He called a wrap on filming for the rest of the day. Only one more day of shooting was necessary, and then the cast and crew departed for Hollywood to complete studio interiors.

Gilbert Roland leads his braves across the Colorado River in *Cheyenne Autumn*.

Jesus (Max von Sydow) preaching the Sermon on the Mount at Grand View Point in Canyonlands National Park.

The Greatest Story Ever Told (1965)

For the next two years, there was no feature film production at all in Moab due largely to Utah's tax-withholding law for out-of-state workers. Television commercials were frequently made in the area, beginning with a series of famous advertisements for Chevrolet showing their Impala sedan perched on top of Castle Rock in Castle Valley. So popular was this approach to automobile promotion that it was repeated three more times in subsequent years.

While competition from other states was a factor in the diminishing number of films made in Moab, so was the changing nature of the film industry, as audiences declined and the Western film became an endangered species. In early 1963, when an exemption was made in Utah's law for movie workers, George Stevens was nearing the end of filming his biblical epic *The Greatest Story Ever Told*. Sam Taylor, a state legislator representing Grand County, went to Utah governor George Clyde and convinced him and a few other legislators to fly to Lake Powell in the state's airplane and persuade Stevens to consider Moab as a location. Stevens and his crew visited Moab, and "when they saw Dead Horse Point, they knew that they had to film at least part of the movie here."[25] In early May 1963, casting began for the location shoot near Moab. Residents lined up outside the high-school gymnasium to fill out applications as extras, or, as the casting director called them, "atmosphere." A friend of Moab resident Ruby Shafer was visiting from Tacoma, Washington, and was signed up on the spot as an extra. While only part of the film was made in the vicinity, the company stayed for nearly three weeks, almost as long as was usually required for a single feature film. It was estimated that the Stevens company spent $60,000 a day while on location, $4,000 of that on the extra talent. Beginning on May 20, 1963, more than four hundred extras got up at 4:00 a.m. to be dressed in drab muslin clothing and sandals. They were then put onto buses that took them to Grand View Point in Canyonlands for the filming of the Sermon on the Mount. Max von Sydow, Sal Mineo, and Michael Ansara had arrived the previous day from Hollywood. Navajos from Bluff, Utah, were brought in to play roles ranging from extras to Roman soldiers. Sal Mineo "was very serious about his work. He insists he is never too tired to sign autographs for the fans after a hard day's work." Michael Ansara, who had been in Moab for *The Comancheros* two years previous, surprised Moabites "dressed in a black tunic-like costume for his part as commander of Herod's army. It is hard to connect this gracious man with a villain role."[26]

Blue (1968)

In 1967, up-and-coming actor Robert Redford was slated by Paramount Pictures to appear in the Western *Blue,* to be filmed in Utah. However, the script was substantially changed from the kind of film Redford originally had agreed to, so he backed out. In retaliation, Paramount sued Redford, with the result that the actor and his ex-agent Richard Gregson formed their own film production company, Wildwood Enterprises, and made *Downhill Racer*. Paramount chose then-popular British actor Terence Stamp to replace Redford. The story, set on the Texas–Mexico border of the 1850s, follows the journey of an American-born youngster (Stamp) who is adopted by a Mexican bandit (Ricardo Montalban) and given the name Azul (Blue) after a raid on a border town. Azul is torn between two cultures, especially when he falls in love with a Caucasian woman (Joanna Pettet), whom he earlier rescued from a rape by a fellow bandit.

Filmed in Panavision and Technicolor by noted cinematographer Stanley Cortez, *Blue* displayed Moab's Professor Valley landscape to such a degree that Utah state officials expected a renaissance of the gradually declining movie business. After nearly three years without any filming in the area, Moabites were gleeful that Paramount had come to town. Old bills were being paid by locals and "markets note an increase in business over last year but often it is hard to sort the Paramount customers from tourists," recorded the *Times-Independent,* which published a special edition of the newspaper, printed in blue ink, about the making of the film.[27] *Blue* was given a first-class premiere at the Utah Theater in Salt Lake City on April 23, 1968. It was preceded by a state reception dinner sponsored by Governor Calvin Rampton, and a special performance for visiting stars Stamp, Montalban, and Joe DeSantis by the Mormon Tabernacle Choir. Said Montalban, who would gain fame on television's *Fantasy Island* a few years later, about the performance, "For the first time, I was able to hear live, the Tabernacle Choir. It was a humbling experience. I had goose pimples up and down my back. I had tears in my eyes."[28]

The production of *Blue* gave the filmmakers an idea, even before cameras rolled in Moab: Why not make a film *about* the film we are making? During location scouting, the producers visited the Doles Ranch in Castle Valley. Referring to the "attractive rosy cheeked Mrs. Doles," Patricia Casey, associate producer to Judd Bernard, marveled at "the uncomplicated easy going life she led in contrast to her own frenzied world."[29] What if a local fell in love with someone from the *Blue* production team? This was the inspiration for a feature-length film, *Fade-In,* starring Burt Reynolds, who had played "Quint" for a couple of years in television's *Gunsmoke* but had not yet broken through as a major actor. The plot of *Fade-In* focuses on the filming of *Blue*, with Moab rancher Reynolds falling in love with the film's editor, played by Barbara Loden, by then an accomplished actress married in real life to famed theater and film director Elia Kazan. Their love grows, but Reynolds realizes that their class differences will not make them happy together. Still photographs show the bare-chested Reynolds riding below Fisher Towers. "They filmed *Blue* in the daytime and *Fade-In* at night," remembered Bette Stanton, an extra in *Fade-In*, and later head of the Moab Film Commission. Stanton also dated the recently divorced Reynolds during the production. "He would talk of his dreams, one of which was to run an actors' school, which he later did in Florida. He was fabulous, very intelligent, not the womanizer image that seemed to stick to him later on. I found him very much a thinker."[30] Stanton remembered hearing that one nude swimming scene in the Colorado River rendered the film too explicit for US theatrical distribution. The film was shown on American television in 1982 and then was never seen again. Certainly one of the most interesting films shot simultaneously with another film, *Fade-In* survives only in video format under the title *The Iron Cowboy* and stands as an important piece of Moab history, as it generously shows many sections of downtown Moab in the 1960s. Reynolds remained generally silent about the film over the years, saying only that "It should have been called Fade-Out."

British star Terence Stamp got the title role in *Blue*, a Western about a teenager who cannot fit in either the Mexican or the American world.

Stuart Whitman and Seeta, the mountain lion, in Moab for the filming of Disney's *Run, Cougar, Run*.

THE APOCALYPSE IN MOAB

From the 1970s on, the number of feature films made in Moab dwindled. Segments of Twentieth Century-Fox's *Vanishing Point*, a contemporary chase film, and *Wild Rovers*, a Western starring William Holden and Ryan O'Neal, were filmed in the surrounding area. The Disney company stayed for eighteen days to make *Run, Cougar, Run,* which began as a two-part drama for *The Wonderful World of Disney* television program. Starring Stuart Whitman, Alfonso Arau, and Harry Carey Jr., the film tells the story of a mountain lion named Seeta, whose mate is killed by trophy hunters. Arau plays a shepherd who befriends Seeta and eventually sees to her escape. Locations used in the film include Locomotive Rock, George White's ranch, Arches National Park, Dead Horse Point State Park, and the Bill McCormick ranch in Castle Valley. "The Utah scenery becomes a star of the film," said the cougar's trainer and handler. "Those in the studio audience to see rushes couldn't believe country like that actually exists. All said they wanted to visit it."[1]

Independent production companies also provided some business for Moab. After releasing their successful feature *Where the Red Fern Grows*, Doty-Dayton Productions chose Utah native Stewart Peterson to appear with screen veterans Richard Boone and Henry Wilcoxon in *Against a Crooked Sky*. The story tells of Indians running off with Peterson's sister and a grizzly old prospector who aids Peterson in his search, along with a native scout who leads them to his camp. The company spent a month filming at a number of area locations.

Moab became a science-fiction netherworld in Ivan Reitman's *Spacehunter: Adventures in the Forbidden Zone*, released by Columbia Pictures. Filmed in the briefly revived 3-D format, *Spacehunter* starred Peter Strauss and Molly Ringwald. Strauss, an interplanetary mercenary, tries to assist three female intergalactic travelers who make an emergency landing on the planet Terra in the year 2136. Hardly the spotless environment defined earlier by *Star Wars,* Terra's Graveyard City is a mélange of worn-out devices and structures,

Peter Strauss with Molly Ringwald in the red canyons near Moab that represented the planet Terra in the year 2136.

filmed inside the Dominion Bridge Works at Vancouver, British Columbia. The Moab location is where most of the action takes place, with working props including Strauss's Scrambler truck and the Ramrod, a battering-ram vehicle used by Strauss's sidekick, played by Ernie Hudson. There is also a Techno Sail Train, a mobile battleship on rails that was constructed on three flat cars at the potash plant fifteen miles west of Moab.

In 1977, the State of Utah established a Film Development Office, with John Earle as its first director. This motivated the people in Moab to formalize their own efforts in movie promotion, and in 1984 the city created the Moab Film Promotion, complete with a board of directors, bylaws, and a greater effort to generate location filming in Grand County. Bette L. Stanton, whose father L. H. "Dude" Larsen was involved in movie production, prepared applications for Grand County that were successful in garnering a Community Development Block Grant for economic planning for the region.

Moab continued to be a setting for the extreme with *Choke Canyon*, a bizarre story of a physicist who tries to capture energy from Halley's Comet in order to help solve the world's energy problem. Downtown Moab was used extensively and the Colorado River's Dewey Bridge is the setting for aerial stunts, car crashes, and daredevil feats with helicopters.

In *Nightmare at Noon*, downtown Moab becomes the city of "Canyonlands, U.S.A." George Kennedy, Wings Hauser, and many local Moab actors manage to live through an attempt by foreign agents to poison the city's municipal water supply, turning residents who drink from it into maniacal killers. More sinister was the straight-to-video release *Sundown: The Vampire in Retreat*, a horror-comedy wherein Moab becomes Purgatory, a Western city inhabited by vampires, headed by David Carradine, who are trying to get out of the "business" by manufacturing a blood substitute. However, another faction, headed by veteran actor John Ireland (who had earlier appeared in *My Darling Clementine* and *Southwest Passage*), wants the vampires to continue their habits "the old-fashioned way."

Efforts to attract filmmakers were heightened in 1989 when Moab Film Promotion celebrated its fortieth anniversary with a Moab Movie Jubilee. Stars John Agar, Virginia Mayo, John Ireland, Marie Windsor, and others spoke at screenings and opened the commission's memorabilia museum. The commission also produced a promotional video, *Filmmaker's Perfect Location*, which was distributed to location managers for the major studios. That same year, San Juan County locations (most importantly Monument Valley) were included in the commission's promotional efforts. The area's Bureau of Land Management created a Moab Movie Tour map so that tourists could visit the sites of forty years' worth of films accessible on public lands.

Cooperation between the Utah Film Commission's executive director, Leigh von der Esch, and Moab Film Promotion's Bette Stanton resulted in a major coup for Grand County film production when director Steven Spielberg's crews found it necessary to switch locations for the opening sequences of *Indiana Jones and the Last Crusade* from Mesa Verde, Colorado, to Arches National Park. Stanton showed the scouts "everything conceivable trying to find ruins and caves as well as scenic areas." Eventually, Spielberg decided to build a cave in the studio and film the exteriors at Double Arch. "Because of the fast turnaround in providing photographs and permissions," remembered von der Esch, "they changed the title printed over the scene from 'Colorado—1914' to 'Utah—1914'."[2] "Having southern Utah at the beginning of a film like that," said Stanton, "was a wonderful thing for this state."[3]

Right: Cisco, Utah, resident and day player Ernest Vandrehoff and Susan Sarandon on the set of *Thelma & Louise*.

Director Ridley Scott was impressed with Grand County's natural setting when he visited Salt Lake City to film a British Airways commercial at the airport. The desert that he saw below his plane en route to Salt Lake City "was absolutely mesmerizing. I couldn't take my eyes off what I was seeing."[4] He remembered that impression two years later when he chose Grand County as a major location for *Thelma & Louise*, one of the most controversial films of the 1990s. The image of Geena Davis and Susan Sarandon—women on the run from a world dominated by manipulative, noncommittal men—careening over a cliff in a vintage 1966 Thunderbird symbolized to many the ultimate escape from contemporary cultural pressures. The precipice, meant to be the Grand Canyon in the film, was actually on a cliff below Dead Horse Point in Canyonlands National Park. Curiously, the preview trailer for *Thelma & Louise* was shot not in Canyonlands but in Monument Valley, which also dominated the film's publicity poster at theaters and the jacket art for its home-video release. Scott's conception of the film was keyed very much to landscape. "My objective was to create a world which was a reflection of the characters, an environment that mirrored the drama, humor or pathos that they were experiencing at any given moment, around any given curve in the road."[5]

In 1993, the Moab Film Commission formally included San Juan County and Monument Valley in its operations, as indicated by the commission's new name: Moab to Monument Valley Film Commission. The organization would officially coordinate film promotion from Moab south to Monticello, Blanding, Mexican Hat, and Monument Valley. The commission's hard work paid off with another major motion picture, Columbia's *Geronimo: An American Legend*. Gene Hackman, Robert Duvall, Jason Patric, and Wes Studi came to the Moab area for weeks of production work. The story, directed by Walter Hill and written by John Milius, begins in 1885 as the US Army is nearing the end of its efforts to put the Chiricahua Apache under Geronimo onto the reservation. "The *Geronimo* company brought 350 people and then hired several hundred more locally," said Stanton. There were also two hundred Native Americans hired from a number of tribes, many of them from the Mescalero/White Mountain Apache tribe in Arizona. Since production work coincided with the tourist season, curiosity was high among visitors to the location of the major set, Fort San Carlos in Professor Valley. "This is where the new era of filmmaking comes in," said Stanton. "In the old days, the movie companies didn't mind tourists visiting the set, as long as they did not interrupt shooting. Now you get a film like *City Slickers II* or *Geronimo,* and it is a closed set. You don't even get out there, even if you're the head of the local film commission."[6]

Because of the flurry of activity and the amount of money coming into the community, there were the usual complaints both from townspeople and from the film company. "We had a big meeting with motel owners, businesses, and residents who were renting their houses to film crews," said Stanton. "Even one of Senator Orrin Hatch's aides as well as the mayor dropped in. You get everybody together and try to identify in writing specific problems and then work out solutions. It is understandable to see how house prices can escalate when someone, say, says he can get $2,000 a month, so another person figures he can get $3,000 per month for his house. It's our responsibility as the film commission to try and keep a balance."[7]

Pontiac Moon, starring Ted Danson and Mary Steenburgen, and segments of Paul Hogan's *Lightning Jack*, directed by Simon Wincer, were filmed at Fisher Towers and Professor Valley, as well as in Monument Valley. The 1994 release of *City Slickers II: The Legend of Curly's Gold,* starring, co-produced, and co-written by comedian Billy Crystal, was substantially filmed in the canyons and parks surrounding Moab. Also in the mix were the many commercial shoots for soft drinks, Federal Express, Marlboro cigarettes, foreign anti-cigarette smoking commercials, various automobile manufacturers, cosmetics, and music videos. The aggressive posture of Stanton and the Moab to Monument Valley Film Commission resulted in a dramatic rise in money left in the area by production companies, from $5.17 million in 1992 to $11 million in 1993.[8]

Left: Wes Studi played a memorable role as Geronimo. Below: Robert Duvall and Gene Hackman relax on set. Right: Fort San Carlos, to which the Apaches were taken by the US Army, was re-created in Professor Valley, north of Moab.

Paul Hogan and Cuba Gooding Jr. in Professor Valley for the comedy Western *Lightning Jack*.

that his choice of Utah as a location was because of the state's "religion and the history it has had with religion," particularly since the film's demonic serial killer is connected with satanic rites.

Hearkening back to the traditional Westerns, actor Ed Harris and wife Amy Madigan produced a version of Zane Grey's classic *Riders of the Purple Sage* for the TNT network. Filmed mostly in the Indian Creek area south of Canyonlands National Park, *Riders of the Purple Sage* belied its television format with stunning visuals of the expansive Dugout Ranch and surrounding area.

Many films made in Moab in the 1980s and '90s went straight to cable and home video. In *Slaughter of the Innocents*, the teenage son of FBI agent Scott Glenn discovers troubling information about the recent "Provo Canyon Massacre" on his computer, and suggests to his father that the authorities are about to execute the wrong man. Unable to stay the execution, Glenn looks for more evidence, as his son, alone, follows his leads to southern Utah, where he discovers the hilltop domain of the killer, who has constructed a modern Noah's ark, mounted on a track, in which are the dead bodies of his victims, both animal and human, to prepare for the apocalypse. The director, James Glickenhaus, whose son Jesse Cameron Glickenhaus played the boy genius of the film, said that *Slaughter of the Innocents* was intended to be a "campfire story" of "ultimate evil and ultimate innocence."[9] Few Utahns, however, would agree with Glickenhaus's statement

In 1996, Disney made Moab the choice for a Martian landscape for part of its science-fiction comedy *RocketMan*. "We had to find an environment that resembled what scientists have told us Mars looks like," said producer Roger Birnbaum, "and that wasn't as easy as it sounds. It was vital that the topography of the area we chose came close to what we all imagine Mars to be like and the Moab area is, I think, as close as we could get." Director Stuart Gillard added that "The area outside of Moab had everything we needed. It has the giant cliffs, the red rocks, the lack of vegetation and the overall scale of what could be a distant planet." *RocketMan* was also a harbinger of Hollywood's new digital age, which threatens the future of on-location film production. "In post-production, we used computer generated imaging

Billy Crystal at Fisher Towers for *City Slickers II: The Search for Curly's Gold.*

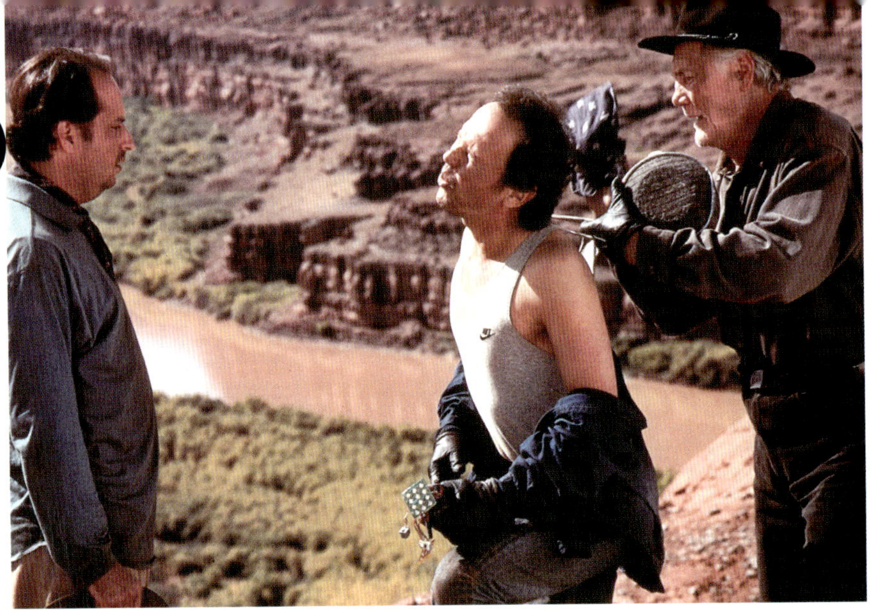

Billy Crystal's sunburn gets salved by old prospector "Duke" at Dead Horse Point.

(CGI) to add volcanoes, six-mile deep craters and twenty-five-mile-high mountains," said Birnbaum. "We changed Moab's blue sky to a soft pink-into-black to give the illusion of an enormous vista somewhere on the Martian plains. I truly felt that all of us—the entire cast and crew—had just spent the last three months and thirty-five million miles to get to Mars and I didn't want to end up on a back lot in Burbank."[10]

The 1990s brought new challenges to film production as efforts by the Southern Utah Wilderness Alliance, beginning in 1993, pressed for a thirty-day inquiry period on movie-company permit applications. "We lost *Broken Arrow* to Arizona because of the long wait period," said Stanton. "If serious questions are raised—which they almost never are—then the time period is extended to ninety days. No film company can deal with a month and a half of uncertainty when bank loans for production are compiling interest and cast and crew are waiting around to get started."[11] Stanton defended the film industry against the criticism of ruining pristine public lands:

> It is one of the cleanest industries you could have. It does nothing but bring money into the area. [The studios] pay a fortune to have environmental-impact assessments, archaeological assessments, and wildlife assessments. The money that they have put into just archaeological assessments has wound up identifying some important sites that probably would not have been otherwise identified. They contribute more to the preservation of these lands than they do in diminishing its value.[12]

Veteran actor Harry Carey Jr. visiting bedridden Moab movie pioneer George White in the mid-1990s. White helped make it possible for John Ford to film *Wagon Master*, which featured Carey, in Moab's Professor Valley.

Husband and wife Ed Harris and Amy Madigan produced and starred in the retelling of Zane Grey's classic *Riders of the Purple Sage*.

SCENE 6

NORTHERN UTAH

1908–2003

CAPITOL MOVIEMAKING

Salt Lake City never intended to become a movie capital, and it certainly had no ambitions to rival Hollywood. However, it did have a brief period when production companies came and went, with movie promoters trying to get a foothold on regular film production in the Beehive State.[1] Surviving records mention the Rocky Mountain Moving Picture Company that existed in Salt Lake City in the summer of 1908, making travelogue films of scenic areas in Utah. The announcement of this firm was followed by these remarks from the editors of the trade paper *Moving Picture World*: "The benefits that will accrue to Utah and the West, in advertisement through the medium of these pictures, which are to be shown throughout the United States, will be far reaching."[2] Virtually nothing is known about the longevity of these early companies or the effects of their films. What is important is that the editors of this important industry trade publication saw the films as being valuable for drawing people to the state for tourism. If Utah's experience was consistent with attempts by film companies to establish a presence in other American cities, the precariousness of the moviemaking business guaranteed a high mortality rate, and these companies quietly went out of business.

Harry Revier was an ambitious filmmaker who established "four buildings, one studio, and three printing and developing laboratories" in the Sugar House area of Salt Lake City in the fall of 1910. Advertisements running in *Moving Picture World* heralded his first production in December of that year. *Love's Sorrow* was promised as "a gripping tale of the West, Real Western scenery, Real Cowboys in their natural surroundings; taken midst the hills and plains of Utah." The next month's issue contained yet another display advertisement from Revier publicizing his studio as "the largest plant in the west."[3] Revier also made what might be the first appeal for outside filmmakers to consider the natural endowments of the Utah landscape: "The natural scenery of the Mormon State is the equal of any the world over for the production of motion pictures."[4] Revier would soon give up on Salt Lake City and establish facilities in Hollywood, where he leased his barn to the newly arrived Cecil B. DeMillle and the Jesse L. Lasky Feature Play Company, precursor to Paramount Pictures.

W. W. Hodkinson opened one of the nation's first movie theaters in Ogden in 1907 and was the first to develop the idea of a motion-picture exchange. Later, he went east and formed a distribution agency, which he named Paramount. For the company's logo, Hodkinson drew an image of a snow-capped peak resembling those along the Wasatch mountain range of his former home. Paramount's current logo is representative of that same Utah peak, and represents an emblematic tie to the state of Utah.[5]

One Hundred Years of Mormonism (1913) may have been the first Hollywood filmmaking venture in Utah. The story recounted the history of The Church of Jesus Christ of Latter-day Saints, from its early years in New York and Ohio to the massive pilgrimage that ended in the valley of the Great Salt Lake in 1847. Directed by Norval MacGregor, the film was the brainchild of Harry A. Kelly, who managed to elicit cooperation from the church, as well as their approval of the film. Unfortunately, no copies of the film are known to exist.[6]

Beginning in the early 1920s, Utah suffered along with the rest of the nation in an economic depression that, although it did not approach the level of the 1929 market crash, was nevertheless significant in its effects. Utah suffered more than most other states due to the depression's long-term impact on local agriculture, especially in the regions of southwestern and southeastern Utah.[7] Money was welcomed from just about any source, and the first taste of Hollywood money coming into the state was at its west-central border in Garrison, Utah, an area that even today is sparsely populated and little traveled. To the east are the petered-out mining boomtowns of Frisco and Newhouse. In 1922, Ogden native and movie director James Cruze showed up to make a film version of Emerson Hough's Western saga *The Covered Wagon*. Cruze's studio crew of 127 was augmented by hundreds of extras, including 750 people from the Bannock tribe in Fort Hall, Idaho. The Baker Ranch, astride the Utah–Nevada border in the Snake Valley, was used for much of the filming, as was the Nevada ranch of Otto Meek. The scenes depicting the crossing of the Platte River were photographed at the lake on Meek's property. Karl Brown, the head cameraman on the production, praised Meek as "an angel in disguise and we valued him as such."[8] Brown was filled with wonder, and perhaps some dread, when he and the advance party detrained in Milford, Utah, and were greeted by Meek, "advancing towards us accompanied by a swarm of his own flies." He drove the group north in his sixteen-cylinder Cadillac over rough roads to the remote wilderness of his ranch, eighty-five miles from the nearest railroad. Director Cruze and Meek sat in the house to review the needed livestock, covered wagons, extras, and other requirements and to tabulate the overall cost of production. Brown noted the lake nearby that could be used as "the crossing of the Platte at or near Julesburg, while one side had two kinds of deserts, the hard pebbly kind with plenty of greasewood and palos verdes, and the other kind, of loose, all but impassible sand."[9]

Three days were spent on Antelope Island, in the Great Salt Lake, where *The Covered Wagon* company photographed buffalo on the run. To get to the island, the camera crew and principal cast members took the train from Milford to Salt Lake City and then boarded an interurban train to the Saltair beach resort, where they all piled into a launch that took them across the lake to the barren island. At times, herding the massive buffalo was a life-threatening task. During the filming of one particular scene, the animals came charging at the movie cameras, which were mounted on fragile triangles of stacked lumber. Cameras were also mounted on horse-drawn wagons to follow the action. "The ground was rough so getting around to follow the capture of the buffalo bull took a lot of hanging on to keep the camera from being pitched out onto the ground," said Brown. "My prize-fighting assistant, Ed Coffee, solved the problem by sitting down under the tripod and hanging onto the tripod head with both hands. That, and a few lash-lines, kept the camera aboard even though my hands were a blur trying to turn the camera handle with one hand and operate the pan and tilt handles with the other. This gave me nothing to hang onto, so I had to roll with the wagon as it spun crazily over the rocks and hummocks of Antelope Island."[10]

***The Covered Wagon*, the first great Western epic, was filmed in primitive conditions near the desert town of Garrison, Utah.**

The Native Americans brought in for the shoot lived in their own lodges set near the movie replica of Fort Bridger. The Hollywood crew watched them with incredulity as they slaughtered "their own on-the-hoof beef supplies" and carefully cleaned and consumed the raw intestines "no doubt pitying us poor whites because we had no appreciation of so delicious a delicacy." Their chief, Yellow Calf, forestalled conflicts between his people and Cruze's production crew by inducting Cruze into the tribe as Chief Standing Bear. According to Brown, his photograph of Yellow Calf "went to the publicity department and from there to the artist who used it as a model for designing the Indian head of the buffalo nickel."[11] At $601,422, the movie was very expensive to make, but it brought handsome returns at the box office, setting the standard for Western epics to follow.

In 1928, minor Hollywood producer George Edward Lewis moved from California to Salt Lake City and created the Pioneer Film Corporation. Lewis's first film, *All Faces West,* was a dramatization of the Mormon pioneer trek to Utah, and was filmed on Utah locations. Also known as *The Exodus,* this Western was completed in November 1928, but the popularity of talking pictures delayed its release until March 1929, when it ran in Salt Lake City for one week. The Pioneer Film Corporation collapsed after the October stock market crash. *The Exodus* was subsequently picked up by a syndicate distributor and released as *Call of the Rockies* or *West of the Rockies* in 1931. Directed by Bernard B. Ray, the film starred the popular Ben Lyon and Marie Prevost.

The Wasatch Mountains east of Salt Lake City were used for filming snow sequences for M-G-M's *The Mortal Storm* (1940), about the growing threat of Nazism in Germany prior to the outbreak of war. There was also a two-week film shoot at the Alta ski resort for Alfred Hitchcock's suspense thriller *Spellbound*. Louise Parry Thomas remembered that not long after the tragic death of her father, Chauncey, in Cedar City, her mother packed up the family belongings and moved to be near her relatives in Salt Lake City. Shortly after their arrival, Helen Parry received a call from Hollywood contacts about second-unit photography for *Spellbound*. The experienced Parry insisted that the crew supply appropriate facilities for the children while filming took place. "She went down the whole list of things that were required for the children. So, we all boarded the bus and went home that day. On the second day, there was a huge camp set up, with food, a fire, and everything she said we had to have. For two weeks we filmed this scene that, on the screen, must have lasted only a few seconds, where we are seen out the window on a hill with all of these little kids on their sleds."[12]

The inspiration for *Carnival of Souls* (1962) came solely from a Utah location: a rotting structure in the Great Salt Lake. Industrial filmmaker Herk Harvey was driving home from a film shoot in the San Francisco Bay Area when he was captivated by the aging hulk of the Saltair resort, closed since 1958. The vacant structure appeared mystical to Harvey: "With the sun setting and the lake in the background, this was the weirdest-looking place I'd ever seen."[13] He drove on to Kansas, where he immediately announced to John Clifford, a screenwriter he worked with, that he wanted to make a feature film constructed around Saltair. Clifford was so enthused that in three weeks he turned out a script about a young woman who, after surviving an automobile accident that kills her two companions, takes a job playing an organ in Salt Lake City. She becomes drawn to the empty Saltair amusement park, where she is plagued by communications from the dead. Harvey obtained help from an electrician to string power out to the Saltair ballroom, after which, to the director's surprise, all of the original lights went on, creating enough light to film the ghoulish *danse macabre* that takes place at the end of the film, played by students recruited from the University of Utah. It was guerilla filmmaking at its leanest, with locations including the City and County Building, the ZCMI department store, the Union Pacific and Greyhound Bus depots, and the sidewalk near Temple Square. The film was distributed independently and only had screenings in the southeastern United States. However, it showed up again in the 1980s on television and has since become a cult classic. Unwittingly, it presents important historical footage of Saltair shortly before it burned to the ground in November 1970.

Combatants take a break from filming a mountaintop battle near Draper, Utah, for *The Devil's Brigade*. Utah Lake is seen in the distance.

In 1968, director Andrew V. McLaglen came to Salt Lake City to film *The Devil's Brigade*, with a stellar cast including William Holden, Cliff Robertson, Dana Andrews, Vince Edwards, and Claude Akins. Most of the story deals with the travails of turning a bunch of ragtag misfits into a dedicated group of fighting men. The Snowbird ski resort and the nearby cities of Alpine and Park City were used as filming locations, but the most dramatic location was at the top of a canyon above Draper, which served as the site of the film's climactic battle in the mountains of Italy between American and German forces. Residents could see and hear explosions, and massed Utah National Guard troops were used as extras. The snow-capped Wasatch and Oquirrh mountains made a fine backdrop, all of which was caught by the wide-screen cameras. The film was budgeted at $4.5 million, and it was estimated that United Artists left $2.5 million in the northern Utah economy.

In the mid-1970s, the Utah Division of Industrial Promotion and the Utah Travel Council made a film featuring Robert Redford to promote film production in the state. "We recognize the splintering of the movie industry," said Industrial Promotion head John Alston. "The big studios no more mean what they used to. The independent producer is the man to contact."[14] Governor Rampton hosted a dinner at the Ambassador Club in Salt Lake City to commence an effort to get more films made in the state. Representatives from Utah regions attended the dinner, where Rampton announced his intention to appoint a person to represent Utah to Hollywood studios. Jack Payne, Moab delegate to the event, remarked on his return from the meeting that the governor's new appointee might create another kind of competition. "Our committee [Moab Movie Committee] will cooperate with the State organization and if the State is successful in attracting a company to Utah, then we will compete with other localities for filming work. We will no longer be competing with entire states but will be working against cities around Utah."[15]

Utah was now prepared to move ahead on a concerted effort to entice Hollywood to Utah. Stanley Kramer, noted producer of *High Noon, The Caine Mutiny,* and *Judgment at Nuremberg,* came to Utah to premiere his latest film, *Bless the Beasts and the Children,* at Brigham Young University. He announced that he would work with Governor Rampton and personally host a Hollywood lunch of independent film executives so that Utah could be promoted for film production. He also urged Utah to appoint a single person to cut through bureaucratic red tape for film companies, a person who "can assure the producer that there will be no last-minute request to review the script, a man who can stave off any denial of the use of such and such a piece of land."[16] Hal Schleuter, head of special projects at the Utah Travel Council, was put in charge as Utah's film promoter.

The luncheon for independent producers hosted by Kramer in Los Angeles was a success. Rampton's visit coincided with a Southern California tour by the Mormon Tabernacle Choir. His strident promotional activity was part of what was referred to as "Rampton's Raiders," a term that described his revitalization of Utah's office of economic development.[17] The following month, director Jerome Courtland came to Salt Lake City to film a one-hour television pilot for the series *Movin' On*. The episode told the story of two race-car drivers who compete with a local man for the affections of a girl who is soon to leave on missionary service for The Church of Jesus Christ. The Bonneville Speedway, Temple Square, and various other locations around Salt Lake City, as well as Bridal Veil Falls in Provo Canyon, were used, but the series did not make it beyond the pilot stage. "It was through his [Governor Rampton's] visits that we became convinced we should visit the Utah areas for possible locations," the director said.[18]

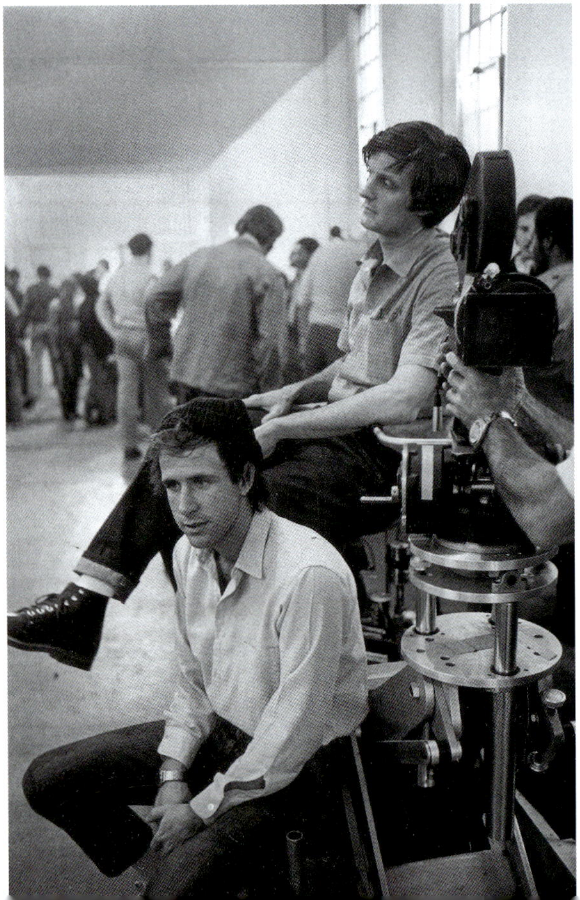

Left: Alan Alda rests between scenes at the Utah State Prison in Draper for the gritty Emmy Award-winning television drama *The Glass House*. Above: Pickpocket ringleader Walter Pidgeon tussles with a mark on the steps of the Utah State Capitol in *Harry in Your Pocket*.

Above, left: Troubleshooter George Kennedy rushes onto the tarmac at Salt Lake City International Airport with pilot Charlton Heston in *Airport 1975*. Above, right: Aerial sequences for *Airport 1975* were photographed over Heber and the Wasatch Mountains east of Salt Lake City.

Soon after *Movin' On*, *The Glass House*, adapted from a Truman Capote story about the stratified life within the prison community, appeared as a television movie. It was filmed entirely at the Utah State Prison at Bluffdale, where prisoners were hired for $3 per day, $100 for a speaking part. The film won an Emmy for director Tom Gries and, with additional footage, was entered into the Cannes Film Festival.

Robert Redford deserved a great deal of credit for steering Warner Bros. to make *Jeremiah Johnson* in Utah instead of Spain. "I showed them where they could produce it in Utah for less than they figured," he said. "Also, I believe this will show the beauty of Utah to many of the right sources. I received the finest cooperation from everyone in the state. Governor Rampton did everything he could for us. The cooperation was magnificent. I have told everyone in Hollywood."[19] After the opening of *Jeremiah Johnson* in late 1972, Redford received letters from all over the country. "There were people who saw the movie and wanted to invest in land here," he said. "I had letters from people who recognized the Utah scenery and were homesick."[20] On another occasion, Redford declared that the film "will show the beauty of Utah to many of the right sources . . . It is the prettiest state around. There is a lot to be protected in this state. There is more to be gained from our past than what we have today. I like the guts it took for the people to get here."[21] He also announced two more Westerns to be made in Utah, although only one of them, *The Electric Horseman*, ended up being filmed in the state.

Film production increased in Salt Lake City with *House of Seven Corpses*, a low-budget horror film made at a number of old mansions in town, including the Kearns Mansion. Contemporary pickpockets were the subject of *Harry in Your Pocket*, filmed on the streets of Salt Lake City and in Seattle. The disaster movie *Airport 1975*, a spin-off from the earlier *Airport*, was photographed mainly at the Salt Lake City airport and over the Wasatch Mountains above the Heber and Salt Lake valleys. Charlton Heston, Myrna Loy, George Kennedy, Karen Black, Linda Blair, Helen Reddy, and Gloria Swanson were in Salt Lake City for a week filming airport sequences. "We thought we would use the new airport in Dallas," said producer William Fry, "but when we got there it was physically not right for us. We then scouted around in New Mexico and Arizona without luck. Then as we were flying into Salt Lake and over these gorgeous mountains,

In *Footloose,* city boy Kevin Bacon comes to a small town where rock music and dancing are prohibited. Scenes were filmed at the Lehi Roller Mills, Payson, Provo, Orem, and American Fork.

we knew this was the place."[22] Later, in the air over Heber Valley, the dramatic and dangerous aerial stunt work was filmed using a Boeing 747 and a small corporate jet.

Whiffs, a drama about chemical weapons and robberies, was filmed near Tooele, west of Salt Lake City, where actual banks were used to stage the robbery scenes. The world premiere opened the new Midtown Trolley theater in Salt Lake City on October 7, 1975. Independent producer-director Lyman Dayton's *Against a Crooked Sky,* filmed in Moab, was also given its premiere in Salt Lake City in December. By this time a delegation from the Industrial Development & Promotion Council was making at least one yearly trip to Hollywood, as were George White from Moab and various individuals from Kanab. It was estimated that from the time of Rampton's trip in 1971, nearly $13 million in movie money had been added to the state's economy.

During the 1970s, Dayton moved his film company from California to Utah and businessman Charles Sellier began Sun International Pictures (later Schick Sunn Classics), making movies out of his base in Park City. His most visible success was the NBC television series *The Life and Times of Grizzly Adams*, a spin-off of his 1974 feature film. By 1980, shortly before Sunn Classic Pictures was sold to Taft International, Sellier reported a studio operation of 305 employees and sales of $40 million.[23]

In 1977, the Utah legislature finally appropriated monies to establish the Utah Film Development office under the Department of Development Services. Independent filmmaker John Earle was hired as its first director. He had worked the previous year with Utah filmmaker Sterling Van Wagenen on the first major American film festival in Utah, held in Salt Lake City. His relentless pursuit of film production, combined with a warm personality, brought many film, television, and documentary projects to Utah. A *Filmmakers Guide to Utah* was published in mid-1978 to "keep Utah in the minds of Hollywood producers."[24] Earle sought to provide regular contact and assistance with local film promoters, particularly in southern Utah. Funds spent by film companies for Utah goods and services relating to construction, meals, lodging, extras, and equipment at the conclusion of his first two years in office were over $10 million, compared to $5.2 million in 1977.[25]

In 1985, John Earle died following a sudden heart attack. His successor, Leigh von der Esch, noted the change wrought by Earle's efforts to attract new movie business: "There was a real shift from being a liaison service and working with companies when they got here to reading the trades, seeing what books are being published and who picked them up for film development. We would then contact these companies, send them photographs, and provide them with information on filmmaking sources within the state. We try to stay a step ahead of the curve. That has made the difference in being proactive instead of reactive."[26]

The Executioner's Song, starring Tommy Lee Jones, was filmed entirely in Utah, and told the unique story of killer Gary Mark Gilmore and his execution at the Utah State Prison. Norman Mailer penned the teleplay, which was based on his own highly publicized novel. Gilmore's case received a great deal of attention because he lobbied for his own execution, which finally occurred on January 17, 1977, making him the first person to be executed after the US Supreme Court reinstated the practice of capital punishment in 1976. The nearly three-hour movie also includes Christine Lahti, Rosanna Arquette, and Eli Wallach in its distinguished cast. The film's gritty realism was rendered by filming at the Utah State Prison, the Utah State Courthouse in Salt Lake City, and at locations in Orem and Provo, Utah.

In the fall of 1989, director Michael Cimino chose a Georgian mansion on Arlington Avenue in Salt Lake City for his remake of the chilling 1955 drama *The Desperate Hours,* originally starring Humphrey Bogart and Fredric March. In Cimino's remake, Mickey Rourke is a killer who escapes from his trial and takes hostage a family led by philandering

An increasing number of television movies were made in northern Utah during the 1980s and '90s, some with Utah-based stories such as *In the Line of Duty: Siege at Marion.* Tess Harper plays the wife of polygamist John Singer. Dennis Franz plays the FBI leader who comes to arrest Adam Swapp.

Above, left: The interior of the home in Salt Lake City, used for exteriors, was replicated at the Osmond Studios in Orem for *Desperate Hours*, for its terrified occupants Anthony Hopkins, Mimi Rogers, and Shawnee Smith. Above, right: Mickey Rourke reprised the role originally played by Humphrey Bogart.

attorney Anthony Hopkins and his wife Mimi Rogers. The Salt Lake City home exterior was used as the visual motif for the movie posters, but the entire interior set was built at the Ventura Entertainment Center in Orem. The football stadium at Brigham Young University and the communities of Coalville, Orem, and Alta were also used, as well as the Federal Courthouse in Salt Lake City. There were also a few scenes filmed at Zion and Capitol Reef national parks.

In the twenty-first century, as films with urban settings became popular, northern Utah eclipsed southern Utah in moviemaking activity. The region that had played host to so much movie activity had now seen its last. "Film is a billboard like no other," concluded Leigh von der Esch, who headed the Utah Film Commission for two decades. "As film commissioner, I knew that we couldn't buy the exposure that came through the movies made in Utah, and to have someone of Robert Redford's stature say, 'I made a movie here and it was easy, the people worked hard, and they were friendly, and you can get to the locations easily,' was a great calling card."[27]

Jeremiah Johnson **acquainted moviemakers with the varied scenery available to them in Utah.**

SCENE 7

Background actors in scene from *Horizon: An American Saga*, Film 1, filmed in Professor Valley, Moab, Utah. The dance hall and tent city of the burgeoning western town of Horizon, the story of which is at the center of Kevin Costner's *Horizon: An American Saga*.

A NEW HORIZON

1994–2024

THE UTAH DISNEY MOVIE HERITAGE

As is evident in this book thus far, Walt Disney Productions has been a presence in Utah for almost seventy years, marked with well over forty motion pictures and television shows, not including television series episodes. Beginning with *Perri* in 1957, and continuing with *Ten Who Dared, One Little Indian, The Apple Dumpling Gang Rides Again, Tall Tale,* and *National Treasure,* Disney Productions has also featured early roles for many later major talents, including Jodie Foster and Patrick Swayze.

In 2007, Disney's most expensive production of the year and the longest running time of any Disney feature up to that time—*Pirates of the Caribbean: At World's End*—made a three-day production shoot on the Bonneville Salt Flats. Where racing car speed records had been set and broken for decades, the Black Pearl, commanded by Jack Sparrow (Johnny Depp) and Barbossa (Geoffrey Rush) appeared stark on the blindingly white Salt Flats west of the Great Salt Lake. A large portion of the ship was erected on the site, with CGI applied in post-production. The occasion brought out Utah Governor Jon Huntsman, Jr. with his family to meet the film's producer, Jerry Bruckheimer, director Gore Verbinski, and Johnny Depp. The cinematically inclined head of state reveled in the movie's magic right in the middle of this salt-encrusted desert.

Two additional major feature film projects undertaken by Disney in the twenty-first century included the much-anticipated film version of Edgar Rice Burroughs' novel *John Carter*, whose main character first appeared in 1911 in what became known as the Barsoom series. Transported to Mars, this Civil War veteran became a powerful warrior, whose exploits against strange beasts were lionized in several novels in the series. The big-budget film version (at an estimated overall cost of $300 million), *John Carter,* was released to theaters in 2012. It was director Andrew Stanton's first live-action film, after having directed two highly profitable Pixar animated features for Disney. Many locales vied for the filming, and principal photography began at Longcross Studios in England. In an effort to attract Disney to southern Utah's otherworldly-like desert landscape for exteriors, Utah began its campaign. Utah's Governor Jon Huntsman, Jr. was a big fan of the John Carter stories, but initially it looked like Utah was out of the running because of inadequate incentive rebate funding. Appeals were made by the Utah Film Commission to the Governor's Office of Economic Development (GOED) to increase the rebate incentive fund. At the eleventh hour,

On-site filming the brief sequence from *Pirates of the Caribbean: At World's End* on the Bonneville Salt Flats (left to right): Producer Jerry Bruckheimer, Director Gore Verbinski, Utah Governor Jon Huntsman, Mary Kay Huntsman, Johnny Depp, and Utah Film Commission staffers Mimi Davis Taylor, Marshall Moore, and Aaron Syrett.

Governor Gary Herbert visits the Moab location of *The Lone Ranger* accompanied by local and state officials. Left to right, front row: Ally Isom (Governor's Chief of Staff), Johnny Depp in costume as Tonto, Tara Penner (Moab to Monument Valley Film Commissioner), Governor Gary Herbert, Marshall Moore (Director, Utah Film Commission, 2007–2014). Second row: second from left, Spencer Eccles, Sr. (Governor's Office of Economic Development, Jesse Anderson (Governor's Security Detail), Larry Campbell (freelance location scout).

money was made available and Disney ended up spending $20 million during the filming in 2009, hiring locals, meal catering, lodging, set construction, and other services needed to film in various Utah desert locations in Grand and Wayne Counties, Kanab in Kane County, and Lake Powell. That was more money than had been spent by a single studio on any one feature film shoot in Utah. "The project itself had a number of challenges regarding permits on public lands," said Marshall Moore. "Some of those permits took as much as a hundred days from application to approval. That's why a production needs those long prep periods that help during this process. We're talking about use of vast public lands in southern Utah. Navigating that was difficult, and sometimes scary, to make certain that their needs could be met in a timely manner."[1]

In 2013, Disney released *The Lone Ranger,* starring Armie Hammer as the masked stranger and Johnny Depp playing the Ranger's decidedly darker and quirky sidekick, Tonto. That production saw filming in New Mexico, Texas, and Arizona before Utah filming began in Moab and Monument Valley. As with *John Carter, The Lone Ranger* was visually dazzling and entertainingly action-packed. However, both films failed to make back their high costs, thus becoming two of the biggest commercial box office failures in motion picture history.

The big promotion for Disney's *The Lone Ranger* included the locomotive used in the film on the Red Carpet at Disneyland visited by Utah Governor Gary Herbert and First Lady Jeanette Herbert. Marshall Moore, Director, Utah Film Commission, is at right.

High School Musical (2019)

Beginning in the early 2000s, the Disney Channel featured numerous locations in Utah from urban settings in *Right on Track* to a working haunted house in *Halloween High*. Yet, for the demographic that consumed Disney Channel product, Disney had not done a musical. At the Disney Channel, Executive Producer Bill Borden conferred with Gary Marsh, then head of Disney Channel's Original Programming about upcoming projects. "Gary asked for a musical set in a high school," remembered Susette Hsiung, executive vice president of Network Production Management and Operations at Disney Channels Worldwide in 2023. "Once we received Peter Barsocchini's script, Kenny Ortega was attached, and the rest is history. Zac Efron, Vanessa Hudgens, and Ashley Tisdale were already in the Disney Channel family."[2]

Future director of the Utah Film Commission, Marshall Moore, was, in 2005, a producer's service executive with the film commission. Part of his duties was to receive and review all scripts submitted by the studios and filmmakers for locations to determine their qualification for participation in the state's rebate incentive fund. "Across my desk came a script called *High School Musical* that had been submitted by Disney. I couldn't believe what I was reading. I said, 'This is like *Grease*, a new *Grease*.' I loved it! I knew that it was going to be a hit. I could sense it. There was something about it that was different. I got so excited. For me, *Grease* had become one of my favorite movies of a lifetime and I saw the similarities in the script to *High School Musical*. Yes, it was different for Disney because it was a musical. A true musical." Inasmuch as the story was set primarily in a high school situated in Albuquerque, New Mexico, Disney was exploring its options to film it in the "land of enchantment." "So, I went to Leigh von der Esch, at that time the director of the Utah Film Commission, and told her that we had a shot at this because we had ties with director Kenny Ortega, who had just directed the dance numbers featured in the Salt Lake City Winter Olympics in 2002. As a result, he was familiar with the extensive, talented dance community in Utah. The obstacle was that we had no money left in the state's incentive program." Von der Esch took the proposal and enthusiastically presented it to the various offices necessary to borrow money against the following year's rebate incentive fund. Finally, the executive officer of the Governor's Office of Economic Development gave the green light. "We were able to tell Disney that there were incentive dollars equal to that being offered by New Mexico." With Kenny Ortega's experience with the Olympics and the solid infrastructure of talent available in Utah, they chose to shoot *High School Musical* in Salt Lake City in 2005. "They were not going to choose Utah," Moore emphasized, "unless there was a way to come with, in some sort of creative way, a rebate." Moore added that studios filming on location find that the local supporting talent is often the driver of their final decision, thus saving significant amounts of money that otherwise would be spent on food and lodging for actors brought from Hollywood to fill supporting roles. "In talking to Kenny Ortega and others, the dance community in Utah is one of the best in the nation."[3]

Producer Ben Worden was shown the various high schools in the Salt Lake City and Ogden metropolitan areas. East High School on the bench of the Wasatch Mountains and near the University of Utah campus was chosen as the site for filming what would become all three *High School Musical* movies. "The cooperation given the production by East High was also a factor in its attractiveness as a location," said Moore. "Filming in the evenings and weekends, roping off the areas during school where students could not go when filming during school hours, East High made it work."[4]

High School Musical turned into a massive hit when it debuted on the Disney Channel in late January 2006. The characters of Troy, Gabriella, Sharpay, Ryan, and Chad embedded themselves in the teen cultural milieu, to the soundtrack of the film's catchy songs, "Start of Something New," "We're All in This Together," "Get'cha Head in the

The principal cast of *High School Musical 3: Senior Year* meets Governor Jon M. Huntsman in the Gold Room at the Utah State Capitol in April, 2008, during their two-month rehearsal period. Left to right: Mary Kay Huntsman (First Lady), Marshall Moore (Director, Utah Film Commission), Olesya Rulin, Monique Coleman, Kenny Ortega (Director and Choreographer), Governor Jon M. Huntsman, Ashley Tisdale, Bill Borden (Producer), Vanessa Hudgens, KayCee Stroh, Corbin Bleu, Ryne Sanborn, Chris Warren. Front row: Kneeling: Lucas Grabeel; Gracie Huntsman, Asha Huntsman.

April 2008

Marshall -

Thanks for your great work.
Keep making Utah Shine!

Jon M Huntsman Jr.
Governor

Brooklyn Moore, daughter of Marshall Moore, spends time off the set of *High School Musical 3: Senior Year* with cast members (left to right): Ryne Sanborn, Vanessa Hudgens, Zac Efron, Kaycee Stroh, Chris Warren, and Matt Prokop.

Game," and others by an array of songwriters that included Matthew Gerrard, Robbie Nevil, David Cham, David Lawrence, and Drew Seeley. To all of this was added the energetic choreography by Charles Klapow, Bonny Story, and the film's director, Kenny Ortega. *High School Musical* was the film that brought stardom to Zac Efron, earning him the Teen Choice Award for Breakout Star. For Hudgens, the high profile given her by the series led to a recording contract and to acting and producing for Netflix.

The East High School cafeteria was the ideal space for dance numbers, and the auditorium sequences were filmed at the nearby Murray High School, as East High's auditorium was undergoing renovation. East High's roof was completely decorated for the many scenes filmed there. So attractive was the design that faculty and students recommended that it be left with its plants and trees, just as it was dressed for the film. For *High School Musical 2* (2007), the story takes place during the students' summer vacation, when they are employed at an upscale golf course. For this, Moore escorted director Ortega to Utah's nine major golf courses, finally settling on the Entrata, an upscale club in the vicinity of St. George in the southwestern desert of the state, adjacent to Snow Canyon State Park. Even amidst their luxurious surroundings, the traditional high schooler's social life of romance, rejection, envy, jealousy, and reconciliation played out once again between plenty of musical dance numbers. *High School Musical 3: Senior Year* (2008) was the only one of the series to be released theatrically, a reflection of the soaring popularity of the first two television movies. The filming budget tripled the amount spent on each of the previous entries and it ended up with a worldwide box office gross of more than $225 million dollars. The pangs of graduation and planning for life and what to do and where to go afterward were temporarily assuaged by bigger-than-ever musical numbers. It was, therefore, no surprise when "specials" were made for Disney Channel, to be followed by four seasons of *High School Musical: The Musical: The Series,* that aired beginning in November 2019, and all filmed in Utah, except for season three that, for story reasons, was located in Los Angeles.

One of the series' biggest boosters—and of moviemaking in Utah—was Governor Huntsman. During the filming of the first two television movies, cast members were invited to the Governor's Mansion to perform at major dinner events. The opportunity to familiarize Utah legislators—from whom development and rebate incentive monies were appropriated—with Hollywood celebrities and movie-making was not lost on the Utah Film Commission. "For *High School Musical 3,*" remembers Moore, who was there, "we were able to take a good portion of the Utah Legislature to the set, meet the actors, and watch the filming of the dance numbers. Many of the major dance scenes were done in the Jon M. Huntsman Center, named for the governor's father, on the campus of the University of Utah, and in the auditorium at the Murray High School." It had its intended effect. "The popularity of that movie really raised eyebrows to legislators," Moore continued, "and the knowledge that its fame pointed all eyes to Utah, where all of them were filmed." The politicians discovered that 90 percent of the crew and supporting players were from Utah and that the incentive rebates applied only to those Utah residents hired who worked on the crew and the cast as well. "When you have those questions addressed right on the set, where they can see the results, it leaves a big impression on them. They can also understand that the economic benefits translate into the other services as well: catering, rental facilities, and computer graphics at Utah's Silicon Slopes."[5]

Following his term as governor, Huntsman served as ambassador of the United States to China and later to Russia. On one of his diplomatic trips to a remote village, he noticed a little girl emerging from a hut wearing a silk-screened shirt branded with the logotype of *High School Musical.* "She didn't speak English at all," as Moore recalled hearing it from the governor, "but he was able to have a conversation with her and he told her that he came from the place where *High School Musical* was filmed. He then realized the international impact that the movie had and the commerce generated by the film industry, as well as by the people wanting to come to Utah to see the locations."[6]

The spirit of *High School Musical,* in all its iterations, from 2006 to 2024, still lives at East High School where, on occasion, tours are given of this venerated location to the high school set. The shocking-pink colored school locker used by the film's primary antagonist, Sharpay Evans (played with ripe spitefulness by Ashley Tisdale), is still at East High. An annual school lottery allows one lucky student to use it during that school year.

Bailey Young poses beside Sharpay Evan's locker still used by students at East High School in Salt Lake City in this 2023 photo.

TOUCHED BY AN ANGEL

"Angels were in the air," remembered Jonathan Levin, once head of drama series development at CBS, from an interview in 2003. "There was an angel on the cover of *Time* magazine. It just seemed like we were entering times when people's sense of spirituality was greatly heightened. Quite frankly, our idea was just to do a twist on *Highway to Heaven* that had a bit more attitude and bite to it."[1] The television airwaves, as well as American popular culture, seemed fascinated with the idea of angels ministering to confused and often problem-ridden mortals during the 1980s and 1990s. Michael Landon's aforementioned *Highway to Heaven* and the long-running series *7th Heaven*, about a minister and his family dealing with the everyday concerns of raising a large family, were the most successful of these entries, followed by shorter-lived series *Heaven Help Us*, *Amen*, and *Nothing Sacred*. John Masius, writer and producer of *St. Elsewhere* and *L.A. Law*, created the pilot for a new kind of angels series, *Touched by An Angel*. It featured two female angels, the blunt-talking angel supervisor Tess (played by African-American singer Della Reese) and her soft-spoken Irish trainee, Monica (Roma Downey), sent to earth to help mortals in crisis. CBS president Andy Hill and producer Bob Gros liked the idea but thought that Masius's vision was not quite the show CBS wanted and offered the job to the young, successful television writer-producer Martha Williamson, who was also a committed Christian. "I watched the pilot. I didn't like the pilot," Williams said to *60 Minutes* host Ed Bradley in 1997. "The angels didn't like each other. They were irreverent."[2] She turned down the offer to be executive producer and writer of the series but advised Hill that they should find someone who could make the angels more friendly and positive. Over time, Williamson had second thoughts about helming the program and reapproached CBS executives and pleaded her case. "If I were going to do it, I would put my heart into it. And that meant writing only what I could stand behind: that angels were messengers of God, not ends in themselves. The angels couldn't be fairies flapping their wings and granting wishes. God had to be Someone to reckon with. And at the end of each episode, the angels wouldn't win. God would. And we would, because people of faith are tired of being depicted on television as stereotypes, mass murderers, abusive parents, fanatics. I was convinced that a show that took spirituality seriously would attract an intelligent, rational audience of people for whom faith has a place in their lives. I explained that we had to ask the hard questions every week. 'If God is god, then why did my baby die? Why did my marriage end? Where was God when I needed Him?' We had to meet head-on the inevitable criticism that faith is a cop-out to avoid dealing with reality, that belief in God is the opiate of the masses. Instead, I told them faith is the most powerful weapon we have. And if audiences could turn off the television at night feeling inspired and empowered, they'd come back next week, and they'd bring more with them."[3]

CBS hired Williamson as the series executive producer and head writer, as well as her MoonWater Productions, and she immediately created a completely new pilot episode, retaining only Downey and Reese in the cast. She then headed for Salt Lake City, where the first episode had to be produced in three and a half weeks. Production head Gros had already explored possible locations for the series and had chosen Salt Lake City as the headquarters. "The reason that CBS chose Utah is pretty basic," said Marshall Moore, location manager for the series for most of its nine seasons. "Every episode of *Touched by An Angel* is in a different town. There was no home for the angels. No standing sets. Utah's versatility and the strength of its crew base and the infrastructure was what drove the decision. You could film in a small-town environment. In the next, you are shooting in Manhattan, and make the couple of blocks in downtown

Salt Lake City look like it."[4] Initially operating out of rooms in a downtown Holiday Inn, Williamson remembered the reputation of the new series was "6-and-out," a reference to the initial order for six episodes and then cancellation. However, we were the little show that could, and *did*."[5]

The first episode, "The Southbound Bus," filmed in Utah and aired September 21, 1994. Following the main title sequence, played to Della Reese's vocal of "I'll Walk with You," its first scene was at a bus stop in the middle of nowhere. Angel-in-training Monica was met by supervisor Tess to begin her earthy mission, only to be met by what Williamson describes as the show's first miracle. "It was so unbearably hot. Crew members were keeling over from dehydration," wrote Williamson. "Finally, Della, an ordained minister as well as a great singer and actor, stepped away from the set and into the desert. She held out her hands to the sky and invoked the following prayer: 'Lord, we need a cloud. And we need one now. Thank you, Father.' She walked back to the cameras as if nothing had happened, but there was something about the way she had just ordered up the weather that made us feel that indeed something was about to happen. Honest to God, fifteen minutes later, there wasn't just a cloud. There was cloud cover over the entire Salt Lake Valley. The

The "Indigo Angel" episode from season two featured five iconic blues artists as guest stars. Standing: Dr. John, Al Hirt, Della Reese, Hal Linden, BB King, John Dye, Roma Downey, Al Jarreau. Kneeling: Franklin Lett Jr. (Della's husband) and executive producers Martha Williamson and Jon Anderson.

temperature dropped ten degrees and we finished the day in the cool summer evening. The astonished crew stared at Della, who just shrugged. 'It's a God thing.' And she smiled."[6]

Jon Andersen, the line producer sent by CBS to monitor expenses for the budding series, remarked that he didn't unpack his luggage for the first seven episodes, so tenuous was the future of *Touched by An Angel* to the network. Gradually, the show's ratings increased. CBS ordered a seventh episode and then more. For its first Christmas episode, "Fear Not," the series moved from its Saturday night slot to Sunday night for the first time, in place of the popular *Murder She Wrote* series. Its star, Angela Lansbury, introduced *Touched by An Angel* to audiences, and ratings took the series into the top 20 on television. The wisdom of choosing its Utah base was confirmed when Utah Film Commissioner Leigh von der Esch "recognized the potential of the series immediately," remembered Williamson. "She was a terrific liaison between the city and the state, becoming a de facto crew member in some ways, a department head, part of the team. She was a godmother to our show. We always knew that if we had a challenge, we could call Leigh and she would help us find a way to resolve it."[7]

Leigh von der Esch, managing director, Utah Office of Tourism and Film 2005–2013.

Williamson quickly took to the Utah locale. "We had something special once we saw Salt Lake and discovered how we could use it as a canvas for anything that came to us. One week we'd be shooting an outer space story and two weeks later we would be doing the assassination of Abraham Lincoln. We attracted a large list of talent who wanted to be in the series and we could bring them out quickly if they were in Los Angeles. It wasn't a huge schlep across the country."[8] Among the approximately 200 enviable talent that guest-starred on *Touched by An Angel* during its nine seasons were Henry "Hank" Aaron, Muhammad Ali, Maya Angelou, Carol Burnett, Kirk Douglas, Patrick Duffy, Faye Dunaway, Gregory Harrison, Melissa Gilbert, James Earl Jones, Brian Keith, B.B. King, Diane Ladd, Janet Leigh, Angela Lansbury, Darrin McGavin, Gerald McRaney, Rosa Parks, Mandy Patinkin, Debbie Reynolds, Sally Ride, John Ritter, Randy Travis, Cecily Tyson, and Stephanie Zimbalist. Casting director David Giella noted that, "From the gate, people were intrigued by the concept. Then when they read the scripts, that would usually seal the deal. They would read it and say, 'Oh, my God, it's not schmaltz! It's smart!' That helped a lot. On *Touched by An Angel,* the guest lead is in fifty of the fifty-two script pages. It has always offered actors something in terms of guest roles that they were never offered before. When you're the guest star, you are the lead—and the angels are supporting players in your story. It's the guest stars who drive the stories."[9]

Distance from Hollywood also proved to the young writer and executive producer that CBS was finally on board with their talented team, both in front of as well as behind the cameras. "I had never executive produced a show before and to have done it essentially out of the Hollywood eye was a gift," said Williamson. "Studio executives are notorious for just showing up on sets and driving people crazy, but we were blessed with distance. Nobody wanted to fly to Salt Lake on a whim. We were blessed with trust. CBS trusted us to make these shows on-time and on-budget and we did. We never, ever had an executive come to the set in Salt Lake City other than to say hello. No one ever came to fix a problem."[10]

Because the series was not tied to a single standing set, in contrast to traditional episodic television, the diverse story locations called for continual advanced scouting throughout Utah. The challenges were momentous. In the season four episode "Netherlands," the now-experienced angel Monica is introduced to her own trainee angel, Gloria, that introduced Valerie Bertinelli to the series. However, Monica is traumatized, and her faith is tested by an intentional bombing of a downtown office building resulting in numerous casualties including a mother and daughter whom she and her new angel trainee were there to help. But where can one blow up a building in a busy urban metropolis? "Oh, how hard that was for us," Moore recalled. "I approached the city about using a building in downtown Salt Lake City that was right across the street from the Federal Building. They said that it is right on the cusp of being torn down, but if we could be quick, we could use it. It was already gutted at this point, everything was out of there, but from the outside it still looked like an active functioning structure. The street was closed off and patrolled by six police officers right in the afternoon of a busy workday. All of our special effects guys had demolition experience. They rigged it all over and made sure that it was properly vented so that no other harmful effects arose from the explosion. Rick Josephson, our special effects head, did a great job of pulling that off, but he created a monster blast. The whole building came down. It knocked out a window at the Federal Building. The windows on homes in a residential area north of downtown shook with the blast."[11]

Left: The fiery explosion of a downtown Salt Lake City building scheduled for demolition enabled this scene in the "Netherlands" episode to be realized. Above: The aftermath of the explosion done by the special effects team of *Touched by An Angel*.

The second major location used in "Netherlands" was crucial to Monica's narrative. Following the explosion, Monica sets out on foot to the isolation of the desert to contemplate her future, where she is picked up by Satan (cunningly played by Mandy Patinkin), who then takes her to a red rock outcrop overlooking a vast canyon gorge. "Come work for me," he intones to the emotionally depleted angel. Mimicking Satan's temptation of Christ during his forty days in the wilderness, this leisure-suited, smooth-talking Satan challenges Monica to jump off the precipice, assuring her that he'll be down below to catch her. Moore, for this dramatic scene, secured the stunning location at Utah's Dead Horse Point State Park, southwest of Moab and a four-hour drive from Salt Lake City. However, there was a problem. "We were about to film Monica, on the edge of Dead Horse Point, against this astounding vista of the red rocks and the Colorado River hundreds of feet below," said Williamson, "when we were informed that some rare hawk was mating with another hawk, and we wouldn't be able to have a helicopter aloft to film in any way that would potentially injure these birds. We called Leigh von der Esch. Not long afterward, we were able to get our impressive aerial pull-out shot of Monica. The hawks mated and we were overjoyed." Williamson remembered this moment with delight, "The two of them, Marshall and Leigh, were a ballet to behold. They worked in concert with each other so beautifully."[12] The scene at Dead Horse Point was so impressive that the next episode opened at the same site showing Tess and Monica, sitting on red upholstered chairs atop Dead Horse Point, discussing the lessons learned after her successful rejection of Satan's temptation.

Over the nine years that *Touched by An Angel* called Utah home, episodes represented myriad story locations: the battlefields of Europe, the Sahara Desert (with the salt

Library square at the Salt Lake City Public Library stands in for Tiananmen Square in "The Spirit of Liberty Moon" episode.

Soldiers patrolling the Beijing marketplace in the "The Spirit of Liberty Moon" episode redressed in suburban Salt Lake City.

flats of the Great Salt Lake standing in for Northern Africa), outer space, and then there was a special two-part episode centered on Beijing, China, and the events surrounding the tense confrontation of protestors and Chinese military in Tiananmen Square in 1989. The planning for filming it all in Salt Lake City became a major operation. "The production designer, Diane Millet, and I flew to Los Angeles to meet with Martha Williamson," recalled Moore. "This *never* happens in episodic television," he added. Millet presented her plans and photographs on how to dress up buildings in downtown Salt Lake City and in other areas to represent downtown Beijing, all of which met with Williamson's and CBS's approval. "The 'hero shot,' with all of the bicycles going down the street, was on Regent Street north of Salt Lake City's downtown Gallivan Center. It took that entire block to be cordoned off," remembered Moore. "Two days before, we hung every possible decoration on the buildings to look like Beijing. It took a herculean effort just to get permission to do that. These were big corporations, but by that time the series was an established presence. That helped considerably. There was another area on the west side of town, a nightclub called Brick's. They had a curved alley, made of all brick, so we closed that off and dressed it up like a marketplace in Beijing. The Chinese-themed International Peace Gardens, south of downtown in Salt Lake City, and one of two peace gardens in the United States, was also an important filming site." The other challenge was how to create Tiananmen Square where

This production shot shows the central character Bai Ling (played by Jean Chang) vocally protesting Chinese oppression in Tiananmen Square, actually on the steps of the Salt Lake City Public Library, in the special two-part episode, "The Spirit of Liberty Moon," from season four.

the climactic events occurred in 1989. "We did that in Library Square in downtown Salt Lake City, which at the time was a big flat concrete square," said Moore. "There were government buildings to the north that looked very nondescript that we were able to dress appropriately."[13]

In season three of *Touched by An Angel*, the opening episode, "Promised Land," aired in September 1996, and served as the pilot for a spin-off series by the same name, also created by Williamson, who also was its executive producer. Her co-executive producer was Ernie Wallengren. It starred Gerald McRaney and Wendy Phillips as the Greenes, who were informed by Tess that God wanted their family to travel the United States to help those in need. The well-reviewed series, also made by MoonWater Productions for CBS, ran for three seasons and all of it was filmed in Utah. Astonishingly, Williamson wrote many of and oversaw the writing of all seventy episodes, concurrently with her work on *Touched by An Angel.*

During its run from 1994 through 2003, and totaling 213 episodes, *Touched by An Angel* was nominated for eleven Primetime Emmy Awards as well as nominations for Downey and Reese. It had often been referred to as a series in the fantasy category, to which Williamson responded, "We're not out there doing fantasy. We are doing something that is real and true. The stories are straight out of the headlines. People recognize the similarities in our shows with what is in the news. *Touched by An Angel* doesn't offer hope by saying 'this is it.' God is it. We don't have all the answers on *Touched by An Angel.* In a show about angels, you have to acknowledge that God exists and by doing that, it asks a lot of questions. We don't treat it as a fantasy. We treat it as a drama about real people with real problems and a real God who is there to help them solve them."[14]

Throughout her nine years in Salt Lake City, Williamson remarked frequently about the reception her team received whenever they came to a neighborhood to film. "The neighbors would come out of their homes, put up folding chairs, and would bring us cookies. There's nothing like Mormon baking to keep you going on a long shoot. It was really hard to leave. Salt Lake City is where I met my husband, Jon Andersen, and where we started our family. No other productions created more hours of entertainment in Utah than *Touched by An Angel* and *Promised Land*. As a result, the production of these series presented an economic opportunity that the state hadn't had before, which was a consistent source of revenue and employment for those in the state. There was a work ethic among those people in Salt Lake City that I had never seen before. We had a joke that you always build in a certain amount of money in your budget to cover loss, which is code for people walking off with stuff. We could always know that we had a bit of a buffer in the budget because nobody walked off with anything. Nobody showed up hung over on Monday morning at 10:00 or missed a call. People were willing to work later if we had a weather challenge or a production challenge because we all believed in the message of the series. The phrase, 'We are all in this one, big family' is overused in Hollywood but, to this day, we stay in touch with all of the folks who worked on that show, and with many of those from the show."[15]

The end of the successful run of *Touched by An Angel* in the late spring of 2003 was perhaps known from the beginning, at least it seems that way, according to Williamson's account of Della Reese, when that venerable vocalist and ordained minister showed up for the mandatory insurance medical examination before the start of the series in 1994. Following the successful exam, the attending nurse reported to Williamson that Reese refused to sign the insurance form stating that the series duration was for six episodes, the initial number ordered by CBS. The nurse explained the reason. "Miss Reese won't sign it until I change it to say ten years," the nurse continued. "She says it's a God thing." Williamson recalled at the time she wrote of this moment in 1997, Della said that she believed in herself. The newly minted executive producer then remembered of that day that Reese "stood up in her little paper gown and said she believed in me as well. And most importantly she believed God had brought us all together. I turned to the nurse, 'I guess you'd better change the form. If Della says ten years, then that's what we ought to plan on.'"[16] Nine years was pretty close. Perhaps not only Reese, but Williamson might conclude that, in Reese's catchphrase uttered in numerous episodes of the series, this, too, "is a God thing."

Roma Downey participated in civic affairs, including carrying the torch to the Olympic site for the 2002 Salt Lake City Olympic Games.

Overview of the Jerusalem set at The Church of Jesus Christ of Latter-day Saints Motion Picture Studio–South Campus, situated on seven hundred and twenty five acres at Goshen, Utah.

THE CHOSEN

Of the more than eighty motion pictures and the television series covered in detail in this book about filming locations and their significance to a production, none is more unusual than that of the streaming phenomenon that is *The Chosen* and the influence of its Utah location on its creator, writers, cast, and crew. This dramatized chronicle of the ministry of Jesus of Nazareth, along with that of his ancient Apostles has, as of 2023, attracted more than 420 million episode views worldwide.[1]

The story of how *The Chosen* was able to be filmed at the Utah location on which a standing set of Jerusalem was, according to its series creator, "closer to Jesus's presence in first-century Jerusalem than Jerusalem is now"[2] is one that involves myriad twists and turns. The tale includes business people of multiple faiths, an innovative method to assure ongoing funding, a lawsuit from four major motion picture studios, a bankruptcy, a desperate public appeal by the series creator to his viewers, a spiritual prompting for a critically timed telephone call, and, according to the series creator and its production company heads, the intervention of that very Being about whose life and teachings *The Chosen* was created.

These many strands of converging people and events began with VidAngel—an entertainment company cofounded by two southern Idaho farm boys, Jeff and

Neal Harmon—that began as an advertising agency, then a provider of clean, stand-up comedy programs streaming under the name *Dry Bar Comedy* that, according to its owners, "created the largest body of stand-up comedy in the world"[3] and that has been viewed, as of 2023, 4.5 billion times. An additional service offered by VidAngel that attracted an even wider audience was their providing copies of existing, commercially produced Hollywood motion pictures that, through a proprietary filtering process, removed offensive content and language from box office champions, including *Titanic* and other mainstream hits. So successful were the results of this venture that the Provo, Utah-based company faced a massive copyright infringement lawsuit in 2016 from Disney Enterprises, Inc., Lucasfilm, 20th Century Fox, and Warner Bros. Played out in the media as a David-and-Goliath confrontation, the long-running suit that began in 2016 resulted in a $62.4 million judgment against VidAngel in 2019, with the company filing for Chapter 11 bankruptcy protection so they could appeal and reorganize their business model.

In the midst of this legal wrangling in Utah, Dallas Jenkins, a young evangelical Christian with dreams of making movies, was on the back side of the commercially unsuccessful release of *The Resurrection of Gavin Stone* (2017) that he directed. As a gift to his local Harvest Bible Chapel in the Chicago suburb of Elgin, Illinois, Jenkins wrote and directed *The Shepherd,* an eighteen-minute short film on the birth of Jesus Christ, filmed on a friend's farm in Marengo, two blocks from the Jenkins home.

The Harmon brothers were still negotiating their company's survival in the wake of a preliminary judgment against VidAngel when chief of content officer Jeff Harmon

Director and series creator Dallas Jenkins directing a scene at the Pool of Bethesda. Filmed during the 2020 COVID pandemic.

received a link to *The Shepherd* from VidAngel's executive producer Matthew Faraci on September 17, 2017, that simply read "screener." "Watching it generated a flood of ideas that poured into my mind that this would be the first project, an Angel original, that wasn't a comedy," remembered Harmon. "There was a flood of information that just came to my mind for the next few hours and into the evening of how to launch it, how to crowdfund it, how to get it to the point that we could fund a series based on it." Jeff passed it onto his brother, Neal, who was initially resistant to such programming for their for-profit company—that is, until he watched it the next day. "It was like I was in this other world, and that I was there at the birth of Jesus," said Neal. "Jeff asked me what I thought? I said that I think this is why we created this company. We saw that it needed to happen because of the impact that it had on us when we watched it."[4]

The day after viewing *The Shepherd,* the Harmons were about to phone Jenkins to discuss a possible series when Jeff discussed with Neal the realities they were up against. "We are filing for bankruptcy; we are involved in a lawsuit with the biggest entertainment company in the world. We do filtering, crowdfunding, and we are members of The Church of Jesus Christ of Latter-day Saints," Jeff said. "All strikes against us." Nevertheless, a two-hour telephone call with Jenkins elicited from the filmmaker an invitation: "Let's talk about it. I'm interested. I'll come out to Utah." Jenkins and his wife, Amanda, made the trip to Utah and attended a Latter-day Saint church service with the Harmons. Jeff remarked, "Dallas said that Mormons were normal, having been told by others about weird seances and oddities that didn't square with Christianity." By the end of the visit, Jeff and Neal declared to Dallas and Amanda: "We want this to be our *Game of Thrones,* our *House of Cards,* but a series with a moral compass. They said yes." However, before the couple left for the airport to return to Illinois, the brothers disclosed the Chapter 11 bankruptcy protection filing within the next two weeks. "You've got to know this because that is what we are facing," said Neal. "It was a good thing that Amanda was there because Dallas's face went white. Then, Amanda said, 'Ah, what the heck, let's do it.'"[5]

"I had a few random conversations with some faith-based companies about my idea for the show, but with no studios," remembered Jenkins. "The Harmons were the first ones to see the short film as a possible pilot and fundraising device for my show idea. . . . I figured that it would never happen because no one was lining up to do a Jesus show. . . . The Harmons saw the potential, got the vision, and had the crazy crowdfunding idea that I thought was odd."[6] Under the aegis of Angel Studios, *The Chosen* became "the king of crowdfunding among TV shows," that included a provision of "equity crowdfunding," permitting donors to have a share in the profits.[7] The lawsuit involving VidAngel was not settled until 2020. Angel Studios was created in the spring of 2021, following the sale of the VidAngel filtering technology. Darral Eves, a Latter-day Saint, joined Jenkins in founding *The Chosen* company, and Loaves & Fishes Productions.

For the next eighteen months, a crowdfunding campaign raised more than $10 million to get production of *The Chosen* underway. The cast, led by Shahar Isaac (Peter), Jonathan Roumie (Jesus), Elizabeth Tabish (Mary Magdalene), and Paras Patel (Matthew), was assembled with the scripts for the initial episodes written by Tyler Thompson, Dallas Jenkins, and Ryan Swanson, with Jenkins directing the episodes. During late 2018, episodes one through four of *The Chosen* were completed in Texas at a replica of the ancient Galilean city of Capernaum, an existing tourist attraction in Weatherford, Texas. Those episodes were streamed, on-demand and for free, thanks to an innovative fundraising program, Pay It Forward. A total of seven seasons were forecast to take the Biblical narrative through Jesus's crucifixion and resurrection, and the missionary activities of the Apostles. The groundswell reaction to this pathbreaking production was encouraging, especially during the pandemic when viewing was offered on *The Chosen* app for free.

Funding was sufficient to move ahead for episodes five through eight of season one that were filmed in Texas

Jesus (Jonathan Roumie) with Peter (Shahar Isaac), John (George H. Xanthis), and Matthew (Paras Patel) on the Jerusalem set at Goshen, Utah.

during the late spring and early summer of 2019. The growing worldwide viewer demand was met by the season's remaining episodes streamed on *The Chosen* app, beginning November 26, 2019. It was then that a crisis developed, not one of audience size or even funding. They had no place to film the second season. *The Chosen* needed a Jerusalem for the series to continue. "The Weatherford set was very small," said Jenkins. "And we had shot all that we could shoot there, turning the camera at every angle to make it look different. We were looking for land in Texas. We even looked at a set where something had been filmed years ago, but it had disintegrated."[8]

In the search for their Jerusalem, Jenkins and his team scoured Europe and the Middle East, going to Malta, Bulgaria, and Morocco, where films with a religious theme, such as Franco Zeffirelli's *Jesus of Nazareth* (1977), had been filmed. They even visited Israel, but it was too urbanized and crowded with tourists, making it impractical for filming. With the onset of COVID-19, local restrictions and the high cost of locating a cast and production team for months at a time in a foreign country were prohibitive. In frustration, the series creator, cowriter, and director concluded, "I had no other options. I didn't have a place to film. We were genuinely at the edge of the Red Sea. There was nowhere else to go. I was so confused."[9]

Enter Utah, right in the vicinity of the Provo headquarters of Angel Studios. Ten years before the crisis faced by Jenkins and Angel Studios, The Church of Jesus Christ of Latter-day Saints had completed a sprawling outdoor Jerusalem set on 725 acres of desert land near Goshen, Utah, about twenty-five miles from Angel Studios. The facility is designated as The Church of Jesus Christ of

Dallas Jenkins directing Pilate (Yoshi Barrigas).

Below: Jesus (Jonathan Roumie) and Matthew (Paras Patel), acting as scribe during Jesus's composing the Sermon on the Mount on the property surrounding the Jerusalem set.

Latter-day Saints Motion Picture Studio–South Campus. Its purpose was to film an ongoing series of short video productions on the life and ministry of Jesus Christ for the church's worldwide Seminary and Institute of Religion programs. Jenkins had been shown photographs of the set more than a year before by his company's partner and executive producer Darral Eves. Jenkins was dazzled by what he saw. However, he was resistant to step foot on it. "I don't want to see it," he told Brad Pelo, a businessman and enthusiast of *The Chosen*. "Don't do this to me." It wasn't until June 25, 2020, that Jenkins walked the entire set for the first time, accompanied by Neal Harmon, Eves, Pelo, and a few others to evaluate for himself this professionally built and creatively weathered movie set—complete with courtyards, pools, grottos, ramparts, and marketplaces designed specifically for motion picture production. "It was the greatest set I'd ever seen," Jenkins remembered from that visit. "I felt God pressing on my heart, telling me that lives are going to be changed because of the work that you will do on the set. I don't have that impression very often, but I felt very strongly that good things had happened on this set so far, that a lot of blood, sweat and tears went into building this set and it hasn't been used to its full potential yet."[10]

According to Pelo, days after Jenkins toured the Jerusalem set, a proposal for its use was submitted to Sheri Dew, executive vice president of Deseret Management, and with whom Pelo had previously worked. Dew forwarded the proposal to administrators at Church headquarters. The answer that came back stunned Jenkins and the Harmon brothers. "They said no," Jenkins remembers telling his wife, Amanda. There were COVID restrictions. The set had not previously been let out to other organizations. "My wife is very in tune with the Spirit, and she said that God had put it on her heart that we will be working on the set. God is taking us to the edge of the Red Sea." Pelo's wife telephoned Jenkins to tell him, "Dallas, it isn't over." To both, Jenkins replied, "Will you stop, please? You're killing me. We have to find a place to film in two months."[11]

During this time, friends of the Harmons had distributed DVD copies of season one of *The Chosen* to Church leaders at all levels, including those in the faith's leading council, the Quorum of the Twelve Apostles. For months prior, VidAngel had mounted a massive publicity campaign to spread the word about *The Chosen*. "We had influencers across Utah promoting *The Chosen* at Easter," described Jeff Harmon. However, it was now July, the month during which the busy globe-trotting LDS Church administrators broke from their busy schedules for vacation. Neal Harmon recalled, "We were getting nos from everyone. I knelt down and prayed, 'God, this is not happening. We need Your help. What more can I do?' And the answer was, 'There's nothing more you can do. I need Dallas to do one more thing.' I called Jeff and shared this answer with him. Meanwhile, not even the director of BYU-tv, the Church's worldwide satellite television station, could give them hope."[12]

Oblivious to Neal Harmon's impressions, Jenkins was, as he described it, "desperate and confused." To find solace and meditation, he returned to the farm in Illinois, where he had filmed *The Shepherd*, to pray and to meditate. This led him to post a Facebook video that then migrated to YouTube on July 6, 2020, appealing to his audience to pray for the breakthrough needed to continue the series. "I am in a difficult place where I don't know the future," Jenkins intoned to his viewers from the farm site. "I don't even know the immediate future. I have a lack of clarity, and I have a lack of wisdom about the next six months and potentially the next few years. As of right now, I can't tell you where we are going to film our show next. I can't tell you even if we are going to film in 2020." As thunder could be heard on the video and rain beginning to fall amidst the gathering clouds, Jenkins concluded, "And, as the captain of the ship, over the next few weeks, I have to make some decisions that are going to tremendously [affect] potentially the next four or five years. And, I don't have answers."[13]

As Jeff Harmon recalled, one of the Harmons' friends who had made a delivery of the season one videos to the office of M. Russell Ballard, the acting president of the Church's Quorum of the Twelve Apostles, felt a prompting on the day that Jenkins posted his video on YouTube to call President Ballard. The call was made. "All of the leadership was out on vacation, but President Ballard was in his office," remembered that individual relating the story to Harmon. "His secretary said, 'I watched the DVD that you gave me last weekend. I'll talk to President Ballard.'" She later returned the call. "'President Ballard has just watched it.'"[14] Then, according to Pelo, President Ballard promised to call Sheri Dew to see what he could do to encourage another review of *The Chosen*'s proposal.[15] A Zoom meeting was soon arranged between Jenkins and Pelo and two members of the Quorum of the Twelve Apostles, Jeffrey Holland and David Bednar, who said that they would forward the proposal to the Church's First Presidency, headed by President Russell M. Nelson. "I think that they [Elders Holland and Bednar] sensed a lack of pretense in me," said Jenkins. "I think that they concluded that I was someone who had surrendered to God's will. The next day, the First Presidency said yes. Amanda was nonplussed. She knew it all the time. I think that God was waiting for me to surrender and say, 'okay,' with whatever He wanted me to do."[16]

Within days the approval was made official, and the agreement drawn up with The Church of Jesus Christ of Latter-day Saints and *The Chosen*. Jeff related to his brother Neal, "I think the reason that it happened this way is because of the opposition that Dallas encountered. God had to show him and us, all of us, because we were all facing so much, that this was Him, not us."[17]

Jenkins reflected, "It was within ten days of posting the video that I was in Utah. I remember people saying after I had posted the video that they started praying and instantly it was as if God was saying, 'I was just waiting for you to surrender. I will part the Red Sea and you will know that it's Me.'"[18]

Concerning the Goshen movie set, Jenkins identified five benefits that it has given to the production of the series: First, for both economic and aesthetic advantages, the set and surrounding property reduced the need for special visual effects. "You don't have to use visual effects when there is something tangible and authentic. You can never convince me that you can replace all of that with visual effects. What's interesting in Utah is that it's not just the mountains that are extraordinarily beautiful, but the space between you and the mountains. You can see them clearly, untouched by pollution or forests. When we are out in Goshen you can see the actors and the set design and whatever we are doing in a scene, it has a full opportunity to breathe. We don't have to shoot around certain things, recreate, or remove anything from the frame. This physical location becomes this massive palate on which to paint, and Utah is unique to almost any location in the entire country where the palate is so wide and so big. You have the room and more space in which to paint and in which to place things intentionally as opposed to something that is there that you wish wasn't there and you're going to have to remove it. That they have preserved those hundreds of acres makes our job that much easier."[19]

Second, Jenkins says there is something uniquely "spiritual" about the Utah property on which *The Chosen* is filmed. "That's the beauty of Goshen," Jenkins told the *Deseret News*. "You don't feel like you're in the middle of industry. You feel like you're in God's country in many ways. I don't have to walk far to get some alone time and feel like I can connect with God each day. . . . Utah is clearly 'Chosen' country."[20] Jenkins further confirmed his sense about the nature of the set. "I do believe that there is something transcendent and spiritual about the location that is owned by people who want to make God known. I saw a woman get out of her car in the parking lot. She saw me and started crying and said, 'I have been painting the sets of your show for two years and I haven't had a chance to meet you. Thank you!' For her, it's her life's mission, her life's calling. She said, 'I'm contributing to Jesus being known.' That doesn't apply to everybody. Not everybody who is on our crew is a believer and not everybody who provides the equipment is a believer. Not even everybody in Utah is a believer, but I do think that there is something special about that property, regardless of our theological differences. It is owned by people who want to make God known. The set was built by people who want to take you back there and you feel that. A location has a physical value, meaning that you don't have to do too much work to make it look good. It gives you that much more time and resources to focus on the actors and the story. You can let the setting support you as opposed to the setting getting in the way. At least for my project, I think there is something spiritually connective about this location and the people that work in it that makes a difference in the show."[21]

Jenkins, as well as Jeff and Neal Harmon, referenced the significance of the prayer offered by Elder Bednar at the on-site dedication of the Jerusalem set on its completion on August 2, 2011, nearly a decade before Jenkins set foot on it. After praying for those who in the future will view the New Testament films to be made there by the Church to "have their hearts touched and their faith in Thy Son strengthened," Elder Bednar then specifically mentioned "that those not of our faith will be inspired by the depth of our conviction of and faith in Jesus Christ, that they may understand the purpose for which this facility was constructed, and that they may join us in honoring and worshipping the Savior." Dallas Jenkins remembered being told that Elder Bednar had "prayed that it would be used to make Jesus known and that it would be used as an opportunity to connect with other denominations. It had always been in his heart to share it."[22] Toward the end of Elder Bednar's dedicatory prayer, he said, "We also ask Thee to bless other believers in the film industry that they will be touched and influenced to inquire how this set might be used to further goodness and righteousness throughout the earth."[23]

Third, Jenkins affirms that the set and the surrounding acreage envelops the cast of the series. "When they get to Utah their job is at least twice as easy because they can lose themselves in the location. Acting is always pretending. The goal is to have as few things to pretend as possible. You want to be as authentic as possible. When they are on that set and when they are in the surroundings in Utah, the mountains, and the deserts, and out in the fields, and on the Jerusalem set, it just becomes so much easier because they don't have to pretend themselves in the place. They feel that they are in *the* place."[24]

Fourth, even the writing of the series is affected positively by its place and by its versatility. "When I directed and cowrote season one, I had no idea where we were going to film. The writing has gotten easier once we got the Utah set to think about. We have a scene in season four that takes place in the mountains, which is not something that we do too often and probably would not have done if we didn't know that we had access to these extraordinary mountains. When you are on a lower-budget project, you are limited. Because of Utah, the scenery, and the set, we now get a chance to improve our set. Instead of placing this on an alleyway, we can now put it in a large field in the mountains. The possibilities increase because of our access to the set."[25]

Fifth, Jenkins counts the reaction by the Utah community to the presence of *The Chosen*. "Everyone is so happy that we are here," he remarked. "The people who volunteer to be extras, to help with some of the set construction, serving meals, just want to contribute. Being in Provo, where we spend a majority of our time, the restaurants and the hotels and people in the street ask, 'What can we do to help?' I get the impression that this is a place where kindness and generosity is pretty common. It's clear that they are very happy to have us. Even the folks at the Utah Film Commission and those at the Church ask, 'What can we do to help?'"[26]

That *The Chosen* has not only reached across viewing audiences identifying as Catholic, Protestant, evangelical Christians, Latter-day Saints, and numerous other denominations, but also to many Jews has been one of the many unintended results of the wide popularity of the series. "We sent a couple of teams to Israel because we were hearing repeatedly that the Jewish population in Israel loves the show because, as we present him, Jesus is so Jewish. Many hadn't known that he was, indeed, a rabbi. We lean into his Jewishness in the show so deeply that non-Messianic Jews gravitate to it. They appreciate the respectful consideration that we are giving them and the accurate portrayal that we are giving of the prayers, the traditions, and the Jewishness of his disciples as well. There are many Jews for whom the disciples have been whitewashed in paintings, by prejudice, and so we are seeing a growing engagement in the show."[27]

The Chosen has grown into a worldwide phenomenon boasting 108 million viewers of at least one episode, and Jenkins and his colleagues have been astonished at the many unexpected results from *The Chosen*.[28] "It's all surprising," reflected Jenkins. "I did this little film for my church on my friend's farm in Illinois, just two blocks from my house. But I will tell you this: Jews in Israel liking the show is no more surprising to me than me sitting with members of The Church of Jesus Christ of Latter-day Saints!"[29] Such is the astonishment to the series creator himself in his series that began as small as "a mustard seed," to borrow from a Biblical parable, and has grown into an international phenomenon.

TAYLOR SHERIDAN'S *YELLOWSTONE*

The movie western is a uniquely American creation, born of pioneering and the cultural doctrine of Manifest Destiny. American authors Owen Wister, Louis L'Amour, and Zane Grey thrived on the drama and the conflicts of the westward movement—the outlaws up against the gunslingers, carving civilization out of chaos to make the growing towns like Dodge City, Shinbone, or Tombstone safe for the school marm from the East as well as the parson and his congregation. As in popular literature, the movies cut their sprocket teeth on "cowboys and Indians" in B movies as well as big-screen spectaculars such as Cinerama's *How the West Was Won*.

In June 2018, the Paramount Network aired "Daybreak," the first episode of what would become one of the most talked-about, controversial, and innovative television series ever, as patriarch John Dutton fought to protect his ranch, bordering on Yellowstone National Park, from poachers, politicians, and those on his other border at the Native American reservation with ambitions of developing its land to include casinos and other revenue-generating activities. Politics, sex, loyalty, land use, and ranching life made *Yellowstone* America's drama of the new West. In many ways the same battles were fought as in classic western films starring John Wayne, Henry Fonda, and James Stewart, only in a modern electronic, media-driven, and litigiously saturated, contemporary Montana. *Yellowstone* was the creation of director-writer-producer Taylor Sheridan, whose 2017 feature film *Wind River* focused on modern-day Native American life and the mysterious murder of a young Native American woman on the Wind River Indian Reservation in Wyoming.

Barn and corral used in *Yellowstone* on the Thousand Peaks Ranch east of Park City.

The cabin occupied by Rip Wheeler (Cole Hauser), the foreman of the Dutton Ranch in *Yellowstone*, situated on the Thousand Peaks Ranch near Park City.

Yellowstone was also an outgrowth of Sheridan's directorial debut, who filmed most of *Wind River* in Utah's Wasatch Mountains and small towns spanning two Utah counties. The chain of events leading to *Yellowstone*'s home base in Utah began in January 2016, when Sheridan attended Park City's Sundance Film Festival. At the time, the relatively new Utah Film Studios in Park City staged a vendor's showcase to acquaint moviemakers with facilities and services available to them when filming in Utah. Sheridan showed up and was met by Marshall Moore, who had recently concluded his stint as the director of the Utah Film Commission and was subsequently the studio's vice president of operations and marketing. "He met our local vendors and hired them on the spot," described Moore, "and told us that he would be using the Utah Film Studios as the base of his operations on a new film, *Wind River*."[1] The studio boasted three large soundstages, offices, internet, and parking for the film crews, everything a production company needed to shoot interiors, from which they could then fan out to shoot on locations in the nearby mountains and valleys.

"When principal photography had been completed on *Wind River*," remembered Moore, "Taylor called me

Utah actress Shae Robins in her brief sequence with Kevin Costner and Wendy Moniz in season two's episode "The Reek of Desperation."

into his office and said, 'I'm working on another show. I don't know what it's going to be, whether a limited series or an ongoing series, but it will be called *Yellowstone*. As soon as we get the green light, we're coming here.' That all had to do with his positive experience shooting *Wind River* at the studio and the surrounding country." When the money was in place and a commitment by Paramount Network locked in, Sheridan purchased a home a few miles from the studio. Filming locations in Salt Lake City, the vast private Thousand Peaks Ranch, and the nearby towns of Coalville, Heber, Oakley, and Kamas filled most of Sheridan's requirements. However, the large, baronial log ranch house belonging to Yellowstone Ranch patriarch John Dutton could not be found in Utah, so the Chief Joseph Ranch in Darby, Montana, was used. "*Yellowstone* had two footprints," added Moore. "The bigger one in Utah and the smaller one in Montana. The log home, the barns, and the corrals were in Montana. Everything else was in Utah. While this is not an official statistic, about 70 percent of *Yellowstone* was filmed in Utah during the three seasons that they were here." The entire Utah Film Studios facility was leased by the *Yellowstone* company for all three years. "They kept their offices here year-round even through the hiatus [nonproduction period]. So, we became like family with the crew and the talent, some of whom purchased homes here in the area and sent their children to local schools."[2]

Kevin Costner came to his role as the Dutton Ranch scion from a credible western film pedigree of *Silverado* (1985), *Dances with Wolves* (1990) that earned him Best Director and Best Film Oscars, the title role in *Wyatt Earp* (1994), and both directing and starring in a critical favorite, *Open Range,* in 2003, with Robert Duvall and Annette Benning. He headed the *Yellowstone* cast and functioned as the series executive producer because "I thought it had a chance to be relevant," Costner said in an interview with the Associated Press, "in that this work [ranching] is still going on in America and most people kind of take it for granted how stuff ends up at their dinner table. . . . We're set in one of the most beautiful places in the world, and I think the idea of mountains and rivers captured people's imagination. But it's a working ranch. It's how it's still done. I think it spoke well of that, with its kind of heightened sense of drama." The drama in the series was often created between Dutton and businessman-tribal chief Thomas Rainwater (played by Gil Birmingham), but Costner saw both sides of the argument. "For them [Native Americans] everything has been stripped away, and they've had this little niche called gambling and even that's being nibbled at. Anytime there's money, there's going to be disputes no matter what culture you're dealing with. . . . The political machinations of what happens on the rez (reservation) are equal to what happens on our national stage. There's bitterness and resentment. So who gets left in the lurch? It's the people."[3]

Location filming in Montana at the Dutton Ranch compound blended seamlessly with the outdoor settings in northern Utah, so much so that when Moore was asked about the variety of beautiful Montana scenes they were watching, he simply replied, "Most of Montana is actually Utah."[4] In addition to Utah's alpine valleys standing in for Montana, Salt Lake City was often the site for urban filming, including office buildings and restaurants.

Utah actress Shae Robins provides a slivered perspective from resident talent working on this major television series. Robins played a waitress in what was a brief restaurant scene with Kevin Costner and Wendy Moniz, playing Montana's governor. Robins had but three lines to deliver to John Dutton and the governor as she served them at their table. The then twenty-eight-year-old married resident of the Salt Lake City suburb of South Jordan grew up in Utah and had, by this time, appeared in numerous stage productions, independent feature films, and television commercials. It was an exciting experience to have even a small part in a hit series, and it led to an unexpected friendly encounter with the series' star.

After arriving at the Pallet restaurant in downtown Salt Lake City, Robins went to the trailer for hair and makeup, then proceeded to the set. "The camera was set on this track to go behind the bar, so I had to maneuver behind the camera and the track," remembers Robins four years later. "I was sitting on the floor and had to wait for the camera to move, then get up and maneuver into position and deliver my lines. They were delivering their lines very quietly, and I had to be very attentive to even hear what they were saying as Kevin spoke so softly. What I remembered *not* to do was to look at him until I delivered my lines. There were a couple of takes and we wrapped the shot from that perspective. After that shot, Kevin asked, 'I'm so sorry. Can you tell me your name?' Further takes from other camera perspectives took another hour-and-a-half, just for that short scene. After that, he apologized for having to ask my name again. I said, 'It's Shae,' and without thinking, I teased—which is my nature—'And, yours is?' He stopped, and then paused as if he was thinking to himself, 'Is she serious?' Then, he realized that I was joking, and he smiled and looked at me and said, 'Thank you.' For the rest of the day we had some other interactions, and he was very kind. Even though my appearance lasted only a few seconds, it took a full day to shoot that scene. After we wrapped, I was back in the kitchen. He waited a good four minutes until I came out to tell me, 'Good job,' even though I only had a few lines and nothing impressive. He could have just as easily left so people wouldn't talk to him."[5]

Cast and crew alike savored their Utah stay, dining at local restaurants and enjoying cultural events. A few of them, including Cole Hauser (who played Rip, the ranch foreman), purchased homes in Utah. However, the persistent struggle over money, referenced by Costner in the Associated Press interview, spun its own real-life drama in the efforts by states to capture and keep lucrative movie and television productions. During *Yellowstone*'s third season in early 2018, Sheridan's production company applied to the Utah Film Commission's rebate incentive fund in planning for the filming of season four in Utah. At the same time, other productions were competing for Utah's limited funds. "When the state has several large productions vying for a rebate—as was the case with both *Yellowstone* and the Disney Channel's *High School Musical* remake—the cap limits what each show can receive, regardless of how much it is spending," Salt Lake City's *Deseret News* reported at the time. "Despite receiving around $7 million in rebates for seasons prior, the available kickback for season four was substantially smaller."[6] Moore lamented, "It's as much a business decision as it is a creative decision. It just so happened that, in the same year, Montana had created a $10 million incentive basically designed for *Yellowstone*. So, when their money became available, ours dried up. This was in 2019 and we were hanging onto hope that Governor Huntsman would be reelected and infuse some of the state's money into the Film Commission's budget, but neither outcome occurred. It broke my heart when we had worked so hard to get a show like this here and [we had to let it go] after three seasons with possibly many seasons left in the popular show. As it turned out, there were only two more seasons left, before it was cancelled after season five."[7] The loss of *Yellowstone* to Montana ended the revenue-rich production into the Utah economy that during its three seasons added $80 million.

In July 2019, semitrucks lined up at the Utah Film Studios to remove all of the standing interior sets built for *Yellowstone* and take them up to Montana. It took six weeks to dismantle and move the sets, which included the dining room and study in the Dutton lodge, the bunkhouse, Rainwater's office at the tribal casino, the interior of Monica (Kelsey Asbille) and Casey's (Luke Grimes) trailer from season one, the upstairs of the Dutton lodge including John Dutton's bedroom and those for adult children Beth (Kelly Reilly) and Jamie (Wes Bentley), the Montana Livestock Association office, the Montana governor's office, Beth's office, as well as the "swing sets" (temporary structures that are moved in and out as filming requires).

Marshall Moore used the occasion to invite a Utah State Senator to the studio on the last day of the move to dramatize its negative effect on the loss of commerce to local businesses. "He was shocked to see how big the sets were and how many jobs had been lost because of the move," remembered Moore. Senator Ron Winterton, from the rural eastern part of Utah, decided on that day to work up a bill to get the incentive fund up to a healthy, competitive level. Under his leadership, the Utah Legislature, in 2022, approved Winterton's bill that targeted motion picture production in Utah's rural areas. "If a company filmed in rural Utah," Moore summarized, "they could lay claim to a $12 million pool of money that was in addition to the established $6.79 million, totaling $19 million that the Utah Film Commission had to work with."[8] The net effect is that it has increased film production within the state, even among budget-minded independent filmmakers.

Interior sets of the Dutton ranch house and other structures from *Yellowstone* on the sound stages of Park City's Utah Film Studios.

KEVIN COSTNER'S *HORIZON: AN AMERICAN SAGA*

In mid-June 2023, on the banks of the Colorado River, just north of Moab, Utah, the unfiltered sunlight made the heat seem much warmer than its 82 degrees. However, there was compensation. That same sun caused the billowing white cumulus clouds to glow against the deep blue sky, made even more arresting against the fiery red sandstone mesas and buttes of Professor Valley and the massive sandstone wall across the river marking the natural southern boundary of Arches National Park. It perhaps looked and felt much like this in the fall of 1949—perhaps a bit cooler—when John Ford first came to Professor Valley to make *Wagon Master*. He returned to this remote desert town, as he had promised its 1,300 residents, to bring John Wayne and Maureen O'Hara to make his next western, *Rio Grande,* one of the pair's best. Moab was then off and running in the movie business and it has never stopped.

Luke Wilson and Todd Allen in a scene from *Horizon: An American Saga*, Film 1, filmed in Warner Valley, Hurricane, Utah.

More than seventy years later, this same area, boasting a population of over 5,000, is the setting for another western, such as the legendary John Ford could never have imagined, helmed by a director he never knew. The film's star is also its director, producer, coscreenwriter, and is the same one who financed the entire enterprise.

Old West. New West. Old Westerns. New Westerns. Those were just a few of the thoughts that ran through my head as I spent the day on location in this storied valley, bounded by the Colorado River to the north and Fisher Towers to the south, with the sixty-eight-year-old veteran filmmaker Kevin Costner as he began day 40 making the second installment of what will be a total of four feature-length films that make up his dream project that collectively he names *Horizon: An American Saga.* Costner finished *Horizon 1* on this same locale the previous year. Filming for *Horizon 2* began in the vicinity of St. George, Utah, in late April 2023, then back to finish the feature film in Professor Valley and the distant, forested La Sal Mountains.

Day 40—out of 48 shooting days—began with filming around 9:00 a.m., but preparations were under way hours earlier with costuming, makeup, and hair for the principals and extras. "*Horizon*," Costner explained, "is the story of a town over a fifteen-year period in the post-Civil War era. America's expansion into the West was one that was fraught with peril and intrigue from the natural elements to the interactions with the indigenous peoples who lived on the land and the determination and, at many times, the ruthlessness of those who sought to settle it. *Horizon* tells the story of that journey in an honest and forthcoming way, highlighting the points of view and consequences of the characters' life-and-death decisions."[1]

Horizon began as a dream more than thirty years earlier in 1988, between his breakout film *Silverado* (1985) and his Best Director, Best Picture Oscar-winning smash, *Dances with Wolves* (1990). He called it *Sidewinder.* "This came at a point in my life that when I decided to make a movie, someone would try and do the same one. When I did *Robin Hood: Prince of Thieves* (1991), then two Robin Hoods came out. So, I just changed the title and hid it so that no one could backtrack and find out what *Sidewinder* was. So, I called it *Horizon.*"[2] It is likely that because this story had been "running through my mind a million times" in the intervening years, Costner never looked at a script, cowritten with friend Jon Baird, as he went from scene to scene on at least four different locations during this very long day.

As we walked to what was called "graffiti rock," next to an elevated portion of the trail, Costner stopped and spread out his hands. "Can you feel it?" he asked softly. "This is where the settlers first see the place that they will make their home. When I first came here, it didn't look like much, but I knew at the time that it would work. As I walked this area for quite a while, I could see that this would be the entrance to their valley. Then, we started to see how much we could do here."[3]

First assistant director Phil Patterson added, "When we were here, we did what we call the wagon wheel. That's where you put the pin in, which is the town of Horizon, then you figure out what else you can shoot. The fort, the town, everything. Then, you pinwheel around. From this position we saw that we could shoot in Castle Valley to the south and in Onion Creek. In the beginning—years ago—we scouted New Mexico. Then, we went to Kanab, St. George, and then here in Moab, and to Price. We looked at the east side, the south side, the northeast side of Moab. Kevin realized that in this location he could do three, four, five other things here as opposed to picking a place where he could only do one. It was a slam-dunk." Patterson paused, then said, "He is walking in the footsteps of John Ford. Ford shot from over there in the red cliffs to the end of this valley, to Fisher Towers and back. This was his playground. Kevin wanted John Ford's playground and he found it here."[4]

So, how did Kevin Costner decide on this area in the first place and be confident enough to lock it up in a long-term lease for four years in order to make his American Saga? "I am haunted when I see this location," Costner continued. "I remember driving from Aspen, Colorado, and coming down this road, Highway 128, that parallels the Colorado River. I had never been on it before, and Monument Valley

Angus Macfadyen in a scene from *Horizon: An American Saga*, Film 1, filmed in Professor Valley, Moab, Utah.

was a location that I was considering as well. I actually drove through here and passed the Red Cliffs Lodge and I said to myself, 'Why am I rushing?' So, I turned around and spent the night. When I passed Mexican Hat, I literally felt a couple of tears because I had this story in my mind for a long time." The sight of all the tourist buses and the teeming crowds at Monument Valley's iconic cathedral-like formations prompted him to return to Moab. "This land was my UFO. I am so happy that I haven't seen a UFO, because how do you walk that back for the rest of your life when you have actually seen one? So, when I dreamed about this western, I saw this land as Utah land. I drove through it and I saw it and I was haunted by it. I can't ignore that I've seen it. I can't walk away from it. I can't disown it. Even when it didn't make economic sense to come here and shoot it, I still came, because it would not have been the same movie."[5]

Commissioner Bega Metzner of the Moab to Monument Valley Film Commission accompanied Costner and *Horizon*'s coproducers Mark Gillard and Glenn Kleczkowski, along with Derek Mellus of the Utah Film Commission, to scout locations. They began in Kanab for an afternoon tour in April 2021. That evening they flew to Moab for a day's reconnoiter of the region. They returned to Moab, this time with Philip Patterson, for a longer, five-day detailed scouting exploration in January 2022. "Kevin liked to act things out," recalled Metzner. "I remember that we were up Castle Valley, on a piece of private property that I had arranged for them to see. He got down on one knee and talked about the tents that would be built here, just to feel if it was the right spot. At other times, he would just wander off and take it in, then call Phil over and discuss it with him, just as he did on this location and on the other side of the hill as a place for the wagon train so it would look like a different location from the others nearby."[6]

We then moved to another shooting location, along with the video tent that consisted of four flat-screen video

Georgia MacPhail, Sienna Miller, Chase Ramsey, and Dalton Baker filmed in Professor Valley, Moab, Utah.

take my seat. It has some corny things in it, but I look past them. There are so many classic lines of dialogue in that movie such as those spoken by the gold-digging female played by Debbie Reynolds. After her gambling husband, played by Gregory Peck, dies, she utters a line that I have built my whole life on. "We made and lost three fortunes and spent our whole life doing it." I've done the same thing. I've mortgaged everything I own to make this movie. I just love her perspective."[7] Indeed, as Costner remarked in another interview, "I mortgaged ten acres on the water in Santa Barbara where I was going to build my last house. But, I did it without a thought. . . . It's my life, and I believe in the idea and the story."[8]

Quickly, Costner is alerted that the scene is ready to shoot. His attention shifts immediately to the video monitors. Then, speaking into his walkie-talkie, Costner says, "Virgil, stay on the alert. You're on your horse. You're wondering how many cattle you are going to have to give up, all right? Same with you, Diamond. OK, ROLLING." Mounted cavalry approaches the wagon master. "We're only going to do this once, if we're lucky," Costner remarks to those on the other end of the wireless system as well as to those in the video tent. "Let's move that black cow out. Just keep rolling! All right, let's roll. Wait a second! We've got a black cow. Get that black cow out. I've got two guys after one cow. We should keep that for the dummy reel. Call it, Phil! ACTION, CAVALRY! Come on, cavalry." The cavalry advances past the video tent and the officer dismounts to talk with the wagon master. "That's a cut!" announces Costner. "Play it back for me, please. Virgil got there a little early, but I really like how it plays out."

The next scene involves pioneer women, played by Isabelle Fuhrman and Ella Hunt, beside a wagon. Three takes and each time, the wagons have to make a wide circle to come back around for the next take, as they must move

monitors and communications equipment mounted on an all-terrain vehicle that could be moved to virtually any location, followed by crew members with chairs and a tent enclosure. Costner could see on the monitors what the four cameras were picking up. Script supervisor Nirvana Adams sat next to Costner as she was responsible for not only script notes, but scene timing, dialogue, and continuity. This one involved a cavalry detachment. As the cameras and wagon train got into position, Costner talked about the movies that influenced his approach to westerns. "*The Searchers,* and *The Man Who Shot Liberty Valance. Liberty Valance* breathes mythology," was his immediate reply. "It travels through time. It circles back to tell the truth. I believe the myth and know how to dig out the truth. You have to believe that the truth is somewhere in between, that it happened. *Horizon* is like a mining expedition to find out the truth that the town is founded on a lie. Myth usually conjures up the notion that something isn't true. But, mythology really is true. I saw *How the West Was Won* when I was seven years old. I know that movie because I never left my seat at the intermission. I didn't want anybody to single file to the side of the stationary wagon where the scene is being played. Costner yells, "Cut!" Fuhrman is invited to watch, alongside her director, the playback of the powerful performance she delivered. Throughout the day, whether at the Horizon town set or the fort compound, the assured Costner either knew exactly what he wanted in each scene—from the nuance of performance, spoken to a performer via earbuds—or he gave instructions to Philip Patterson.

At times, Costner tends to remind one of the way silent-film directors coached and molded the performances of the actors and a scene, without the worry of a microphone intruding modern-day reality of the New West into his depiction of the Old West. The connection between moviemaking in 2023 and the way a western was made a hundred years ago, in the days when Tom Mix came to Utah to make *The Deadwood Coach,* seemed to fuse past with present at this flash point. As day 40 ended, Costner's dream fueled an energy level that never seemed to falter. I left the location at 7:00 that night, and there were still additional shots left to make before Costner and his band of players and support crew called it a wrap.

What emerged from that experience reminded me of something that Costner said just prior to the start of *Horizon 2* in St. George. He's a storyteller. "My background is hunting and fishing. I've sat around campfires with my father and watched older men talk. I got to know who the real storytellers were. Time doesn't matter if your story is interesting. I'm not a gambler. People might look at this and say, 'Oh, this is a gamble.' And I go, 'Well, I guess it is, but do I want to go to Las Vegas and gamble?' No, I am not that kind of gambler. I gamble on the love of story. I'm gambling on people. In a sense, I can't make them go to the theater, but if they get there, I'm going to try to take care of them the best I possibly can. That's what I count on, like that guy at the campfire."[9]

Costner's sense of story, his obvious love of the craft of moviemaking, and a pointed focus on his audience links him with the makers of movies that last, many of those made on the Utah landscapes and in its studios for the past century. "The state of Utah, with its intrinsic beauty, is the perfect backdrop for the story of *Horizon,*" Costner said as *Horizon 2* began filming in St. George. "And it can be said to be its own character in our story."[10]

As Utah concludes its first century of moviemaking, Costner is representative of how this same land, in its varied landscapes, can shape and inspire innumerable new filmmakers for the state's next hundred years. In *Butch Cassidy and the Sundance Kid,* there is a memorable scene showing the pair of outlaws on horseback traveling on a shallow portion of the Virgin River filmed in Zion National Park. Butch (Paul Newman) tells his partner Sundance (Robert Redford), "Boy, you know every time I see Hole-in-the-Wall again, it's like seeing it fresh for the first time." How filmmakers have seen Utah's mountains, deserts, river gorges, salt flats, sand dunes, alpine forests, even its urban centers, freshen not only the imaginations of those living in this intermountain state, but those who come to Utah from *their* familiar places, bringing those cinematic moments with them. Actor James Stewart once referred to the movies as captured "pieces of time." They also capture a place that leaves viewers with indelible images that are associated with the vision of a writer, director, and a performer such as Kevin Costner is doing in his "saga" fashion. These kinds of viewers would agree with Kevin Costner, when he said, "I believe in the movies, the power of them." Especially, in his final phrase, "I believe in their longevity."[11]

Between scenes, Kevin Costner and the author on location in Professor Valley near Moab for *Horizon 2*.

EPILOGUE

"You're travelling through another dimension, a dimension not only of sight and sound but of mind; a journey into a wondrous land whose boundaries are that of imagination. There's a signpost up ahead—your next stop, the Twilight Zone!" With these words, host Rod Serling opened each episode of the phenomenally influential television series. As I watch so many of the films covered in this book and visit the locations where they were made, the "zone experience" becomes pronounced. The Mohawk War of the American Revolution did not happen in the mountains above Cedar City—and yet, standing there as cattle graze on the lush grass, I am convinced that it did. Buffalo Bill and a contingent of US Cavalry *did* fight the Battle of War Bonnet Gorge in the sun-baked desert canyon of Paria, and then again, they did not. Cochise and his son, Taza, made peace with the US government in Arches National Park. Or so it seems. And Jesus's Sermon on the Mount occurred in Canyonlands National Park, in *The Greatest Story Ever Told*, even as in *The Chosen* He walked the streets of Jerusalem and in the fields of Galilee in Utah County.

Orson Welles referred to movies as "ribbons of dreams," and Jimmy Stewart called them "pieces of time." When we watch a movie, what we see is already *past*. Yet our physiological ability to process moving images fixes them in our memory. The magic of the movies leaves an indelible imprint. Nearly seventy years ago, a movie crew filmed the Lone Ranger as he reared up on his horse in Kanab Canyon. That time is gone forever. But today I can stand at that same spot, touch it, photograph it, and view it from every angle. And so, in a way, the Lone Ranger lives on.

The movies made in Utah hewed to no particular standard, except those governed by market forces and the tastes of a changing audience. To borrow from a non-Utah-based Western, many of these movies contained generous helpings of the good, the bad, and the ugly. But their collective legacy will forever exert an influence, as will Utah's landscapes, a "wondrous land whose boundaries are that of the imagination" that drew Hollywood back again and again.

NOTES

CEDAR CITY AND THE PARRY BROTHERS

1. Inez S. Cooper, "Biography of Gronway Robert Parry (1889–1969)," May 5, 1969, 6, Gronway Parry Collection MS 18, Box 3 Fd. 28, Special Collections, Gerald R. Sherratt Library. Southern Utah University.

2. William O. Tufts, "Memorandum in regard to concessioners in Mukuntuweap National Monument," February 17, 1917, Dena S. Markoff Collection ZION 11887, Zion National Park Museum.

3. William O. Tufts, "Memorandum for Mr. Albright in regard to application for concession in Mukuntuweap National Monument," March 3, 1917, Markoff Collection.

4. "Articles of Incorporation of the National Park Transportation and Camping Company," April 14, 1917, Markoff Collection. Formal granting of the concession to Wylie and the Parrys was communicated to them by Horace Albright on April 27, 1917. Initially, Gronway and Chauncey Parry competed with Wylie for the transportation concession as late as early April. Wylie also had the backing of Utah governor Simon Bamberger. However, when businessman A. S.Wilson of Salt Lake City made an application, it was feared that he had an inside track because of the endorsement by Douglas White, General Industrial Agent for the Los Angeles & Salt Lake Railroad, whose schedules would coincide with that of the park buses. Wylie and the Parrys hastily joined forces and submitted a joint proposal that eventually carried the day for them. See: Letter, Governor Simon Bamberger to Hon. Samuel Mather, February 10, 1917; Letter, G. C. Parry to Jos. J. Cotter, March 3, 1917; Letter, Douglas White to Hon. James H. Mays, February 24, 1917; Letter, W. W. Wylie to Horace M. Albright, April 8, 1917; Telegram, Horace Albright to W. W. Wylie, April 27, 1917; Letter, William W. Wylie, Clinton W. Wylie, Gronway R. Parry, Chauncey G. Parry to J. J. Cotter, April 12, 1917. All in Markoff Collection.

5. Dale Parry, interview by Janet Seegmiller, July 4, 2004, 5, Utah Parks Company Oral History Projects UPC #59, Special Collections, Gerald R. Sherratt Library, Southern Utah University.

6. Quoted in James D'Arc, "They Came This 'A Way," *Mountainwest* (March 1978).

7. Janet B. Seegmiller, "Selling the Scenery: Chauncey and Gronway Parry and the Birth of Southern Utah's Tourism and Movie Industries," September 2005, Narrative of PowerPoint presentation, p. 6, Special Collections, Gerald R. Sherratt Library, Southern Utah University.

8. "Down the Colorado River by Canoe," *Salt Lake Tribune,* May 9, 1926; "Rare Beauty Greets Party," *Salt Lake Tribune,* May 10, 1926; "Dern Prepared to Aid Rescue," *Salt Lake Tribune,* May 11, 1926. The journal entries for the trip, the form in which the newspaper coverage was published, were made by Grimes, who was Governor Dern's secretary; Ruby, a family friend of Chauncey and Helen Parry, was described as an "unofficial representative of the governor of Colorado." Ruby and Parry married in the years following Chauncey's death in 1943; Rust, from Kanab, had "made several trips down the river, and acted as guide and chief of the party." See also Frederick H. Swanson, *Dave Rust: A Life in the Canyons* (Salt Lake City: University of Utah Press, 2007), 189–91.

9. Quoted in Inez S. Cooper, 6.

10. Louise Parry Thomas, interview by Janet Seegmiller, July 18, 2003, Utah Parks Company Oral History Projects, UPC15b, 6, Special Collections, Gerald R. Sherratt Library, Southern Utah University.

11. J. W. Thomas, "Chauncey Gardner Parry–Modern Pioneer," n.d., 12, unpublished typescript. In possession of the author.

12. Caleb Whitney Parry, "Resume of My Educational Qualifications and Professional Experience," [1941], 3, photocopy in Grayce Beckett Pike Papers MSS SC 1257, L. Tom Perry Special Collections, Brigham Young University.

13. Grayce Beckett Pike, interview by author, July 1977, 15, L. Tom Perry Special Collections, Brigham Young University.

14. Ralph Beckett, interview by author, July 1977, 18, L. Tom Perry Special Collections, Brigham Young University.

15. Ralph Beckett interview, 22–23.

16. Shirley Ricks, "Memory Lane," July 20, 1977, 12, unpublished typescript, Pike Papers, Brigham Young University.

17. Calvin Johnson, interview by author, March 1995.

TOM MIX AND *THE DEADWOOD COACH*

1. Kloma Flake, "Tale of a Town," *Movieland* (November 1944), 53. Flake had access to the two surviving Parry brothers, Gronway and Whit, for her story. Although, beyond this article, there is no other source to corroborate Grey's suggesting the Utah locations to Mix, such information would likely have been shared with Gronway and Whit by their brother Chauncey prior to his death in 1943. There is a local tradition that Grey wrote some of his novels while staying in Kanab, and, in fact, a number of his stories were set in Utah locales. Also, a reference to Grey's lodging in Kanab at the historic Stewart-Wooley home, in: "Mary E. Woolley Chamberlain: Handmaiden of the Lord," n.p. [Kanab, UT], n.d. [ca. 1960s], 93. Privately printed family history, copy at Kanab Heritage Museum.

2. "'The Orphan' To Be Filmed Here Soon," *Iron County Record,* August 15, 1924.

3. *Iron County Record.*

4. *Iron County Record,* August 22, 1924.

5. *Iron County Record.*

6. *Iron County Record.*

7. *Iron County Record.* Paul Mix wrote of his father that "Fox used Tom's boyish nature to make a strong appeal to the youthful audience. . . . Youngsters also frequently appeared in Tom's pictures and Tom always proved worthy of their trust and friendship. He was a first-class hero for any little boy or girl." Paul E. Mix, *The Life and Legend of Tom Mix* (South Brunswick & New York: A. B. Barnes, 1972), 99.

8. *Iron County Record.* The matter of "influence" should be more correctly read as "mention" of the Mormon church in the 1925 remake of *Riders of the Purple Sage,* starring Mix.

9. J. L. Crawford, interview by author, March 18, 2000.

10. J. L. Crawford, "When Hollywood Discovered Zion," n.d., typescript in possession of the author.

11. Vilo DeMille, interview by author, August 30, 2008.

12. Rupert Ruesch, interview by author, January 6, 2001.

13. *Iron County Record,* September 5, 1924.

14. *Iron County Record.*

15. *Iron County Record.*

16. *Iron County Record.*

17. *Iron County Record.*

18. *Iron County Record,* January 9, 1925.

19. Crawford, "When Hollywood Discovered Zion," 3.

20. Ruesch interview.

21. Sylvan Johnson, interview by author, March 12, 2000.

THE SHEPHERD OF THE HILLS, RAMONA, AND THE "BATTLE" OF CEDAR BREAKS

1. "Movie Companies Fight for Location," *Iron County Record,* September 16, 1927.

2. "Movie Companies Fight for Location."

GLORY DAYS FOR CEDAR CITY

1. *Annual Report of Extension Work, Agricultural Agent-Iron County 1936*, U.S. Department of Agriculture, Utah State Agricultural College and County Farm Bureaus, 63.
2. "Film Director Lauds Scenery of South Utah for Locations," *Salt Lake Tribune*, November 20, 1938.
3. Louise Parry Thomas, interview by Janet Seegmiller, July 18, 2003, Utah Parks Company Oral History Project UPC #15b, 3. In the interview, Thomas refers to Cecil B. DeMille as the director giving her mother instructions. However, it was Rosson, and not DeMille, who supervised the second-unit production at Iron Springs.
4. Arthur S. Winton, "Southern Utah Again Furnishes Setting for Movie Makers," *Salt Lake Tribune*, October 15, 1939.
5. Contract, Twentieth Century-Fox Film Corporation and Anderson Boarding & Supply Company, June 28, 1939, Twentieth Century-Fox Archives.
6. Winton.
7. Merle Morris, interview by author, October 29, 2008.
8. Jackie Rife, interview by author, March 23, 1995.
9. Mary Gaye Evans, interview by author, October 17, 2008.
10. Evans interview.
11. "Movie Group Expects to Complete Outdoor Shots for Picture This Week," *Kane County Standard*, July 28, 1939.
12. Winton.
13. Letter, Charles G. Clarke to Richard Alan Nelson, June 12, 1977. Copy in possession of the author.
14. Frederick C. Othman, "Chamber of Commerce Please Note," *Citizen-News* (Hollywood, CA), August 11, 1944.
15. Review, *Variety*, December 14, 1944.
16. "'Mid Utah Scenes Deanna Sings!" *Salt Lake Tribune*, January 28, 1945.
17. Grady Johnson, "Goldwyn's 'Rebels' Take to the High Ground," *New York Times*, October 13, 1957.
18. J. L. Crawford, interview by author, March 18, 2000.

FROM SILENTS TO SOUND

1. Charles Reed Jones, ed., *Breaking Into the Movies* (New York: Unicorn, 1927), 35.
2. Jones, 155.
3. J. L. Crawford, "When Hollywood Discovered Zion," 2, unpublished manuscript in possession of the author.
4. Crawford, 3.
5. Advertisement, *Photoplay*, ca. 1929.
6. "Fox Co. Will Film Picture in County," *Washington County News*, April 19, 1928. No title or subject of the film for which they were searching for locations was mentioned in this account.
7. Raoul Walsh, *Each Man in His Time* (New York: Farrar, Strauss & Giroux, 1978), 220–21.
8. Walsh, 222.
9. Walsh, 223.
10. Walsh, 224.
11. Vilo DeMille, interview by author, August 30, 2008.
12. Vilo DeMille interview.
13. "Highlights on 'The Arizona Kid,' From Victor M. Shapiro, Director of Publicity, Wm. Fox West Coast Studios," [1930], 1, Twentieth Century-Fox Archive.
14. *Variety*, review, October 2, 1934.
15. Crawford, 4.
16. Sylvan Johnson, interview by author, March 16, 2000.
17. Crawford, 4.

UTAH'S CENTENNIAL FILM

1. Memorandum, n.a., n.d. [1943], Department of Publicity & Industrial Development, Series 1138, Box 22, Utah State Archives. Hereafter cited as PID.
2. Letter, Tracy Barham to Governor Herbert B. Maw, March 18, 1943, PID, Box 22.
3. Letter, H. J. Plumhof to Newton B. Drury, May 6, 1943, PID, Box 22. See "Order No. 1472," April 20, 1940, United States Department of the Interior, Washington, 4 pp., in PID, Box 22. This informative document signed by Harold Ickes itemizes the various categories of permissions and fees that were available from the department to motion-picture companies desiring to produce feature motion pictures in the National Parks that formed the basis for Plumhof's and the studios' concern. One example justifying the concerns by studios for high fees charged by the National Park Service is evident from the Park Service's response to Atherton Productions, the company that had previously filmed *The Dude Ranger* in the park in 1934. The company applied in February 1935 to film "Cowboy Millionaire" in Zion National Park. "I have heard indirectly," wrote the park ranger in his monthly report, "that the secretary's [of the Department of the Interior] office wired the company that [the] permit would be granted only on payment of $5,000." This exorbitant amount would likely represent up to 10 percent of the modest film's production budget, an inordinate amount. The film was ultimately made in Arizona. See: *United States Department of Interior, National Park Service Monthly Report for February, 1935,* 8, ZION 1156/07, Zion National Park Museum.
4. Telegram, A. S. Brown to Senator Abe Murdock, March 17, 1943, PID, Box 22.
5. Letter, H. J. Plumhof to Louis Shapiro, July 18, 1944, PID, Box 22.
6. "'Buffalo Bill' Producer Enthusiastic Over Utah's Scenic Splendor," *Salt Lake Telegram*, May 17, 1943.
7. "Zion Park Setting for $1,750,000 Picture 'Ramrod,'" *Washington County News*, June 20, 1946.
8. "Premiere of Utah-Made Film Set for Friday," *Salt Lake Tribune*, February 16, 1947.
9. Andre de Toth, interview by author, March 24, 1996.
10. Rupert Ruesch, interview by author, January 6, 2001.
11. Gordon Bench, interview by author, September 22, 2008.
12. Ed Buscombe, *The BFI Companion to the Western* (London: British Film Institute, 1988), 336.
13. Gordon Bench interview.
14. Andre de Toth interview.
15. "Premiere of 'Ramrod' is High, Wide and Handsome Affair," *Salt Lake Tribune*, February 22, 1947.
16. "Yesterday's Star Parade That Made History," *Salt Lake Tribune*, February 22, 1947. The screen credit touting Utah locations was apparently only on original release prints. Subsequent copies transferred to home video do not contain this credit.
17. "Solons Would Remove Utah Seal From Ramrod," *Deseret News*, February 24, 1947.
18. "Centennial Officials Defend 'Ramrod' Premiere," *Deseret News*, February 25, 1947.
19. Howard Pearson, "Premiere of 'Ramrod' Brings Utah Benefits," *Deseret News*, February 25, 1947.
20. "Republic Picture Corporation to Film Movie Here," *Iron County Record*, June 17, 1943.
21. Gordon Bench interview.
22. "Motion Picture Cast Expected Early Next Week," *Iron County Record*, June 24, 1943.

THE CONQUEROR

1. "Columbia Pictures Have Unit Here Shooting Scene of 'Plane No.4,'" *Washington*

County News, January 12, 1939.

2. "Observations with Nora R. Lyman," *Washington County News,* May 13, 1954.

3. John L. Scott, "Mongol Hordes Clash on Utah Plains," *Los Angeles Times,* August 8, 1954.

4. Betty Motter, interview by author. October 29, 2008.

5. Louie K. Smith, "Deluxe Chuck Wagon Serves RKO Cast Lunch on 'The Conqueror' Set," *Washington County News,* June 24, 1954.

6. "Observations by Nora R. Lyman," *Washington County News,* June 10, 1954.

7. Linn Unkefer, "RKO Radio Pictures, Inc., Stars Clown in Baseball Elks Benefit; Fun for All," *Washington County News,* July 8, 1954.

8. "Observations by Nora R. Lyman," *Washington County News,* July 8, 1954.

9. "Observations by Nora R. Lyman," *Washington County News,* July 1, 1954.

10. "Rain Deluge Plays Havoc With RKO Sets Saturday; Stars, Extras Take Cover," *Washington County News,* July 1, 1954.

11. "RKO Radio Pictures, Inc., Begin Trek to California as Shooting Nears End," *Washington County News,* July 15, 1954.

12. "Observations by Norma R. Lyman," *Washington County News,* July 29, 1954.

13. "RKO Radio Pictures, Inc., Begin Trek to California as Shooting Nears End," *Washington County News,* July 15, 1954.

14. Cobbett Steinberg, *Reel Facts* (New York: Vintage, 1978), 347.

15. Oscar Millard, "Un-Khan Words for John Wayne," *Los Angeles Times,* June 28, 1981, Calendar section, 18.

16. Harry Medved and Michael Medved, *The Golden Turkey Awards* (New York: Perigee, 1980), 47–48.

17. Patricia Newman, "A Flinty Grandmother Battles for the victims of Utah's Nuclear Tragedy," *People* (October 1, 1979), 26–29; "The Children of John Wayne, Susan Hayward and Dick Powell Fear That Fallout Killed Their Parents," *People* (November 10, 1980), 42–47.

18. "Fallout Take Won't Hold Water, says Wayne's Son, Michael," *Washington County News,* August 9, 1979.

19. "Restranteur [*sic*] Doubts Wayne Cancer Link," *Washington County News*, September 6, 1979.

VANISHED AMERICANS

1. "Observations by Nora R. Lyman," *Washington County News,* January 19, 1956.

2. "St. George C of C Talk, Local Motion Pictures, Christmas Street Lights," *Washington County News,* November 18, 1954.

3. "Chamber of Commerce Hears Mining Industry," *Washington County News,* April 7, 1955; "Chamber of Commerce Hear Discussions," *Washington County News,* April 14, 1955. Columnist Nora Lyman was concerned for such a structure because of the damage done by vandals on many local structures located far from town. "Observations by Nora R. Lyman," *Washington County News,* April 21, 1955. So far as is known, the street was never built.

4. "Chamber of Commerce Hear Dairy Association Officer Give Local Data," *Washington County News,* June 16, 1955; "Chamber of Commerce Hold Interesting Meeting to Discuss Vital Matters," *Washington County News,* June 23, 1955.

5. Lyn Tornabene, *Long Live the King* (New York: Putnam, 1976), 352.

6. "Observations by Nora R. Lyman," *Washington County News,* May 24, 1956.

7. Samuel Fuller, *A Third Face* (New York: Knopf, 2002), 337. "He was always fun to be with. Over cigars and drinks, Walsh told me he loved his actors but hated the script he was shooting. When I told him my story, he liked it better than his own. 'Why don't we swap!' he suggested one evening. 'Swap?' I said. 'Sure, Sammy!' Raoul laughed, winking at me with his one good eye. 'You do my picture and I'll do yours!' I laughed with him, but explained how much this picture meant to me . . . . Every time he'd come over to our set, Raoul would continue to rib me, saying with a twinkle in that good eye, 'Just let me do a few scenes, Sammy!'"

8. Fuller, 338.

9. "'They Came to Cordura' Is Nearing Completion," *Washington County News,* November 13, 1958.

10. Louise Parry Thomas, interview by author, January 6, 2001.

11. Lyman Hafen, "Gary Cooper's Final Scenes," *St. George Magazine* (Spring 1984), 31.

12. "Another Movie Company Interested in St. George," *Washington County News,* December 4, 1958.

13. "St. George Area Attracts Major 'Western' Movie," *Washington County News,* July 25, 1968.

14. Lyman Hafen, "Redford on St. George," *St. George Magazine* (Spring 1984), 29.

15. This movie house stood for years until partiers built a fire in the fake fireplace and burned the structure to the ground.

16. Leigh von der Esch, interview by author, December 9, 2008.

17. Billie Frei, interview by author, November 3, 2008.

18. "St. George Area . . ."

19. Conrad Hall, audio commentary for the DVD of *Butch Cassidy and the Sundance Kid,* Blu-Ray disc, Twentieth Century-Fox Home Entertainment, 2007.

20. Pressbook, Universal Studios, n.d. [1977], p. 10.

21. Pressbook.

22. Billie Frei interview.

23. Errol Foremaster, "'The Car' Is in Town!," *Washington County News,* August 5, 1976; Errol Foremaster, "'The Car' Draws Local Talent," *Washington County News,* August 12, 1976; "'The Car' Filming in Kanab Area," *Southern Utah News,* August 26, 1976.

24. "'Electric Horseman' Shocks Leeds," *Washington County News,* January 25, 1979.

25. "Redford Speaks Out at LDS Function," *Washington County News,* March 29, 1979.

26. Hafen, "Redford on St. George."

UTAH'S HOLLYWOOD

1. Jonreed Lauritzen, "Kanab, Utah's Hollywood," *The Utah Magazine* (May 1946), 16.

2. "Utah's Hollywood," *Life* (September 19, 1949), 156–59.

3. Caleb Whitney Parry, "Resume of My Educational Qualifications and Professional Experience," [ca. 1941], typescript photocopy, 3. Photocopy in author's possession.

4. Book N, Page 132, Official Kane County Records.

5. "Kanab to Have New Hotel," *Kane County Standard,* March 27, 1931; "City May Sell Light Plant," *Kane County Standard,* May 1, 1931; June 26, 1931. The lodge was initially known as the Parry System Hotel, no doubt referring to part of the brothers' transportation system of loop tours of Cedar Breaks National Monument, Zion, Bryce, and Grand Canyon national parks. In June 1935, it became known as the Parry Lodge & Café.

6. "Hotel Closes for Season," *Kane County Standard,* November 4, 1932.

7. "'Kanab Kid' Title of New Scenario," *Kane County Standard,* September 30, 1938.

8. "Big Movie Dance Set for Jan. 20," *Kane County Standard,* January 13, 1939.

9. "Grand Opening Dance Held at 'Utah's Hollywood,'" *Kane County Standard,* January 27, 1939.

10. "Early Settlement theme of Movie," *Kane County Standard,* May 12, 1939. It appears

that Dixon/Adamson (1880–1972) was quite a character, using the name of Art Mix when appearing as an actor. "In the world of low-budget western filmmaking, there are a number of jack-of-all-trade figures, one of the most enterprising being the ubiquitous Victor Adamson," wrote Wheeler W. Dixon and Audrey Brown Fraser in *I Went That-A-Way* (Metuchen, NJ: Scarecrow, 1990), 3. Dixon produced many of his own low-budget features. His son, Al Adamson, was a film producer-director of economical exploitation horror films. Three of these, *The Female Bunch* (1969), *Five Bloody Graves* (1970), and *Jessi's Girls* (1975), were filmed (in Utah's Wayne County) at various locations that included Capitol Reef National Monument, Torrey, and Hanksville.

11. "Two Companies Take Films Here," *Kane County Standard,* June 16, 1939. Additional cast members included Dorothy McKinnon, "who takes the role of the leading lady," Tom Wynn, William Wood, and Oscar Gaham. For historical purposes, it is fortunate that the newspaper published a lengthy recitation of the film's plot: "Scenes used in the picture are all familiar to people in this locality and the country in and around Zion National Park. With a song echoing through the wastelands of southwestern Utah, the wagon train, piloted by a man named Willard Smith, who the writer says characterizes Jacob Hamblin, crosses the Virgin River, after an Apache Indian has sighted it. From the high cliff overlooking the evening camp, Jud and Vic Gunnison, enemies to the Mormons, watch the movements of the pioneers and plan to kill an Indian in a way that they feel will arouse the enmity of the Red man against the defenseless settlers. The Gunnisons are owners of a saloon and disliked by the Mormons because they try to demoralize the settlers and to get them to drink. When camp is made, Lucy Lane, one of the party, goes out to hunt rabbits and upon hearing a shot finds Chris Ferril, a young man from Santa Fe, bending over a dead Indian. They are almost immediately surrounded by Apaches, who carry off Chris, but allow Lucy to go to camp. That evening, while the body of the dead Indian is being burned by his friends, Smith, the leader of the wagon train, arrives and through his influence and good will the Indians allow Chris and an Indian brave to hunt down the killers. Realizing that their plans have failed to arouse the Indians against the Mormons, the Gunnisons kill more Indians with the thought that the Red men will seek revenge and attack the settlers at Kanab. A hat, shot from Gunnison's head in the fray, is found by Chris and the Indian who are still seeking the killers, and Chris now knows Jud is the man he is trailing for murder. The wagon train arrives at Kanab and Bonnie, a little girl Chris has found on the trail, is left with an old scout, who goes to sleep. As she is playing with a little boy, Gunnison kidnaps them and locks them in the back of his saloon. Chris trails Jud Gunnison to the saloon and tells him that the Indians are coming to seek revenge, but not from the Mormons. The Mormons, who see them approaching, seek divine deliverance in prayer and feel that their appeal has been answered when the Indians surround and burn the saloon. While it is in flames, Chris learns that the children are there and rescues them. The next day he calls upon Lucy Lane to tell he that he loves her." "Local Movie Enjoyed by Group," *Kane County Standard,* July 14, 1939.

IN GLORIOUS TECHNICOLOR!

1. Jack Richmond, "Western Union," *Screen Life* (January 1941), 83.
2. Review, *Newsweek* (February 17, 1941), 68.
3. Bosley Crowther, "When is an 'Epic'?" *New York Times,* February 9, 1941.
4. Jack Richmond, 82.
5. "Rescued by Hollywood," *New York Times,* January 26, 1941.
6. Dale Parry, interview by Janet Seegmiller, July 4, 2004, Utah Parks Company Oral History Projects, 29, Special Collections, Gerald R. Sherratt Memorial Library, Southern Utah University.
7. Grayce Pike, interview by author, July 1977.
8. *First Report of the Department of Publicity & Industrial Development to the Governor, Ended June 30, 1942,* State of Utah, 34, Department of Publicity & Industrial Development Papers, Utah State Archives.
9. "Colorful South Utah Stars in Newest Picture Epic," *Salt Lake Tribune,* February 7, 1943.
10. "Utah Grandeur Again Furnishes Film Setting," *Salt Lake Tribune,* March 28, 1943.
11. "Columbia Pictures Begins production of Technicolor Western Near Kanab," *Kane County Standard,* June 26, 1942.
12. Telegram, Jack Lawton to State Department of Agriculture (Salt Lake City, UT), August 19, 1942, Universal Pictures Papers, Box 269/8742, USC Cinematic Arts Library.
13. Jack Adams, interview by author, September 29, 2008.
14. Louise Parry Thomas, interview by author, January 6, 2001.
15. Louise Parry Thomas interview.
16. Telegram, Whit Parry to Gronway Parry, March 6, 1943. In possession of Louise Parry Thomas.
17. Louise Parry Thomas interview.
18. "Funeral Services for Chauncey Gardner Parry, held at The Deseret Mortuary, Salt Lake City, Utah on Saturday, March 13, 1943," typescript, 21. Copy in possession of Louise Parry Thomas.
19. The deed to the Parry Lodge was transferred from Helen Parry, Chauncey's widow, to Whit Parry on February 16, 1944. Book 3, p. 17–18, Official Kane County Records.
20. Jack Adams interview.
21. Jack Adams interview.
22. "Vanguards of Twentieth-Century Fox Here Arranging for a Feature Picture," *Kane County Standard,* May 25, 1945.
23. *Smoky* grossed $4 million. *My Friend Flicka* was the sixth-top money earner for the studio on its release in 1943, at $2.4 million. See: Aubrey Solomon, *Twentieth Century-Fox: A Corporate and Financial History* (Metuchen, NJ: Scarecrow, 1988), 220–21.
24. Review, *Film Daily,* June 14, 1946.
25. Review, *New Yorker,* July 6, 1946.
26. Florabel Muir, "The Town That Learned to Act," *Saturday Evening Post* (February 17, 1945), 25–26.
27. Murray Moler, "Out Where the Horse-Operas Grow," *Coronet* (December 1946), 114.
28. Jack Adams, interview by author, April 10, 2001.
29. Jack Adams interview. A local historian identified that the structure, dating back to 1871, was purchased by Whit Parry on January 21, 1944, from a Kanab physician. The building's demise was occasioned by a late-night forced entry by "five boys ages eight to twelve," who initially wanted to steal soda pop, and then tried to pry loose the cashbox to get coins to play the three slot machines. Whit's anger on discovering

the following morning the damage to his pop machine and till prompted him to sue the boys he suspected had broken into the Black Cat. However, "one of the boy's fathers counter-charged on the grounds that Mr. Parry was the first lawbreaker, by having the slot machines with which to tempt the boys." While the suit progressed, a carelessly discarded cigarette butt smoldered after closing one night and by morning engulfed the log structure in flames, thus spelling the end of this unique episode of Kanab history. See: Adonis Findlay Robinson, *Romance of the Black Cat* ([Kanab, UT]: Kanab Heritage Council, 2002), 5–6.

30. "Secretary of State Represents Governor in Ceremonies," *Kane County Standard,* September 23, 1949.
31. Articles of Incorporation of Kanab Pictures Corporation, November 26, 1947. L. H. Larsen was listed as president, Clyde Jackman as vice president, H. R. [Denver] Brandon, Clark Veater, and Donald Swapp as directors. Larsen's daughter, Bette Stanton, claimed that Jackman was brought into the company to handle production and distribution details for *Stallion Canyon,* but ended up taking "his money, did little toward putting the picture together, nothing about distribution, and left the country." See: Bette Stanton, "Making of the Movie *Stallion Canyon,* Kanab Pictures Corporation," n.d., unpublished typescript, 3 pp. Author's possession.
32. Jackie Rife, interview by author, November 10, 2008.
33. "Movie Title Changed to Red Canyon," *Kane County Standard,* October 22, 1948.
34. "Air-Port News," *Kane County Standard,* October 1, 1948; "Kanab Airport Dedication 24th," *Kane County Standard,* October 22, 1948; Universal-International press release, October 28, 1948, in the Universal Pictures Papers, USC Cinematic Arts Library; "$106,357 Available for Airport," *Kane County Standard,* October 17, 1947, in which it was stated that "An airport, which can accommodate larger ships is a MUST for Kanab and Southern Utah. At present the Fredonia airport is the only means for ships to land. However, Arizona has a very stiff compensation law and according to Whit Parry, the Fox studio executives, who have flown in most of their equipment and personnel for this latest picture [*Fury at Furnace Creek*], are hesitating to continue to do so."
35. Jack Breed, "First Motor Sortie into Escalante Land," *National Geographic* (September 1948), 369–404; Maurine Whipple, "Anybody's Gold Mine," *Saturday Evening Post* (October 1, 1948).
36. "Kanab Runs Hollywood Close Second on Movies," *Deseret News,* November 12, 1948. No byline on the story suggests an Associated Press or United Press International wire story that was also picked up by other newspapers in the United States.
37. Ted Harbert, "Cooperation Evident on Movie Setting," *Kane County Standard,* August 26, 1949.
38. *Motion Pictures Present the Kanab K'Ola.* Springville, UT: Art City Publishing Co., 1948. Copy in possession of Norm Jackson.
39. "Utah's Hollywood," *Life* (September 19, 1949), 156–58; "County Again Gets National Publicity, *Kane County Standard,* September 30, 1949.

WILLIAM WELLMAN'S *BUFFALO BILL*

1. Memorandum, [n.d., ca. 1943], 2 pp. typescript, Department of Publicity & Industrial Development Papers, Box 22, Utah State Historical Society.
2. "'Buffalo Bill,' the Greatest Picture to be Filmed in Kane County, Will be Done in Technicolor," *Kane County Standard,* August 5, 1943.
3. Richard Schickel, *The Men Who Made the Movies* (New York: Antheneum, 1975), 227.
4. "Over 200 of 20th Century-Fox Co. in Kanab Filming Picture," *Kane County Standard,* August 12, 1943.
5. "One Day on Location," *Kane County Standard,* August 19, 1941. Some spelling and punctuation added for clarity.
6. James F. Denton, "The Red Man Plays Indian," *Collier's* (March 18, 1944).
7. "Please Give Us A Break," *Kane County Standard,* June 22, 1943.
8. Schickel, 228.
9. Review, *Hollywood Reporter,* March 15, 1944.
10. Sylvan Johnson, interview by author, March 16, 2000. The entire battle sequence was used in two other films, *Pony Soldier* (1952) and *Siege at Red River* (1954), the latter being distinguished by having been filmed at both Kanab and Moab, Utah.
11. Quoted in Michael Sheridan, "Town With A Movie Career," *Magazine Digest* (n.d., ca. 1945), 106.
12. Mayor R. C. Lundquist, "Kanab's Responsibility," *Kane County Standard,* December 7, 1945.

THE RUSTLER FROM KANAB

1. Edward Buscombe, ed. *The BFI Companion to the Western* (New York: Atheneum, 1988/1993) rev. ed., 426–28.
2. Arthur Rowan, "Westward the Women," *American Cinematographer* (January 1952), 45.
3. Rowan.
4. Louis Berg, "400 Women—and Bob Taylor," *This Week* (July 8, 1951).
5. Calvin Johnson, interview by author, August 27, 2009.
6. Jackie Rife, interview by author, September 10, 1999.
7. Frank Thompson, *William A. Wellman* (Metuchen, NJ: Scarecrow, 1983), 235.
8. Sylvan Johnson, interview by author, March 16, 2000.
9. Memorandum, Carl Benoit to W. L. Guthrie, July 21, 1951, Warner Bros. Papers, USC Cinematic Arts Library.
10. Memorandum, Frank Mattison to T. C. Wright, August 9, 1951, Warner Bros. Papers.
11. Pressbook, *The Lion and the Horse*, Warner Bros. Papers.
12. "Sinatras Arrive in Cedar City," *Deseret News,* July 13, 1953.
13. Howard Pearson, "Filmmakers Quit High-Priced Utah," *Deseret News,* August 3, 1950.
14. Pearson.
15. Dale Parry, interview by Janet Seegmiller, July 4, 2004, 33, Utah Parks Company Oral History Projects, UPC #59, Special Collections, Gerald R. Sherratt Library, Southern Utah University.
16. Calvin Johnson, interview by author, March 1995.
17. Letter, Jeanne Bithers to Del Dorius, Intermountain Editor, *Deseret News,* August 4, 1950, Howard Pearson Papers MSS 2147, Box 10, Fd. 22, L. Tom Perry Special Collections, Brigham Young University.
18. Jeanne Bithers letter.
19. Dale Parry interview.

HOWARD KOCH AND BEL-AIR PRODUCTIONS

1. Howard W. Koch, interview by author, May 18, 1995.
2. George Schenck, interview by author, April 7, 2001.
3. George Schenck interview.
4. Peter Graves, interview by

author, October 1, 2008.
5. Peter Graves interview.
6. "Movie Company Schedules October Filming," *Kane County Standard,* October 2, 1953.
7. Howard W. Koch, interview by author and Dennis Rowley, November 10, 1976.
8. Peter Graves interview.
9. Jackie Rife, interview by author, March 23, 1995.
10. Review, *The Hollywood Reporter,* December 14, 1953.
11. Lisa Davis, interview by author, July 7, 2008.
12. Paul Wurtzel, interview by author, June 11, 2001.
13. The song was composed by noted musician Les Baxter and his brother Jim Baxter. Les Baxter wrote the scores for many Schenck-Koch films.
14. Lisa Davis interview.
15. Paul Wurtzel interview.
16. Lisa Davis interview.
17. Jackie Rife interview.
18. Ina Fay Frost, interview by author, March 23, 1995.
19. Calvin Johnson, interview by author, March 22, 1995.
20. George Russell Aiken, *The Doc Aiken Story* (n.p. [Kanab, Utah], 1989), 84.
21. "Kanab Community Groups Reach A Complete Understanding here Thursday On Film Making Problems," *Southern Utah News,* June 6, 1957. Simultaneous with the strike by Kanab extras was the thorny problem of Utah's withholding of tax by out-of-state workers that adversely affected moviemaking in Moab as well as in Kanab. This unresolved matter may have exerted additional motivation for Kanab extras not to make the labor situation even more difficult for movie companies. See: "New Setup in Kanab to Win Hollywood; Tax Bogey Scouted," *Hollywood Reporter,* October 14, 1957.
22. "Around Kanab with the Roving Reporter," *Southern Utah News,* June 28, 1956.
23. Paul Wurtzel interview.
24. Marie Windsor, interview by Tom Weaver, in Tom Weaver, *Monsters, Mutants and Heavenly Creatures* (Baltimore: Midnight Marquee Press, 1996), 222–23.
25. Jay Robert Nash and Stanley Ralph Ross, eds., *The Motion Picture Guide* (Chicago: Cinebooks, 1985), vol. 3, 1017.
26. "New Owners Take Over Management of Parry's Lodge," *Southern Utah News,* July 18, 1957. According to Calvin Johnson, the sale of the Parry Lodge did not actually go through, and after some months Whit Parry was back in charge of the Lodge. Calvin Johnson, interview by author, December 1, 2008.
27. "Public Forum—by the Readers," letter from C. W. Parry, *Southern Utah News,* April 9, 1956.
28. Errol G. Brown, "We Offer Our Apologies," *Southern Utah News,* May 10, 1956.
29. Ina Fay Frost interview.
30. Jackie Rife interview.
31. Ina Fay Frost interview.
32. "Missing Items From Movie Needed," *Southern Utah News,* August 25, 1961.
33. "'Koch Day' Fans Revival of Filmmaking," *Southern Utah News,* October 22, 1990.
34. Jeanette Rusk, "Koch and Kanab is Mutual Love Affair," *Southern Utah News,* November 5, 1990.

REEL CHANGE IN KANAB

1. "Warner Brothers Studio and Belair Productions to Film Three Movies Near Kanab," *Southern Utah News,* July 28, 1955.
2. Sara Hamilton, Review, *Los Angeles Examiner,* February 9, 1956.
3. Philip K. Scheuer, Review, *Los Angeles Times,* February 9, 1956.
4. "Movie Producers Disapprove of State Income Tax Collection," *Washington County News,* January 23, 1958. A delegation of southern Utah business leaders appealed without success to Utah governor George Clyde over the withholding tax exemption.
5. Memorandum, Kenneth Cox to G. F. Greenlaw and W. L. Guthrie, June 24, 1957, Warner Bros. Papers, USC Cinematic Arts Library. *Copper Sky* (1957) and *Ride A Violent Mile* (1957) were the two films made by Filmaster during this time.
6. Scott Boyter, interview by author, November 18, 2008.
7. Review, *Hollywood Reporter,* January 23, 1958.
8. "No Mirages Here—They're Just Old Movie Remains," *Salt Lake Tribune,* November 9, 1959.
9. Review, *Motion Picture Herald,* August 16, 1966.
10. Hollis Alpert, ed., *Charlton Heston: The Actor's Life, Journals 1967–1976* (New York: Dutton, 1978), 159.
11. Ken Darby, *Hollywood Holyland: The Filming and Scoring of The Greatest Story Ever Told* (Metuchen: Scarecrow, 1992); Jean Duffy, "The Greatest Story Ever Told," *Arizona Highways* (January 1965), 4–11.
12. Bruce Braithwaite, *The Films of Jack Nicholson* (Bembridge: BCW Publishing, 1977). For a detailed account of these two films, see Patrick McGilligan, *Jack's Life* (New York: Norton, 1994), 151–162.
13. "Poitier Shows What Films Teach," *Catholic Standard and Times* (Philadelphia, PA), July 28, 1967, 3. On the Durango set, see "UA Cancels 'Duel' as Mex Production," *Variety*, April 21, 1965.
14. Alpert.
15. Forace Green, "Move Boosters Set Dec. 11 As Organizational Meeting," *Southern Utah News*, November 30, 1967.
16. Loren Webb, "Parry Lodge; A Landmark Then and Now," *Southern Utah News*, August 6, 1981, 7.
17. Phyllis Stewart interview.
18. Linda Adams Crosby, interview by author, January 6, 2001.
19. John Skow, "OK, Julie is a Beautiful, Mute, Nymphomaniac Indian Girl," *Saturday Evening Post* (June 1, 1968), 73.
20. Review, *Hollywood Reporter,* August 9, 1967.
21. Bill Heaton, "Nothing Like A 'Shooting'," *Deseret News,* September 28, 1972.
22. Heaton.
23. Dennis Judd, interview by author, March 23, 1995.
24. "'Friends of Utah' Honor Movie Makers," *Southern Utah News,* October 2, 1969.
25. Elayne Waering Fitzpatrick, "Where Have All the Movies Gone?" *Salt Lake Tribune,* December 23, 1973.
26. Howard W. Koch, interview by author, November 10, 1976.
27. "There'll Be a Hot Time in the Old Town," *Southern Utah News,* June 22, 1978.

JOHN FORD'S MONUMENT VALLEY

1. Raymond Carlson, "The Valley Nobody Knows," *Arizona Highways* (April 1956), 13–25. The entire issue was devoted to Monument Valley and to the films made there by John Ford.
2. Samuel Moon, *Tall Sheep* (Norman: University of Oklahoma Press, 1991), 7–9. Moon's book, consisting of lengthy interviews with Harry Goulding between 1974 and 1979, are used for Goulding's chronology of events in this account. For another interview with Goulding, with slight variations on Moon's account, see Todd McCarthy, "John Ford and Monument Valley," *American Film* (May 1978), 10–16. Goulding's basic story is supported by H. Jackson Clark, who, as a boy in 1939, heard the account from Goulding himself on a visit with

his family to Monument Valley. See: H. Jackson Clark, *The Owl in Monument Canyon* (Salt Lake City: University of Utah Press, 1993), 32–49.

3. H. Jackson Clark, *The Owl in Monument Canyon* (Salt Lake City: University of Utah Press, 1993), 19–31.

4. Peter Bogdanovich, *John Ford* (Berkeley: University of California Press, 1978), rev. and enlarged ed., 69–70.

5. Maurice Zolotow, *Shooting Star* (New York: Simon and Schuster, 1974), 150.

6. Virginia Greene, "Some of the Photos that Sold Monument Valley," *Arizona Highways* (September 1981), 33. Greene interviewed Josef and Joyce Muench, wherein they described the spiral-bound portfolio of twenty-four images, glued back-to-back, that Goulding took to California in 1938.

7. Garry Wills, *John Wayne's America* (New York: Simon & Schuster, 1997), 86–87. Wills makes a persuasive case regarding the Wetherills' connection with movie companies. They were the first to set up a trading post in Monument Valley, briefly, in 1906, but moved it to Kayenta, Arizona, in 1910, eleven years before the arrival in Monument Valley of the Gouldings. John Wetherill assembled the party that first discovered Rainbow Bridge in southern Utah in 1909. Tourists, as well as Zane Grey, used the Kayenta trading post as the base from which to explore the surrounding regions of northern Arizona and southeastern Utah.

8. Thomas H. Pauly, *Zane Grey: His Life, His Adventures, His Women* (Urbana: University of Illinois Press, 2005), 138.

9. Zane Grey, "The Heights of Wild Horse Mesa," *The Country Gentleman* (April 12, 1924), 13.

10. *The Vanishing American,* souvenir program published by Famous Players-Lasky Corporation [1925], 4.

11. *The Vanishing American* souvenir program.

12. Harry Perry, with Col. Oscar Estes, autobiography, unpublished typescript, chapter 7, 76. Photocopy in possession of the author.

13. Andrew Sinclair, *John Ford* (New York: Dial/James Wade, 1979), 82.

14. Moon, 150, 152.

15. Neil M. Clark, "Desert Trader," *Saturday Evening Post* (March 29, 1947), 115.

16. *First Report of Department of Publicity & Industrial Development to the Governo, Ended June 30, 1942,* State of Utah, 34, Department of Publicity & Industrial Development Papers, Utah State Archives.

17. Harry Carey Jr., *Company of Heroes* (Metuchen: Scarecrow, 1994), 67–68.

18. In 1953, the old rock cabins were torn down and a motel built adjacent to the trading post.

19. This footage has been added as a supplementary item on the home video version of *The Searchers.*

20. Dan Ford, *Pappy* (Englewood Cliffs: Prentice-Hall, 1979), 272.

21. Bogdanovich's visit with Ford is recounted with some detail in Peter Bogdanovich, 2–5.

22. Quoted in Todd McCarthy, 16.

23. Joseph McBride and Michael Wilmington, *John Ford* (New York: DaCapo, 1975), 9.

24. Robert H. Woody, "Goulding's Belongs to Utah By Mere Half Mile," *Salt Lake Tribune,* June 24, 1990).

MOAB MEANS MOVIES

1. Patrick Ford, interview by author, April 25, 1979.

2. Susan Lyman Whitney, "Resident Had Leading Role in Attracting Filmmakers," *Deseret News,* May 4, 1989.

3. Bette L. Stanton, *Where God Put the West: Movie Making in the Desert. A Moab-Monument Valley Movie History* (Moab: Four Corners Publications, 1994. Second ed., 2008), 8. Stanton walked the filming sites with George White in 1983, long before White's later debilitating illness, and talked extensively about showing Ford around Moab and the Colorado River area.

4. Jack Goodspeed, interview by author, August 14, 2002. In 2002, Sam Taylor, son of Loren Taylor, said that his father, George White, and a few others went down to Monument Valley to "buttonhole" Ford for a visit to Moab. Sam Taylor, interview by author, June 25, 2002.

5. "Southern Utah Again Chosen as Setting for Picture," *Kane County Standard,* October 2, 1941. Frank E. O'Brien, of Utah's Department of Publicity & Industrial Development, announced that Sherman was to make a film entitled "Utah" under the Paramount Pictures banner and had been in Moab for "several days in the vicinity of Moab last spring." Sherman also traveled down the San Juan River to the Hole-in-the-Rock and "joined the annual pilgrimage to this famed spot." While "Utah" was never made, the visit undoubtedly influenced the producer for his choice of Kane County and Grand County as locations for later films.

6. George White, interview by author, March 27, 1995.

7. "Argosy Productions Will Film Utah Pioneers Picture at Moab," *Times-Independent,* October 6, 1949.

8. Harry Carey Jr., *Company of Heroes* (Metuchen: Scarecrow, 1994), 87.

9. "Movie Goers Will View Moab But Won't Believe It True," *Times-Independent,* November 17, 1949. The reference to Shangri-La was taken from James Hilton's novel *Lost Horizon.* "Filming of 'Wagon Master' Started Monday Near Moab," *Times-Independent,* December 1, 1949.

10. "Filming of 'Wagon Master' Started Monday Near Moab," *Times-Independent,* June 29, 1950.

11. "Utah's Road Needs Cited," *Times-Independent,* January 12, 1950. In his letter, Ford mistook Castle Valley for Professor Valley, the actual location for all filming connected with *Wagon Master.*

12. Review, *New York Times,* June 19, 1950.

13. Review, *Variety,* April 12, 1950.

14. Harry Carey Jr., 107.

15. Karl Tangren, interview by author, March 26, 1995. Sam Taylor, who played one of the army troopers, remembered riding in the limousine that took O'Hara to the location: "I was so disgusted with her. All the way, she bellyached how dusty it was, how hot it was, and about the mosquitoes. She couldn't wait to get out of town." Sam Taylor interview.

16. Sam Taylor interview.

17. "Picture Stars Put on Great Show at Moab," *Times-Independent,* June 29, 1950.

18. Sam Taylor interview.

19. Barbara Burck Cathey, interview by author, August 15, 2002.

20. "*Border River* Production Notes," typescript mimeograph, Universal Pictures Papers, Box 421/12260, USC Cinematic Arts Library.

21. Barbara Burck Cathey interview.

22. *Border River* Production Notes.

23. Review, *Variety,* March 16, 1955.

24. Don Holyoak, interview by author, March 26, 1995.

25. Sam Taylor interview.

26. "Movies Mean Money to Moab Area," *Times-Independent,* May 23, 1963.

27. n.a., "Two Movie Productions at One Time Keep Moab on the Go," *Times-Independent,* August 3, 1967.

28. Howard Pearson, "Stunning Premiere for 'Blue,'" *Deseret News,* April 24, 1968.

29. Maxine Newell, "Film Exec., Patricia Casey, Holds a Top Hollywood Job," *Times-Independent,* August 3, 1967, Section C.

30. Bette L. Stanton, interview by author, June 22, 2002.

THE APOCALYPSE IN MOAB

1. "Disney Plans Big Film Premiere," *Deseret News*, July 22, 1972.
2. Leigh von der Esch, interview by author, December 9, 2008.
3. Bette L. Stanton, interview by author, March 26, 1995.
4. Ridley Scott, telephone interview by Jeff Vice, quoted in Jeff Vice, "Made In Utah," *Deseret News*, February 27, 1998.
5. *Thelma & Louise*: About the Production, Pathe Entertainment, [1991], typescript, 6.
6. Bette L. Stanton interview.
7. Bette L. Stanton interview.
8. Bette L. Stanton, *Where God Put the West: A Moab-Monument Valley Movie History* (Moab: Four Corners Publications, 1994. Second ed., 2008), 22.
9. *Slaughter of the Innocents*, laserdisc commentary by James Glickenhaus and Scott Glenn.
10. *RocketMan* Production Information, Walt Disney Pictures [1997], 12.
11. Christopher Smith, "BLM Permits Bad for 'Biz,'" *Salt Lake Tribune*, February 20, 1995. Part of *Broken Arrow* (1996), directed by John Woo and starring John Travolta and Christian Slater, was ultimately photographed partially on Utah locations, primarily over the Glen Canyon National Recreation Area.
12. Christopher Smith.

CAPITOL MOVIEMAKING

1. For a full presentation of Utah's early filmmaking companies and their activities, see Richard Alan Nelson, "Utah Filmmakers of the Silent Screen," *Utah Historical Quarterly* 43:1 (Winter 1975), 5–25.
2. *Moving Picture World* (August 29, 1908).
3. *Moving Picture World* (December 3, 1910).
4. *Moving Picture World,* (October 1, 1910).
5. When Paramount celebrated its 75th anniversary, Utah Film Commission head Leigh von der Esch scouted Utah's Wasatch front for the mountain that inspired Hodkinson for the Paramount logo. She identified it as Mt. Nebo in Utah County and contacted Paramount, which planned on including a dissolve from their modernized logo to a view of Mt. Nebo, as photographed by von der Esch, before the appearance of the main title credits of *Indiana Jones and the Last Crusade* (1989). This was to have been the only connection between the Utah Film Commission and this third installment in the successful Indiana Jones franchise until the fortuitous location switch from Colorado to Utah for the film's opening scene. The Paramount Pictures Web site identifies Ben Lomond Peak, near Hodkinson's home in Ogden, Utah, as the mountain representing the studio logo. See: Leigh von der Esch, interview by author, December 9, 2008.
6. Richard Alan Nelson, "From Antagonism to Acceptance: Mormons and the Silver Screen," *Dialogue* 10 (Spring 1977); Nelson, "A History of Latter-day Saint Screen Portrayals in the Silent Film Era, 1905–1936," (Masters Thesis, Brigham Young University, 1975).
7. Karl Brown, unpublished typescript, n.d., chapter 4, 6; chapter 5, 1. Typescript in possession of Kevin Brownlow. According to Thomas G. Alexander, an agricultural boom in rural Utah after World War went bust in the early 1920s, the impact of which was enhanced with the stock-market crash in 1929. In its wake, in 1932–33, Utah's 36 percent unemployment rate was significantly higher than the national average unemployment rate of 25 percent. See: Thomas G. Alexander, *Utah: The Right Place* (Layton: Gibbs Smith, 2003), 311.
8. Brown, chapter 5, 7.
9. Brown, chapter 6, 5.
10. Brown, chapter 8, 4.
11. Brown, chapter 8, 6.
12. Louise Parry Thomas.
13. Herk Harvey, 1989 interview for *Carnival of Souls* in the DVD edition, Criterion Collection, 2002. For information on Saltair, see Nancy D. McCormick and John S. McCormick, *Saltair* (Salt Lake City: University of Utah Press, 1985). Saltair appeared in one more film, a straight-to-video production, *Neon City* (1992). Directed by Monte Markham, this futuristic drama, inspired by the *Mad Max* films, was partially filmed at what was left of Saltair's main structure, following the 1970 fire and subsequent efforts to rebuild it by a private party.
14. Howard Pearson, "Utahns Seek Recovery of Moviemaking Role," *Deseret News*, July 8, 1970.
15. "Movie Committeeman Reports on SLC Reception," *Times-Independent*, February 26, 1970.
16. Robert Woody, "Kramer to Advocate Utah Film-Making," *Salt Lake Tribune*, August 24, 1971.
17. Thomas G. Alexander, 380–81. The popular Rampton was elected in 1964 and was the only Utah governor to serve three successive terms. The state entity was the Department of Development Services, with Hal Schleuter as its first head, under the administrative umbrella of the Utah Travel Council. Schleuter traveled to Hollywood two or three times a year, spending from a week to ten days on each trip visiting the various studios.
18. Clint Barber, "Hollywood Lens Catches S.L. Scenes for Movie," *Deseret News*, November 6, 1971; Don C. Woodward, "Pitch Lures Film to Utah," *Deseret News*, October 23, 1971.
19. Howard Pearson, "Redford Plans Two More Films to be Made in Utah," *Deseret News*, December 19, 1972.
20. Josephine Zimmerman, "Redford Wants to Make Utah Film Capital," *Daily Herald*, November 16, 1982.
21. Howard Pearson.
22. Celebrities on Hand for 'Airport 1975,'" *Salt Lake Tribune*, May 29, 1974.
23. Max B. Knudsen, "Utah Great for 'On Location' Film Production," *Deseret News*, November 3, 1980.
24. Rick Hassett, "Utah to Promote Production of Movies," *Salt Lake Tribune*, June 15, 1978.
25. Statistics on file with the Utah Film Commission.
26. Leigh von der Esch, interview by author, 1994.
27. Leigh von der Esch, interview by author, December 9, 2008.

THE UTAH DISNEY MOVIE HERITAGE AND *HIGH SCHOOL MUSICAL*

1. Marshall Moore interview by James D'Arc. Park City, Utah. 30 May 2023. In author's possession.
2. Susette Hsiung interview by James D'Arc. Written questions and answers. 5 June 2023. In author's possession.
3. Moore interview.
4. Moore interview.
5. Moore interview.
6. Moore interview.

TOUCHED BY AN ANGEL

1. Ray Richmond, "Heaven on Earth," *Hollywood Reporter*, 13 February 2003, S-1.
2. "An Extended Version of Executive Producer Martha Williamson's *60 Minutes* Interview with Ed Bradley," *Touched by An Angel: The Complete First Season on DVD*. Disc 4. Paramount/CBS DVD. 2004.
3. Martha Williamson and Robin Sheets,

Touched by An Angel: Stories from the Hit Television Series! (Grand Rapids, MI: Zondervan, 1997), 28.

4. Marshall Moore interview by James D'Arc, 23 May 2023. In possession of the author.

5. Martha Williamson telephone interview by James D'Arc, 23 May 2023. In possession of the author.

6. Williamson and Sheets, 51, 52.

7. Williamson interview.

8. Williamson interview.

9. Ray Richmond, "Talent Show," *Hollywood Reporter*, 13 February 2003, S–2.

10. Williamson interview.

11. Moore interview.

12. Williamson interview.

13. Moore interview.

14. "Martha Williamson Talks About *Touched by An Angel*." Undated. *Touched by An Angel: The Complete First Season on DVD*. CBSDVD/Paramount. 2004. Disc 4.

15. Williamson interview. Marshall Moore estimates that both series brought more than $215 million into the Utah economy.

16. Williamson and Sheets, 17.

THE CHOSEN

1. Press release, *The Chosen*, 9 December 2022. Modified, 27 March 2023.

2. Dallas Jenkins interview, by James D'Arc. 16 June 2023. Mapleton, Utah. In author's collection.

3. Jeff Harmon and Neal Harmon interview, by James D'Arc. 9 June 2023. Provo, Utah. In author's possession.

4. Jeff Harmon and Neal Harmon interview.

5. Jeff Harmon and Neal Harmon interview.

6. Email, Dallas Jenkins to James D'Arc, 7 July 2023.

7. Paul Bond, "Largest-Ever Crowdfunding Campaign for a TV Show Issues Equity to Investors," *Hollywood Reporter*, 5 January 2019.

8. Jenkins interview.

9. Jenkins interview.

10. Jenkins interview.

11. Jenkins interview.

12. Jeff Harmon and Neal Harmon interview.

13. Dallas Jenkins, "I'm in a tough spot," YouTube Video, posted 6 July 2020.

14. Jeff Harmon and Neal Harmon interview.

15. Brad Pelo interview, by James D'Arc. 13 July 2023. Telephone. In author's possession. In December 2021, Pelo became executive producer of *The Chosen*. He became president of The Chosen, Inc. in March 2022.

16. Jenkins interview.

17.Jeff Harmon and Neal Harmon interview.

18. Jenkins interview. While Jenkins declared that "One of the joys of this project is my relationship with so many friends and brothers and sisters in the LDS faith," the set is used as a rental facility for *The Chosen*. Its use by the production company does not imply any endorsement of *The Chosen* by The Church of Jesus Christ of Latter-day Saints, nor is the Church in any way involved in the production of the series. The Church-owned BYU-tv was granted broadcast rights to the series in the fall of 2020. Cassidy Wixom, "The Chosen' resonates with believers who see authenticity in its characters," *The Daily Universe* [Brigham Young University], 26 May 2021.

19. Jenkins interview.

20. Trent Toone, "Why cast and crew of 'The Chosen' love filming in Utah's version of the Holy Land," *Deseret News*, 28 October 2020.

21. Jenkins interview. The figure cited is from 2022.

22. Jenkins interview.

23. "Remarks and Dedicatory Prayer, Elder David A. Bednar, August 2, 2011." The Jerusalem Set. Goshen, Utah. CR1038, p. 4. Church History Library. The Church of Jesus Christ of Latter-day Saints. Salt Lake City, Utah.

24. Jenkins interview.

25. Jenkins interview.

26. Jenkins interview.

27. Jenkins interview. David Nekrutman, an Orthodox Jewish theologian, was hired as an advisor for season four. Patrick B. McGuigan, "Orthodox Jewish Theologian David Nekrutman is chosen as an advisor to 'The Chosen'," *Oklahoma City Sentinel*. Nekrutman joined the existing advisory panel that included a Catholic priest, a Messianic rabbi, and a professor of New Testament from Biola University. Jim Graves, "Watch 'The Chosen,' the online series on the life of Jesus," *Aleteia*, 29 May 2019.

28. Ruth Graham, "Jesus Christ, Streaming Star," *New York Times*, 25 November 2022.

29. Jenkins interview.

TAYLOR SHERIDAN'S *YELLOWSTONE*

1. Marshall Moore interview by James D'Arc. 30 May, 2023. Park City, Utah. In author's possession.

2. Moore interview.

3. Lynn Elber, "Kevin Costner: Returning 'Yellowstone' Is a Hit On Own Terms," *US News & World Report*, 11 November 2022.

4. Quoted in Kyle Dunphey, "What Utah lost when 'Yellowstone' left—and what it stands to gain from the film industry," *Deseret News*, 7 December 2021.

5. Shae Robins interview by James D'Arc, telephone, 23 July 2023. In author's possession.

6. Kyle Dunphey.

7. Moore interview.

8. Moore interview.

KEVIN COSTNER'S *HORIZON: AN AMERICAN SAGA*

1. Mike Fleming, Jr., "Kevin Costner Sets Late Summer Start for His Passion Film 'Horizon,' Epic Period Western," *Deadline*, 28 January 2022.

2. Kevin Costner interview by James D'Arc. Moab, Utah. 13 June 2023. In author's possession.

3. Costner interview.

4. Philip A. Patterson interview by James D'Arc. Moab, Utah. 13 June 2023. In author's possession.

5. Costner interview.

6. Bega Metzner interview by James D'Arc. Moab, Utah. 13 June 2023. In author's possession.

7. Costner interview.

8. Mike Fleming, Jr., "Mavericks Francis Ford Coppola and Kevin Costner on Risking Their Fortunes Bankrolling Passion Pics 'Megalopolis' And 'Horizon,'" *Deadline*, 18 May 2023.

9. Fleming, Jr., Coppola-Costner interview.

10. Ladd Egan, "Filming begins in St. George for Kevin Costner's 'Horizon, an American Saga'," *KSL-TV*, 2 May 2023.

11. Fleming, Jr., Coppola and Costner interview.

BIBLIOGRAPHY

BOOKS

Aiken, George Russell. *The Doc Aiken Story.* [Kanab, UT]: n.p., 1989.

Alexander, Thomas G. *Utah: The Right Place.* Rev. & updated ed. Salt Lake City: Gibbs Smith, 2003.

Alpert, Hollis, ed. *Charlton Heston: The Actor's Life, Journals 1956–1976.* New York: Dutton, 1978.

Alter, Douglas D., and Karl F. Brooks. *A History of Washington County: From Isolation to Destination.* Salt Lake City: Utah Historical Society/Washington County Commission, 1996.

Bogdanovich, Peter. *John Ford.* Rev. & enlarged ed. Berkeley: University of California Press, 1978.

Bona, Damien. *Starring John Wayne as Genghis Khan: Hollywood's All-Time Worst Casting Blunders.* Secaucus: Citadel Press, 1996.

Bradley, Martha Sonntag. *A History of Kane County.* Salt Lake City: Utah State Historical Society, 1999.

Braithwaite, Bruce. *The Films of Jack Nicholson.* Bembridge: BCW Publishing, 1977.

Brownlow, Kevin. *The Parade's Gone By.* New York: Alfred A. Knopf, 1969.

———. *The War, the West, and the Wilderness.* New York: Alfred A. Knopf, 1979.

Buscombe, Edward, ed. *The BFI Companion to the Western.* Rev. ed. New York: Atheneum, 1993.

Carey, Jr., Harry. *Company of Heroes.* Metuchen: Scarecrow, 1994.

Carmichael, Deborah A. *The Landscape of Hollywood Westerns.* Salt Lake City: University of Utah Press, 2006.

Clark, H. Jackson. *The Owl in Monument Canyon.* Salt Lake City: University of Utah Press, 1993.

Darby, Ken. *Hollywood Holyland: The Filming and Scoring of The Greatest Story Ever Told.* Metuchen: Scarecrow, 1992.

Eyman, Scott. *Print the Legend: The Life and Times of John Ford.* New York: Simon & Schuster, 1999.

Firmage, Richard. *A History of Grand County.* Salt Lake City: Utah State Historical Society and Grand County, 1996.

Ford, Dan. *Pappy.* Englewood Cliffs: Prentice-Hall, 1979.

Fuller, Samuel. *A Third Face.* New York: Alfred Knopf, 2002.

Gaberscek, Carlo. *Cinema Western in California.* Udine, Italy: Stamp Litografia Designgraf, 1991.

———. *Dove Hollywood Ha Creato Il West.* Udine, Italy: n.p., 1988.

———. *Il West di John Ford.* Udine, Italy: Arti Grafiche Friulane, 1994.

Hart, E. Richard, ed. *That Awesome Space: Human Interaction With the Intermountain Landscape.* Salt Lake City: Westwater Press, 1981.

Hulse, Ed. *Filming the West of Zane Grey.* Lone Pine: Beverly and Jim Rogers Museum of Lone Pine History, 2007.

Jones, Charles Reed, ed. *Breaking Into the Movies.* New York: Unicorn, 1927.

Lamar, Howard R., ed. *The New Encyclopedia of the American West.* New Haven & London: Yale University Press, 1998.

McBride, Joseph and Michael Wilmington. *John Ford.* New York: DaCapo, 1975.

McGilligan, Patrick. *Jack's Life.* New York: Norton, 1994.

Medved, Harry and Michael. *Golden Turkey Awards.* New York: Perigree Books, 1980.

Mix, Paul E. *The Life and Legend of Tom Mix.* South Brunswick & New York: A.S. Barnes, 1972.

Moon, Samuel. *Tall Sheep.* Norman: University of Oklahoma Press, 1991.

Nash, Jay Robert and Stanley Ralph Ross, eds. *The Motion Picture Guide.* 10 vols. Chicago: Cinebooks, 1985.

Pauly, Thomas H. *Zane Grey: His Life, His Adventures, His Women.* Urbana: University of Illinois Press, 2005.

Platt, Lyman E. and Karen L. *Grafton: Ghost Town on the Rio Virgin.* St. George: Tonaquint Press, 1998.

Robinson, Adonis Findlay. *History of Kane County.* Kane County: Kane County Daughters of the Utah Pioneers, 1970.

———. *Romance of the Black Cat.* [Kanab]: Kanab Heritage Council, 2002.

Schickel, Richard. *The Men Who Made the Movies.* New York: Atheneum, 1975.

Seegmiller, Janet. *History of Iron County: Community Above Self.* Salt Lake City: Utah State Historical Society/Iron County (Utah) Commission, 1988.

Sillitoe, Linda. *A History of Salt Lake County.* Salt Lake City: Utah State Historical Society/ Salt Lake County Commission, 1996.

Sinclair, Andrew. *John Ford.* New York: Dial/James Wade, 1979.

Slide, Anthony. *The New Historical Dictionary of the American Film Industry.* Lanham, MD: Scarecrow, 1998.

Solomon, Aubrey. *Twentieth Century-Fox: A Corporate and Financial History.* Metuchen: Scarecrow, 1988.

Stanton, Bette L. *"Where God Put the West:" Movie Making in the Desert. A Moab–Monument Valley Movie History.* 2d ed. Moab: Four Corners Publications, 2008.

Steinberg, Cobbett. *Reel Facts.* New York: Vintage, 1978.

Stier, Kenny. *The First Fifty Years of Sound Westerns Movie Locations (1929–1979).* Rialto: Corriganville Press, 2006.

Swanson, Frederick H. *Dave Rust: A Life in the Canyons.* Salt Lake City: University of Utah Press, 2007.

Thompson, Frank. *William A. Wellman.* Metuchen: Scarecrow, 1983.

Tornabene, Lyn. *Long Live the King.* New York: Putnam, 1976.

Walsh, Raoul. *Each Man in His Time.* New York: Farrar, Giroux & Strauss, 1978.

Weaver, Tom. *Monsters, Mutants and Heavenly Creatures.* Baltimore: Midnight Marquee Press, 1996.

Weiss, Ken. *To Be Continued: American Sound Serials 1929–1956.* 3rd ed. New Rochelle, NY: Love's Labor/Cummington, 2008.

Williamson, Martha, and Robin Sheets. *Touched by An Angel: Stories from the Hit Television Series!* Grand Rapids: Zondervan, 1997.

Wills, Gary. *John Wayne's America.* New York: Simon & Schuster, 1997.

Zolotow, Maurice. *Shooting Star.* New York: Simon & Schuster, 1974.

MAGAZINES AND JOURNALS

Berg, Louis. "400 Women—and Bob Taylor." *This Week* (July 8, 1951).

Breed, Jack. "First Motor Sortie into Escalante Land." *National Geographic Magazine* (September 1948).

Carlson, Raymond. "The Valley Nobody Knows." *Arizona Highways* (April 1956).

Clark, Neil M. "Desert Trader." *Saturday Evening Post* (March 29, 1947).

D'Arc, James V. "They Came This 'A Way." *Mountainwest Magazine* (March 1978).

Denton, James F. "The Red Man Plays Indian." *Collier's* (March 18, 1944).

Duffy, Jean. "The Greatest Story Ever Told." *Arizona Highways* (January 1965).

Elber, Lynn. "Kevin Costner: Returning 'Yellowstone' Is a Hit on Own Terms." *Us News & World Report* (November 11, 2022).

Flake, Kloma. "A Tale of A Town." *Movieland* (November 1944).

Greene, Virginia. "Some of the Photos That Sold Monument Valley." *Arizona Highways* (September 1981).

Hafen, Lyman. "Gary Cooper's Final Scenes." *St. George Magazine* (Spring1984).

———. "Redford on St. George." *St. George Magazine* (Spring 1984).

McCarthy, Todd. "John Ford and Monument Valley." *American Film* (May 1978).

Moler, Murray. "Out Where the Horse-Operas Grow."*Coronet* (December 1946).

Muir, Florabel. "The Town That Learned to Act." *Saturday Evening Post* (February 17, 1945).

n.a. "Utah's Hollywood." *Life* (September 19,1949).

Nelson, Richard Alan. "Utah Filmmakers of the Silent Screen." *Utah Historical Quarterly* 43:1 (Winter 1975).

———. "From Antagonism to Acceptance: Mormons and the Silver Screen." *Dialogue* 10 (Spring 1977).

Newman, Patricia. "A Flinty Grandmother Battles for the Victims of Utah's Nuclear Tragedy." *People* (October 1, 1979).

———. "The Children of John Wayne, Susan Hayward and Dick Powell Fear That Fallout Killed Their Parents." *People* (November 10, 1980).

Richmond, Jack. "Western Union." *Screen Life* (January 1941).

Rowan, Arthur. "Westward the Women."*American Cinematographer* (January, 1952).

Skow, Jack. "OK, Julie is a Beautiful, Mute, Nymphomaniac Indian Girl."*Saturday Evening Post* (June 1, 1968).

NEWSPAPERS

Aleteia.org

Citizen-News. Hollywood, California.

Daily Herald. Provo, Utah.

Daily Universe (Brigham Young University). Provo, Utah.

Deadline.com

Deseret News. Salt Lake City, Utah.

The Hollywood Reporter. Hollywood, California.

Iron County Record. Cedar City, Utah.

Kane County Standard. Kanab, Utah.

KSLtv.com

Los Angeles Examiner. Los Angeles, California.

Los Angeles Times. Los Angeles, California.

Motion Picture Herald. Los Angeles, California.

Moving Picture World. New York, New York.

New York Times. New York, New York.

Oklahoma City Sentinel. Oklahoma City, Oklahoma.

Salt Lake Tribune. Salt Lake City, Utah.

Southern Utah News. Kanab, Utah.

Times-Independent. Moab, Utah.

Variety. Hollywood, California. New York, New York.

Washington County News. St. George, Utah.

RECORDED MEDIA

Butch Cassidy and the Sundance Kid. Blu-ray disc. 1969. Audio Commentary by Conrad Hall. Fox Home Entertainment. 2246813. 2007.

Carnival of Souls. DVD. 1962. Audio commentary by John Clifford and Herk Harvey. Criterion Collection. CC15530. 2000.

The Searchers. Blu-ray disc. 1956. *Warner Bros. Presents* supplementary material. Warner Home Video.111532. 2006.

Slaughter of the Innocents. Laserdisc. 1993. Audio commentary by James Glickenhaus. MCA Universal Home Video. 41650. 1994.

Touched by An Angel: The Complete First Season on DVD. Paramount/CBS DVD. 2004.

ARCHIVAL COLLECTIONS & UNPUBLISHED ITEMS

n.a., *Annual Report of Extension Work, Agricultural Agent—Iron County 1936.* N.p.: U.S. Department of Agriculture, Utah State Agricultural College and County Farm Bureaus. Special Collections, Gerald R. Sherratt Library. Southern Utah University. Cedar City, UT.

Bison Archives. Hollywood, CA.

Brown, Karl. N.t. Unpublished typescript. Courtesy of Kevin Brownlow.

Cooper, Inez. "Biography of Gronway Robert Parry (1889–1969)." Gronway Parry Collection MS 18. Special Collections. Gerald R. Sherratt Library. Southern Utah University. Cedar City, UT.

Crawford, J.L. "When Hollywood Discovered Zion." N.d., unpublished typescript in author's possession.

Dena S. Markoff Collection ZION 11887. Zion National Park Museum. Springdale, UT.

Department of Publicity & Industrial Development. Utah State Archives. Salt Lake City, UT.

Howard Pearson Papers MSS 2147. L. Tom Perry Special Collections. Harold B. Lee Library. Brigham Young University. Provo, UT.

Jean Adams Crosby Collection MSS 7520. L. Tom Perry Special Collections. Brigham Young University. Provo, Utah.

Lex Chamberlain Collection MSS 7522. L. Tom Perry Special Collections. Harold B. Lee Library. Brigham Young University. Provo, UT.

"Mary E. Woolley Chamberlain: Handmaiden of the Lord," n.p. [Kanab, UT], n.d. [ca. 1960s].

Kanab Heritage Museum. Kanab, UT.

Motion Picture Publicity Collection MSS 2544. L. Tom Perry Special Collections. Brigham Young University. Provo, UT.

Motion Picture Stills Collection P-768. L. Tom Perry Special Collections. Harold B. Lee Library. Brigham Young University. Provo, UT.

Nelson, Richard Alan. "A History of Latter-day Saint Screen Portrayals in the Silent Film Era, 1905–1936." Master's thesis, Brigham Young University, 1975.

Perry, Harold, with Col. Oscar Estes. "Autobiography." Unpublished typescript. Courtesy of Kevin Brownlow.

Seegmiller, Janet. "Selling the Scenery: Chauncey and Gronway Parry and the Birth of Southern Utah's Tourism and Movie Industries." Powerpoint. September 2005. Special Collections. Gerald R. Sherratt Library. Southern Utah University. Cedar City, UT.

Stanton, Bette L. "Making of the Movie *Stallion Canyon,* Kanab Pictures Corporation." N.d., unpublished typescript in author's possession.

Thomas, J. W. "Chauncey Gardner Parry—Modern Pioneer." N.d., unpublished typescript in author's possession.

Twentieth Century-Fox Corporate Archives. Beverly Hills, CA.

Universal Pictures Papers. Cinematic Arts Library. University of Southern California. Los Angeles, CA.

Utah Parks Company Oral History Projects. Special Collections. Gerald R. Sherratt Library. Southern Utah University. Cedar City, UT.

Warner Bros. Papers. Cinematic Arts Library. University of Southern California. Los Angeles, CA.

INTERVIEWS

All interviews are by the author and are in his possession, unless otherwise indicated.

Jack Adams. Northridge, CA. April 10, 2001; Indian Wells, CA. September 29, 2008.

Ralph L. Beckett. Pasadena, CA. July, 1977.

Gordon Bench. Alpine, UT. September 22, 2008.

Scott Boyter. Provo, UT. November 18, 2008.

Barbara Burfk Cathey. Moab, UT. August 15, 2002.

Kevin Costner. Moab, UT. June 13, 2023.

J. L. Crawford. St. George, UT. March 18, 2000.

Linda Adams Crosby. Kanab, UT. January 6, 2001.

Lisa Davis. Telephone. July 7, 2008.

Andre de Toth. Burbank, CA. March 24, 1996.

Vilo DeMille. Rockville, UT. August 30, 2008.

Mary Gae Evans. Telephone. October 17, 2008.

Patrick Ford. Torrance, CA. April 25, 1979.
Billie Frei. Telephone. November 3, 2008.
Ina Fay Frost. Kanab, UT. March 23, 1995.
Jack Goodspeed. Moab, UT. August 14, 2002.
Peter Graves. Santa Monica, CA. October 1, 2008.
Jeff Harmon and Neal Harmon. Provo, UT. June 9, 2023.
Don Holyoak. Moab, UT. March 26, 1995.
Susette Hsiung. Written. June 5, 2023.
Dallas Jenkins. Mapleton, UT. June 16, 2023.
Calvin Johnson. Kanab, UT. March 1995; August 27, 2009.
Sylvan Johnson. Johnson Canyon, UT. March 16, 2000.
Dennis Judd. Kanab, UT. March 23, 1995.
Howard W. Koch. With Dennis Rowley, Hollywood, CA., November 10, 1976; Paria, UT. May 18, 1995.
Bega Metzner. Moab, UT. June 13, 2023.
Marshall Moore. Park City, UT. May 30, 2023.
Merle Morris. Telephone. October 29, 2008.
Betty Motter. Telephone. October 29, 2008.
Dale Parry. By Janet Seegmiller. July 4, 2004. Utah Parks Company Oral History Projects, 29. Special Collections, Gerald R. Sherratt Memorial Library. Southern Utah University. Cedar City, UT.
Philip A. Patterson. Moab, UT. June 13, 2023.
Brad Pelo. Telephone. July 13, 2023.
Grayce Beckett Pike. Pasadena, CA. July, 1977. Grayce Beckett Pike Papers MSS SC 1257. L. Tom Perry Special Collections. Brigham Young University. Provo, UT.
Jackie Rife. Kanab, UT. March 23, 1995; September 10, 1999; November 10, 2008.
Shae Robins. Telephone. July 23, 2023.
Rupert Ruesch. Springdale, UT. January 6, 2001.
George Schenck. Los Angeles, CA. April 7, 2001.
Bette L. Stanton. Moab, UT. March 26, 1995; June 22, 2002.
Karl Tangren. Moab, UT. March 26, 1995.
Sam Taylor. Moab, UT. June 25, 2002.
Louise Parry Thomas. By Janet Seegmiller. July 18, 2003. Utah Parks Company Oral History Project, UPC #15b. Special Collections, Gerald R. Surratt Memorial Library. Southern Utah University. Cedar City, UT.
Louise Parry Thomas. Hurricane, UT. January 6, 2001.
Leigh von der Esch. Salt Lake City, UT. 1994; December 9, 2008.
George White. Moab, UT. March 27, 1995.
Martha Williamson. Telephone. May 23, 2023.
Paul Wurtzel. Los Angeles, CA. June 11, 2001.

MOTION PICTURES AND TELEVISION PRODUCTIONS MADE IN UTAH

Any list of motion pictures claiming to be comprehensive is immediately challenged by frequent lack of documentation, the fact that many productions simply no longer exist, and the sheer enormity of the number of films included. In later years, straight-to-video releases were often released with titles other than those by which they were known at the time of production. I have attempted to include here significant feature films, television shows, and documentaries that, in one form or another, found their way into theatrical, television, or home-video release in various formats. Finally, you will note occasional references to Utah filming locations in counties not covered in the chapters of this book.

Titles of motion pictures are listed below, followed by production company and releasing studio. The year in which the production is placed is the actual year of release (in theaters, television, cable, and video), which is not usually the same year of production. An asterisk (*) denotes that the film is in color through 1965. After 1965, all titles are in color. Director (DIR); lead members of the cast (CAST); and the known Utah locations (LOC). Entries of many films include other locations (OL) outside of Utah, even when the primary location is in Utah.

The Utah filming locations identified after LOC do not always mean that they were the primary locations. The narrative chapters in this book will guide you to those titles for which Utah locations served as the primary filming sites. The simple designation of "Utah" as the LOC indicates that the motion picture or television series episode was either unavailable for viewing or that the specific Utah locations are thus far unidentified. Every effort has been made to corroborate the accuracy of the information gleaned from contemporary newspapers, studio documents, viewing of the films and television programs, and from entries on Imdb.com.

All listings are movies unless identified as television.

1913:

One Hundred Years of Mormonism (Utah Moving Picture Co.). DIR: Norval MacGregor. LOC: Salt Lake City, Daniels Canyon, Heber.

1923:

The Covered Wagon (Paramount). DIR: James Cruze. CAST: J. Warren Kerrigan, Lois Wilson, Ernest Torrence. LOC: Garrison. OL: eastern Nevada.

1924:

The Deadwood Coach (Fox Film Corp.). DIR: Lynn Reynolds. CAST: Tom Mix, George Bancroft, DeWitt Jennings. LOC: Cedar Breaks, Zion, Springdale, Bryce Canyon, Johnson Canyon. Note: lost film.

1925:

The Vanishing American (Paramount). DIR: George B. Seitz. CAST: Richard Dix, Lois Wilson, Noah Beery. LOC: Monument Valley, Rainbow Bridge. OL: Tuba City, Sagi Canyon, AZ.

1926:

Forlorn River (Paramount). DIR: John Waters. CAST: Jack Holt, Raymond Hatton, Arlette Marchal. LOC: Zion, Bryce Canyon, Cedar Breaks. Note: lost film.

1927:

Arizona Bound (Paramount). DIR: John Waters. CAST: Gary Cooper, Betty Jewel, El Brendel. LOC: Bryce Canyon. Note: lost film.

Lightning (Tiffany Prods.). DIR: James C. McKay. CAST: Jobyna Ralston, Margaret Livingston, Robert Frazier. LOC: Sevier Mountains. Note: lost film.

Nevada (Paramount). DIR: John Waters. CAST: Gary Cooper, Thelma Todd, William Powell. LOC: Zion, Bryce Canyon, Cedar Breaks.

1928:

The Shepherd of the Hills (First National). DIR: Albert S. Rogell. CAST: Alec B. Francis, Molly O'Day, John Boles. LOC: Cedar Breaks, Dixie National Forest. Note: lost film.

Under the Tonto Rim (Paramount). DIR: Herman Raymaker. CAST: Richard Arlen, Mary Brian, Jack Luden. LOC: Undetermined [*Salt Lake Tribune* ad, 18 February 1928]. Note: lost film.

The Vanishing Pioneer (Paramount). DIR: John Waters. CAST: Jack Holt, Jack Holt Jr. (Tim Holt), William Powell. LOC: Zion, Springdale. Note: lost film.

Ramona (Inspiration Pictures/United Artists). DIR: Edwin Carewe. CAST: Dolores del Rio, Warner Baxter, Roland Drew. LOC: Zion, Springdale, Cedar Breaks.

The Night Flyer (James Cruze Prods./Pathe). DIR: Walter Lang. CAST: William Boyd, Jobyna Ralston, Philo McCullough. LOC: Thistle. Note: lost film.

1929:

In Old Arizona (Fox Film Corp.). DIR: Irving Cummings. CAST: Warner Baxter, Edmund Lowe, Dorothy Burgess. LOC: Zion, Grafton. OL: Mojave Desert, CA.

All Faces West [originally "The Exodus." 1931 sound version "Call of the Rockies"] (Pioneer Film Corp.). DIR: George Edward Lewis. CAST: Ben Lyon, Marie Prevost, Andrus Randolph. LOC: Salt Lake City.

The Great Divide (First National). DIR: Reginald Barker. CAST: Dorothy Mackaill, Ian Keith, Lucien Littlefield. LOC: Zion.

1930:

The Arizona Kid (Fox Film Corp.). DIR: Alfred Santell. CAST: Warner Baxter, Mona Maris, Carole Lombard. LOC: Grafton, Rockville Road, Zion.

Billy the Kid (M-G-M). DIR: King Vidor. CAST: Johnny Mack Brown, Wallace Beery, Kay Johnson. LOC: Zion. OL: Gallup, NM; Grand Canyon, AZ; Porter Ranch, San Fernando Valley, CA.

The Lone Star Ranger (Fox Film Corp.). DIR: A. F. Erickson. CAST: George O'Brien, Sue Carol, Walter MacGrail. LOC: Monument Valley, Rainbow Bridge.

1934:

Cross Country Cruise (Universal). DIR: Edward Buzzell. CAST: Lew Ayres, June Knight, Alice White. LOC: Salt Lake City.

The Dude Ranger (Fox Film Corp.). DIR: Edward F. Cline. CAST: George O'Brien, Irene Hervey, LeRoy Mason. LOC: Johnson Canyon, Springdale, Zion, Virgin River. OL: Grand Canyon, AZ.

1935:

When a Man's a Man (Fox Film Corp.). DIR: Edward F. Cline. CAST: George O'Brien, Dorothy Wilson, Paul Kelly. LOC: Zion.

1937:

The Painted Stallion (Republic). 15-chapter serial. DIR: William Witney, Alan James, Ray Taylor. CAST: Ray Corrigan, Hoot Gibson, LeRoy Mason. LOC: Snow Canyon.

The Good Earth (M-G-M). DIR: Sidney Franklin. CAST: Paul Muni, Luise Rainer, Walter Connolly. LOC: Parowan.

The Bad Man of Brimstone (M-G-M). DIR: J. Walter Reuben. CAST: Wallace Beery, Virginia Bruce, Dennis O'Keefe. LOC: Johnson Canyon, the Gap, Kanab Canyon, Zion, Springdale.

1938:

The Great Adventures of Wild Bill Hickok (Columbia). 15-chapter serial. DIR: Sam Nelson, Mack V. Wright. CAST: William Elliott, Monte Blue, Carole Wayne. LOC: Johnson Canyon, Three Lakes, Parry Lodge.

1939:

Feud on the Range (Metropolitan). DIR: Harry S. Webb. CAST: Bob Steele, Richard Cramer, Gertrude Messenger. LOC: Cave Lakes, Johnson Canyon.

Drums Along the Mohawk* (Twentieth Century-Fox). DIR: John Ford. CAST: Claudette Colbert, Henry Fonda, Edna May Oliver. LOC: Duck Creek, Strawberry Valley, Aspen Mirror Lake, Navajo Lake, Sidney Valley, Cedar Breaks.

Westbound Stage (Monogram). DIR: Spencer Gordon. CAST: Tex Ritter, Muriel Evans, Reed Howes. LOC: Johnson Canyon, Cave Lakes, Kanab Canyon.

The Mormon Conquest (Security National Pictures). DIR: Denver Dixon (Victor Adamson). CAST: Dorothy McKinnan, Tom Wynn, Bonnie Chamberlain. LOC: Kanab Canyon, Three Lakes, Cedar Mountain, Strawberry Valley, Zion, Bryce Canyon. Note: lost film.

Union Pacific (Paramount). DIR: Cecil B. DeMille. CAST: Barbara Stanwyck, Joel McCrea, Robert Preston. LOC: Iron Springs

20,000 Men a Year (Twentieth Century-Fox). DIR: Alfred E. Green. CAST: Randolph Scott, Preston Foster, Margaret Lindsay. LOC: Zion.

Stagecoach (Walter Wanger/United Artists). DIR: John Ford. CAST: John Wayne, Claire Trevor, Thomas Mitchell. LOC: Monument Valley. OL: Newhall, Kern River, Lucerne Dry Lake, Victorville, CA.

Only Angels Have Wings (Columbia). DIR: Howard Hawks. CAST: Cary Grant, Jean Arthur, Richard Barthelmess. LOC: St. George, Zion.

Overland With Kit Carson (Columbia). 15-chapter serial. DIR: Sam Nelson, Norman Deming. CAST: William Elliott, Iris Meredith, Richard Fiske. LOC: Johnson Canyon, Kanab Canyon. OL: Kiabab Forest, AZ.

Lure of the Wasteland* (Al Lane Pictures/Monogram). DIR: Harry Fraser. CAST: Grant Withers, LeRoy Mason, Marion Arnold. LOC: Johnson Canyon.

1940:

Roll Wagons Roll (Monogram). DIR: Al Herman. CAST: Tex Ritter, Muriel Evans, Nelson McDowell. LOC: Johnson Canyon, Cave Lakes, Kanab Canyon.

Brigham Young (Twentieth Century-Fox). DIR: Henry Hathaway. CAST: Tyrone Power, Linda Darnell, Dean Jagger. LOC: Plains west of Parowan Gap, Utah Lake for seagull sequences. OL: Lone Pine, CA.

The Mortal Storm (M-G-M). DIR: Frank Borzage. CAST: Margaret Sullavan, James Stewart, Robert Young. LOC: Salt Lake City/Alta.

The Fargo Kid (RKO). DIR: Harry Fraser. CAST: Tim Holt, Harry Carey, Gertrude Messenger. LOC: Paria.

The Thief of Bagdad* (Korda/United Artists). DIR: Ludwig Berger, Tim Whelan, Michael Powell. CAST: Sabu, John Justin, June Duprez. LOC: Bryce Canyon.

Wagon Train (RKO). DIR: Edward Killy. CAST: Tim Holt, Ray Whitley, Martha O'Driscoll. LOC: Kanab Canyon, Cave Lakes, Paria, the Gap.

Kit Carson (Edward Small/United Artists). DIR: George B. Seitz. CAST: Jon Hall, Dana Andrews, Lynn Bari. LOC: Monument Valley, San Juan River, Mexican Hat.

1941:

Western Union* (Twentieth Century-Fox). DIR: Fritz Lang. CAST: Randolph Scott, Robert Young, Dean Jagger. LOC: Johnson Canyon, Paria, the Gap, Alton. OL: Fredonia, AZ.

Billy the Kid* (M-G-M). DIR: David Miller. CAST: Robert Taylor, Brian Donlevy, Chill Wills. LOC: Monument Valley.

1942:

Arabian Nights* (Universal). DIR: John Rawlins. CAST: Sabu, Jon Hall, Maria Montez. LOC: Coral Pink Sand Dunes.

King of the Stallions (Monogram). DIR: Edward Finney. CAST: Chief Thundercloud, Dave O'Brien, Sally Caims. LOC: Monument Valley, Crater Canyon, CA.

1943:

My Friend Flicka* (Twentieth Century-Fox). DIR: Harold Schuster. CAST: Roddy McDowall, Preston Foster, Rita Johnson. LOC: Duck Creek, Aspen Mirror Lake, Rockville Road, Strawberry Valley, Johnson Canyon, Zion, Cedar Breaks.

In Old Oklahoma (aka "War of the Wildcats") (Republic). DIR: Albert S. Rogell. CAST: John Wayne, Martha Scott, Albert Dekker. LOC: Johnson Canyon, Paria, Cedar City, Virgin.

The Desperadoes* (Columbia). DIR: Charles Vidor. CAST: Randolph Scott, Glenn Ford, Claire Trevor. LOC: Johnson Canyon, Kanab Canyon, the Gap, Paria.

1944:

Buffalo Bill* (Twentieth Century-Fox). DIR: William Wellman. CAST: Joel McCrea, Maureen O'Hara, Linda Darnell. LOC: Johnson Canyon, Paria.

Can't Help Singing* (Universal). DIR: Frank Ryan. CAST: Deanna Durbin, Robert Paige, Akim Tamiroff. LOC: Johnson Canyon, Cascade Falls, Duck Creek, Strawberry Point, Navajo Lake, Cedar Breaks.

City of Brigham Young* (M-G-M). DIR: James A. FitzPatrick. Documentary. LOC: Salt Lake City.

Monumental Utah* (M-G-M). NARRATOR: James A. FitzPatrick. LOC: Zion, Bryce Canyon.

Days of Glory (RKO). DIR: Jacques Tourneur. CAST: Tamara Toumanova, Gregory Peck, Alan Reed. LOC: Cedar City.

1945:

Thunderhead, Son of Flicka* (Twentieth

Century-Fox). DIR: Louis King. CAST: Roddy McDowall, Preston Foster, Rita Johnson. LOC: Duck Creek, Strawberry Valley, Kanab Canyon, Navajo Lake, Glendale, Zion.

Spellbound (Selznick/RKO). DIR: Alfred Hitchcock. CAST: Gregory Peck, Ingrid Bergman, Leo G. Carroll. LOC: Alta.

1946:

Smoky* (Twentieth Century-Fox) DIR: Louis King. CAST: Fred MacMurray, Anne Baxter, Burl Ives. LOC: Zion, Kanab Race Track, Cave Lakes, Aspen Mirror Lake, the Gap, Rockville Road, Kanab Canyon, Ogden, Cedar Breaks, Three Lakes. OL: Fredonia, AZ; Cheyenne, WY; Burbank and Saugus, CA.

The Harvey Girls* (M-G-M). DIR: George Sidney. CAST: Judy Garland, Angela Lansbury, John Hodiak. LOC: Monument Valley.

My Darling Clementine (Twentieth Century-Fox). DIR: John Ford. CAST: Henry Fonda, Victor Mature, Cathy Downs, Linda Darnell. LOC: Monument Valley.

Avalanche (Producers Releasing Corporation). DIR: Irving Allen. CAST: Bruce Cabot, Roscoe Karns, Helen Mowery. LOC: Wasatch Mountains.

Little Mr. Jim (M-G-M). DIR: Fred Zinnemann. CAST: Jackie "Butch" Jenkins, James Craig, Frank Gifford. LOC: Fort Douglas.

1947:

Slave Girl* (Universal). DIR: Charles Lamont. CAST: Yvonne De Carlo, George Brent, Broderick Crawford. LOC: Paria Canyon, Coral Pink Sand Dunes.

Ramrod (Enterprise/United Artists). DIR: Andre de Toth. CAST: Veronica Lake, Joel McCrea, Preston Foster. LOC: Zion, Grafton.

Thunder in the Valley* (original release title: "Bob, Son of Battle") (Twentieth Century-Fox). DIR: Louis King. CAST: Lon McCallister, Edmund Gwenn, Peggy Ann Garner. LOC: Duck Creek, Strawberry Valley, Strawberry Point, Kanab Canyon, Navajo Lake, Blue Springs.

Angel and the Badman (Republic). DIR: James Edward Grant. CAST: John Wayne, Gail Russell, Harry Carey. LOC: Monument Valley under main title only. OL: New Mexico.

1948:

Green Grass of Wyoming* (Twentieth Century-Fox). DIR: Louis King. CAST: Charles Coburn, Peggy Cummings, Lloyd Nolan. LOC: Strawberry Valley, Three Lakes, Kanab Race Track, Rockville Road, Panguitch Lake, Cedar Breaks.

Fury at Furnace Creek (Twentieth Century-Fox). DIR: H. Bruce Humberstone. CAST: Victor Mature, Coleen Gray, Glenn Langan. LOC: Zion, Virgin River, Springdale, Johnson Canyon. OL: Arizona Strip, AZ.

Black Bart* (Universal). DIR: George Sherman. CAST: Yvonne De Carlo, Dan Duryea, John McIntire. LOC: Kanab Canyon, Strawberry Valley, Strawberry Point.

Fort Apache (Argosy Pictures/RKO). DIR: John Ford. CAST: John Wayne, Henry Fonda, Shirley Temple. LOC: Monument Valley, San Juan River at Mexican Hat.

1949:

The Big Cat* (William Moss Pictures/Eagle Lion). DIR: Phil Karlson. CAST: Lon McCallister, Peggy Ann Garner, Preston Foster. LOC: Cedar Breaks, Parowan Canyon, Hoosier Lake, Strawberry Point.

Calamity Jane and Sam Bass* (Universal). DIR: George Sherman. CAST: Yvonne De Carlo, Howard Duff, Dorothy Hart. LOC: Johnson Canyon, Kanab Race Track, Vermillion Cliffs, Kanab Canyon, the Gap.

Red Canyon* (Universal). DIR: George Sherman. CAST: Howard Duff, Ann Blyth, George Brent. LOC: Duck Creek, Cascade Falls, Kanab Canyon, Kanab Race Track, Aspen Mirror Lake, Paria, Tibbets Valley, Bryce Canyon.

She Wore a Yellow Ribbon* (Argosy Pictures/RKO). DIR: John Ford. CAST: John Wayne, John Agar, Harry Carey. LOC: Monument Valley, San Juan River at Mexican Hat.

Stallion Canyon* (Kanab Pictures/Astor). DIR: Harry Fraser. CAST: Ken Curtis, Carolina Cotton, Shug Fisher. LOC: St. George, Ivins, Escalante.

1950:

The Outriders* (M-G-M). DIR: Roy Rowland. CAST: Joel McCrea, Arlene Dahl, Claude Jarman. LOC: Duck Creek, Aspen Mirror Lake, Strawberry Valley, Paria, Long Valley, Asay Creek.

Wagon Master (Argosy Pictures/RKO). DIR: John Ford. CAST: Ben Johnson, Harry Carey, Ward Bond. LOC: Professor Valley, Colorado River, Spanish Valley.

Rio Grande (Republic). DIR: John Ford. CAST: John Wayne, Maureen O'Hara, Ben Johnson. LOC: Ida Gulch, Professor Valley, Colorado River, Onion Creek Narrows.

Sierra* (Universal-International). DIR: Alfred E. Green. CAST: Audie Murphy, Wanda Hendrix, Dean Jagger. LOC: Kanab Canyon, Aspen Mirror Lake, Duck Creek, Cascade Falls, Cedar Breaks.

1951:

Cattle Drive* (Universal-International). DIR: Kurt Neumann. CAST: Joel McCrea, Dean Stockwell, Chill Wills. LOC: Paria. OL: Death Valley, CA.

Oh! Susanna* (Republic). DIR: Joe Kane. CAST: Rod Cameron, Forrest Tucker, Chill Wills. LOC: Aspen Mirror Lake, Strawberry Valley.

Best of the Badmen* (RKO). DIR: William D. Russell. CAST: Robert Ryan, Bruce Cabot, Claire Trevor. LOC: Paria, Johnson Canyon, Strawberry Valley, the Gap, Kanab Canyon.

Westward the Women (M-G-M). DIR: William A. Wellman. CAST: Robert Taylor, Denise Darcel, Hope Emerson. LOC: Johnson Canyon, Kanab Canyon, the Gap, Paria, Surprise Valley.

1952:

The Lion and the Horse* (Warner Bros.). DIR: Louis King. CAST: Steve Cochran, Ray Teal, Harry Antrim. LOC: Rockville Road, Kanab Canyon, Cave Lakes, Barracks Canyon, Three Lakes.

Bugles in the Afternoon* (Warner Bros.). DIR: Roy Rowland. CAST: Ray Milland, Hugh Marlowe, Forrest Tucker. LOC: Johnson Canyon, Long Canyon, Asay Creek, Kanab Canyon, Aspen Mirror Lake, Strawberry Valley.

The Battle at Apache Pass* (Universal-International). DIR: George Sherman. CAST: Jeff Chandler, John Lund, Susan Cabot. LOC: Professor Valley, Ida Gulch, Courthouse Wash, Arches, Colorado River, Sand Flats.

The Toughest Man in Arizona (Republic). DIR: R. G. Springsteen. CAST: Vaughn Monroe, Joan Leslie, Edgar Buchanan. LOC: Snow Canyon.

This is Cinerama* (Lowell Thomas Co./Cinerama Productions). SEQUENCE SUPERVISORS: Lowell Thomas, Merian C. Cooper, Michael Todd. LOC: Salt Lake City (Kennecott open-pit mine), Zion.

Ride the Man Down (Republic). DIR: Joseph Kane. CAST: Brian Donlevy, Rod Cameron, Forrest Tucker. LOC: Kanab Canyon, Johnson Canyon, Cave Lakes.

1953:

Taza, Son of Cochise* (Universal-International). DIR: Douglas Sirk. CAST: Rock Hudson, Barbara Rush, Jeff Chandler. LOC: Castle Valley, Professor Valley, Sand Flats, Devil's Garden, Arches.

Ride, Vaquero!* (M-G-M). DIR: John Farrow. CAST: Robert Taylor, Ava Gardner, Howard Keel. LOC: Kanab Canyon, Johnson Canyon.

Pony Express* (Paramount). DIR: Jerry Hopper. CAST: Charlton Heston, Rhonda Fleming, Forrest Tucker. LOC: Kanab Creek, Kanab movie fort, the Gap, Johnson Canyon.

1954:

Border River* (Universal-International). DIR: George Sherman. CAST: Joel McCrea, Yvonne De Carlo, Pedro Armendáriz. LOC: Colorado River, Professor Valley, Courthouse Wash.

Siege at Red River* (Panoramic Prods./Twentieth Century-Fox). DIR: Rudolph Mate. CAST: Van Johnson, Joanne Dru, Richard Boone. LOC: Professor Valley, Colorado River, Castle Valley, Dead Horse Point. OL: Durango, CO.

Southwest Passage* (Edward Small/United Artists). DIR: Ray Nazarro. CAST: John Ireland, Rod Cameron, Joanne Dru. LOC: Johnson Canyon, Coral Pink Sand Dunes.

The Yellow Tomahawk* (Bel-Air/United Artists). DIR: Lesley Selander. CAST: Rory Calhoun, Peggie Castle, Lee Van Cleef. LOC: Turkey Crossing, Kanab movie fort, Kanab Creek, Kanab Canyon, Three Lakes.

Smoke Signal* (Universal-International). DIR: Jerry Hopper. CAST: Dana Andrews, Piper Laurie, Pat Hogan. LOC: Big Bend of the Colorado River, Professor Valley, Ida Gulch, Courthouse Wash, San Juan River.

1955:

Canyon Crossroads (MTP/United Artists). DIR: Alfred L. Werker. CAST: Richard Basehart, Phyllis Kirk, Stephen Elliott. LOC: Professor Valley, Ninemile Bottom, Sevenmile Canyon, Dead Horse Point, Castle Valley, downtown Moab.

Santa Fe Passage* (Republic). DIR: William Witney. CAST: John Payne, Faith Domergue, Rod Cameron. LOC: Snow Canyon.

Fort Yuma* (Camden/United Artists). DIR: Lesley Selander. CAST: Peter Graves, Joan Vohs, John Hudson. LOC: Kanab movie fort, Kanab Creek, Kanab Canyon.

A Man Alone* (Republic). DIR: Ray Milland. CAST: Ray Milland, Mary Murphy, Ward Bond. LOC: Sand dunes outside St. George.

1956:

The Lone Ranger* (Warner Bros.). DIR: Stuart Heisler. CAST: Clayton Moore, Jay Silverheels, Lyle Bettger. LOC: Kanab Canyon, Barracks Canyon, Johnson Canyon.

Quincannon: Frontier Scout* (Bel-Air/United Artists). DIR: Lesley Selander. CAST: Tony Martin, Peggie Castle, John Bromfield. LOC: Kanab Canyon. OL: Pipe Springs, AZ.

Ghost Town (Bel-Air/United Artists). DIR: Allen Miner. CAST: Kent Taylor, John Smith, Marian Carr. LOC: Johnson Canyon, Kanab movie fort.

The Conqueror* (RKO). DIR: Dick Powell. CAST: John Wayne, Susan Hayward, Pedro Armendáriz. LOC: Snow Canyon, Warner Valley, Pine Valley, Leeds, Harrisburg.

The Searchers* (C. V. Whitney/Warner Bros.). DIR: John Ford. CAST: John Wayne, Jeffrey Hunter, Vera Miles. LOC: Monument Valley, San Juan River at Mexican Hat.

The King and Four Queens* (Russ-Field-Gabco/United Artists). DIR: Raoul Walsh. CAST: Clark Gable, Eleanor Parker, Jo Van Fleet. LOC: Snow Canyon, Santa Clara River.

Trooper Hook (Fielding Prods./United Artists). DIR: Charles Marquis Warren. CAST: Joel McCrea, Barbara Stanwyck, Rodolfo Acosta. LOC: Kanab Canyon, Three Lakes, the Gap.

Stagecoach to Fury (Regal /Twentieth Century-Fox). DIR: William Claxton. CAST: Forrest Tucker, Mari Blanchard, Wally Ford. LOC: the Gap.

Television:

Cavalry Patrol. (CBS). Series. LOC: Kanab.

1957:

Raiders of Old California (Allied Artists). DIR: Albert Ganaway. CAST: Jim Davis, Arleen Whelan, Lee Van Cleef. LOC: Kanab Canyon.

Copper Sky (Regal Films/Twentieth Century-Fox). DIR: Charles Marquis Warren. CAST: Jeff Morrow, Coleen Gray, Strother Martin. LOC: Johnson Canyon, Kanab Canyon.

War Drums* (Bel-Air/United Artists) DIR: Reginald Le Borg. CAST: Lex Barker, Joan Taylor, Ben Johnson. LOC: Kanab Canyon, Johnson Canyon.

Perri* (Disney/Buena Vista) DIR: Paul Kenworthy Jr. LOC: Salt Lake City, Uintah National Forest.

The Badge of Marshal Brennan (Allied Artists). DIR: Albert C. Gannaway. CAST: Jim Davis, Carl Smith, Arleen Whelan. LOC: Kanab Canyon, Johnson Canyon.

Dragoon Wells Massacre (Allied Artists). DIR: Harold Schuster. CAST: Barry Sullivan, Dennis O'Keefe, Mona Freeman. LOC: Kanab Canyon, Johnson Canyon, the Gap, Kanab movie fort.

Revolt at Fort Laramie* (Bel-Air/United Artists). DIR: Lesley Selander. CAST: John Dehner, Gregg Palmer, Frances Helm. LOC: Kanab movie fort, Kanab Creek.

Tomahawk Trail (Bel-Air/United Artists). DIR: Lesley Selander. CAST: John Smith, Chuck Connors, Lisa Montell, Kanab movie fort, Johnson Canyon.

The Girl in Black Stockings (Bel-Air/United Artists). DIR: Howard W. Koch. CAST: Lex Barker, Anne Bancroft, Mamie Van Doren. LOC: Kanab, Three Lakes, Moqui Cave. OL: Fredonia, AZ.

Run of the Arrow* (RKO/Universal-International). DIR: Samuel Fuller. CAST: Rod Steiger, Sarita Montiel, J. C. Flippen. LOC: Snow Canyon, Pine Valley Lake.

The Dalton Girls (Bel-Air/United Artists). DIR: Reginald Le Borg. CAST: Merry Anders, Penny Edwards, Lisa Davis. LOC: Kanab Canyon, Kanab Creek, Johnson Canyon.

Television:

Boots and Saddles. (NBC). Series. LOC: Kanab Canyon.

1958:

Fort Bowie (Bel-Air/United Artists). DIR: Howard W. Koch. CAST: Ben Johnson, Jan Harrison, Kent Taylor. LOC: Kanab Canyon, Johnson Canyon, Kanab movie fort.

Warlock* (Twentieth Century-Fox). DIR: Edward Dmytryk. CAST: Richard Widmark, Henry Fonda, Anthony Quinn. LOC: Dead Horse Point, Kings Bottom, Professor Valley, Arches, Sand Flats.

Fort Dobbs (Warner Bros.). DIR: Gordon Douglas. CAST: Clint Walker, Virginia Mayo, Brian Keith. LOC: Duck Creek, Aspen Mirror Lake, Paria, Kanab Canyon, Cave Lakes Canyon, Kanab movie fort, Colorado River, Mat Martin Wash, Professor Valley.

Proud Rebel* (Sam Goldwyn/Buena Vista). DIR: Michael Curtiz. CAST: Alan Ladd, Olivia de Havilland, David Ladd. LOC: Cedar Mountain, Rush Lake, Johnson Canyon.

Snowfire (Snowfire Prods./Allied Artists). DIR: Dorell McGowan. CAST: Don Megowan, Molly McGowan, Claire Kelly. LOC: Bryce Canyon Nat'l Park.

1959:

They Came to Cordura* (Columbia). DIR: Robert Rosson. CAST: Gary Cooper, Rita Hayworth, Van Heflin. LOC: Snow Canyon, Harrisburg. OL: Indio, CA.

Timbuktu (Imperial Pictures/United Artists). DIR: Jacques Tourner. CAST: Victor Mature, Yvonne De Carlo, George Dolenz. LOC: Coral Pink Sand Dunes.

Television:

Death Valley Days (Madison Prods.). Series. LOC: Kanab.

1960:

Ten Who Dared* (Disney/Buena Vista). DIR: William Beaudine. CAST: John Beal, Brian Keith, Ben Johnson. LOC: Big Bend of the Colorado River, Professor Valley, Arches, Dead Horse Point, Dewey, Castle Valley, Westwater Canyon.

Sergeant Rutledge* (Warner Bros.). DIR: John Ford. CAST: Jeffrey Hunter, Woody Strode, Constance Towers. LOC: Monument Valley, San Juan River at Mexican Hat.

Seven Ways From Sundown* (Universal). DIR: Harry Keller. CAST: Audie Murphy, Barry Sullivan, Venetia Stevenson. LOC: St. George.

Television:

Death Valley Days (Madison Prods.). Series. LOC: Kanab.

1961:

Gold of the Seven Saints (Warner Bros.). DIR: Gordon Douglas. CAST: Clint Walker, Roger Moore, Chill Wills. LOC: Professor Valley, Fisher Towers, Arches, Dead Horse Point, Kane Creek Canyon, King's Bottom, Sevenmile Wash, Klondike Flats.

The Comancheros* (Twentieth Century-Fox). DIR: Michael Curtiz. CAST: John Wayne, Stuart Whitman, Ina Balin. LOC: Professor Valley, Dead Horse Point, King's Bottom, LaSal Mountains, Fisher Valley, Onion Creek, Hurrah Pass, Haver Ranch.

Half Way to Hell (Victor Adamson Prods.). DIR: Al Adamson. CAST: Al Adamson, David Lloyd, Sergio Virel. LOC: Salt Lake City, Capitol Reef. OL: Chihuahua, Mexico

Television:

Death Valley Days (Madison Prods.). Series. LOC: Kanab.

1962:

Sergeants 3* (Essex-Claude/United Artists). DIR: John Sturges. CAST: Frank Sinatra, Dean Martin, Sammy Davis Jr. LOC: Johnson Canyon, Paria, Kanab movie fort, Bryce Canyon. OL: House Rock Valley, AZ.

Carnival of Souls (Herts-Lion). DIR: Herk Harvey. CAST: Candace Hilligoss, Herk Harvey, Frances Feist. LOC: Salt Lake City, Saltair Resort at Great Salt Lake.

Six Black Horses* (Universal-International). DIR: Harry Keller. CAST: Audie Murphy, Dan Duryea, Joan O'Brien. LOC: Snow Canyon, Leeds.

Television:

Death Valley Days (Madison Prods.). Series. LOC: Kanab.

1963:

How the West Was Won* (M-G-M). DIR: George Marshall, Henry Hathaway, John Ford. CAST: Gregory Peck, George Peppard, Debbie Reynolds. LOC: Monument Valley.

Television:

Death Valley Days (Madison Prods.). Series. LOC: Kanab.

1964:

Bullet for a Badman* (Universal). DIR: R. G. Springsteen. CAST: Audie Murphy, Darren McGavin, Ruta Lee. LOC: Snow Canyon, Virgin River.

Cheyenne Autumn* (Warner Bros.). DIR: John Ford. CAST: Richard Widmark, Caroll Baker, Ricardo Montalban. LOC: Monument Valley, San Juan River at Mexican Hat, Professor Valley, Castle Valley, Colorado River, Fisher Canyon, Arches.

Rio Conchos* (Twentieth Century-Fox). DIR: Gordon Douglas. CAST: Richard Boone, Stuart Whitman, Edmond O'Brien. LOC: Professor Valley, Fisher Towers, Castle Valley, Arches, Dead Horse Point.

Ballad of a Gunfighter (Bill Ward Pictures). DIR: Bill Ward. CAST: Marty Robbins, Joyce Redd, Robert Barron. LOC: Kanab Canyon.

Television:

Death Valley Days (Madison Prods.). Series. LOC: Kanab.

1965:

Duel at Diablo* (United Artists). DIR: Ralph Nelson. CAST: James Garner, Sidney Poitier, Bibi Andersson. LOC: Paria, Kanab Canyon, Tom's Canyon, Glen Canyon, Vermillion Cliffs, White Cliffs, Kiabab National Forest.

Fort Courageous (Twentieth Century-Fox). DIR: Lesley Selander. CAST: Fred Bier, Harry Lauter, Donald Barry. LOC: Kanab movie fort, Johnson Canyon, the Gap.

The Greatest Story Ever Told* (George Stevens/United Artists). DIR: George Stevens. CAST: Max von Sydow, Charlton Heston, Carroll Baker. LOC: Lake Powell, Canyonlands, Island in the Sky, Dead Horse Point.

Convict Stage (Steve Prods./Twentieth Century-Fox). DIR: Lesley Selander. CAST: Harry Lauter, Don "Red" Barry, Jodi Mitchell. LOC: Kanab movie fort, the Gap.

Television:

Daniel Boone. (Arcola Pictures/NBC). Series. LOC: Kane County.

Death Valley Days (Madison Prods.) Series. LOC: Kanab.

Branded (Madison Prods./NBC). Series. LOC: Kanab movie fort, Kanab Canyon.

1966:

Gunpoint (Universal). DIR: Earl Bellamy. CAST: Audie Murphy, Joan Staley, Warren Stevens. LOC: Kanab Canyon.

The Appaloosa (Universal). DIR: Sidney J. Furie. CAST: Marlon Brando, Anjanette Comer, John Saxon. LOC: Hurricane, Virgin River.

The Plainsman (Universal). DIR: David Lowell Rich. CAST: Don Murray, Guy Stockwell, Abby Dalton. LOC: Kanab Canyon, Kanab movie fort, Paria.

The Shooting (Santa Clara). DIR: Monte Hellman. CAST: Warren Oates, Millie Perkins, Jack Nicholson. LOC: Kanab Canyon, Calvin Johnson Ranch, Glen Canyon.

Ride in the Whirlwind (Proteus Films). DIR: Monte Hellman. CAST: Jack Nicholson, Millie Perkins, Cameron Mitchell. LOC: Kanab Canyon, Calvin Johnson Ranch, Paria, Glen Canyon.

Television:

Death Valley Days (Madison Prods.). Series. LOC: Kanab.

1967:

Brighty of the Grand Canyon (Stephen F. Booth Prods.). DIR: Norman Foster. CAST: Joseph Cotten, Dick Foran, Pat Conway. LOC: Colorado River. OL: Grand Canyon, AZ.

Rough Night in Jericho (Universal). DIR: Arnold Laven. CAST: Dean Martin, George Peppard, Jean Simmons. LOC: Glen Canyon, Kanab Canyon, Paria, the Gap.

The Ride to Hangman's Tree (Universal). DIR: Al Rafkin. CAST: Jack Lord, James Farentino, Don Galloway. LOC: Cedar Breaks, Strawberry Valley, Strawberry Point.

A Time for Killing (Sage Western Pictures/Columbia). DIR: Phil Karlson, Roger Corman (uncredited). CAST: Glenn Ford, George Hamilton, Inger Stevens. LOC: Zion, Glen Canyon, Kanab movie fort, Paria, Coral Pink Sand Dunes. OL: Old Tucson, AZ.

Television:

Death Valley Days (Madison Prods.). Series. LOC: Kanab.

1968:

Blue (Paramount). DIR: Silvio Narizzano. CAST: Terence Stamp, Ricardo Montalban, Karl Malden. LOC: Professor Valley, Sevenmile Canyon, Long Valley, Kane Creek Road, Sand Flats, LaSal Mountains, Klondike Flats.

Fade-In (video title: "Iron Cowboy") (BCW/ Paramount). DIR: Allen Smithee (Jud Taylor). CAST: Burt Reynolds, Barbara Loden, Noam Pitlik. LOC: Professor Valley, Castle Valley, Hittle Bottom, Moab, Dead Horse Point, Arches.

2001: A Space Odyssey (M-G-M). DIR: Stanley Kubrick. CAST: Keir Dullea, Gary Lockwood, William Sylvester. LOC: Monument Valley.

Head (Raybert Prods./Columbia). DIR: Bob Rafelson. CAST: Peter Tork, Davy Jones, Micky Dolenz. LOC: Valley Music Hall auditorium.

Planet of the Apes (Twentieth Century-Fox). DIR: Franklin G. Shaffner. CAST: Charlton Heston, Roddy McDowall, Kim Hunter. LOC: Lake Powell, Glen Canyon. OL: Malibu Mountains, Twentieth Century-Fox Ranch, CA.

The Devil's Brigade (David L. Wolper/ United Artists). DIR: Andrew V. McLaglen. CAST: William Holden, Cliff Robertson, Vince Edwards. LOC: Park City, Lehi, Alpine, Solitude, Granite Mountain.

Bandolero! (Twentieth Century-Fox) DIR: Andrew V. McLaglen. CAST: James Stewart, Dean Martin, Raquel Welch. LOC: Kanab Canyon, Glen Canyon. OL: Del Rio, TX.

Television:

Death Valley Days (Madison Prods.). Series. LOC: Kanab. OL: Pipe Spring, AZ.

1969:

Body Fever (Guilty Pleasures). DIR: Ray Dennis Steckler. CAST: Carolyn Brandt, Bernard Fein, Gary Kent. LOC: Bonneville Salt Flats; OL, Los Angeles, North Hollywood, Hollywood, San Pedro, CA.

Butch Cassidy and the Sundance Kid (Twentieth Century-Fox). DIR: George Roy Hill. CAST: Paul Newman, Robert Redford, Katharine Ross. LOC: Snow Canyon, Grafton, Zion. OL: Silverton, CO; Taos, Chama, NM.

Carnival of Fools (Pan American Pictures). DIR: John Carr. CAST: Meredith Haze, Rick Barnes, J. Martin Sellers. LOC: Salt Lake City.

Downhill Racer (Wildwood/Paramount). DIR: Michael Ritchie. CAST: Robert Redford, Camilla Sparv, Gene Hackman. LOC: Sundance. OL: Boulder, CO.

Easy Rider (Columbia) DIR: Dennis Hopper. CAST: Peter Fonda, Dennis Hopper, Jack Nicholson. LOC: Monument Valley.

Love Is a Funny Thing (Films 13, Films Ariane, Majestic Films/United Artists) DIR: Claude Lelouch. CAST: Jean-Paul Belmondo, Annie Girardot, Farrah Fawcett. LOC: Monument Valley, Goulding Trading Post.

Mackenna's Gold (Columbia). DIR: J. Lee Thompson. CAST: Gregory Peck, Omar Sharif, Camilla Sparv. LOC: Kanab Canyon, Paria, Sink Valley, Glen Canyon, Panguitch Fish Hatchery, Monument Valley. OL: Canyon de Chelly, AZ; Medford, OR.

Once Upon A Time in the West (Paramount). DIR: Sergio Leone. CAST: Charles Bronson, Henry Fonda, Claudia Cardinale. LOC: Monument Valley. OL: Spain.

Television:

Death Valley Days (Madison Prods.). Series. LOC: Kanab.

1970:

The Grasshopper (National General). DIR: Jerry Paris. CAST: Jacqueline Bisset, Jim Brown, Joseph Cotten. LOC: Heber.

Five Bloody Graves (Independent Int'l). DIR: Victor Adamson. CAST: Robert Dix, Scott Brady, Jim Davis. LOC: Capitol Reef.

Television:

Cutter's Trail (CBS). DIR: Vincent McEveety. CAST: John Gavin, Manuel Padilla Jr., Marisa Pavan. LOC: Kanab movie fort.

1971:

Vanishing Point (Twentieth Century-Fox). DIR: Richard C. Sarafian. CAST: Barry Newman, Victoria Medlin, Cleavon Little. LOC: Cisco, Thompson Springs, route I-70. OL: Goldfield, NV; Denver, CO.

Wild Rovers (M-G-M). DIR: Blake Edwards. CAST: William Holden, Ryan O'Neal, Karl Malden. LOC: Monument Valley, Professor Valley, Arches. OL: Old Tucson, Sedona, AZ.

Toklat (Sun Int'l). DIR: Robert W. Davidson. CAST: Leon Ames, Dick Robinson, Bette Bennett Penney. LOC: Uinta National Forest.

Brandy in the Wilderness (New Line Cinema). DIR: Stanton Kaye. CAST: Scott Glenn, Elizabeth Hartman, Chris King. LOC: Kanab Canyon, Moqui Cave, Kanab.

The Moviemakers (Professional Films/ Robins Nest Prods.). DIR: Ronald Saland. CAST: Julie Andrews, John Dehner, Blake Edwards. LOC: Monument Valley.

Television:

The American West of John Ford (CBS). DIR: Dennis Sanders. Documentary. LOC: Monument Valley.

Directed by John Ford (American Film Institute). DIR: Peter Bogdanovich. Documentary. LOC: Monument Valley.

The Devil and Miss Sarah (Universal). DIR: Michael Caffey. CAST: Gene Barry, Janice Rule, James Drury. LOC: Paria Canyon, Glen Canyon.

Alias Smith and Jones (Universal/ABC). Series. LOC: Castle Valley, Professor Valley.

Gunsmoke. (CBS). Series. LOC: Kanab.

1972:

The Female Bunch (Dalia). DIR: Al Adamson. CAST: Jennifer Bishop, Russ Tamblyn, Lon Chaney Jr. LOC: Hanksville, Capitol Reef. OL: Las Vegas, NV.

Jeremiah Johnson (Warner Bros). DIR: Sidney Pollack. CAST: Robert Redford, Will Geer, Stefan Gierasch. LOC: Wasatch Mountains, Snow Canyon, Zion, Ashley National Forest, Wasatch-Cache National Forest.

Run, Cougar, Run (Disney/Buena Vista). DIR: Jerome Courtland. CAST: Stuart Whitman, Frank Aletter, Lonny Chapman. LOC: Castle Valley, Arches, Sevenmile Canyon, Dead Horse Point, LaSal Mountains.

Television:

Alias Smith and Jones (Universal/ ABC). Series. LOC: Arches.

The Glass House (aka "Truman Capote's The Glass House") (Tomorrow Ent./ CBS). DIR: Tom Gries. CAST: Vic Morrow, Alan Alda, Billy Dee Williams. LOC: Draper (Utah State Prison).

Movin' On (Screen Gems/NBC). Series. LOC: Salt Lake City, Heber, Midway.

1973:

The Man Who Loved Cat Dancing (M-G-M). DIR: Richard G. Sarafian. CAST: Burt Reynolds, Sarah Miles, Lee J. Cobb. LOC: St. George–Hurricane area, Zion, Virgin River, Silver Reef.

One Little Indian (Disney/Buena Vista). DIR: Bernard McEveety. CAST: James Garner, Vera Miles, Jodie Foster. LOC: Kanab Canyon, the Gap, Kanab movie fort, Coral Pink Sand Dunes.

Electra Glide in Blue (United Artists). DIR: James William Guercio. CAST: Robert Blake, Billy Green Bush, Mitchell Ryan. LOC: Monument Valley.

Harry in Your Pocket (United Artists). DIR: Bruce Geller. CAST: James Coburn,

Trish Van Devere, Walter Pidgeon. LOC: Salt Lake City. OL: Seattle, WA.

Television:

Birds of Prey (Tomorrow Ent./CBS). DIR: William A. Graham. CAST: David Janssen, Ralph Meeker, Elayne Heilveil. LOC: Salt Lake City, Wendover, Canyonlands, Sevenmile Canyon.

1974:

The Trial of Billy Jack (Taylor-Laughlin/ Warner Bros.). DIR: Frank Laughlin. CAST: Tom Laughlin, Delores Taylor, Teresa Laughlin. LOC: Monument Valley.

The House of Seven Corpses (Television Corporation of America). DIR: Paul Harrison. CAST: John Ireland, Faith Domergue, John Carradine. LOC: Salt Lake City.

When the North Wind Blows (Sunn Classic Pictures). DIR: Stewart Raffill. CAST: Henry Brandon, Herbert Nelson, Dan Haggerty. LOC: Summit County.

Run to the High Country (Sun Int'l). DIR: Keith Larsen. CAST: Jim Davis, Nick Nolte. LOC: Uinta National Forest, Zion, Springdale.

Television:

The Six Million Dollar Man (Universal). Series. LOC: Kanab.

1975:

Airport 1975 (Universal). DIR: Jack Smight. CAST: Charlton Heston, Karen Black, George Kennedy. LOC: Salt Lake City Int'l Airport, aerials over Heber Valley and Wasatch Mountains.

Birth of a Legend (American National Enterprises). D: Dick Robinson. Documentary. LOC: Brian Head and Mammoth.

The Life and Times of Grizzly Adams (Sunn Classic Pictures). DIR: Richard Friedenberg. CAST: Dan Haggerty, Don Shanks, Lisa Jones. LOC: Uinta National Forest, Wasatch National Forest, Park City.

The Adventures of the Wilderness Family (Pacific International Enterprises). DIR: Stewart Ranfill. CAST: Robert Logan, Susan Damante-Shaw, Hollye Holmes. LOC: Summit County.

Jessi's Girls (Manson Int'l). DIR: Al Adamson. CAST: Sondra Currie, Geoffrey Land, Ben Frank. LOC: Capitol Reef, Dee Cooper Ranch.

Land of No Return (Int'l Picture Show Co.). DIR: Kent Bateman. CAST: Mel Torme, William Shatner, Donald Moffat. LOC: undetermined.

Against a Crooked Sky (Doty-Dayton). DIR: Earl Bellamy. CAST: Richard Boone, Stewart Petersen, Henry Wilcoxon. LOC: Professor Valley, Martin Ranch, Pace Creek, Castle Valley, Dud's Bottom, Arches, Dead Horse Point, Dolores River.

The Eiger Sanction (Warner Bros.). DIR: Clint Eastwood. CAST: Clint Eastwood, George Kennedy, Jack Cassidy. LOC: Monument Valley, Zion, Wasatch Mountains.

A Genius (Rafran Cinematografica). DIR: Damiano Damiani. CAST: Terence Hill, Miou Miou, Robert Charlebois. LOC: San Juan River, Monument Valley.

Whiffs (Brut/Twentieth Century-Fox). DIR: Ted Post. CAST: Elliott Gould, Eddie Albert, Harry Guardino. LOC: Dugway, Stockton, Tooele.

White Line Fever (Columbia). DIR: Jonathan Kaplan. CAST: Jan-Michael Vincent, Kay Lenz, Slim Pickens. LOC: Monument Valley.

The Outer Space Connection (Landsburg Prods./Sunn Classic Pictures). DIR: Fred Warshofsky. LOC: Park City.

1976:

The Adventures of Frontier Fremont (Sunn Classic Pictures). DIR: Richard Friedenberg. CAST: Dan Haggerty, Denver Pyle, Tony Mirrat. LOC: Park City, Kamas, Uinta National Forest.

Joshua (Larry Spangler/ Po' Boy Prods.). DIR: Larry Spangler. CAST: Fred Williamson, Calvin Bartlett, Isela Vega. LOC: LaSal National Forest, Colorado River, Arches, Valley of the Gods.

The Outlaw Josey Wales (Malpaso/Warner Bros.). DIR: Clint Eastwood. CAST: Clint Eastwood, Chief Dan George, Sondra Locke. LOC: Kanab Canyon, Stout Canyon, Paria, Glen Canyon, Coral Pink Sand Dunes. OL: Mescal, Old Tucson, AZ; Oroville, CA.

Television:

The Six Million Dollar Man. (ABC). Series. LOC: Kanab.

The Donny and Marie Show (Osmond Prods./NBC). Variety series. LOC: Orem (Osmond Studios).

The Life and Times of Grizzly Adams (Sunn Classic Pictures). Series. LOC: Uinta National Forest.

Mayday at 40,000 Feet (Andrew Fenady Prods./Warner Bros/CBS). DIR: Robert Butler. CAST: David Janssen, Don Meredith, Broderick Crawford. LOC: Salt Lake City.

Across the Great Divide (Pacific Int'l enterprises). DIR: Stewart Rafill. CAST: Robert Logan, Heather Rattray, Mark Edward Hall. LOC: Kane County. OL: Alberta, British Columbia, Canada.

1977:

Guardian of the Wilderness (aka "Mountain Man") (Sunn Classic Pictures). DIR: David O'Malley. CAST: Denver Pyle, Ken Berry, John Dehner. LOC: Uinta National Forest, Wasatch National Forest, Kamas, Mirror Lake, Capitol Reef.

Brigham (aka "Savage Journey") (Sunset Films). DIR: Tom McGowan. CAST: Maurice Grandmason, Richard Moll, John Mason. LOC: Salt Lake City, Kanab Canyon.

The Lincoln Conspiracy (Sunn Classic Pictures). DIR: James L. Conway. CAST: Bradford Dillman, John Dehner, John Anderson. LOC: Park City.

The Car (Universal). DIR: Elliot Silverstein. CAST: James Brolin, Kathleen Lloyd, John Marley. LOC: St. George, Hurricane Bridge, Zion, Kanab, Crazy Horse Canyon, Glen Canyon.

Exorcist II: The Heretic (Warner Bros.). DIR: John Boorman. CAST: Linda Blair, Richard Burton, Louise Fletcher. LOC: Glen Canyon.

Damnation Alley (Twentieth Century-Fox). DIR: Jack Smight. CAST: Jan-Michael Vincent, George Peppard, Dominique Sanda. LOC: Glen Canyon. OL: Imperial County, CA.

In Search of Noah's Ark (Sunn Classic Pictures). DIR: James L. Conway. CAST: Vern Adix, Brad Crandall. LOC: Park City.

Television:

The Donny and Marie Show (Osmond Prods./NBC). Variety series. LOC: Orem (Osmond Studio).

The Life and Times of Grizzly Adams (Sunn Classic Pictures). Series. LOC: Uinta National Forest.

Incredible Rocky Mountain Race (Sunn Classic Pictures/NBC). DIR: James L. Conway. CAST: Parley Baer, Whit Bissell, Dan Haggerty. LOC: Summit County.

The Last of the Mohicans (Sunn Classic Pictures/NBC). DIR: James L. Conway. CAST: Steve Forrest, Ned Romero, Andrew Prine. LOC: Summit County. OL: Pipe Spring, AZ.

1978:

Baker's Hawk (Doty-Dayton). DIR: Lyman Dayton. CAST: Clint Walker, Burl Ives, Diane Baker. LOC: Provo, Uinta National Forest.

Beyond and Back (Sunn Classic Pictures).

DIR: James L. Conway. CAST: Vern Adix, Linda Bishop, Janet Bylund. LOC: Park City, Salt Lake City, Heber.

The Great Brain (Osmond Prods.). DIR: Sidney Levin. CAST: Jimmy Osmond, James Jarnigan, Len Birman. LOC: Salt Lake City, Provo, Orem (Osmond Studio).

The Further Adventures of the Wilderness Family (Pacific Int'l Enterprises). DIR: Frank Zuniga. CAST: Robert Logan, Susan Damante-Shaw, Hollye Holmes. LOC: Uinta National Forest.

The Fall of the House of Usher (Sunn Classic Pictures). DIR: James L. Conway. CAST: Martin Landau, Charlene Tilton, Ray Walston. LOC: Kamas, Park City, Heber.

Take Down (American Film Consortium/ Buena Vista). DIR: Kieth Merrill. CAST: Edward Herrmann, Kathleen Lloyd, Lorenzo Lamas. LOC: American Fork.

Land of No Return (Int'l Picture Shows). DIR: Kent Bateman. CAST: Mel Torme, William Shatner, Donald Moffatt. LOC: undetermined.

Teen Alien (Prism Ent.). DIR: Peter Semelka. CAST: Vern Adix, Michael Dunn, Keith Nelson. LOC: Salt Lake City.

Television:

Donner Pass: The Road to Survival (Sunn Classic Pictures/NBC). DIR: James L. Conway. CAST: Robert Fuller, Andrew Prine, Michael Callan. LOC: Kanab Canyon, Tom's Canyon, Kanab movie fort. OL: Pipe Springs National Monument, AZ.

The Donny and Marie Show (Osmond Prods./NBC). Variety series. LOC: Orem (Osmond Studio).

Mel and Susan Together (Osmond Prods.). Series. LOC: Orem (Osmond Studio).

The Life and Times of Grizzly Adams (Sunn Classic Pictures). Series. LOC: Uinta National Forest.

The Time Machine (Sunn Classic Pictures/ NBC). DIR: Henning Schellerup. CAST: R. G. Armstrong, Parley Baer, Priscilla Barnes, John Beck. LOC: Kamas.

1979:

Encounter with Disaster (Sunn Classic Pictures). DIR: Charles E. Sellier Jr. NARRATOR: Brad Campbell. LOC: Park City.

Beyond Death's Door (Sunn Classic Pictures). DIR: Henning Schellerup. CAST: Tom Hallick, John Brooks Aspiras, Jesse Bennett. LOC: Park City, Kamas, Heber.

The Bermuda Triangle (Sunn Classic Pictures). DIR: Richard Friedenberg. CAST: Donald Albee, Lin Berlitz, Howard W. Bishop Jr. LOC: Park City.

Mountain Family Robinson (Sunn Classic Pictures). DIR: John Cotter. CAST: Robert Logan, Susan Damante-Shaw, Heather Rattray. LOC: Uinta National Forest.

The Apple Dumpling Gang Rides Again (Disney/Buena Vista). DIR: Vincent McEveety. CAST: Tim Conway, Don Knotts, Tim Matheson. LOC: Kanab movie fort, Kanab Creek.

The Electric Horseman (Columbia/Universal). DIR: Sidney Pollack. CAST: Robert Redford, Jane Fonda, Valerie Perrine. LOC: St. George, Snow Canyon, Virgin River, Zion.

Head Over Heels (Triple Play Prods./ United Artists). DIR: Joan Micklin Silver. CAST: John Heard, Mary Beth Hurt, Peter Reigert. LOC: Salt Lake City.

Savage Water (Talking Pictures). DIR: Paul Kener. CAST: Bridget Agnew, Ron Berger, Pat Comer. LOC: Colorado River.

In Search of Historic Jesus (Sunn Classic Pictures). DIR: Henning Schellerup. CAST: John Rubinstein, John Anderson, Nehemiah Persoff. LOC: Heber, Provo, Park City.

The Villain (Columbia). DIR: Hal Needham. CAST: Kirk Douglas, Arnold Schwarzenegger, Ann-Margaret. LOC: Monument Valley.

Concorde: Airport '79 (Universal). DIR: David Lowell Rich. CAST: Alain Delon, Susan Blakely, Robert Wagner. LOC: Alta.

Wanda Nevada (Hayward-Fonda/United Artists). DIR: Peter Fonda. CAST: Peter Fonda, Brooke Shields, Henry Fonda. LOC: Glen Canyon, Monument Valley, Mexican Hat, Colorado River.

Television:

Christmas Lilies (Osmond Prods.). DIR: Ralph Nelson. CAST: Timmy Arnell, Julie Delgado, Sam Di Bello. LOC: Salt Lake City, Orem (Osmond Studio).

The Donny and Marie Show (Osmond Prods./NBC). Variety series. LOC: Orem (Osmond Studio).

1980:

Cataclysm (Mill Creek Ent.). DIR: Phillip Marshak, Tom McGowan, Gregg C. Tallas. CAST: Cameron Mitchell, Charles Moll, Marc Lawrence. LOC: Salt Lake City. OL: San Diego, CA.

Hangar 18 (Sunn Classic Pictures). DIR: James Conway. CAST: Gary Collins, Robert Vaughn, James Hampton. LOC: Salt Lake City. OL: Big Spring, TX.

Knocking at Heaven's Door (Linton/7 Star). DIR: John Linton. CAST: Kristina David. LOC: Moab.

Windwalker (Pacific International Enterprises). DIR: Kieth Merrill. CAST: Trevor Howard, Nick Ramus, James Remar. LOC: Wasatch Mountains.

Stir Crazy (Columbia). DIR: Sidney Poitier. CAST: Gene Wilder, Richard Pryor, Georg Stanford Brown. LOC: St. George.

Melvin and Howard (Universal). DIR: Jonathan Demme. CAST: Jason Robards, Paul Le Mat, Mary Steenburgen. LOC: Salt Lake City, Willard. OL: Las Vegas, NV.

The Nude Bomb (Universal). DIR: Clive Donner. CAST: Don Adams, Sylvia Kristel, Rhonda Fleming. LOC: Salt Lake City.

My Road (Dakota Lines Prods.). DIR: Kikuo Kawasake. CAST: John Denos, Laura Fanning, Wendy Hoffman. LOC: Moab, Dead Horse Point.

Honky Tonk Freeway (Kendon/ Universal). DIR: John Schlesinger. CAST: Jeffrey Combs, Beau Bridges, Beverly D'Angelo. LOC: Salt Lake City. OL: Mount Dora, Sarasota, FL.

Television:

The Legend of Sleepy Hollow (Sunn Classic Pictures). DIR: Henning Schellerup. CAST: Jeff Goldblum, Meg Foster, Paul Sand. LOC: Park City.

Christmas Mountain (Osmond Prods.). DIR: Pierre De Moro. CAST: Mark Miller, Slim Pickens, Fran Ryan. LOC: Utah County, Salt Lake City.

Mr. Krueger's Christmas (Bonneville Ent). DIR: Kieth Merrill. CAST: James Stewart, Beverly Rowland, Kamee Aliessa. LOC: Salt Lake City.

1981:

Harry's War (Taft Int'l). DIR: Kieth Merrill. CAST: Edward Herrmann, Geraldine Page, Karen Grassle. LOC: St. George.

Legend of the Wild (Taft Int'l). DIR: James L. Conway. CAST: Dan Haggerty, Denver Pyle, Don Shanks. LOC: Uinta Mountains, Wasatch National Forest.

Conspiracy to Kill the President (Sunn Classic Pictures). DIR: James L. Conway. LOC: Park City.

Don't Go Into the Woods (Seymour Borde & Assoc.). DIR: James Bryan. CAST: James McClelland, Mary Gail Artz, James P. Hayden. LOC: Brighton.

The Boogens (Taft Int'l). DIR: James L. Conway. CAST: Rebecca Balding, Fred McCarren, Anne-Marie Martin. LOC: Park City, Kamas, Ontario Mine, Mayflower Mine, Heber.

The Legend of the Lone Ranger (Universal). DIR: William A. Fraker. CAST: Klinton Spilsbury, Jason Robards, Richard Farnsworth. LOC: Monument Valley, Marble Arch.

Television:

Child Bride of Short Creek (Schiller-Monash Prods.). DIR: Robert Lewis. CAST: Christopher Atkins, Diane Lane, Helen Hunt. LOC: Grafton, Rockville Road, Rockville Bridge.

Adventures of Nellie Bly (Schick Sunn Classics/Taft Int'l.). DIR: Henning Schellerup. CAST: Gene Barry, Jay Bernard, Linda Purl. LOC: Park City, Salt Lake City.

California Gold Rush (Sunn Classic Pictures/ Taft Int'l). DIR: Jack B. Nively. CAST: Dan Haggerty, Ken Curtis, John Dehner. LOC: Wasatch and Summit counties.

Earthbound (Taft Int'l). DIR: James L. Conway. CAST: Burl Ives, Christopher Connelly, Meredith MacRae. LOC: Park City.

Incident at Crestridge (CBS). DIR: Jud Taylor. CAST: Tip Boxell, Eileen Brennan, Bruce Davison. LOC: Park City.

Nashville Grab (Taft Int'l/NBC). DIR: James L. Conway. CAST: Jeff Conway, Henry Gibson, Mari Gorman. LOC: Heber.

1982:

Octopussy (M-G-M/UA). DIR: John Glen. CAST: Roger Moore, Maud Adams, Louis Jourdan. LOC: Hurricane Mesa, LaVerkin-Hurricane Bridge, New Harmony.

The Dream Chaser (P.I.E.). DIR: Arthur R. Dubs, David Jackson. CAST: Harold Gould, Justin Dana, Jeffrey Tambor. LOC: Washington County. OL: southern Oregon.

Television:

The Executioner's Song (Film Communications Inc.). DIR: Lawrence Schiller. CAST: Tommy Lee Jones, Christine Lahti, Rosanna Arquette. LOC: Draper (Utah State Prison), Provo.

The Capture of Grizzly Adams (Shick/ Taft Int'l). DIR: Don Kesslar. CAST: Dan Haggerty, Denver Pyle, Noah Beery Jr. LOC: Park City, Uinta National Forest, Wasatch National Forest.

Side by Side: The Osmond Story (Osmond Prods./NBC). DIR: Russ Mayberry. CAST: Joseph Bottoms, Marie Osmond, Karen Alston. LOC: Orem (Osmond Studio).

1983:

Lost. DIR: Al Adamson. CAST: Sandra Dee, Gary Kent, Jack Elam. LOC: Capital Reef.

Thunder (USA video title "Thunder Warrior") (European Int'l Films). DIR: Fulvia De Angelis. CAST: Bo Svenson, Mark Gregory, Raymond Harmstorf. LOC: Monument Valley; OL: Marble Canyon, Sedona, AZ.

Hidden Secrets of the Grand Canyon (IMAX). DIR: Kieth Merrill. CAST: Daniel T. Majetich, Coby Jordan, Bruce Simballa. LOC: Kanab. OL: Grand Canyon, AZ.

Cujo (Sunn Classic Pictures/Taft Int'l/Warner Bros.). DIR: Lewis Teague. CAST: Dee Wallace, Danny Pintauro, Daniel Hugh Kelly. LOC: Salt Lake County. OL: Glen Ellen, Mendocino, Petaluma, Santa Rosa, CA.

Superman III (Warner Bros.). DIR: Richard Lester. CAST: Christopher Reeve, Richard Pryor, Jackie Cooper. LOC: Glen Canyon. OL: Calgary, Canada.

Koyaanisqatsi (New Cinema). DIR: Godfrey Reggio. Documentary. LOC: Monument Valley.

Spacehunter: Adventures in the Forbidden Zone (Columbia). DIR: Lamont Johnson. CAST: Peter Strauss, Molly Ringwald, Ernie Hudson. LOC: Kane Creek, Bull Canyon, Colorado River, Potash, Lower Shafer Trail, Potash Settling Ponds, Grey Hills, U.S. Highway 91, south of Canyonlands Airport.

The Returning (Willow Productions). DIR: Joel Bender. CAST: Susan Strasberg, Gabriel Walsh, Ruth Warrick. LOC: Salt Lake City, Arches, Professor Valley, Fisher Towers, La Sal Mountains, Dewey.

Savannah Smiles (Gold Coast). DIR: Pierre DeMoro. CAST: Mark Miller, Donovan Scott, Bridgette Andersen. LOC: Salt Lake City, Provo Canyon.

Footlose (Paramount). DIR: Herbert Ross. CAST: Kevin Bacon, Lori Singer, John Lithgow. LOC: Lehi, Orem, Payson.

Revenge of the Ninja (Cannon Films/ Golan-Globus). DIR: James Firstenberg. CAST: Sho Kosugi, Keith Vitali, Virgil Frye. LOC: Salt Lake City.

National Lampoon's Vacation (Warner Bros.). DIR: Harold Ramis. CAST: Chevy Chase, Beverly D'Angelo, Imogene Coca. LOC: Monument Valley. OL: Flagstaff, Sedona, Grand Canyon, AZ; Arcadia, Magic Mountain (Valencia), CA; St. Louis, MO.

Television:

Ghost Dancing (Titus Prods./ABC). DIR: David Greene, Don Taylor. CAST: John Bellah, Scotch Byerly, Robert Clotworthy. LOC: St. George.

Uncommon Valor (Sunn Classic Pictures/ CBS). DIR: Rodney Amateau. CAST: Julie Cobb, Norman Fell, Sherry Hursey. LOC: Salt Lake City. OL: Kaui, HI.

A Killer in the Family (Sunn Classic Pictures). DIR: Richard T. Heffron. CAST: Robert Mitchum, James Spader, Lance Kerwin. LOC: St. George.

1984:

Skipper (Frameline Prods.). DIR: Roberto Malenotti. CAST: Gianni Garko, Fabio Testi. LOC: Torrey, Capitol Reef.

In Search of a Golden Sky (Generic Films/ Comworld). DIR: Jefferson Richard. CAST: Charles Napier, George "Buck" Flower, Clifford Osmond. LOC: Heber, Midway, Kamas, Uinta Mountains.

Snowballing (Sunn Classic Pictures). DIR: Charles E. Sellier Jr. CAST: Alan Sues, P. R. Paul, Mary McDonough. LOC: Park City.

Warning Sign (Twentieth Century-Fox). DIR: Hal Barwood. CAST: Sam Waterston, Kathleen Quinlan, Yaphet Kotto. LOC: Payson.

The Philadelphia Experiment (New World). DIR: Stewart Raffill. CAST: Michael Pare, Nancy Allen, Eric Christmas. LOC: Salt Lake City, Wendover. OL: Denver, CO; Santa Paula, CA; Charleston, SC.

Romancing the Stone (El Corrazon Producciones/Twentieth Century-Fox). DIR: Robert Zemeckis. CAST: Michael Douglas, Kathleen Turner, Danny De Vito. LOC: Snow Canyon.

Starman (Columbia). DIR: John Carpenter. CAST: Jeff Bridges, Karen Allen, Charles Martin Smith, Richard Jaeckel. LOC: Monument Valley.

Jupiter Menace (Youngstar). Documentary. DIR: Lee Auerbach, Peter Matulavick. NARRATORS: George Kennedy, Lindsay Workman, Clarissa Bernhart. LOC: Professor Valley, Fisher Towers.

Silent Night, Deadly Night (TriStar Pictures). DIR: Charles Sellier. CAST: Lilyan Chauvin, Gilmer McCormick, Toni Nero. LOC: Salt Lake City, Heber.

Television:

Airwolf (Belisarius/Universal/CBS). Series. LOC: Monument Valley.

Scorned and Swindled. (Cypress Point Productions) DIR: Paul Wendkos. CAST: Tuesday Weld, Keith Carradine, Peter Coyote. LOC: Ogden, Roy.

Single Bars, Single Women (Sunn Classic Pictures). DIR: Harry Winer. CAST: Tony Danza, Paul Michael Glaser, Shelly Hack. LOC: Provo

1985:

Static (NFI Prods.). DIR: Mark Romanek.

CAST: Keith Gordon, Amanda Plummer, Bob Gunton. LOC: Lake Powell; OL, Page, AZ.

California Dreaming (Sognando la California) (Filmauro). DIR: Carlo Vanzina. CAST: Massimo Boldi, Maurizio Ferrini. LOC: Moki Dugway, Mexican Hat, Monument Valley.

Better Off Dead (A&M Films/CBS Films). DIR: Savage Steve Holland. CAST: John Cusack, David Ogden Stiers, Kim Darby. LOC: Alta, Brighton, Snowbird.

Konrad (Bonneville World Enterprises/ PBS). DIR: Nell Cox. CAST: Max Wright, Polly Holliday, Huckleberry Fox. LOC: Salt Lake City.

Fletch (Douglas-Greisman/Universal Pictures). DIR: Michael Ritchie. CAST: Chevy Chase, Dana Wheeler-Nicholson, Tim Matheson. LOC: Salt Lake City Int'l Airport, Provo, Orem.

Night Train to Terror (aka "Shiver"). (Visto). DIR: John Carr, Phillip Marshak, Tom McGowan, Jay Schlossberg-Cohen, Gregg C. Tallas. CAST: John Phillip Law, Richard Moll (as Charles Moll). LOC: Salt Lake City. OL: La Jolla, San Diego, CA.

Nutcracker (Hyperion-Kushner-Locke/ Atlantic Releasing Corp.). DIR: Carroll Ballard. CAST: Hugh Bigney, Vanessa Sharp, Patricia Barker. LOC: Salt Lake City.

Choke Canyon (United Film Distribution). DIR: Chuck Bail. CAST: Stephen Collins, Janet Julien, Bo Svenson. LOC: Onion Creek, Professor Valley, Sand Flats, Dead Horse Point, Byrd's Ranch, Squaw Park, Moab.

Jewel of the Nile (Twentieth Century-Fox). DIR: Lewis Teague. CAST: Michael Douglas, Kathleen Turner, Danny DeVito. LOC: Zion National Park. OL: Cannes, Cote d'Azur, France; Monte Carlo, Monaco; Morocco.

Solo (Dayton-Stewart). DIR: Lyman Dayton. CAST: Randy Hamilton, Sandra Kearns, Richard Auer. LOC: St. George.

1986:

Riders of the Storm (Kewash/Miramax). DIR: Maurice Phillips. CAST: Jon Alderson, James Aubrey, Dennis Hopper. LOC: Glen Canyon.

The American Way (Kerrash Ltd., Tamburra Films/Mirimax). DIR: Maurice Phillips. CAST: Dennis Hopper, Michael J. Pollard, Eugene Lipinski. LOC: Glen Canyon.

Television:

The Deliberate Stranger (Stuart Phoenix/ Lorimar). DIR: Marvin J. Chomsky. CAST: Mark Harmon, Frederic Forrest, George Grizzard. LOC: Salt Lake City, Draper (Utah State Prison), Farmington. OL: Seattle, WA.

A Hobo's Christmas (Joe Byrne/Phoenix Ent. Group.). DIR: Will Mackenzie. CAST: Barnard Hughes, Gerald McRaney, Wendy Crewson. LOC: Salt Lake City.

Louis L'Amour's Down the Long Hills (Disney/ABC). DIR: Burt Kennedy. CAST: Bruce Boxleitner, Bo Hopkins, Michael Wren. LOC: Heber.

Ordinary Heroes (Crow Prods./Juniper Releasing). DIR: Will Mackenzie. CAST: Richard Dean Anderson, Valerie Bertinelli, Matthew Laurance. LOC: Salt Lake City, Magna.

1987:

Thunder (aka "Thunder Warrior I") (European Int'l/Trans World Ent.). DIR: Larry Ludham [Fabrizio DeAngelis]. CAST: Mark Gregory, Bo Svenson, Raymond Hamstorf. LOC: Monument Valley.

Thunder II (USA video title: "Thunder Warrior II") (European Int'l Films). DIR: Fulvia De Angelis. CAST: Bo Svenson, Mark Gregory, Raymond Harmstorf. LOC: Monument Valley.

Million Dollar Mystery (De Laurentiis Ent.). DIR: Richard Fleischer. CAST: Eddie Deezen, Michael J. Pollard, Eugene Lifinski. LOC: Glen Canyon.

Berserker (American Video Group/Shapiro Ent.). DIR: Jefferson Richard. CAST: Joseph Alan Johnson, Valerie Sheldon, Greg Dawson. LOC: Big Cottonwood Canyon.

P. K. and the Kid (Petaluma Pride Prods.). DIR: Lou Lombardo. CAST: Paul Le Mat, Molly Ringwald, Alex Rocco. LOC: undetermined. OL: Glenwood Springs, CO; Monterey, Petaluma, San Francisco, CA.

Red Fury (Dayton-Stewart). DIR: Lyman Dayton. CAST: William Jordan, Katherine Cannon, Calvin Bartlett. LOC: St. George.

Wall Street (Twentieth Century-Fox). DIR: Oliver Stone. CAST: Michael Douglas, Charlie Sheen, Daryl Hannah. LOC: Snowbird.

Three O'Clock High (Universal). DIR: Phil Joanou. CAST: Casey Siemaszko, Anne Ryan, Richard Tyson. LOC: Ogden High School.

Promised Land (aka "Young Hearts") (Wildwood Prods./Vestron). DIR: Michael Hoffman. CAST: Jason Gedrick, Kiefer Sutherland, Meg Ryan. LOC: Salt Lake City, Midvale, Wendover, Provo.

Over the Top (Warner Bros.). DIR: Menahem Golan. CAST: Sylvester Stallone, Robert Loggia, Susan Blakely. LOC: Monument Valley.

The Survivalist (Precision Films). DIR: Sig Shore. CAST: Steve Railsback, Sandra Lea, Tara Trimble. LOC: Moab.

Television:

At Mother's Request (ITC, CBS). DIR: Michael Tuchner. CAST: Stefanie Powers, Doug McKeon, Frances Sternhagen. LOC: Salt Lake City.

Desperado (Charles E. Sellier Prods./ Universal TV). DIR: Virgil Vogel. CAST: Alex McArthur, David Warner, Yaphet Kotto. LOC: Monument Valley; OL: Old Tucson, Mescal, Patagonia, AZ.

Werewolf (Tri-Star/Sony Pictures). Series. DIR: David Hemmings. CAST: John J. York, Lance LeGault, Chuck Connors. LOC: Salt Lake City.

Stranger on My Land (Taft Ent./ABC). DIR: Larry Elikann. CAST: Tommy Lee Jones, Dee Wallace Stone, Ben Johnson. LOC: Salt Lake City, Kamas.

1988:

Halloween 4: The Return of Michael Myers (Trancas Ent./Galaxy Int'l). DIR: Dwight H. Little. CAST: Donald Pleasence, Ellie Cornell, Danielle Harris. LOC: Salt Lake City.

Television:

Hemingway (Alcor). Miniseries. DIR: Bernhard Sinkel. CAST: Scott Weinger, Jacques Balutin, Lisa Banes. LOC: Kamas, Ogden.

Evil in Clear River (Phoenix Ent. Group/ Tisch). DIR: Karen Arthur. CAST: Lindsay Wagner, Randy Quaid, Thomas Wilson Brown. LOC: Kamas, Salt Lake City.

1989:

Iced (aka "Blizzard of Blood") (Mikon Releasing Corp.). DIR: Jeff Kwinty. CAST: Debra Delisio, Doug Stevenson, Ron Kologie. LOC: Big Cottonwood Canyon.

Indiana Jones and the Last Crusade (Paramount). DIR: Steven Spielberg. CAST: Harrison Ford, Sean Connery, River Phoenix. LOC: Arches, Sevenmile Canyon.

Halloween 5: The Revenge of Michael Myers (Magnum Pictures/Galaxy Int'l). DIR: Dominique Othenin-Girard. CAST: Donald Pleasence, Danielle Harris, Donald L. Shanks. LOC: Salt Lake City.

On Our Own (Dayton Filmcorp). DIR: Lyman Dayton. CAST: Leigh Lombardi, Sam Hennings, Scott Warner. LOC: St. George.

Wait Until Spring, Bandini (Zoetrope/Orion). DIR: Dominique Deruddere. CAST: Joe Mantegna, Ornella Muti, Faye Dunaway. LOC: Orem (Sunrise Studio), Ogden.

Tripwire (New Line Cinema). DIR: James Lemmo. CAST: Terence Knox, David Warner, Isabella Hofmann. LOC: Park City.

Television:

Blind Witness (Shadowplay Films). DIR: Richard A. Colla. CAST: Victoria Principal, Paul Le Mat, Stephen Macht. LOC: Salt Lake City.

Incident at Dark River (Farrell/Minoff/TNT). DIR: Michael Pressman. CAST: Mike Farrell, Tess Harper, Helen Hunt. LOC: Ogden.

Encyclopedia Brown (Howard David Deutsch/HBO). Series. LOC: Provo.

Rescue 911 (MTM/Fox-TV). Series. LOC: undetermined.

It Nearly Wasn't Christmas (Osmond Ent.). DIR: Burt Brinkerhoff. CAST: Beverly Rowland, Charles Durning, Risa Schiffman. LOC: undetermined.

Mothers, Daughters and Lovers (Katz-Huyck/NBC). DIR: Matthew Robbins. CAST: Helen Shaver, David MacIlwraith, Claude Akins. LOC: Provo, Solitude.

1990:

China O'Brien/China O'Brien 2 (Golden Harvest). DIR: Robert Clouse. CAST: Cynthia Rothrock, Richard Norton. LOC: Park City.

The Dream Machine (Epperson/Dayton/Sorenson). DIR: Lyman Dayton. CAST: Randall England, Tracy Fraim, Corey Haim. LOC: Salt Lake City.

Ski Patrol (Trans World Ent.). DIR: Richard Correll. CAST: Roger Rose, T. K. Carter, Paul Feig. LOC: Park City, Snowbird.

Snow Kill (Wilshire Court). DIR: Thomas J. Wright. CAST: Terence Knox, Patti D'Arbanville, Jon Cypher. LOC: Heber, Park City, Uinta National Forest.

Desperate Hours (M-G-M/UA). DIR: Michael Cimino. CAST: Mickey Rourke, Anthony Hopkins, Mimi Rogers. LOC: Salt Lake City, Echo Junction, Orem, Zion, Capitol Reef.

Dragonfight (Warner Bros.). DIR: Warren A. Stevens. CAST: Robert Z'Dar, Paul Coufos, Michael Pare. LOC: Glen Canyon. OL: Arizona.

Back to the Future III (Paradox/Universal). DIR: Robert Zemeckis. CAST: Michael J. Fox, Christopher Lloyd, Mary Steenburgen. LOC: Monument Valley.

Nightmare at Noon (Omega Ent.). DIR: Nico Mastorakis. CAST: Wings Hauser, Bo Hopkins, George Kennedy. LOC: Moab, Ken's Lake, Colorado River, Arches.

Sure Fire (Complex). DIR: Jon Jost. CAST: Tom Blair, Kristi Hager, Robert Ernst. LOC: Circleville.

Legacy (Bonneville Int'l). DIR: Kieth Merrill. CAST: Kathleen Beller, LOC: Salt Lake City. OL: Nauvoo, IL; New York; Wyoming.

Sundown: Vampire in Retreat (Vestron Video). DIR: Anthony Hickox. CAST: David Carradine, Morgan Brittany, Bruce Campbell. LOC: Moab, Spanish Valley, Thompson Springs, Hittle Bottom, Arches.

Television:

Cop Rock (20th Century Fox). Series. LOC: Grantsville.

My Life as a Babysitter (Cornerstone/Disney). CAST: Shane Meier, Michele Abrams, Thom Adcox-Hernandez. LOC: Salt Lake City.

Teen Angel Returns (Cornerstone/Disney). Series. LOC: Salt Lake City.

Troll 2 (Filmirage [Italy]). DIR: Claudio Fragasso. CAST: Michael Stephenson, George Hardy, Margo Prey. LOC: Porterville.

1991:

Thelma & Louise (Pathe/M-G-M). DIR: Ridley Scott. CAST: Susan Sarandon, Geena Davis, Harvey Keitel. LOC: Shafer Overlook, Monument Valley, La Sal Mountains, La Sal Junction, Cisco, Old Valley City Reservoir, Thompson Springs, Arches, Crescent Junction. OL: Bakersfield, Long Beach, CA.

K-2: The Ultimate High (Miramax Films/Paramount). DIR: Franc Roddam. CAST: Michael Biehn, Matt Craven, Raymond J. Barry. LOC: Snowbird.

In Your Wildest Dreams (Feature Films for Families-Video). DIR: Bruce Neibaur. CAST: Trevor Black, Lise Wilburn, Sarah Schaub. LOC: Salt Lake County.

Fast Getaway (Cinetel/New Line Cinema). DIR: Spiro Razatos. CAST: Corey Haim, Cynthia Rothrock, Leo Rossi. LOC: Park City.

Grand Canyon (Twentieth Century-Fox). DIR: Lawrence Kasdan. CAST: Danny Glover, Kevin Kline, Steve Martin. LOC: Glen Canyon. OL: Los Angeles, Canoga Park, CA; Grand Canyon, AZ.

A Midnight Clear (A&M Films). DIR: Keith Gordon. CAST: Peter Berg, Kevin Dillon, Arye Gross. LOC: Park City.

Motorama (Planet Prods.). DIR: Barry Shils. CAST: Jordan Christopher Michael, Martha Quinn, Michael Naegel. LOC: Glen Canyon. OL: Page, AZ.

Wind (Zoetrope/Tri-Star). DIR: Carroll Ballard. CAST: Matthew Modine, Jennifer Grey, Cliff Robertson. LOC: Green River, Wendover, Bonneville Salt Flats.

Equinox (Identical Co./SC Ent.). DIR: Alan Rudolph. CAST: Matthew Modine, Lara Flynn Boyle, Fred Ward. LOC: Crescent Junction, Moab. OL: St. Paul/Minneapolis, MN.

Warlock (New World). DIR: Steve Miner. CAST: Julian Sands, Lori Singer, Richard E. Grant. LOC: Bonneville Salt Flats.

Rubin and Ed (Working Title Films). DIR: Trent Harris. CAST: Howard Hesseman, Crispin Glover, Karen Black. LOC: Hanksville, Factory Butte, Goblin Valley, Salt Lake City.

Beastmaster 2: Through the Portal of Time (New Line Cinema). DIR: Sylvio Tabet. CAST: Marc Singer, Kari Wuhrer, Sarah Douglas. LOC: Glen Canyon.

Dream Machine (Live Video). DIR: Lyman Dayton. CAST: Cory Haim, Jeremy Slate, Randall England. LOC: Salt Lake City.

Television:

Love Kills (Paramount/USA). DIR: Brian Grant. CAST: Virginia Madsen, Lenny von Dohlen, Eric Anderson. LOC: Salt Lake City.

The Witching of Ben Wagner (Leucadia). DIR: Paul Annett. CAST: Sam Bottoms, Sylvia Sidney, Bettina Ray. LOC: Mirror Lake.

1992:

Boraka (Magdison Films/Samuel Goldwyn). DIR: Ron Frickle. Feature-length environmental documentary. LOC: Canyonlands, Arches. OL: dozens of major cities and scenic areas throughout the world.

The Bulkin Trail. DIR: Michael J. Nathanson. CAST: Tony Burton, David Hasselhoff, Jeremy Jackson. LOC: Park City.

The ButterCream Gang (Feature Films for Families-Video). DIR: Bruce Neibaur. CAST: Jason Johnson, Michael D. Weatherred, Brandon Blaser. LOC: Draper, Riverton.

Carving the White (RAP Ent.). DIR: James Angrove, Jon Long. CAST: James Angrove (narrator). LOC: Park City. OL: Big Sky, MT; Valdez, AK; Taos, NM; Banff, Alberta, Canada.

Highway to Hell (Helmdale). DIR: Ate de Jong. CAST: Patrick Bergin, Chad Lowe, Kristy Swanson. LOC: Glen Canyon. OL: Arizona.

Memoirs of an Invisible Man (Warner Bros.). DIR: John Carpenter. CAST: Chevy Chase, Daryl Hannah, Sam Neill. LOC: Snowbird.

Neon City (Vidmark EnterprisesBVideo). DIR: Monte Markham. CAST: Michael Ironside, Lyle Alzado, Monte Markham. LOC: Salt Lake, Draper.

Split Infinity (Feature Films for Families-Video). DIR: Stan Ferguson. CAST:

Trevor Black, Derric Anderlin, Talia Argyle. LOC: Salt Lake City.

Point Break (Largo/Twentieth Century-Fox). DIR: Kathryn Bigelow. CAST: Patrick Swayze, Keanu Reeves, Gary Busey. LOC: Lake Powell. OL: Edola State Park, Wheeler, OR; Malibu, Manhattan Beach, Santa Monica, Venice, Fox Hills Mall, CA.

Seasons of the Heart (Feature Films for Families-Video). DIR: T. C. Christensen. CAST: Sam Hennings, Claude Akins, Jay Dee Bateman. LOC: Salt Lake City.

The Goodbye Bird (Leucadia-Video). DIR: William Clark, William Tannen. CAST: Christopher Pettiet, Cindy Pickett, Concetta Tomei. LOC: Salt Lake City.

Television:

Ancient Secrets of the Bible (Sunn Int'l/CBS). DIR: Henning Schellerup. CAST: William Devane, Jesse Bennett, Douglas Caputo. LOC: Salt Lake City.

Battling for Baby (Von Zerneck Sertner Films/CBS). DIR: Art Wolff. CAST: Suzanne Pleshette, Debbie Reynolds, Courteney Cox. LOC: Salt Lake City.

Deliver Them From Evil: The Taking of Alta View [Video title: "Take Down"] (Citadel Films). DIR: Peter Levin. CAST: Harry Hamlin, Teri Garr, Terry O'Quinn. LOC: Lehi.

Double Jeopardy (Boxleitner/Bernstein Prods./CBS-TV). DIR: Lawrence Schiller. CAST: Rachel Ward, Bruce Boxleitner, Sela Ward. LOC: Salt Lake City, Highway 279, Rainbow Rocks, Tombstone Butte.

The President's Child (Lauren Films/CBS). DIR: Sam Pillsbury. CAST: Jesse Bennett, J. Scott Bronson, Joyce Cohen. LOC: Salt Lake City.

In the Line of Duty: Siege at Marion (aka "Children of Fury") (Patchett Kaufman Ent./World Int'l Network). DIR: Charles Haid. CAST: Ed Begley Jr., Dennis Franz, Tess Harper. LOC: Midway, Deer Creek Reservoir.

The Boys of Twilight (New World Television). Series. LOC: Park City.

Legend of Wolf Mountain (Majestic Ent). DIR: Craig Clyde. CAST: Peadair S. Addie Sr., Lance August, Jonathan Best. LOC: Wasatch Mountains.

Little Heroes (KOAN). DIR: Craig Clyde. CAST: Raeanin Simpson, Katherine Willis, Reta Patterson. LOC: Salt Lake County.

Miracles & Other Wonders. Series. LOC: Salt Lake City.

1993:

Dark Blood (Fine Line). DIR: George Sluizer. CAST: River Phoenix, Jonathan Pryce, Judy Davis. LOC: Factory Butte. OL: Gallup, NM.

Teenage Bonnie and Klepto Clyde (Trimark). DIR: John Shepphird. CAST: Maureen Flannigan, Scott Wolf, Bentley Mitchum. LOC: Salt Lake City.

This Boy's Life (Warner Bros.). DIR: Michael Caton-Jones. CAST: Robert De Niro, Ellen Barkin, Leonardo DiCaprio. LOC: La Sal Mountains loop road.

Josh and S.A.M. (Castle Rock). DIR: Billy Weber. CAST: Jacob Tierney, Martha Plimpton, Noah Fleiss. LOC: Arches, Highway 191, Lisbon Valley, Spanish Valley.

A Home of Our Own (A&M Films/Polygram). DIR: Tony Bill. CAST: Kathy Bates, Edward Furlong, Clarissa Lassig. LOC: Heber, Wasatch Mountain State Park, Midvale.

Knights (Kings Road Ent.). DIR: Albert Pyun. CAST: Kathy Long, Kris Kristofferson, Lance Henriksen. LOC: Mushroom Rock at Pucker Pass, Long Canyon, Professor Valley, La Sal Mountains, Needles Overlook, Monument Valley.

Rigoletto (Feature Films for Families-Video). DIR: Leo D. Paur. CAST: Joseph Paur, Ivey Lloyd, Scott Wilkinson. LOC: Helper.

Mountain of the Lord (The Church of Jesus Christ of Latter-day Saints—Video). DIR: Peter Johnson. LOC: Provo (BYU Motion Picture Studio).

Benefit of the Doubt (Benefit Prods.). DIR: Jonathan Heap. CAST: Donald Sutherland, Amy Irving, Rider Strong. LOC: Glen Canyon. OL: Camp Verde, Clarkdale, Cottonwood, Sedona, AZ.

The Sandlot (Island World Group/Twentieth Century-Fox). DIR: David Mickey Evans. CAST: Tom Guiry, Mike Vitar, Patrick Renna. LOC: Salt Lake City.

Share the Moon (Crew Prods.). DIR: Gregory C. Haynes. CAST: Michelle Michaels, Bernard Baski, Wendell Pace. LOC: Logan.

Geronimo: An American Legend (Columbia). DIR: Walter Hill. CAST: Wes Studi, Gene Hackman, Robert Duvall. LOC: Professor Valley (San Carlos Fort), Onion Creek, Potash, Dead Horse Point, Needles Overlook, Bates Ranch, Lawson Ranch, Ruby Ranch Road.

Lightning Jack (Savoy/Buena Vista). DIR: Simon Wincer. CAST: Paul Hogan, Cuba Gooding Jr., Beverly D'Angelo. LOC: Fisher Towers, Professor Valley, Onion Creek, Arches, Hall's Crossing, Mexican Hat, Valley of the Gods. OL: Australia, Old Tucson, AZ; Colorado.

Rockwell (Heritage). DIR: Richard Lloyd Dewey. CAST: Randy Gleave, Karl Malone, Scott Christopher. LOC: Emigration Canyon, Spanish Fork. OL: Nauvoo, IL.

The ButterCream Gang in Secret of Treasure Mountain (Feature Family Films—Video). DIR: Scott Swofford. CAST: Brandon Blaser, Jason Glenn, Jason Johnson. LOC: Draper, Riverton.

Television:

Slaughter of the Innocents (Shapiro-Glickenhaus Ent./HBO). DIR: James Glickenhaus. CAST: Scott Glenn, Jesse Cameron Glickenhaus, Jim Gardner. LOC: Salt Lake City, Provo Canyon, Provo airport, Draper (Utah State Prison), Moab, Castle Rock Valley, Salina, Valley of the Gods.

Beyond Suspicion (aka "Appointment For A Killing") (Von Zerneck-Sertner Films/NBC). DIR: William A. Graham. CAST: Markie Post, Corbin Bernsen, Kelsey Grammer. LOC: Salt Lake City.

Shattered Trust: The Shari Karney Story (CBS). DIR: Bill Corcoran. CAST: Melissa Gilbert, Kate Nelligan, Shirley Douglas. LOC: Salt Lake City.

Harmful Intent (Rosemount Prods.). DIR: John D. Patterson. CAST: Tim Matheson, Emma Samms, Robert Pastorelli. LOC: Salt Lake City, Ogden.

The Man With Three Wives (CBS). DIR: Peter Levin. CAST: Beau Bridges, Pam Dawber, Joanna Kerns. LOC: Salt Lake City.

Chantilly Lace (Showtime). DIR: Linda Yellen. CAST: Lindsay Crouse, Jill Eikenberry, Martha Plimpton. LOC: Sundance Resort, Provo Canyon.

Wind Dancer (KOAN/Majestic Ent.). DIR: Craig Clyde. CAST: Mel Harris, Matt McCoy, Raeanin Simpson. LOC: St. George.

1994:

City Slickers II: The Search for Curly's Gold (Columbia). DIR: Paul Weiland. CAST: Billy Crystal, Daniel Stern, Jack Palance. LOC: Arches, Dugout Ranch, Professor Valley, Goblin Valley.

Fate of the Universe. DIR: Diane Beam. Documentary. LOC: Washington County. OL: Cambridge, England.

The Flintstones (Amblin/Universal). DIR: Brian Levant. CAST: John Goodman, Elizabeth Perkins, Rick Moranis. LOC: Glen Canyon. OL: Los Angeles County, CA.

Forrest Gump (Paramount). DIR: Robert Zemeckis. CAST: Tom Hanks, Robin

Wright, Gary Sinise. LOC: Monument Valley. OL: Los Angeles, CA; Savannah, GA; Glacier National Park, MT; Pritchardville, Varnville, Fripp Island, SC; Asheville, NC; Washington, DC; Flagstaff, AZ.

Halloween: The Curse of Michael Myers (Nightfall Prods./Miramax). DIR: Joe Chappelle. CAST: Donald Pleasence, Paul Stephen Rudd, Marianne Hagan. LOC: Salt Lake City.

Maverick (Warner Bros.). DIR: Richard Donner. CAST: Mel Gibson, Jodie Foster, James Garner. LOC: Lake Powell, Warm Creek. OL: Lee's Ferry, Marble Canyon, AZ; Lone Pine, Manzanar, Big Pine, Yosemite National Park, CA; Columbia River Gorge, OR.

Pontiac Moon (Paramount). DIR: Peter Medak. CAST: Ted Danson, Mary Steenburgen, Ryan Todd. LOC: Cisco, Crescent Junction, Ruby Ranch Road, Arches.

The Great Bikini Off-Road Adventure (Imperial Ent.). DIR: Gary Orona. CAST: Eric Abrahamson, Avalon Anders, Fred Begay. LOC: Moab.

Tread (Oak Creek Films). Documentary. DIR: Bill Snider. CAST: Hans Rey, Greg Herbold. LOC: Sand Flats, White Rim.

Windrunner (Leucadia-Video). DIR: William Clark. CAST: Russell Means, Jason Wildes, Margot Kidder. LOC: Kanab, Kanab Canyon, Gunnison (Central Utah Correctional Facility).

Television:

Heaven Sent (KOAN). DIR: Craig Clyde. CAST: David Bowe, Wilford Brimley, Vincent Kartheiser. LOC: Salt Lake City.

Mortal Fear (Von Zerneck/Sertner Films). DIR: Larry Shaw. CAST: Joanna Kerns, Gregory Harrison, Max Gail. LOC: Salt Lake City.

Out of Annie's Past (Moore/Weiss Prods./USA). DIR: Stuart Cooper. CAST: Catherine Mary Stewart, Scott Valentine, Dennis Farina. LOC: Salt Lake City.

Parallel Lives (Sundance/Showtime). DIR: Linda Yellen. CAST: James Belushi, James Brolin, LaVar Burton. LOC: Salt Lake City. OL: California.

The Stand (Laurel Ent./ABC). Miniseries. DIR: Mick Garris. CAST: Gary Sinise, Molly Ringwald, James Sheridan. LOC: Salt Lake City, Draper (Utah State Prison), Sundance, Orem, Provo Canyon, Salina.

Three Things I've Learned (Epicenter Films). DIR: Lory Smith. CAST: Jonathan Gochberg, Oscar Rowland. LOC: Salt Lake City.

Touched by An Angel (MoonWater Prods./CBS-Caroline Prods.). Series: Season 1. CREATOR: John Masius. CAST: Roma Downey, Della Reese, John Dye. EPISODES: 11. Aired September 21, 1994 through March 4, 1995. LOC: Salt Lake City, and throughout Utah.

Miracles and Other Wonders. Series. LOC: Undetermined.

1995:

Species (M-G-M). DIR: Roger Donaldson. CAST: Ben Kingsley, Michael Madsen, Forest Whitaker. LOC: Brigham City, Dugway Proving Ground.

Plan 10 From Outer Space (Leo Films). DIR: Trent Harris. CAST: Patrick Michael Collins, Karen Black, Stefene Russell. LOC: Salt Lake City, Great Salt Lake.

Breaking Free (Leucadia). DIR: David Mackay. CAST: Jeremy London, Gina Phillips, Megan Gallagher. LOC: Farmington, Millcreek Canyon, Big Cottonwood Canyon, Park City.

Friendships Field (Feature Films for Families-Video). DIR: Bruce Neibaur. CAST: Dallen Gettling, Jonathan Hernandez, Kate Maberly. LOC: Salt Lake City. OL: Idaho.

Outbreak (Warner Bros.). DIR: Wolfgang Petersen. CAST: Dustin Hoffman, Rene Russo, Morgan Freeman. LOC: Dugway Proving Ground. OL: Ferndale, CA; Kauai, Hawaii.

Behind the Waterfall (Feature Films for Families). DIR: Scott Murphy. CAST: Gary Burghoff, Luke Baird, Alyssa Hansen. LOC: Murray.

Dumb & Dumber (New Line). DIR: Peter Farrelly. CAST: Jim Carrey, Jeff Daniels, Loren Holly. LOC: Salt Lake City, Park City, Ogden, American Fork Canyon.

Tall Tale (Disney/Buena Vista). DIR: Jeremiah Chechik. CAST: Patrick Swayze, Oliver Platt, Nick Stahl. LOC: Monument Valley, San Juan River.

Desert Winds (Achilles Films). DIR: Michael A. Nickles. CAST: Heather Graham, Jessica Hamilton, Jack Kehler. LOC: Utah. OL: Los Angeles.

The Undercover Kid (Leucadia). DIR: Linda Shayne. CAST: Bradley Pierce, Melora Hardin, Nicolas Surovy. LOC: Salt Lake City.

Waiting to Exhale (Twentieth Century-Fox). DIR: Forest Whitaker. CAST: Whitney Houston, Angela Bassett, Loretta Devine. LOC: Monument Valley. OL: Chandler, Fountain Hills, AL; Phoenix, Paradise Valley, AZ.

Pure Race (Cornerstone Films). DIR: Rocco DeVilliers. CAST: Fred Hunting, Gregory C. Haynes, Marvin Payne. LOC: undetermined. OL: Idaho; Arizona.

Windrunner (Leucadia-Video). DIR: William Clark. CAST: Jason Wiles, Russell Means, Margot Kidder. LOC: Kanab, Salt Lake City.

To Wong Fu Thanks for Everything, Julie Newmar (Amblin/Universal). DIR: Beeban Kidron. CAST: Wesley Snipes, Patrick Swayze, John Lequizamo. LOC: Monument Valley, Mexican Hat, Valley of the Gods; OL, Lincoln, Loma, Hooper, NE; Montclair, NJ; Cornwall & New York City, NY.

The 32nd Day of August on Earth (Max Films). DIR: Dennis Villeneuve. CAST: Paule Baillergeon, Emmanuel Bilodeau, Pascale Bussieres. LOC: Bonneville Salt Flats, SLC Int'l Airport; OL, Montreal, Quebec, Canada.

Television:

Unforgivable (Brayton-Carlucci Prods.). DIR: Graeme Campbell. CAST: John Ritter, Harley Jane Kozak, Kevin Dunn. LOC: Salt Lake City.

Avenging Angel (Curtis-Lowe Prods./TNT). DIR: Craig R. Baxley. CAST: Tom Berenger, James Coburn, Charlton Heston. LOC: Salt Lake City, Morgan, Great Salt Lake.

Touched by An Angel (MoonWater Prods./CBS-Caroline Prods.). Series: Season 2. CREATOR: John Masius. CAST: Roma Downey, Della Reese, John Dye. EPISODES: 24. Aired September 23, 1995 through May 18, 1996. LOC: Salt Lake City, and throughout Utah.

Into the Paradise (Slickrock). DIR: Curtis Briggs. CAST: Cristi Briggs, Tony Carlin, Greg Collins. LOC: Snow Canyon, St. George.

Deadly Invasion: The Killer Bee Nightmare (Von Zerneck Films). DIR: Rockne S. O'Bannon. CAST: Robert Hays, Nancy Stafford, Ryan Phillippe. LOC: Salt Lake City.

In the Shadow of Evil (Vin De Bona Prods./ABC). DIR: Daniel Sackheim. CAST: Treat Williams, Margaret Colin, Joe Morton. LOC: Salt Lake City.

It Was Him or Us (MTD Prods./Warner Bros.). DIR: Robert Iscove. CAST: Ann Jillian, Richard Grieco, Monique Lanier. LOC: Salt Lake City.

Just Like Dad (Leucadia). DIR: Blair Treu. CAST: Wallace Shawn, Ben Diskin, Nick Cassavetes. LOC: Salt Lake City.

Nothing Lasts Forever (Gerber/ITC Entertainment Group). Miniseries. DIR: Jack Bender. CAST: Gail O'Grady, Brooke Shields, Vanessa Williams. LOC: Salt Lake City.

Out of Annie's Past (MCA Television). DIR: Stuart Cooper. CAST: Catherine Mary Stewart, Scott Valentine, Dennis Farina. LOC: Salt Lake City.

Whose Daughter Is She? (Michael Greenwald Prods). DIR: Frank Arnold. CAST: Joanna Kerns, Stephanie Zimbalist, Michael Shulman. LOC: Salt Lake City.

1996:

Jagged Alliance: Deadly Games (Sertner Films). DIR: Ian Currie. CAST: Carl Alacci, Sonja Ball, Jude Beny. LOC: Salt Lake City.

Cheyenne (Halo Films). DIR: Dimitri Logothetis. CAST: Gary Hudson, Bobbie Phillips, Bo Svenson. LOC: Moab, Professor Valley, Mill Creek Canyon, Pucker Pass, Potash Road, Arches.

Clubhouse Detectives (Ridgewood Assoc.). DIR: Eric Hendershot. CAST: Michael Ballam, Michael Galeota, Jimmy Galeota. LOC: St. George.

Cosmic Voyage (IMAX). DIR: Bayley Silleck. LOC: Canyonlands. OL: Netherlands; Hawaii; Greece; Holland; Italy.

Coyote Summer (LeucadiaBVideo). DIR: Matias Alvarez. CAST: Vinessa Shaw, Adam Beach, Bruce Weitz. LOC: St. George, Salt Lake City.

Broken Arrow (Twentieth Century-Fox). DIR: John Woo. CAST: John Travolta, Christian Slater, Samantha Mathis. LOC: Lake Powell, Glen Canyon. OL: Lewistown, Fergus County, Denton, MT.

Tight Spot (Western Visuals-Video). DIR: Robert McCallum. CAST: Shanna McCullough, Tony Martino, John Decker. LOC: Park City. OL: Mazatlan, Mexico.

Larger Than Life (United Artists). DIR: Howard Franklin. CAST: Bill Murray, Janeane Garofalo, Matthew McConaughey. LOC: Professor Valley, Green River City. OL: Los Angeles, CA; Colorado.

Mulholland Falls (Largo/M-G-M-UA). DIR: Lee Tamahori. CAST: Nick Nolte, Melanie Griffith, Chazz Palminteri. LOC: Wendover. OL: Los Angeles, Malibu, CA.

Sarah's Child (Desert Rim). DIR: Ron Beckstrom. CAST: Mary Parker Williams, Michael Berger, Ruth Hale. LOC: Tooele. OL: Twin Falls, ID.

Same River Twice (KOAN/Feature Films for Familes--Video). DIR: Scott Featherstone. CAST: Robert Curtis Brown, John Putch, Shea Ferrell. LOC: Green River.

The Undercover Kid (CINAR/Sandstar Family Entertainment). DIR: Linda Shayne. CAST: Bradley Pierce, Melora Hardin, Nicolas Surovy. LOC: Salt Lake City: Liberty Park. OL: Los Angeles, CA.

Unforgivable (Brayton-Carlucci Prods./ CBS). DIR: Graeme Campbell. CAST: John Ritter, Harley Jane Kozak, Kevin Dunn. LOC: Salt Lake City.

Unhook the Stars (Miramax). DIR: Nick Cassavetes. CAST: Gena Rowlands, Marisa Tomei, Gerard Depardieu. LOC: Salt Lake City. OL: San Francisco, CA.

Wish Upon A Star (Leucadia-Video). DIR: Blair Treu. CAST: Katherine Heigl, Danielle Harris, Lois Chiles. LOC: West Valley City.

The Sunchaser (Regency/Warner Bros.). DIR: Michael Cimino. CAST: Woody Harrelson, Jon Seda, Anne Bancroft. LOC: Moab. OL: Jerome, AZ; Ouray, CO.

Zion Canyon: Treasure of the Gods (World Cinemax Prods.). DIR: Douglas Memmott, Kieth Merrill. LOC: Zion.

The Paper Brigade (LeucadiaBVideo). DIR: Blair Treu. CAST: Kyle Howard, Robert Englund, Travis Wester. LOC: Salt Lake City.

Television:

Invasion of Privacy (Fontana Filmproduktions GmbH). DIR: Anthony Hickox. CAST: Johnathon Schaech, Mili Avital. LOC: Salt Lake City, Canyonlands.

Raven Hawk (Ravenhawk/HBO). DIR: Albert Pyun. CAST: Rachel McLish, John Enos, Ed Lauter, Matt Clark. LOC: Glen Canyon. OL: Page, AZ; Santa Fe, NM.

Terror in the Family (Hallmark/Von Zerneck-Sertner Films). DIR: Gregory Goodell. CAST: Joanna Kerns, Hilary Swank, Dan Lauria. LOC: Salt Lake City.

In the Blink of An Eye (Grossbart Barnett Prods./ABC) DIR: Mick Dickoff. CAST: Polly Bergen, Carlos Gomez, Veronica Hamel. LOC: Farmington, Salt Lake City.

A Loss of Innocence (Manti Films/ABC). DIR: Graeme Clifford. CAST: Jenni Garth, Rob Estes, Polly Holliday. LOC: Salt Lake City.

Promised Land (MoonWater Prods./ CBS). Series. Seaton 1. CREATOR: Martha Williamson. CAST: Gerald McRaney, Wendy Phillips, Austin O'Brien. EPISODES: 24. Aired September 17, 1996 through May 26, 1997. LOC: Salt Lake City, and throughout Utah.

Face of Evil (Larry Thompson Ent./CBS). DIR: Mary Lambert. CAST: Tracey Gold, Perry King, Don Harvey. LOC: Salt Lake City.

Unabomber: The True Story (USA). DIR: Jon Purdy. CAST: Robert Hays, Dean Stockwell, Tobin Bell. LOC: Salt Lake City, Park City.

Riders of the Purple Sage (Amer-Rosemont-Zeke Prods/Turner Ent.). DIR: Charles Haid. CAST: Ed Harris, Amy Madigan, Henry Thomas. LOC: Dugout Ranch, Indian River Valley, Mill Creek Canyon, Ten Mile, Pucker Pass/Long Valley.

Touched by An Angel (MoonWater Prods./ CBS-Caroline Prods.). Series. Season 3. CREATOR: John Masius. CAST: Roma Downey, Della Reese, John Dye. EPISODES: 28. Aired from September 15, 1996 through May 18, 1997. LOC: Salt Lake City, and throughout Utah.

Walker, Texas Ranger (Amadea Film Prods.). Series. LOC: Salt Lake City.

The Last Resort (Dayton Studios/Destiny Prods.) DIR: Lyman Dayton. CAST: Dave Buzzotta, Stephanie Dicker, Justin Walker. LOC: Glen Danyon, Oak Grove, Orem, Salt Lake City, St. George, Sunset Mesa. OL: Alpine Canyon, Jackson Hole, Snake River, WY; Lake Powell, AZ.

1997:

The Rage (Imperial/Miramax). DIR: Sidney J. Furie. CAST: Lorenzo Lamas, Kristin Coke, Gary Busey. LOC: Heber City.

Breakdown (Paramount). DIR: Jonathan Mostow. CAST: Kurt Russell, Kathleen Quinlan, J. T. Walsh. LOC: Moab.

Crayoluv (SSOP Prods.). DIR: Tucker Dansie. CAST: Daniel Barton, Jana Dietlein, Quinn Dietlein. LOC: Salt Lake City.

Just in Time (Leucadia-Video). DIR: Shawn Levy. CAST: Rebecca Chambers, Steven Eckholdt, Frank Gerrish. LOC: Salt Lake City.

Con Air (Touchstone). DIR: Simon West. CAST: Nicolas Cage, John Cusack, John Malkovich. LOC: Salt Lake City, Ogden, Canyonlands. OL: Elkhart, Goshen, IN; Las Vegas, NV.

Life Less Ordinary (PolyGram/Twentieth Century-Fox). DIR: Danny Boyle. CAST: Ewan McGregor, Cameron Diaz, Holly Hunter. LOC: Salt Lake City, Utah State Fair Park, Layton, Uinta National Forest, Deer Valley.

Truth or Consequences, N.M. (Higgins-Messick-Wayne/Sony Pictures). DIR: Kiefer Sutherland. CAST: Vincent Gallo, Mykelti Williamson, Kevin Pollak. LOC: Grafton, Rockville, St. George, Pine Valley.

RocketMan (Caravan/Disney). DIR: Stuart Gillard. CAST: Harland Williams, Jessica Lundy, William Sadler. LOC: Moab. OL: Houston, TX.

Address Unknown (Leucadia-Video). DIR: Shawn Levy. CAST: Kyle Howard, Johna Stewart-Bowden, Corbin Allred. LOC: Salt Lake City, Park City.

The Appleby Sensation (Houston Pictures). DIR: Aaron Orullian. CAST: Edward Anderson, Marion Bentley (Narrator), David Bohn. LOC: Provo, Salt Lake City. OL: New York City, NY; Los Angeles, CA.

The Last Time I Committed Suicide (Bates Ent.). DIR: Stephen T. Kay. CAST: Thomas Jane, Keanu Reeves, Tom Bower. LOC: Ogden. OL: Los Angeles, CA.

The Last Resort (Dayton Family Pictures). DIR: Lyman Dayton. CAST: Dave Buzzotta, Scott Caan, Maria Carr. LOC: Salt Lake City, Orem, St.George, Oak Grove, Sunset Mesa, Virgin River, Glen Canyon. OL: Alpine Canyon/Snake River, Jackson Hole, WY.

Television:

Heaven or Vegas (Storm Ent.) DIR: Gregory C. Haynes. CAST: Richard Grieco, Yasmine Bleeth, Sarah Schaub. LOC: Logan.

Night Sins (Scripps Howard Ent.). Miniseries. DIR: Robert Allan Ackerman. CAST: Valerie Bertinelli, Harry Hamlin, Karen Sillas. LOC: Park City.

Mr. Atlas (Windmill Prods.). DIR: Karen Arbeeny. CAST: T. J. Lowther, Laura Johnson, Timothy Bottoms. LOC: Heber, Provo, Sandy.

Vanishing Point (Fox TV). DIR: Charles Robert Carner. CAST: Viggo Mortensen, Christine Elise, Steve Railsback. LOC: Monument Valley. OL: Tucson, AZ; New Mexico; Riddle, ID.

Divided by Hate (Great Falls Prods./USA). DIR: Tom Skerritt. CAST: Dyan Walsh, Andrea Roth, Jim Beaver. LOC: American Fork, Provo, Lehi, Pleasant Grove, Payson.

Dying to Belong (Hallmark/NBC). DIR: William A. Graham. CAST: Hilary Swank, Sarah Chalke, Mark-Paul Gosselaar. LOC: Salt Lake City.

Detention: The Siege at Johnson High (Hill/Field Ent.). DIR: Michael W. Watkins. CAST: Rick Schroeder, Henry Winkler, Freddie Prinze Jr. LOC: Sandy.

The Ticket (CNM Ent.) DIR: Stuart Cooper. CAST: Shannen Doherty, James Marshall, Phillip Van Dyke. LOC: Park City.

In My Sister's Shadow (Steinhart Baer/CBS). DIR: Sandor Stern. CAST: Janet Leigh, Nancy McKeon, Thomas McCarthy. LOC: Salt Lake City.

Lost Treasure of Dos Santos (MTM Ent./Family Channel). DIR: Jorge Montesi. CAST: Michele Greene, David Carradine, Cathy Lee Crosby. LOC: Moab.

Mercenary (Conquistador Ent./HBO-Showtime). DIR: Avi Nesher. CAST: Olivier Gruner, John Ritter, Robert Culp. LOC: undetermined. OL: Los Angeles and San Diego, CA; Israel; Mexico City.

Dead by Midnight (Midnight Man Prods./ABC). DIR: Jim McBride. CAST: Timothy Hutton, Suzy Amis, John Glover. LOC: Salt Lake City.

Mother Knows Best (ABC). DIR: Larry Shaw. CAST: Joanna Kerns, Christine Elise, Grant Show. LOC: Salt Lake City.

Money Play$ (Showtime). DIR: Frank D. Gilroy. CAST: Roy Scheider, Sonia Braga, Jon Polito. LOC: Salt Lake City, Wendover. OL: Las Vegas, NV.

Not in This Town (Chelsea Avenue Prods./USA). DIR: Donald Wrye. CAST: Kathy Baker, Adam Arkin, Ed Begley Jr. LOC: Salt Lake City, Utah County.

Touched by An Angel (MoonWater Prods./CBS-Caroline Prods.). Series. Season 4. CREATOR: John Masius. CAST: Roma Downey, Della Reese, John Dye. EPISODES: 27. Aired September 21, 1997 through May 17, 1998. LOC: Salt Lake City, and throughout Utah.

Promised Land (MoonWater Prods./CBS). Series. Season 2. CREATOR: Martha Williamson. CAST: Gerald McRaney, Wendy Phillips, Austin O'Brien. EPISODES: 23. Aired September 25, 1997 through May 14, 1998. LOC: Salt Lake City, and throughout Utah.

Something Borrowed, Something Blue (JCS Ent./CBS). DIR: Gwen Arner. CAST: Connie Sellecca, Twiggy Lawson, Jameson Parker. LOC: Salt Lake City.

1998:

Alyson's Closet (Film in a Suitcase). DIR: Rick Page. CAST: Tobijah Tyler, Suzanne Douglass, Melinda Renee. LOC: Salt Lake City.

Angels in the Attic (Promark Ent. Group). DIR: Eric Hendershot. CAST: Clayton Taylor, Stephen Losak, Dalin Christiansen. LOC: Provo.

Aurora (Rara Avis Films). DIR: Christopher Kulikowski. CAST: Christopher J. Stapleton, Markus Botnick, Micheal DiMaggio. LOC: Moab, Lake Powell. OL: Malibu, North Hollywood, Dumont Dunes, CA; Warm Creek, AZ; Lake Mead, Valley of Fire State Park, NV.

Bench at the Edge (Bateman Prods.). DIR: Kent Bateman. CAST: Cory Dangerfield, Davyd Daniels, Elaine Eaton. LOC: Canyonlands Nat'l Park, Park City.

Dead Ringer (Speedy Films). DIR: Eric Hendershot. CAST: Clayton Taylor, Mace Melbros, David Gardner. LOC: Salt Lake City, Orem.

The Face on the Barroom Floor (Face Prods.). DIR: Paul Gibran Begum. CAST: Cory Dangerfield, Rob Diamond, Lincoln Hoppe. LOC: Salt Lake City.

Freeriders (Warren Miller Ent.). DIR: Brian Sisselman. NARRATOR: Warren Miller. Ski documentary. LOC: Park City, The Canyons. OL: ski resorts throughout the world.

Letters From a Killer. (J&M Ent.) DIR: David Carson. CAST: Patrick Swayze, Gia Carides, Kim Myers. LOC: Salt Lake City, Wendover, Jordanelle Reservoir, Echo Reservoir. OL: Los Angeles, Lone Pine, Sacramento, CA; New Orleans, LA.

Meet the Deedles (Disney). DIR: Steve Boyum. CAST: Steve Van Wormer, Paul Walker, A. J. Langer. LOC: Park City; OL: O'ahu, HI.

The Only Thrill (Prestige Prods.). DIR: Peter Masterson. CAST: Diane Keaton, Sam Shepard, Diane Lane. LOC: Moab.

Only Once (Bristone Films). DIR: Rocco DeVilliers. CAST: Austin O'Brien, Britt Leary, David Jensen. LOC: Salt Lake City.

No More Baths (Feature Films for Families-Video). DIR: Timothy J. Nelson. CAST: Garrett M. Brown, Gretchen Carr, Victoria Jackson. LOC: Salt Lake City.

Passion in the Desert (Roland Films/Fine Line Features). DIR: Lavinia Currier. CAST: Ben Daniels, Michael Piccoli, Paul Meston. LOC: Mill Creek Canyon, Dead Horse State Park, Whitewash Sand Dunes.

Route 66 (TAG Ent.). DIR: Steve Austin. CAST: Alana Austin, Diane Ladd, Richard Moll. LOC: Torrey, Capitol Reef.

Clay Pigeons (Gramercy Pictures). DIR: David Dobkin. CAST: Joaquin Phoenix, Vince Vaughn, Janeane Garofalo. LOC: Brigham City, Deweyville, Garland, Hyrum Lake. OL: Lancaster, CA.

Zack and Reba (Itasca Pictures). DIR: Nicole Bettaver. CAST: Sean Patrick Flanery, Martin Mull, Brittany Murphy. LOC: Salt Lake City.

Television:

Perfect Getaway (Gaslight Pictures). DIR: Armand Mastroianni. CAST: Adrian Pasdar, Antonio Sabato Jr., Kelly

Rutherford. LOC: Moab, Salt Lake City.
Legion of Fire: Killer Ants! (Producers Ent. Group/Fox TV). DIR: Jim Charleston, George Manasse. CAST: Eric Lutes, Julie Campbell, Mitch Pileggi. LOC: Kamas, Heber.
No Laughing Matter (Great Falls Prods./Universal). DIR: Michael Elias. CAST: Suzanne Somers, Chad Christ, Selma Blair. LOC: Salt Lake City.
Martian Law (Rysher Ent.). Series. LOC: Moab.
Everest (MacGillivray Freeman Films/ Miramax). DIR: David Breashears, Stephen Judson, Greg MacGillivrey. NARRATOR: Liam Neeson. CAST: Beck Weathers, Jamling Tenzing Norgay. LOC: Moab. OL: Mt. Everest, Nepal; India; Colorado; New Hampshire.
A Town Has Turned to Dust (Sci-Fi Channel). DIR: Rob Nilsson. CAST: Gabriel Olds, Ron Perlman, Stephen Lang. LOC: Utah County.
Touched by An Angel (MoonWater Prods./ CBS-Caroline Prods.). Series. Season 5. CREATOR: John Masius. CAST: Roma Downey, Della Reese, John Dye. EPISODES: 26. Aired September 20, 1998 through May 23, 1999. LOC: Salt Lake City, and throughout Utah.
Promised Land (MoonWater Prods./ CBS). Series. Season 3. CREATOR: Martha Williamson. CAST: Gerald McRaney, Wendy Phillips, Austin O'Brien. EPISODES: 22. Aired October 1, 1998 through May 20, 1999. LOC: Salt Lake City. OL: Colorado: Denver.
Before He Wakes (CBS). DIR: Michael Scott. CAST: Jaclyn Smith, Diana Scarwid, Timothy Carhart. LOC: Salt Lake City.
Virtual Obsession (Germain Prods./ Hallmark Ent.). DIR: Mick Garris. CAST: Peter Gallagher, Mimi Rogers, Jack Lloyd. LOC: Salt Lake City, Provo.
Walker, Texas Ranger (Amadea Film Prods.). Series. LOC: Salt Lake City.
Independent's Day (Graceful Pictures/ Sundance Channel). DIR: Marina Zenovich. CAST: Ira Deutchman, Jeff Dowd, Roger Ebert. LOC: Park City. OL: New York City; Los Angeles, CA.

1999:

Colors: Up Close & Personal. DIR: Tucker Dansie. Documentary. LOC: Salt Lake City, Logan. OL: Las Vegas, NV.
Fifty (Warren Miller Ent.). DIR: Kurt Miller, Peter Speek. Documentary. LOC: Snowbird. OL: various ski resorts around the world.
Blue Ridge Fall (Filmwaves). DIR: James Rowe. CAST: Peter Facinelli, Jay R. Ferguson, Rodney Eastman. LOC: Salt Lake City.
The Creator's Game (American Int'l Media). DIR: Bruce Troxell. CAST: Dakota House, Al Harrington, Bryce Chamberlain. LOC: Utah County.
The Old Woman (Films for the Humanities and Sciences). DIR: Durane Andersen. CAST: Bryan D. Moss, Anna Platanova, Eric Bjarnson. LOC: Salt Lake City.
Galaxy Quest (Dream Works SKG). DIR: Dean Parisot. CAST: Tim Allen, Sigourney Weaver, Alan Rickman. LOC: Goblin Valley, Green River. OL: Los Angeles, Malibu, CA.
Drive Me Crazy (Grand March Prods./ Twentieth Century-Fox). DIR: John Schultz. CAST: Melissa Joan Hart, Adrian Grenier, Stephen Collins. LOC: Salt Lake City, Ogden.
Fortune Cookie (J&L Prods.). DIR: Clay Essig. CAST: Matt Barker, Rachel Kimsey, Chris Marley. LOC: Salt Lake City, Bountiful.
Friends & Lovers (Laguna Ent.). DIR: George Haas. CAST: Stephen Baldwin, Danny Nucci, George Newbern. LOC: Salt Lake City, Heber, Deer Valley, Park City.
The Right Temptation (Award Ent.). DIR: Lyndon Chubbuck. CAST: Kiefer Sutherland, Rebecca De Mornay, Dana Delany. LOC: Salt Lake City.
The Runner (Aspect Ratio). DIR: Ron Moler. CAST: Ron Eldard, Courteney Cox, John Goodman. LOC: Salt Lake City. OL: Wendover, NV.
SLC Punk! (Beyond-Straight Edge/ Sony). DIR: James Merendino. CAST: Matthew Lillard, Michael Goorjiam, Annabeth Gish. LOC: Salt Lake City, Great Salt Lake. OL: Evanston, WY.
Wild Wild West (Warner Bros.). DIR: Barry Sonnenfeld. CAST: Will Smith, Kevin Kline, Kenneth Branagh. LOC: Monument Valley.
Chill Factor (Morgan Creek Prods.). DIR: Hugh Johnson. CAST: Cuba Gooding Jr., Skeet Ulrich, Peter Firth. LOC: Vernal. OL: Liberty, SC.
Almost Anything (New Tribe Films). DIR: Raymond T. Asante. CAST: Karen Yvonne Taylor, Frances Black, Roger Ontiveros. LOC: Salt Lake City.
Bats (Destination Films/Sony). DIR: Louis Morneau. CAST: Lou Diamond Phillips, Dina Meyer, Bob Gunton. LOC: American Fork, Magna, Park City.
The Argument (Mazzola Film Co.). DIR: Donald Cammel. CAST: Myriam Gibril, Kendrew Lascelles. LOC: Arches.
Shepherd (Shepherd Prods.). DIR: Peter Hayman. CAST: C. Thomas Howell, Roddy Piper, Heidi von Palleske. LOC: Park City, Heber, Salt Lake City.
The Switch (Digital Options/SSOP Prods.). DIR: Tucker Dansie. CAST: Megan Back, Spencer Burnbridge, Leslie Golden. LOC: Murray.
Made Men (Decade Pictures/Columbia Tri-Star). DIR: Louis Morneau. CAST: James Belushi, Michael Beach, Timothy Dalton. LOC: Spanish Fork, Eureka.
Shiloh 2: Shiloh Season (Warner Bros.). DIR: Sandy Tung. CAST: Zachary Browne, Scott Wilson, Michael Moriarty. LOC: undetermined.
Television:
Absence of the Good (Columbia Tri-Star). DIR: John Flynn. CAST: Stephen Baldwin, Tyne Daly, Elizabeth Barondes. LOC: undetermined.
Anya's Bell (Universal). DIR: Tom McLoughlin. CAST: Della Reese, Mason Gamble, Thomas Cavanagh. LOC: Salt Lake City.
Stray Dog (Lynch Ent.). Series. LOC: Salt Lake City, Woodland.
The Long Road Home (KOAN). DIR: Craig Clyde. CAST: Michael Ansara, T. J. Lowther, Sandra Shotwell. LOC: undetermined.
Don't Look Under the Bed (Salty Pictures/ Disney/ABC). DIR: Kenneth Johnson. CAST: Eric Ty' Hodges, Robin Riker, Steve Valentine. LOC: Salt Lake City.
Johnny Tsunami (Film Roman/Disney Channel). DIR: Steve Boyum. CAST: Brandon Baker, Yuji Okumoto, Mary Page Keller. LOC: Brighton. OL: Hawaii.
A Secret Life (Carlo Singer Prods.). DIR: Larry Peerce. CAST: Roma Downey, Penny Johnson, Kristina Molota. LOC: Salt Lake City.
Substitute 3: Winner Take All (Artisan). DIR: Robert Radler. CAST: Treat Williams, David Jensen, Barbara Jean Reams.
Touched by An Angel (MoonWater Prods./ CBS-Caroline Prods.). Series. Season 6. CREATOR: John Masius. CAST: Roma Downey, Della Reese, John Dye. EPISODES: 26. Aired September 26, 1999 through May 21, 2000. LOC: Salt Lake City, and throughout Utah.
Murder at 75 Birch (Nicki Film Prods). DIR: Michael Scott. CAST: Melissa Gilbert, Gregory Harrison, Vyto Ruginis. LOC: Salt Lake City.

2000:

Baby Bedlam (Promark Ent.). DIR: Eric Hendershot. CAST: Joe Piscopo, Julie Hagerty, Reggie Theus. LOC: Salt Lake City.

Overnight Sensation (Burnside). DIR: Glen Trotiner. CAST: Sean Dugan, Maxwell Caulfield, Seth William Meier. LOC: Park City.

Vertical Limit (Columbia/Sony). DIR: Martin Campbell. CAST: Chris O'Donnell, Robin Tunney, Stuart Wilson. LOC: Monument Valley. OL: Southern Alps and Otago, New Zealand; Karakoram Mountain Range, Pakistan.

Baby Bedlam (Speedy Films). DIR: Eric Hendershot. CAST: Robert Costanzo, Julie Hagerty, Joe Piscopo. LOC: Salt Lake City.

Mission: Impossible 2 (Paramount). DIR: John Woo. CAST: Tom Cruise, Dougray Scott, Thandie Newton. LOC: Dead Horse Point.

Christmas in the Clouds (Clouds Prods.). DIR: Catherine Montgomery. CAST: Rita Coolidge, Graham Greene, M. Emmett Walsh. LOC: Salt Lake City, Sundance, Heber City.

Cowboys and Angels (Smokin' Dawks). DIR: Gregory C. Haynes. CAST: Mia Kirshner, Radha Mitchell, Adam Trese. LOC: Salt Lake City.

The Dream Catcher (Film Society of Lincoln Center/Independent Feature Project). DIR: Edward A. Radtke. CAST: Maurice Compte, Paddy Connor, Jeanne Heaton. LOC: Utah. OL: Dayton, Beavercreek, Springfield, Yellow Springs, OH.

Partners in Crime (Daly Harris Prods.). DIR: Jennifer Warren. CAST: Rutger Hauer, Paulina Porizkova, Andrew Dolan. LOC: Salt Lake City.

Crow: The Salvation (Edward Presssman Films). DIR: Bharat Nalluri. CAST: Kirsten Dunst, Eric Mabius, Jodi Lyn O'Keefe. LOC: Salt Lake City.

Belong (Talefeather Prods.). DIR: Joseph Bagley. CAST: Jesse Fluck, Jason Hopkins, July Krause. LOC: Mapleton, Springville, Spanish Fork, Payson.

Way of the Gun (Artisan). DIR: Christopher McQuarrie. CAST: Ryan Phillippe, Benicio Del Toro, James Caan. LOC: Salt Lake City, Delle, Skull Valley.

Primary Suspect (Boxer Prods.). DIR: Jeff Celentano. CAST: William Baldwin, Brigitte Bako, Lee Majors. LOC: Salt Lake City.

Overnight Sensation (Freewheel Prods.). DIR: Glen Trotiner. CAST: Sean Dugan, Seth William Meier, Maxwell Caulfield. LOC: Park City. OL: New York City and Parksville, NY.

Net Worth (Curb Ent.). DIR: Kenny Griswold. CAST: Craig Sheffer, Todd Field, Daniel Baldwin. LOC: Park City, Salt Lake City.

Peroxide Passion (Terence Michael Prods.). DIR: Monty Diamond. CAST: Adam Alexi-Malle, Lorri Bagley, Billy Campion. LOC: Salt Lake City.

Return to the Secret Garden (Feature Films for Families-Video). DIR: Scott Featherstone. CAST: Mercedes Kastner, Michelle Horn, Josh Zuckerman. LOC: Salt Lake City.

Slow Burn (Blue Rider Pictures/ Artisan). DIR: Christian Ford. CAST: Jennifer Ann Evans, Stuart Wilson, Nicole Fellows. LOC: Wendover.

The Testaments: One Fold and One Shepherd (The Church of Jesus Christ of Latter-day Saints). DIR: Kieth Merrill. CAST: Rick Macy, Jeremy Elliott, Arianna Marsden. LOC: Provo, Spanish Fork. OL: Hawaii.

The Road to Redemption (Dean River Prods.). DIR: Robert Vernon. CAST: Pat Hingle, Julia Condra, Leo Rossi. LOC: undetermined.

Little Secrets (Columbia Tri-Star). DIR: Blair Treu. CAST: Evan Rachel Wood, Michael Angarano, David Gallagher. LOC: Salt Lake City

How the Grinch Stole Christmas (Universal). DIR: Ron Howard. CAST: Jim Carrey, Jeffrey Tambor, Christine Baranski. LOC: Salt Lake City. OL: Universal Studios, CA.

How to Smoke Pot (Freedom Filmmakers). DIR: Thomas Camoin. CAST: David F. Camoin, Marie Watkins Crocker, Matthew Crocker. LOC: Salt Lake City, Skull Valley.

Stranger Than Fiction (Bergman Lustig Prods.). DIR: Eric Bross. CAST: Mackenzie Astin, Todd Field, Dina Meyer. LOC: Salt Lake City. OL: Los Angeles, CA; Washington, DC; New York, NY.

Wind River (Ivy Entertainment). DIR: Tom Shell. CAST: Blake Heron, A Martinez, Russell Means. LOC: Park City, St. George. OL: California: Death Valley.

Television:

Perfect Murder, Perfect Town (TVM Prods./CBS). Miniseries. DIR: Lawrence Schiller. CAST: Marg Helgenberger, Kris Kristofferson, Ronny Cox. LOC: Salt Lake City. OL: Boulder, CO.

The Right Temptation (Award Ent./ Columbia). DIR: Lyndon Chubbuck. CAST: Kiefer Sutherland, Rebecca De Mornay, Dana Delany. LOC: Salt Lake City.

Shot in the Heart (Home Box Office). DIR: Agnieszka Holland. CAST: Anne Kathryn Parma, Ashley Edwards, Evyn Clark. LOC: Salt Lake City.

Cover Me: Based on the True Life of an FBI Family (Shaun Cassidy Prods./USA). Series. LOC: Salt Lake City, Wendover, Summit County. OL, San Diego, CA.

Touched by An Angel (MoonWater Prods./ CBS-Caroline Prods.). Series. Season 7. CREATOR: John Masius. CAST: Roma Downey, Della Reese, John Dye. EPISODES: 25. Aired October 15, 2000 through May 20, 2001. LOC: Salt Lake City, and throughout Utah.

Beyond the Prairie: The True Story of Laura Ingalls Wilder (CBS). DIR: Marcus Cole. CAST: Terra Allen, Alandra Bingham, J. Scott Bronson. LOC: Salt Lake City.

The Darkling (USA). DIR: Po-Chih Leong. CAST: F. Murray Abraham, Aidan Gillen, Lisa Linde. LOC: Salt Lake City, Taylorsville, Great Salt Lake.

Under Contract (USA).Series. LOC: Salt Lake City.

Many Wives: Vows of Silence. DIR: Menasheh Fogel, Steven Pecchia-Bekkum. CAST: Ron Allen, Owen Allred, Patty Brown. LOC: Brigham City, Hildale, Salt Lake City, Tropic.

The Huntress (USA). Series. LOC: Salt Lake City, OL: Los Angeles, Santa Clarita, CA.

Stolen From the Heart (Leonard HillFilms/CBS). DIR: Bruce Pittman. CAST: Tracey Gold, Lisa Zane, William R. Moses. LOC: undetermined.

Phantom of the Megaplex (Grossbart Barnett/Disney Channel). DIR: Blair Treu. CAST: Taylor Handley, Corrine Bohrer, Caitlin Wachs. LOC: Salt Lake City. OL: Toronto.

2001:

Brigham City (Main Street Movie Co./Excel). DIR: Richard Dutcher. CAST: Richard Dutcher, Matthew A. Brown, Wilford Brimley. LOC: Provo Canyon, Springville, Mapleton.

Dumb Luck (Tag Ent.). DIR: Craig Clyde. CAST: Scott Baio, Tracy Nelson, Richard Moll. LOC: Salt Lake City.

The Forsaken (Sandstorm). DIR: J.S. Cordone. CAST: Kerr Smith, Brendan Fehr, Izabella Miko. LOC: Utah; OL, Flagstaff, Wellton, Yuma, AZ.

Horse Crazy (Pure Ent.). DIR: Eric Hendershot. CAST: Michael Glauser, Brittany Armstrong, Jonathan Cronin.

LOC: St. George. OL: Littlefield, AZ.
Joe Dirt (Columbia). DIR: Dennie Gordon. CAST: David Spade, Brittany Daniel, Dennis Miller. LOC: Dead Horse Point. OL: Carson, El Segundo, Santa Paula, CA; Twin Arrows, AZ.
Joy Ride (New Regency). DIR: John Dahl. CAST: Steve Zahn, Paul Walker, Leelee Sobieski. LOC: Delle, Skull Valley. OL: Wells, Battle Mountain, Hazen, I-80, NV; Lancaster, Long Beach, Redlands, Playa del Rey, CA.
Le Peuple Migrateur [Winged Migration] (Bac Films). DIR: Jacques Perrin, Jacques Cluzaud. Documentary. LOC: Glen Canyon, Lake Powell, Monument Valley.
Almost Anything (New Tribe Films). DIR: Raymond T. Asante. CAST: Ryan Parks, Karen Yvonne Taylor, Frances Black. LOC: Salt Lake City. OL: Hermosa Beach, Los Angeles, Paso Robles, CA.
Nobody's Baby (Artisan). DIR: David Seltzer. CAST: Skeet Ulrich, Gary Oldman, Radha Mitchell. LOC: Salt Lake City, Thompson, Lake Powell, Summit County.
Planet of the Apes (Twentieth Century-Fox). DIR: Tim Burton. CAST: Mark Wahlberg, Tim Roth, Helena Bonham Carter. LOC: Lake Powell. OL: Los Angeles, Ridgecrest, Santa Clarita, CA; Sydney, Australia.
Road to Redempton (Dean River Prods.). DIR: Robert Vernon. CAST: Pat Hingle, Julie Condra, Wes Studi. LOC: Moab.
Twice Today (Weird Chief Pictures). DIR: Joshua Tai Taeoalii. CAST: Emilee Barber, Rebecca Hunt, Michael Kempner. LOC: Salt Lake City.
Wind River (Mad Dog Prods./Lions Gate Films). DIR: Tom Shell. CAST: Blake Heron, A. Martinez, Russell Means. LOC: Park City, St. George. OL: Death Valley Nat'l Park, CA.
Television:
The Ballad of Lucy Whipple (CBS). DIR: Jeremy Kagan. CAST: Glenn Close, Jena Malone, Bruce McGill. LOC: Park City.
The Luck of the Irish (Hal Roach/Disney Channel). DIR: Paul Hoen. CAST: Ryan Merriman, Henry Gibson, Alexis Lopez. LOC: Draper, Farmington.
Hounded (Hal Roach/Disney Channel). DIR: Neal Israel. CAST: Tahj Mowry, Shia La Beouf, Craig Kirkwood. LOC: /Salt Lake City.
The Poof Point (Hal Roach/Disney Channel). DIR: Neal Israel. CAST: Tahj Mowry, Dawnn Lewis, Mark Curry. LOC: Salt Lake City.
Touched by An Angel (MoonWater Prods./CBS-Caroline Prods.). Series. Season 8. CREATOR: John Masius. CAST: Roma Downey, Della Reese, John Dye. EPISODES: 22. Aired September 20, 2001 through May 11, 2002. LOC: Salt Lake City, and throughout Utah.

2002:

Charly (Cinergy Films/Excel Ent.). DIR: Adam Thomas Anderegg. CAST: Jeremy Elliott, Randy King, Heather Beers. LOC: Salt Lake City, Springville. OL: New York City, NY; Los Angeles, CA.
Austin Powers in Goldmember (New Line). DIR: Jay Roach. CAST: Mike Myers, Beyonce Knowles, Seth Green. LOC: Moab. OL: Reno, NV; Los Angeles, CA; South Bank, London, UK; St. Albans, Herts, UK.
Gerry (Epsilon Motion Pictures/My Cactus). DIR: Gus Van Sant. CAST: Casey Affleck, Matt Damon LOC: Bonneville Salt Flats.
The Climb (Dean River Productions). DIR: John Schmidt. CAST: Jason Winston George, Ned Vaughn, Dabney Coleman LOC: Provo.
Con Express (PM Ent.). DIR: Terry Cunningham. CAST: Sean Patrick Flanery, Arnold Vosloo, Ursula Karven. LOC: Utah.
Double Teamed (Hal Roach Prods.). DIR: Duwayne Dunham. CAST: Poppi Monroe, Annie McElwain, Teal Redmann. LOC: Salt Lake City.
Getting There (Dualstar Ent. Group). DIR: Steve Purcell. CAST: Mary-Kate Olsen, Ashley Olsen, Billy Aaron Brown. LOC: Park City, Salt Lake City.
Just a Dream (DBA Movie Prods.). DIR: Danny Glover. CAST: Carl Lumbly, Robby Benson, Ally Sheedy LOC: Salt Lake City.
Poolhall Junkies (Gold Circle/Samuel Goldwyn). DIR: Mars Callahan. CAST: Chazz Palmenteri, Rick Schroeder, Rod Steiger. LOC: Salt Lake City.
Singles Ward (Halestorm Ent.). DIR: Kurt Hale. CAST: Will Swenson, Connie Young, Daryn Tufts LOC: Provo, Salt Lake City.
I Saw Mommy Kissing Santa Claus (Regent). DIR: John Shepphird. CAST: Connie Sellecca, Corbin Bernsen, Cole Sprouse. LOC: Sandy.
Windtalkers (M-G-M). DIR: John Woo. CAST: Nicolas Cage, Adam Beach, Peter Stromare. LOC: Monument Valley. OL: O'ahu, HI; Acton, CA.
Clubhouse Detectives in Big Trouble (Promark Ent.) DIR: Eric Hendershot. CAST: Jonathan Cronin, Brittany Armstrong, Michael Glauser. LOC: St. George.
Clubhouse Detectives in Search of a Lost Princess (Promark Ent.). DIR: Eric Hendershot. CAST: Jonathan Cronin, Brittany Armstrong, Michael Glauser. LOC: St. George.
The Core (David Foster Prods./Paramount). DIR: John Amiel. CAST: Aaron Eckhart, Hilary Swank, Delroy Lindo. LOC: Wendover; OL, British Columbia, Manitoba, Canada; Everett, WA; Dumont Dunes, CA.
The Good War (MiBAC). DIR: Giorgio Serafini. CAST: Robert Farrior, Roy Scheider, Luca Zingaretti. LOC: Utah; OL, Bulgaria.
Television:
Beyond the Prairie, Part 2: The True Story of Laura Ingalls Wilder (CBS). DIR: Marcus Cole. CAST: Lindsay Crouse, Walt Goggins, Tess Harper. LOC: Strawberry Reservoir, Heber City, Promontory. OL: Texas.
Touched by an Angel. (Caroline Prods./CBS-TV). Series. LOC: SLC/Salt Lake City and various locations throughout Utah.
Firestarter 2: Rekindled (USA Films/Sci-Fi Channel). DIR: Robert Iscove. CAST: Marguerite Moreau, Malcolm McDowell, Dennis Hopper. LOC: SLC/Salt Lake City; WeC/Ogden.
Everwood. Series. LOC: SLC/Salt Lake City.
Double Teamed (Just Singer Entertainment/Disney Channel). Movie. DIR: Duwayne Dunham. CAST: Poppi Monroe, Annie McElwain, Teal Redmann. LOC: Salt Lake City: Capitol Theater, Regency Apts., Judge Memorial High School, Hillcrest High School.

2003:

Abby Singer (Wembly Hall Theatre Co.). DIR: Ryan R. Williams. CAST: Ryan R. Williams, Gloria Smith, Clint J. Palmer. LOC: Park City, Sundance, Park City, Salt Lake City; OL, Santa Monica, Culver City, CA.
The Book of Mormon Movie, Volume 1: The Journey (Halestorm Ent.). DIR: Gary Rogers. CAST: Noah Danby, Jacque Gray, Bryce Chamberlain. LOC: Ogden, Moab, Goblin Valley. OL: Universal Studios, CA; Kaua'i, HI.
The Collectors (JKL Ent.). DIR: John Lyde. CAST: Adam Abram, Jesse Angeles, Joseph Brickey. LOC: Utah.
Clubhouse Detectives in Scavenger Hunt. (Promark Ent.). DIR: Eric Hendershot. CAST: Jonathan Cronin, Brittany Armstrong, Michael Glauser. LOC: St. George.
Day of Defense (NuWorlds Prods.). DIR:

Adam Lawson. CAST: Andrew Lenz, Brooks Utley, Michelle Wright. LOC: Salt Lake City.

The R.M. (Halestorm Ent.). DIR: Kurt Hale. CAST: Kirby Heyborne, Daryn Tufts, Will Swenson. LOC: Salt Lake County, Utah County.

Saints and Soldiers (Go Films/Excel). DIR: Ryan Little. CAST: Corbin Allred, Alexander Polinsky, Kirby Heyborne. LOC: Highland, Alpine.

White Rush (Screen Media). DIR: Mark L. Lester. CAST: Judd Nelson, Louis Mandylor, Sandra Vidal. LOC: Salt Lake City.

The Work and the Story (Do It Now Prods.). DIR: Nathan Smith Jones. CAST: Nathan Smith Jones, Jen Hoskins, Eric Artell. LOC: Salt Lake City.

Hulk (Universal). DIR: Ang Lee. CAST: Eric Bana, Jennifer Connelly, Sam Elliott. LOC: Arches, Wendover.

Legally Blonde 2: Red, White, and Fabulous (M-G-M). DIR: Charles Herman-Wurmfeld. CAST: Reese Witherspoon, Sally Field, Regina King. LOC: Salt Lake City.

Top Speed (MacGillivray Freeman Films). DIR: Greg MacGillivray. CAST: Tim Allen, Marion Jones, Lucas Luhr. LOC: undetermined.

The Core (David Foster Prods.). DIR: Jon Amiel. CAST: Aaron Eckhart, Hillary Swank, Delroy Lindo. LOC: Wendover.

Television:

It's a Miracle (Weller/Grossman Prods.). Series. LOC: Utah.

Edge of America (Showtime). DIR: Chris Eyre. CAST: James McDaniel, Irene Bedard, Delanna Studi. LOC: Salt Lake City.

The Maldonado Miracle (Showtime). DIR: Salma Hayek. CAST: Peter Fonda, Mare Winningham, Ruben Blades. LOC: Eureka, Morgan; Salt Lake County.

Right on Track (Disney/Disney Channel). DIR: Duwayne Dunham. CAST: Beverly Mitchell, Brie Larson, Jon Lindstrom. LOC: Salt Lake City.

Touched by An Angel (MoonWater Prods./CBS-Caroline Prods.). Series. Season 9. CREATOR: John Masius. CAST: Roma Downey, Della Reese, John Dye. EPISODES: 22. Aired September 28, 2002 through April 27, 2003. LOC: Salt Lake City, and throughout Utah.

2004:

American Fork (American Fork Prods.). DIR: Chris Bowman. CAST: Hubbel Palmer, William Baldwin, Mary Lynn Rajskub. LOC: Salt Lake City, West Valley.

Baptists at Our Barbecue (Halestorm Ent.). DIR: Christian Vuissa. CAST: Steve Anderson, Heather Beers, Wayne Brennan. LOC: Provo, Springville, Lehi, Logan, Holden, Delta.

Benji: Off the Leash (Mulberry Square). DIR: Joe Camp. CAST: Nick Whitaker, Chris Kendrick, Nate Bynum. LOC: Salt Lake City, Ogden.

The Home Teachers (Halestorm Ent.). DIR: Kurt Hale. CAST: Danny Allen, Jim Bennett, Michael Birkeland. LOC: Provo, Springville, Goshen, Wallsburg, Elberta, Echo.

National Treasure (Disney). DIR: Jon Turteltaub. CAST: Nicolas Cage, Diane Kruger, John Voight. LOC: Wasatch County.

Slow (Jacko Films). DIR: Gregory C. Haynes. CAST: Kage Ahanou, Heather Ashton, Lauren Renee Boyer. LOC: Salt Lake City.

Sons of Provo (Halestorm Ent.). DIR: Will Swenson. CAST: Will Swenson, Kirby Heyborne, Danny Tarasevich. LOC: Provo, Orem, St. George.

Television:

A Boyfriend for Christmas (Hallmark). DIR: Kevin Connor. CAST: Kelli Williams, Patrick Muldoon, Charles Durning. LOC: Salt Lake City.

The Elevator Movie (Pathfinder Home Ent.). DIR: Zeb Haradon. CAST: Zeb Haradon, Robin Ballard, Alissa Hooper. LOC: Salt Lake City.

Going to the Mat (Disney Channel). DIR: Stuart Gillard. CAST: Andrew Lawrence, Alessandra Torresani, Khelo Thomas. LOC: Salt Lake City.

Halloween High (Disney Channel). DIR: Mark A. Z. Dippe. CAST: Kimberly J. Brown, Debbie Reynolds, Judith Hoag. LOC: Salt Lake City.

Paradise (Showtime). DIR: Frank Pierson. CAST: David Strathairn, Barbara Hershey, Kirk Acevedo. LOC: Salt Lake County, Utah County.

Pixel Perfect (Disney Channel). DIR: Mark A. Z. Dippe. CAST: Ricky Ullman, Leah Pipes, Spencer Redford. LOC: Salt Lake City.

Plainsong (Hallmark/CBS). DIR: Richard Pearce. CAST: Aidan Quinn, Rachel Griffiths, America Ferrera. LOC: Salt Lake City.

2005:

The Bag Man (Prescribed Films). DIR: Insane Mike Saunders. CAST: Chris Alexander, Jeff Alexander, Melissa Alexander. LOC: Park City; OL, Iowa.

The First Christmas (Lightstone Prods.). DIR: Dennis Angle, Jr. CAST: Lauren Faber, Dallyn Vale Bayles, Daniel Beck. LOC: Provo.

Jupiter Landing (Saffire Systems Prods.). DIR: Stacy Dymalski. CAST: Tod Huntington, Bryce Wagoner, Monique Lanier. LOC: Salt Lake City.

Mormons and Mobsters (Halestorm Ent.). DIR: John E. Moyer. CAST: Mark DeCarlo, Jeanette Puhich, Clayton Taylor. LOC: Springville.

Mr. Dungbeetle (Reel Focus Prods.). DIR: Thomas Russell. CAST: Aaron Allen, Dane Allred, Stephen Allred. LOC: undetermined. OL: Colorado.

Urban Legends: Bloody Mary (NPP Prods.). DIR: Mary Lambert. CAST: Kate Mara, Robert Vito, Tina Lifford. LOC: Salt Lake City (West High School, Salt Lake City Cemetery).

The Crow: Wicked Prayer (Dimension Films). DIR: Lance Mungia. CAST: Yuji Okumoto, Marcus Chong, Tito Ortiz. LOC: Salt Lake City.

Don't Come Knocking (Sony). DIR: Wim Wenders. CAST: Sam Shepard, Jessica Lange, Tim Roth. LOC: Salt Lake City, Arches, Moab. OL: Butte, MT; Elko and Wendover, NV; Los Angeles, CA.

Down and Derby (Stonehaven). DIR: Eric Hendershot. CAST: Greg Germann, Lauren Holly, Adam Hicks. LOC: St. George.

The World's Fastest Indian (2929 Prods.). DIR: Roger Donaldson. CAST: Anthony Hopkins, Diane Ladd, Paul Rodriguez. LOC: Salt Lake City, Bonneville Salt Flats, Skull Valley, Tooele.

Piggy Banks (Hudson River Ent.). DIR: Morgan J. Freeman. CAST: Jake Muxworthy, Lauren German, Gabriel Mann. LOC: Salt Lake City, Magna.

This Divided State (Minority Films). DIR: Steven Greenstreet. CAST: Kay Anderson, Jim Bassi, Sean Vreeland. LOC: undetermined.

Television:

Go Figure (Disney Channel). DIR: Francine McDougall. CAST: Jordan Hinson, Whitney Sloan, Christine Rose. LOC: Salt Lake City.

Life Is Ruff (Disney Channel). DIR: Charles Haid. CAST: Kyle Massey, Kay Panabaker, Michael Musso. LOC: Salt Lake City.

Buffalo Dreams (Disney Channel). DIR: David Jackson. CAST: Adrienne Bailon, Simon Baker, Duy Beck. LOC: Antelope Island, Lonerock, Skull Valley, Park City.

Everything You Want (Dream Guy Prods./ABC Family). DIR: Ryan Little. CAST:

Shiri Appleby, Nick Zano, Alexandra Holden. LOC: Salt Lake City.

Alien Express (Dead Rail Prods.). DIR: Turi Meyer. CAST: Sean Bott, Steven Brand, Todd Bridges. LOC: Ogden.

I Shouldn't Be Alive (Darlow Smithson Prods./Discovery Channel). Series. LOC: Grand County and San Juan County.

2006:

Blind Dating (Catfish/Samuel Goldwyn). DIR: James Keach. CAST: Chris Pine, Eddie Kaye Thomas, Anjali Jay. LOC: Salt Lake City, Ogden.

Bonneville (Twentieth Century-Fox). DIR: Christopher N. Rowley. CAST: Jessica Lange, Kathy Bates, Joan Allen. LOC: Salt Lake City, Bonneville Salt Flats, Skull Valley, Bryce Canyon.

Church Ball (Halestorm Ent.). DIR: Kurt Hale. CAST: Fred Willard, Andrew Wilson, Clint Howard. LOC: Utah County.

The Fall of '55 (Entendre Prods.). DIR: Seth Randal. CAST: Ron Bess, Peter Boag, Jack Butler. LOC: Salt Lake City; OL, Boise, ID; Portland, OR; San Francisco, CA.

Fire Creek (Bridgestone). DIR: Jed Wells. CAST: Seth Packard, Kim Abunuwara, John Cannon. LOC: Provo, Silver City, Wallsburg.

Jack's Law (11 Pictures). DIR: Gil Medina. CAST: Danny Trejo, Robert John Burke, Clarissa Costa. LOC: Salt Lake City.

The Letter Writer (Mirror Films). DIR: Christian Vuissa. CAST: Bernie Diamond, Cathleen Mason, Nicholas Neve. LOC:

Man vs. Wild (Discovery Channel). Series. LOC: Salt Lake City.

Outlaw Trail: The Treasure of Butch Cassidy (Go Films). DIR: Ryan Little. CAST: Brian Wimmer, Michael Van Wagenen, Brock Ricardos. LOC: Provo Canyon, Heber, Circleville, Kanab.

Pirates of the Great Salt Lake (Blueshift Ent.). DIR: E. R. Nelson. CAST: Kirby Heyborne, Trenton James, Larry Bagby. LOC: St. George.

Propensity (7Films7). DIR: Rob Diamond, Dave Sapp. CAST: Kent Bateman, Heather Beers, Julie Ann Birch. LOC: Salt Lake City. OL: Las Vegas, NV.

The Saxon Chronicles (EveningStar Prods.). DIR: Jeshua De Horta. CAST: Darin Southam, Bryce Bishop, Jason Brunner. LOC: Ogden, Provo.

Sunset in the Valley (Ellacia Prods.). DIR: Alex Cassun. CAST: Christian Skelley, Judy Shepard, Dick Hoppins. LOC: Salt Lake City; OL, Phoenix, AZ; Desert Hot Springs, Palm Springs, CA.

Take a Chance (Halestorm Ent.). DIR. John Lyde. CAST: Corbin Allred, Sarah Bell, Kirby Heyborne. LOC: American Fork.

Unaccompanied Minors (Warner Bros.). DIR: Paul Feig. CAST: Lewis Black, Wilmer Valderrama, Tyler James Williams. LOC: Salt Lake City Int'l Airport, West Valley, Sandy, Echo Junction.

Unrest (YMIR Prods.). DIR: Jason Todd Ipson. CAST: Corri English, Marisa Petroro, Ben Livingston. LOC: Salt Lake City.

The Utah Murder Project (Spear Films). DIR: Charles Hage. CAST: Oz Perkins, Jeff Conaway, Sarah Lieving. LOC: Kanab; OL: Fullerton, CA.

Television:

Not on the First Date. Series. LOC: Salt Lake City.

High School Musical (Disney Channel). DIR: Kenny Ortega. CAST: Zac Efron, Vanessa Hudgens, Ashley Tisdale. LOC: Salt Lake City, Murray.

Lightspeed (FEW Picture Co./Sci-Fi Channel). DIR: Don E. FauntLeRoy. CAST: Jason Connery, Nicole Eggert, Daniel Goddard. LOC: Salt Lake City.

Read It and Weep (Salty Pictures/Disney Channel). DIR: Paul Hoen. CAST: Kay Panabaker, Danielle Panabaker, Alexandra Krosney. LOC: Salt Lake City, Murray.

Return to Halloweentown (Disney Channel). DIR: David Jackson. CAST: Sarah Paxton, Judith Hoag, Lucas Grabeel. LOC: Salt Lake City, Ogden, Provo.

Big Love (Playtone Prods./HBO). Series. LOC: Salt Lake City. OL: Fillmore, Santa Clarita, CA.

I Shouldn't Be Alive (Darlow Smithson Prods./Discovery Channel). Series. LOC: Grand County and San Juan County.

2007:

American Pastime (Warner Bros.). DIR: Desmond Nakano. CAST: Aaron Yoo, Olesya Rulin, Carlton Bluford. LOC: Copperton, Magna, Salt Lake City, Skull Valley.

Bag Boy (National Lampoon Prods.). DIR: Mort Nathan. CAST: Dennis Farina, Paul Campbell, Marika Dominczyk. LOC: Salt Lake City, West Valley.

Believe (Kaleidoscope Prods.). DIR: Loki Mulholland. CAST: Larry Bagby, Lincoln Hoppe, Vanessa DeHart. LOC: Salt Lake City, Provo.

The Dance (Flynn-Daines/Promethean Fire). DIR: McKay Daines. CAST: Michael Flynn, Joyce Cohen, K. C. Clyde. LOC: Salt Lake City. OL: Cambridge, MA (Harvard University).

Dark Matter (Myriad Pictures). DIR: Shi-Zheng Chen. CAST: Ye Liu, Meryl Streep, Aidan Quinn. LOC: Salt Lake City, Orem. OL: Toronto.

Desert of Eden (Invictus Prods.). DIR: Thor Wixom. LOC: Hanksville, Moab.

Dickie Smalls: From Shame to Fame (Slight Chance). DIR: Ryan Hixson, Vick Smith. CAST: James Brandon Waterman, Alison Brie, Chris Blasman. LOC: Salt Lake City; OL, Los Angeles, CA.

The Fleapit Three (ShineBox). DIR: Elias Pate, Bryan Young. CAST: Shawn Bird, Derek Hunter, Warren Miles. LOC: Orem.

The Haunting of Marsten Manor (Arcadian Pictures). DIR: Dave Sapp. CAST: Brianne Davis, Ken Lukey, Janice Knickrehm. LOC: Salt Lake City.

Heber Holiday (Flynn-Daines/Peace Arch Home Ent.). DIR: McKay Daines. CAST: Torrey DeVitto, Jackie Winterrose-Fuller, K. C. Clyde. LOC: Salt Lake City, West Jordan, Provo.

House of Fears (Lonesome Highway Prods.). DIR: Ryan Little. CAST: Corri English, Sandra McCoy, Michael J. Pagan. LOC: Salt Lake City.

Ice Spiders (Regent Prods.). DIR: Tibor Takacs. CAST: Patrick Muldoon, Vanessa Williams, Thomas Calabro. LOC: Salt Lake City.

It is Fine. Everything is Fine! (Volcanic Eruptions). DIR: David Brothers, Crispin Glover. CAST: Margit Carstensen, Jamie Ferrell, Bruce Glover. LOC: Salt Lake City.

The Last Sin Eater (Twentieth Century-Fox). DIR: Michael Landon Jr. CAST: Louise Fletcher, Henry Thomas, Liana Liberato. LOC: Salt Lake City, Snowbasin, American Fork Canyon.

Moola (Freeze Frame). DIR: Don Most. CAST: William Mapother, Treat Williams, Charlotte Ross. LOC: Salt Lake City, Provo. OL: Los Angeles, CA.

Moving McCallister (Revel Ent.). DIR: Andrew Black. CAST: Ben Gourley, Mila Kunis, Jon Heder. LOC: Arches, OL: Jacksonville and St. Augustine, FL.

Passage to Zarahemla (Candlelight Media). DIR: Chris Heimerdinger. CAST: Summer Naomi Smart, Moronai Kanekoa, Brian Kary. LOC: St. George, Leeds, Cedar City.

Pirates of the Caribbean: At World's End (Disney/Buena Vista). DIR: Gore

Verbinski. CAST: Johnny Depp, Geoffrey Rush, Orlando Bloom. LOC: Bonneville Salt Flats, Wendover. OL: Guadalupe, Rancho Palos Verdes, Redondo Beach, Santa Clarita, Palmdale Regional Airport, CA; O'ahu, HI; Dominica, Bahamas.

Saving Sarah Cain (Twentieth Century-Fox). DIR: Michael Landon Jr. CAST: Abigail Mason, Lisa Pepper, Elliott Gould. LOC: Salt Lake City, Kamas.

The Singles 2nd Ward (Halestorm Ent.). DIR: Kurt Hale. CAST: Michael Birkeland, Erin Chambers, Kirby Heyborne. LOC: Salt Lake City, Provo.

Spiritual Warriors (Scott J-R Prods.). DIR: David Raynr. CAST: Robert Easton, Jsu Garcia, Shyla Marlin. LOC: Moab. OL: Jordan; Syria; Cairo and Luxor, Egypt; Los Angeles, CA.

Teenius (Opposite Ent.) DIR: Mya Stark. CAST: Madison Dominguez Aragon, Karen Camp, John de Lancie. LOC: Salt Lake City.

The Thickness of Delerium (Bartoli Filmworks). DIR: Brian James McGuire. CAST: Brian James McGuire, Leann Slaby, Kat Berlik. LOC: Ogden: OL, Cheyenne & Laramie, WY; Ogallala, NE; Milwaukee, WI; Iowa.

Unearthed (Ambush Ent.). DIR: Matthew Leutwyler. CAST: Emmanuelle Vaugier, Luke Goss, Charles Q. Murphy. LOC: Salt Lake City, Tooele County.

Whisper Island (Dreamchaster Ent.) DIR: Mark Goodman. CAST: Steve Anderson, Austin Archer, Bryce Chamberlain. LOC: Antelope Island, Great Salt Lake.

Television:

High School Musical 2 (Disney). DIR: Kenny Ortega. CAST: Zac Efron, Vanessa Hudgens, Ashley Tisdale. LOC: Salt Lake City, Midvale, St. George.

Tracker (2B Films). DIR: Brian Brough. CAST: Noah Sunday, Anne Mangum, Chris Coppel. LOC: Utah County.

I Shouldn't Be Alive (Darlow Smithson Prods./Discovery Channel). Series. LOC: Grand County and San Juan County.

Big Love (Playtone Prods./HBO). Series. LOC: Salt Lake City. OL: Fillmore, Santa Clarita, CA.

Taking 5 (ABC). DIR: Andrew Waller. CAST: Alona Tal, Daniella Monet, Christy Carlson Romano. LOC: Salt Lake City.

2008:

10,000 A.D.: The Legend of the Black Pearl (Northern Fire Prods.). DIR: Raoul Gasteazoro, Giovanni Messner. CAST: Raoul Gasteazoro, Julian Perez, Russ Russo. LOC: Monument Valley; OL, Italy, Puerto Rico.

Adventures of Food Boy (Cold Fusion Films). DIR: Dane Cannon. CAST: Lucas Grabeel, Brittany Curran, Kunal Sharma. LOC: undetermined.

Adventures of Power (Andrea Sperlong Prods.) DIR: Ari Gold. CAST: Ari Gold, Michael McKean, Jane Lynch. LOC: Salt Lake City, Helper.

Animals (T&C Films). DIR: Douglas Aarniokoski. CAST: Marc Blucas, Naveen Andrews, Nicki Aycox. LOC: Salt Lake City.

Beau Jest (Prostorm Pictures). DIR: James Sherman. CAST: Seymour Cassel, Robyn Cohen, Greg Comer. LOC: Salt Lake City, Provo.

Blank Slate (Turner). DIR: John Harrison. CAST: Eric Stoltz, Lisa Brenner, Clancy Brown. LOC: Provo.

Darkroom (Black Sheep Prods.). DIR: Joshua Tai Taeoalii. CAST: Sila Agavale, John Bell, John Bill. LOC: Salt Lake City, Murray.

Deep Winter (Gigantic Pictures). DIR: Mikey Hilb. CAST: Eric Lively, Kellan Lutz, Michael Madsen. LOC: Park City. OL: Alaska; Austria.

Dragon Hunter (Dragon Hunter Films). DIR: Steven Shimek. CAST: Kelly Stables, Brad Johnson, Newell Alexander. LOC: undetermined.

Dying Days (Howie Mett Prods.). DIR: Joel Henry. CAST: Michael Patrick Breen, Shawn Colten, Michael Gene Conti. LOC: Monument Valley, Thompson; OL, Chesterton, Michigan City, Valparaiso, Wheeler, IN; Painted Desert, Grand Canyon, AZ.

The Flyboys (Dark Coast Pictures). DIR: Rocco DeVilliers. CAST: Jesse James, Reilely McClendon, Stephen Baldwin. LOC: Hurricane, St. George; OL, Mesquite, NV.

Forever Strong (Go Films). DIR: Ryan Little. CAST: Gary Cole, Sean Faris, Neal McDonough. LOC: Salt Lake City.

High School Musical 3: Senior Year (Walt Disney). DIR: Kenny Ortega. CAST: Zac Efron, Vanessa Hudgens, Ashley Tisdale. LOC: Salt Lake City.

HottieBoombahLottie (Black Sheep Prods.). DIR: Seth Packard. CAST: Seth Packard, Lauren McKnight, Matthew Webb. LOC: Provo, Orem; OL, Capitola, CA.

Red Canyon (Red Canyon Pictures). DIR: Giovanni Rodriguez. CAST: Christine Lakin, Tim Draxl, Norman Reedus. LOC: Cainville.

Together Again for the First Time (Brownie/Asgaard/Ocean Park). DIR: Jeff Parkin. CAST: Julie Duffy, David Ogden Stiers, Kirby Heyborne. LOC: Provo, Salt Lake Int'l Airport.

Weiners (Braveart Films/Screen Gems). DIR: Mark Steilen. CAST: Kenan Thompson, Zachary Levi, Fran Kranz. LOC: Salt Lake City, Farmington.

Television:

American Mall (MTV). DIR: Shawn Ku. CAST: Nina Dobrev, Rob Mayes, Autumn Reeser. LOC: Salt Lake City, Provo.

Big Love (Playtone Prods./HBO). Series. LOC: Salt Lake City. OL: Fillmore, Santa Clarita, CA.

Fearless (Science Fiction). Series. DIR: Kevin M. Townshend. CAST: Eileen Barker, James DeMalignon, Darren Dowler. LOC: Moab; OL, Colorado.

I Shouldn't Be Alive (Darlow Smithson Prods./Discovery Channel). Series. LOC: Grand County and San Juan County.

Minutemen (Salty Pictures/Disney Channel). DIR: Lev L. Spiro. CAST: Jason Dolley, Luke Benward, Nicholas Braun. LOC: Salt Lake City, Murray.

2009:

Billy Was A Deaf Kid (Rhett & Burke Pictures). DIR: Burke Lewis, Rhett Lewis. CAST: Rhett Lewis, Candyce Foster, Zachary Christian. LOC: Logan.

The Canyon (Pierce-Williams Ent.). DIR: Richard Harrah. CAST: Yvonne Strahovski, Will Patton, Eion Bailey. LOC: Moab. OL: Williams, AZ.

The Cell 2 (Warner Bros.). DIR: Tim Iacofano. CAST: Tessie Santiago, Chris Bruno, Frank Whaley. LOC: Salt Lake City (SpringMobile Ball Park).

Father in Israel (Mirror Films). DIR: Christian Vuissa. CAST: Tim Threlfall, Pam Eichner, Talon G. Ackerman. LOC: undetermined.

Fire Creek (Campus Studios). DIR: Jed Wells. CAST: Seth Packard, John Cannon, Dayne Rockwood. LOC: Wallsburg, Spring City.

Gentlemen Broncos (Rip Cord/Fox Searchlight). DIR: Jared Hess. CAST: Michael Angarano, Sam Rockwell, Jennifer Coolidge. LOC: Salt Lake City. OL: Los Angeles, CA.

Hatching Pete (Salty Ent.). DIR: Stuart Gillard. CAST: Jason Dolley, Mitchell Musso, Tiffany Thornton. LOC: Midvale (Hillcrest HS).

Lock and Roll Forever (T&C Pictures/Sony Music). DIR: Chris Grismer. CAST:

Lucas Grabeel, Ike Barinholtz, Taylor Negron. LOC: Salt Lake City. OL: Tokyo, Sakai, Osaka, Japan; Los Angeles, CA.

The Legend of Awesomest Maximus (National Lampoon Prods.). DIR: Jeff Kanew. CAST: Will Sasso, Kristanna Loken, Tiffany Claus. LOC: Great Salt Lake, Antelope Island.

The Mine (Savage Pictures). DIR: Jeff Chamberlain. CAST: Alexa Vega, Reiley McClendon, Adam Hendershott. LOC: Cedar Fort, Ophir, Heber.

Minor Details (Mainstay Prods.). DIR: John Lyde. CAST: Kelsey Edwards, Caitlin E. J. Meyer, Danielle Chuchran. LOC: Utah County.

My Girlfriend's Boyfriend (fiftyfilms). DIR: Daryn Tufts. CAST: Alyssa Milano, Christopher Gorham, Beau Bridges. LOC: Salt Lake City.

Scout Camp (Three Coin Prods.). DIR: Garrett Batty. CAST: Kirby Heyborne, Shawn Carter, Nate Harper. LOC: Mapleton.

S Darko (Silver Nitrate/Twentieth Century-Fox). DIR: Chris Fisher. CAST: Daveigh Chase, Briana Evigan, James Lafferty. LOC: Salt Lake City, Magna, Delle, Echo.

Snowmen (Mpower Pictures). DIR: Robert Kirbyson. CAST: Bobby Coleman, Josh Flitter, Ray Liotta. LOC: Park City.

Summer of the Eagle (Focus Light Films). DIR: Mark Knudsen. CAST: Quintin Bell, Al Harrington, Jeremy Jacobsen. LOC: undetermined.

Sweatshop (Bloodline Prods.). DIR: Stacy Davidson. CAST: Ashley Kay, Peyton Wetzel, Brent Himes. LOC: Salt Lake City; OL, Houston, TX.

Waiting for Forever (Catfish Prods.). DIR: James Keach. CAST: Rachel Bilson, Jaime King, Richard Jenkins. LOC: Salt Lake City Int'l Airport, Ogden, Echo.

White On Rice (Brainwave). DIR: Dave Boyle. CAST: Hiroshi Watanabe, Nae Takada, Mio Takada. LOC: Salt Lake City (Wells Fargo Bldng.); OL, Los Angeles, CA.

The Wild Stallion (Film More Ent./Halestorm). DIR: Craig Clyde. CAST: Mirand Cosgrove, Danielle Chuchran, Fred Ward. LOC: Salt Lake City.

The Yankles (DZB Prods.). DIR: David R. Brooks. CAST: Brian Wimmer, Bart Johnson, Don Most. LOC: Salt Lake City.

Television:

Big Love (Playtone Prods./HBO). Series. LOC: Salt Lake City. OL: Fillmore, Santa Clarita, CA.

Dadnapped (Salty Pictures/Disney Channel). DIR: Paul Hoen. CAST: Emily Osment, David Henrie, Jason Earles. LOC: Magna.

Hatching Pete (Just Singer Entertainment/Disney Channel). DIR: Stuart Gillard. CAST: Jason Dolley, Mitchel Musso, Tiffany Thornton. LOC: Midvale: Hillcrest High School.

2010:

127 Hours (Cloud 8 Films/20th Century Fox). DIR: Danny Boyle. CAST: James Franco, Kate Mara, Amber Tamlyn. LOC: Canyonlands Nat'l Park, Blue John Canyon, Sugarhouse.

Bad Fever (Kickstarter). DIR: Dustin Guy Defa. CAST: Kentucker Audley, Allison Barr, Hayward Buchanan. LOC: Salt Lake City.

A Christmas Wish (Halestorm Ent.). DIR: Craig Clyde. CAST: Kristy Swanson, Aline Andrade, Danielle Chuchran. LOC: Mapleton, Spanish Fork.

Civil War 2 (Salty Horror Prods.). DIR: Mario De Angelis. CAST: Antonio Lexerot, Christopher Robin Miller, Rebecca Zeimet. LOC: Salt Lake City.

The Deception (Cinemaair Prods.). DIR: Gary Travis. CAST: Tina Travis, Dan Pahl, Kipp Martin. LOC: Utah.

Den Brother (Salty Pictures). DIR: Mark Taylor. CAST: Hatch Dano, G. Hannelius, Maurice Godin. LOC: West Valley City.

Denizen (Tunis Prods.). DIR: J.A. Steel. CAST: J.A. Steel, Jessica M. Blair, Dianne Sullivan. LOC: Salt Lake City, Tooele; OL, Muskogee, OK.

Exile (Midnight Sun Ent.). DIR: Mike Conway. CAST: Jake Bass, Mike Conway, Sheila Conway. LOC: Utah; OL, Las Vegas, NV.

Frozen (A Bigger Boat/Anchor Bay). DIR: Adam Green. CAST: Emma Bell, Shawn Ashmore, Kevin Zegers. LOC: Snowbasin.

Horse Crazy 2: The Legend of Girzzly Mountain (Artist View Entertainment/Candlelight Media Group) DIR: Eric Hendershot. CAST: Brittany Armstrong, David Candland, Dalin Christiansen. LOC: Heber; OL, Howell, MI.

I Love You Bernie Summersby (Mirror Films). DIR: Alla Volkova. CAST: Lynne Carr, Bob Walkingshaw, Marjorie Wilson. LOC: Salt Lake City.

The Kane Files: Life of Trial (Revel Ent.). DIR: Benjamin Gourley. CAST: Drew Fuller, Ethan Embry, William Devane. LOC: Salt Lake City, Spanish Fork, Provo.

Lovers of Hate (Invisible Kids). DIR: Bryan Poyser. CAST: Chris Doubek, Heather Kafka, Alex Karpofsky. LOC: Park City; OL, Austin, TX.

Maro Charitra (Artistry Films). DIR: Ravi Yadav. CAST: Shradha Das, Anita Galler, Srinivasa Rao Kota. LOC: Bonneville Salt Flats; OL, Las Vegas, NV; Niagara Falls, NY; Overland Park, KS; Hyderabad Andhra Pradesh, India.

Memorias Del Desarrollo (Piramide). DIR: Miguel Coyula. CAST: Eileen Alana, Trent Harris, Abraham Ampka. LOC: Torrey; OL, Las Vegas, NV; New York, NY; London, UK; Tokyo, Japan; Paris, France.

The Maze (Ground Glass Ent.). DIR: Stephen Shimek. CAST: Shalania Castle, Brandon Sean Pearson, Clare Niederpruem. LOC: Provo, Tremonton.

My Girlfriend's Boyfriend (Fifty Fifty Prods.). DIR: Daryn Tufts. CAST: Christopher Gorham, Chantel Flanders, Kelly Packard. LOC: Salt Lake City.

Snowmen (Mpower Pictures). DIR: Robert Kirbyson. CAST: Bobby Coleman, Josh Flitter, Ray Liotta. LOC: Huntsville, Park City.

Waiting For Forever (PCH Films). DIR: James Keach. CAST: Rachel Bilson, Tom Sturridge, Richard Jenkins. LOC: Provo.

Wes and Ella (Stakedance Films). DIR: Christopher Curti. CAST: Jocelin Donahue, Scoot McNairy, Sean Bott. LOC: Utah.

You're So Cupid! (Poppy Prods.). DIR: John Lyde. CAST: Lauren Holly, Brian Krause, Jeremy Sumpter. LOC: Utah.

Television:

Big Love (Playtone Prods./HBO). LOC: Salt Lake City, Sandy, Tooele, Antelope Island.

2011:

17 Miracles (Remember Films/Excel). DIR: T.C. Christensen. CAST: Jason Wade, Emily Wadley, Jason Celaya. LOC: Nephi, Provo, Skull Valley.

Age of the Dragons (KOAN). DIR: Ryan Little. CAST: Danny Glover, Vinnie Jones, Corey Sevier. LOC: Provo.

Archangel Alpha (Chance Studios). DIR: Aaron D. Martin. CAST: Nichelle Aiden, Katherine Joan Taylor, Don Lee. LOC: Salt Lake City.

Blue Door (LunaStudios). DIR: Sohrab Mirmontazeri. CAST: Renny Grames, Tod Huntington, Brighton Hertford. LOC: Salt Lake City, Kamas, Park City.

Guns, Girls, and Gambling (Freefall Films). DIR: Michael Winnick. CAST: Gary Oldman,

Christian Slater, Megan Park. LOC: Salt Lake City, Midvale, Tooele, Wendover.

Midway to Heaven (Cosmic Pictures). DIR: Michael Flynn. CAST: Curt Doussett, Kirby Heyborne, Michelle Money. LOC: Midway.

Remember I'll Always Love You (MOOVIE The Art of Entertainment GmbH). DIR: Carlo Rola. CAST: Bart Johnson, Anja Nejarri, Dennenesch Zoude. LOC: Salt Lake City, Pleasant Grove; OL: Germany.

Tree of Life (Fox Searchlight). DIR: Terrence Malick. CAST: Brad Pitt, Sean Penn, Jessica Chastain. LOC: Goblin Valley State Park, Hwy 24 near Green River; OL: Texas; Death Valley National Park, CA.

2012:

12 Dogs of Christmas: Great Puppy Rescue (12 Dogs II, Kragen/Merrill Family Films). DIR: Kieth Merrill. CAST: Sean Patrick Flanery, Danielle C. Ryan, Skyler Holman. LOC: Salt Lake City.

Blood Fare (Warrior Entertainment). DIR: J.A. Steel. CAST: Gil Gerard, Michelle Wolff, Brandi Lynn Andersen LOC: Ogden, Salt Lake City (University of Utah).

Changing Hearts (Silver Peak Prods.). DIR: Brian Brough. CAST: Brad Johnson, Brian McNamara, Daphne Zuniga. LOC: Midway.

Charly 10th Anniversary Encore (Focused Light Films/Epic World Entertainment). DIR: Adam Thomas Anderegg. CAST: Heather Beers, Jeremy Hoop, Adam Johnson. LOC: Utah; New York.

Chick Magnets (Island Park Pictures). DIR: Brian Douros. CAST: Josh Putnam, Dashiell Wolf, Ataum Langton. LOC: American Fork, Bountiful, Kaysville, Mapleton, Pleasant Grove, Salt Lake City, West Bountiful, West Valley City.

Darling Companion (Kasdan Pictures/ Sony Pictures Classics). DIR: Lawrence Kasdan. CAST: Meg Kasdan, Kevin Kline, Dianne Wiest. LOC: Salt Lake City (airport). OL: Telluride, CO.

Death Canyon (Fade-IN Pictures). DIR: Tyler Mitchell, Bethany Pelton. CAST: Brett Blackham, Travis Lincoln Cox, Whitney Morgan Cox. LOC: Death Canyon.

Electrick Children (Live Wire Films, UK). DIR: Rebecca Thomas. CAST: Julia Garner, Laim Aiken, Billy Zane. LOC: Grafton, Hurricane. OL: Las Vegas & Indian Springs, NV; San Onofre Beach, CA.

Heaven's Door (Stone Five Studios). DIR: Craig Clyde. CAST: Kaden Billen, Mark Brocksmith, Annalaya Brown. LOC: Utah.

John Carter (Walt Disney). DIR: Andrew Stanton. CAST: Taylor Kitsch, Lynn Collins, Samantha Morton. LOC: Moab, Big Water, Millard County.

Missing Pieces (Contraction Entertainment). DIR: Kenton Bartlett. CAST: Mark Boone Junior, Melora Walters, Elizabeth Alexander. LOC: Utah; Birmingham, AL; Kansas; Colorado; South Dakota.

Must Come Down (Malatova Prods.). DIR: Kenny Riches. CAST: Ashly Burch, David Fetzer, Liberty Cordova. LOC: Salt Lake City.

Osombie (Arrowstorm Films). DIR: John Lyde. CAST: Cory Sevier, Eve Mauro, Jason Wade. LOC: Utah.

Path of Souls (High Definition Pictures, Canada). DIR: Jeremy Torrie. CAST: Adam Beach, Laura Harris, Corey Sevier. LOC: Salt Lake City; Canyonlands Nat'l Park; OL: Devil's Tower Nat'l Monument, WY; Chaco Canyon, NM; Bannock Point & Winnipeg, Manitoba, Canada.

Redemption Boys (Ship-to-Shore, France). DIR: Bernie Garcia. CAST: Gerry Garcia, Cory McMillan, Jason Mertlich. LOC: Salt Lake City (University of Utah). OL: Los Angeles, CA.

Saints and Soldiers: Airborne Creed (GoFilms/KOAN). DIR: Ryan Little. CAST: Corbin Allred, David Nibley, Jason Wade. LOC: Alpine, Midway, Provo, Vineyard.

The Mine (Mountainbridge Films). DIR: Jeff Chamberlain. CAST: Reiley McClendon, Adam Hendershott, Valerie C. Walker. LOC: Cedar Fort, Fairfield, Heber, Ophir. OL: Death Valley Nat'l Park.

Unicorn City (Deep Studios). DIR: Bryan Lefler. CAST: John Gries, Matt Mattson, Clint Vanderlinden. LOC: Alpine; American Fork.

Wide Boyz (Alstrin Films). Jay Anderson, Tom Randall. LOC: Canyonlands Nat'l Park.

Television:

Day Zero (Altare Prods.). "Betrayal," Season 1, Episode 4. DIR: Cal Nguyen. CAST: Scott Smith, Cal Nguyen, Richard Scott Dean. LOC: Ogden, Salt Lake City, West Jordan. "Dementia," Season 1, Episode 6. DIR: Cal Nguyen. CAST: Can Nguyen, Richard Scott Dean, Tim Sabuco. LOC: West Jordan, Roy, Salt Lake City, Ogden.

Gary the Unicorn (SuperJoy Media Group). CREATORS: Matt Daniels, Joshua Aukai Ligari. CAST: Trenton James, Matt Daniels, Jaclyn Hales. LOC: West Jordan (Daybreak community).

Meet the Preppers: My Pink Pistol. (BASE Prods.). Reality. CAST: Adria Burns, Kelly Allwood, Phil Burns. LOC: Utah.

The Mistle-Tones (Disney/ABC) DIR: Paul Hoen. CAST: Tia-Mowry Hardrict, Jonathan Patrick Moore, Andy Gala. LOC: Pleasant Grove; Ogden; Salt Lake City (Trolley Square).

[RE]Mind (End of Eternity Prods.). Series. Various episodes. LOC: Utah.

Proper Manors (Ten Spoke Prods.) Series. Various episodes. LOC: Ogden.

2013:

After Earth (Overlook Entertainment/ Columbia Pictures) DIR: M. Night Shaymalan. CAST: Jaden Smith, David Denman, Will Smith. LOC: Utah. OL: Humbolt County, CA; La Fortuna, San Carlos, Costa Rica; Arsenal Volcano Nat'l Park, Costa Rica.

An Ordinary Hero: The True Story of Joan Trumpauer Molholland (Taylor Street Films). DIR: Loki Mulholland. CAST: Luvaughn Brown, Dion Diamond, Erick Etheridge. LOC: Utah. OL: Washington DC; Idaho; Maryland; Mississippi; Tennessee; Virginia.

As You Like It By William Shakespeare (Mellenheads Prods.). DIR: Vance Mellen. CAST: Ashley Lammi, Matt Christensen, Matt Gallacher. LOC: Utah.

Begin Again (Exclusive Media Group). DIR: John Carney. CAST: Kiera Knightley, Mark Ruffalo, Adam Levine. LOC: Utah; New York City.

Bilet na Vegas (3 Days in Vegas, Russia). DIR: Gor Kirakosian. CAST: Ivan Stebunav, Ingrid Olarinskaya, Vladimir Yaglych. LOC: Utah; Las Vegas, NV; Russia.

Border Run (Voltage Pictures, Philippines). DIR: Gabriela Tagliavini. CAST: Sharon Stone, Billy Zane, Amy Kolquist. LOC: Utah. OL: Los Angeles, CA.

Dragonfyre (Arrowstorm Entertainment). DIR: Kohl Glass. CAST: Rusty Joiner, Masiela Lusha, Wesley John. LOC: Salt Lake City. OL: Los Angeles, CA.

Ephraim's Rescue (EPH Films). DIR: T.C. Christensen. CAST: Darin Southam, Richard Benedict, James Gaisford. LOC: Utah.

Gravity (Warner Bros.). DIR: Alfonso Cuaron. CAST: Sandra Bullock, George Clooney, Ed Harris. LOC: Lake Powell. OL: Shepperton Studios, Pinewood Studios, England.

I Am Death (Building Dreams Entertainment/ Banyan Tree Prods.). DIR: Paul Orehovec. CAST: Zacc Duckowitz,

G.W. Bailey, Charlene Amola. LOC: Utah. OL: California, Colorado.

Skinwalker Ranch (Deep Studios). DIR: Devin McGinn, Steve Berg. CAST: Britani Bateman, Taylor Bateman, Steve Berg. LOC: Utah.

Storm Rider (Stone Five Studios). DIR: Craig Clyde. CAST: Kevin Sorbo, Kristy Swanson, Danielle C. Ryan. LOC: Utah.

Templar Nation (Joseph James Films). DIR: Brian Vance, Lilliana Corona. CAST: Erik Estrada, Richard Dutcher, Joseph James. LOC: St. George.

The Cyclist (Opus Distribution). DIR: John Lawrence. CAST: K.C. Clyde, K. Danor Gerald, Frank Gerrish. LOC: Moab, Salt Lake City (Rocky Mountain Raceways), Park City.

The Freemason (Joseph James Films). DIR: Sohrab Mirmont. CAST: Sean Astin, Randy Wayne, Alex McKenna. LOC: Salt Lake City.

The Lone Ranger (Walt Disney). DIR: Gore Verbinski. CAST: Johnny Depp, Armie Hammer, William Fitchner. LOC: Moab, Monument Valley, Dead Horse State Park. OL: Alamosa & Creed, CO; Angel Fire, Hurley, Shiprock, NM; Canyon de Chelle National Monument, AZ.

The Misadventures of the Dunderheads (Montana Amazon Prods.). DIR: D.G. Brock. CAST: Phil Proctor, Olympia Dukakis, Alison Brie. LOC: Monument Valley. OL: Grand Teton National Park, WY; Mojave Nat'l Preserve, CA; Grand Canyon, AZ; Las Vegas, NV.

The Saratov Approach (Saratov Films). DIR: Garrett Batty. CAST: Corbin Allred, Maclain Nelson, Nakita Bogolyubov. LOC: Salt Lake City. OL: Kiev, Ukraine.

Us in the U.S. (Italian International Films). DIR: Carlo Vanzina. CAST: Vincenzo Salemme, Ambra Angiolini, Ricky Memphis. LOC: Lake Powell. OL: Mt. Rushmore Nat'l Memorial, SD; Aspen, CO; Las Vegas, NV.

Zombie Hunter (Arrowstorm Entertainment). DIR: Kevin King. CAST: Danny Trejo, Martin Copping, Clare Niederpruem. LOC: Wendover.

Television:

Beauty and the Least: The Misadventures of Ben Banks. (Signal Films, Canada). DIR: Bryce Clark. CAST: Ben Banks, Katharine Towne, Mischa Barton. LOC: Salt Lake City, St. George. OL: Las Vegas, NV.

Day Zero (Altare Prods.). Series. Various episodes. LOC: Ogden, Salt Lake City, West Jordan.

Granite Flats (Vineyard Film Prods./BYU-TV). Series. All episodes. CREATOR: James Shores. CAST: Jonathan Morgan Heit, Richard Gunn, Charlie Plummer. LOC: Copperton, Magna (downtown Granite Flats), Provo Canyon (Olmstead Power Plant), Salt Lake City (Granite High School).

Kings of Crash (Fisher Prods.). Series. Reality. Various episodes. LOC: Utah. OL: Evanston, WY.

Proper Manors (Ten Spoke Prods.). Series. Various episodes. LOC: Ogden, Salt Lake City.

2014:

108 Stitches (Psycho Rock Prods.). DIR: David Roundtree. CAST: Bruce Davison, Erin Cahill, Kate Vernon. LOC: Orem. OL: Los Angeles, CA.**A Light in the Woods** (Thunder Media Group). DIR: Elizabeth Hansen. CAST: Ryan Lambert, Dee Macaluso, Courtney Scott. LOC: Vivian Park in Provo Canyon.

A Million Ways to Die in the West (Bluegrass Films). DIR: Seth MacFarlane. CAST: Seth MacFarlane, Charlize Theron, Liam Neeson. LOC: Monument Valley. OL: Santa Fe, Jemez Pueblo, NM; Antonio, CO; Mexican Water, AZ.

Dark Blood (Fine Line Features). DIR: George Slulzer. CAST: River Phoenix, Judy Davis, Jonathan Pryce. LOC: Capitol Reef Nat'l Park. OL: Los Angeles, CA; Gallup, NM.

Haunt (Covert Media, Kuwait). DIR: Mac Carter. CAST: Jacki Weaver, Liana Liberato, Harrison Gilbertson. LOC: Salt Lake City.

Inspired Guns (Pitch White Entertainment). DIR: Adam White. CAST: Shona Kay, Anson Bagley, Alix Maria Taulbee. LOC: Salt Lake City, Provo, Heber, Midway, Orem. OL: Chicago, IL; New York City, NY.

Left Behind (Stoney Lake Entertainment). DIR: Vic Armstrong. CAST: Nicholas Cage, Lea Thompson, Cassi Thomson. LOC: Provo (Provo Towne Centre). OL: Baton Rouge, LA.

Love a la Carte (Indie Rights). DIR: Tim McSpadden. CAST: Aaron-Ginn Forsberg, Kimber Leigh, Chauna Mae. LOC: Monument Valley. OL: Phoenix, Sedona, Winslow, AZ; Sierra Nevada Mountains, CA.

Mythica: A Quest for Heroes (Arrowstorm Entertainment). DIR: Anne K. Black. CAST: Melanie Stone, Adam Thompson, Jake Storemoen. LOC: Utah.

Need for Speed. (DreamWorks). DIR: Scott Waugh. CAST: Aaron Paul, Dominic Cooper, Imogen Poots. LOC: Moab, Bonneville Salt Flats. OL: Atlanta, Macon, Rome, Blue Ridge, GA; Phenix City, AL; San Francisco, CA.

Number Runner (Palm Tree Prods., UK). DIR: Robbie Moffat. CAST: Jon-Paul Gates, Fernanda Romero, Martin Cove. LOC: St. George.

SAGA: Curse of the Shadow (Arrowstorm Entertainment). DIR: John Lyde. CAST: Danielle C. Ryan, Richard McWilliams, Paul D. Hunt. LOC: Utah.

Saints and Soldiers: The Void (GoFilms/KOAN). DIR: Ryan Little. CAST: Adam Gregory, Timothy S. Shoemaker, Michael Todd Behrens. LOC: Alpine, Cottonwood Heights, Provo.

SEAL Patrol (Quorum Entertainment). DIR: Nicolas Mezzanatto. CAST: Rich McDonald, Kristina Anapau, Joshua St. James. LOC: Salt Lake City.

Survivor (Arrowstorm Entertainment). DIR: John Lyde. CAST: Danielle C. Ryan, Kevin Sorbo, Rocky Myers. LOC: Utah.

The Adventures of RoboRex (Wulf/Gorley Prods.). DIR: CAST: Ben Browder, Kalvin Stinger, Ethan Phillips. LOC: Salt Lake City.

The Christmas Dragon (Arrowstorm Entertainment). DIR: John Lyde. CAST: Bailee Michelle Johnson, Paris Warner, David DeVilliers. LOC: Utah.

The Giver (Tonik Prods.). DIR: Phillip Noyce. CAST: Brenton Thwaites, Jeffs Bridges, Meryl Streep. LOC: Brighton (mountain cabin). OL: Cape Town, Johannesburg, Paarl Arboretum, South Africa.

The Mentor (Creative Arts Entertainment Group). DIR: Anthony Lefrense. CAST: Jes Macallan, Aaron Douglas, Nic Bishop. LOC: Salt Lake City (North Star Elementary School).

Till Blood Do Us Part (Kith Films). DIR: Levi Robinson. CAST: Levi Robinson, Jordan Howard, Chet Watson. LOC: Salt Lake City. OL: Franklin County, ID.

Transformers: Age of Extinction (Paramount Pictures). DIR: Michael Bay. CAST: Mark Wahlberg, Nicola Peltz, Jack Reynor. LOC: Moab, Monument Valley: OL: Arizona, Illinois, Texas, Michigan; Beijing, Hongkong, China.

Television:

The Big Bang Theory (Chuck Lorre Prods./Warner Bros. TV). CREATORS: Chuck Lorre, Bill Prady. "The Locomotion Interruption," Season 8, Episode 1. DIR: Mark Cendrowski. CAST: Johnny Galecki, Jim Parsons, Kaley Cuoco. LOC: Moab.

Christmas Under Wraps (Hybrid). DIR: Peter Sullivan. CAST: Candace Cameron

Bure, David O'Donnell, Robert Pine. LOC: Salt Lake City, Heber, Payson.

Cloud 9 (Blonde Girl Prods.). DIR: Paul Hoen. CAST: Luke Benward, Dove Cameron, Kiersey Clemons. LOC: Utah.

Day Zero (Altare Prods.). "Return to Sender," Season 2, Episode 5. DIR: Cal Nguyen. CAST: Colin McDermott, Keith Hottinger, Marilee Crockett. LOC: Murray, Salt Lake City.

Granite Flats (Vineyard Film Prods./BYU-TV). Series. All episodes. CREATOR: James Shores. CAST: Jonathan Morgan Heit, Richard Gunn, Charlie Plummer. LOC: Copperton, Magna, Provo Canyon, Salt Lake City.

How We Make Movies (We Make Movies). Series. Talk. 11 episodes. LOC: Park City (Park City Studio).

Nowhere Safe (Gradual Elevate Media). DIR: Brian Brough. CAST: Natasha Henstridge, Jamie Kennedy, Danielle C. Ryan. LOC: Utah.

Proper Manors. (Ten Spoke Prods.). Series. Various episodes. LOC: Ogden, Salt Lake City.

Scooby-Doo and the Doggie Style Adventures. Season 1, Episode 8. "FVB: Fred vs. Batman." DIR: Luke Ostermiller. CAST: Ryan Seemy, Brian Coleman, Kelsey White. LOC: Utah. OL: Denver & Arvada, CO; Las Vegas, NV.

Sundance Dispatch (We Make Movies). Series. Talk. Various episodes. CAST:

2015:

Christmas Eve Miracle (Sony Pictures). DIR: R. Michael Givens. CAST: Olivia d'Abo, Anthony Starke, Josh Reid. LOC: Utah.

Area 15 (Aramid Entertainment). DIR: Oren Peli. CAST: Reid Warner, Darrin Bragg, Ben Rovner. LOC: Salt Lake City. OL: Las Vegas, Rachel, NV; Santa Clarita, CA.

Art & Libby (Center for Media Innovation). DIR: Phil Tuckett. CAST: Melanie Camire, Aaron Hall, Jillian Joy. LOC: St. George.

Blue Door (Mirmont Pictures). DIR: Sohrab Mirmont. CAST: Renny Grames, Tod Huntington, Chelsea Earlwine. LOC: Utah.

Don Verdean (Buffalo Film Co.). DIR: Jared Hess. CAST: Sam Rockwell, Amy Ryan, Jemaine Clement. LOC: Utah.

I'm Not Ready for Christmas (Mayor Entertainment). DIR: Sam Irvin. CAST: Alicia Witt, George Stults, Brigid Brannah. LOC: Salt Lake City.

Inner Fear. DIR: Spencer Brod. CAST: Scott Bailey, Nikohl Boosheri, Austin James. LOC: Moab. OL: Agua Dulce, Santa Monica, CA.

Jackie & Ryan (Main Street Films). DIR: Ami Canaan Mann. CAST: Katherine Heigl, Ben Barnes, Clea DuVall. LOC: Salt Lake City, Ogden (train station interiors).

Just Let Go (Number 7 Entertainment). DIR: Christopher S. Clark, Patrick Henry Parker. CAST: Henry Ian Cusik, Jacob Buster, Brenda Vaccaro. LOC: Salt Lake City.

Missed Connections (Candlelight Media Group). DIR: Brandon Ho. CAST: Kevin O'Keefe, Tatum Langton, Lawrence Fernandez. LOC: Provo.

Nightlight (Herrick Entertainment/ Lionsgate). DIR: Scott Beck, Bryan Woods. CAST: Shelby Young, Carter Jenkins, Chloe Bridges. LOC: Alpine, Heber City, Layton, North Ogden, Ogden, Provo, Spanish Fork, Springville. OL: Thousand Oaks, CA.

Not on the List (Power & Industry). DIR: Tyson Frost. CAST: Scott 'Skippy' Jessop, Mckenna London, John E. Moyer. LOC: Salt Lake City. OL: California.

Once I Was a Beehive (Main Dog Prods.). DIR: Maclain Nelson. CAST: Paris Warner, Lisa Clark, Halley Smith. LOC: Utah.

Sorrow (Films Verite Prods.). DIR: Millie Loredo. CAST: Vanessa Vasquez, Andrew Sensenig, Melissa Mars. LOC: Moab. OL: Houston, Beaumont, Texas.

Last Man(s) on Earth (Last Mans Prods.). DIR: Arthur Hultgren. CAST: Charan Prabhakar, Brady Bluhm, Darin Southam. LOC: Salt Lake City. OL: Los Angeles, CA.

Thine Enemy's Eyes (Dragon Fleet Studios). DIR: Tonya Adolphson. CAST: Steve Warky Nunez, Tonya Adolphson, Dartanian Richards. LOC: Salt Lake City. OL: Boise, ID.

Thirst (Cosmic Entertainment). DIR: Greg Kiefer. CAST: John Redlinger, Jes Macallan, Karl Makinen. LOC: Utah.

Vacation (New Line Cinema). DIR: John Francis Daley, Jonathan M. Goldstein. CAST: Ed Helms, Christina Applegate, Skyler Gisondo. LOC: Kanab (old courthouse). OL: Atlanta, Austell, GA; Charlotte, NC.

Venatus (Carl Jackson Entertainment). DIR: Carl Jackson. CAST: Brittanie Hitchcock, Jennifer Scibetta, Xavier Ray. LOC: Utah.

War Pigs (Schuetzle Co. Prods.). DIR: Ryan Little. CAST: Luke Goss, Dolph Lundgren, Chuck Liddell. LOC: Utah.

Wild Horses (Patriot Pictures). DIR: Robert Duvall. CAST: Robert Duvall, James Franco, Darlen Willardson. LOC: Bluffdale, Magna, Riverton (Riverbend Ranch Equestrian Center), Salt Lake City.

Television:

Christmas Land (Mayor Entertainment/ The Hallmark Channel). DIR: Sam Irvin. CAST: Nikki Deloach, Luke Macfarlane, Maureen McCormick. LOC: Salt Lake City, Riverton, Farmington (Lagoon Amusement Park as Christmas Land).

Granite Flats (Vineyard Film Prods./ BYU-TV. Series. All episodes. CREATOR: James Shores. CAST: Jonathan Morgan Heit, Richard Gunn, Charlie Plummer. LOC: Copperton, Magna, Provo Canyon, Salt Lake City.

Proper Manors (Ten Spoke Prods.). Various episodes. LOC: Ogden.

Rosemont (Enderby Entertainment). DIR: Daniel Petrie, Jr. CAST: Brad Dourif, Lochlyn Munro, Grace Zabriskie. LOC: Brian Head (lodge), Salt Lake City.

The Veronica Exclusive (Molvolio 15 Prods.). Miniseries. CAST: Casey Nicol Caplin, Megan Lambie, Lizzy Phipps. LOC: Salt Lake City. OL: Idaho, Michigan, Colorado, Scotland, Mexico, Germany.

2016:

10,000 Miles (Dream Started, Singapore). DIR: Simon Hung. CAST: Sean Huang, Megan Lai, Talu Wang. LOC: Utah. OL: Taiwan, China.

Adopting Trouble (Rare Legend Films). DIR: Lee Gardner. CAST: Ryan Templeman, Heather Murdock, Ariana Escalante. LOC: Utah.

Alienate (Film Base/Shumway Studios). DIR: Michael Shumway. CAST: Blake Webb, Tatum Langton, Jaclyn Hales. LOC: Salt Lake City. OL: Denver, CO.

American Nobody (Salsa Media Group). DIR: Josh Wilson. CAST: Connor Williams, Amy Atkins, Bryce Bishop. LOC: Salt Lake City (Biz Vision Studio).

Angels in Scrubs (NICH Entertainment). DIR: Will Taylor. CAST: Daphne Ballanger. LOC: Salt Lake City.

Being Charlie (Castle Rock Entertainment). DIR: Rob Reiner. CAST: Nick Robinson, Common, Cary Elwes. LOC: Rush Valley (gas station), Salt Lake Valley, Tooele. OL: Los Angeles, CA.

Black Tar Road (Abovo Films). DIR: Amber Dawn Lee & 4 collaborating directors. CAST: Maria Olsen, James Black, Arda Janean Fenstermaker. LOC: Roy, Salt Lake City. OL: Colorado City, AZ; Las Vegas, NM; Pearblossom, CA; Huntsville, TX.

The Christmas Project (Big Blue Marble Media). DIR: Michael Buster. CAST: Jacob Buster, Anson Bagley, Josh Reid. LOC: Mapleton.

Code of Honor (Premiere Entertainment Group). DIR: Michael Winnick. CAST: Steven Seagal, Craig Sheffer, James Russo. LOC: Salt Lake City (city under siege).

Consumption (Iodine Sky Prods.). DIR: Brandon Scullion. CAST: Sarah Greyson, Arielle Brachfield, David Lautman. LOC: Brian Head. OL: Los Angeles, CA.

Drop Off (Doty-Dayton Prods.). DIR: Lyman Dayton. CAST: Jaque Gray, Paul D. Hunt, Porter Nielsen. LOC: St. George.

Further Back Slightly (Tanglewood Pictures Int'l). DIR: Brian James McGuire. CAST: Sasha Bauer, Janette Bloom, Kathleen Burke. LOC: Bonneville Salt Flats, Ogden. OL: Brookfield, Mineral Point, Milwaukee, WI; Dubuque, IO; Los Angeles, CA.

Hollow Point (Atlas Independent). DIR: Gonzalo Lopez-Gallego. CAST: Patrick Wilson, Lynn Collins, Ian McShane. LOC: Salt Lake City, Toolele.

Independence Day: Resurgence (20th Century Fox). DIR: Roland Emmrich. CAST: Liam Hemsworth, Jeff Goldblum, Bill Pullman. LOC: Bonneville Salt Flats (final battle). OL: West Wendover, NV; Albuquerque, NM (studios); Tower Bridge, London; Dubai, UAE; Marina Bay Sands, Singapore.

K-9 Adventures: Legend of the Lost Gold (Escapology/Wulf-Gorley Prods.). DIR: Stephen Shimek. CAST: Luke Perry, Brooke Langton, Ariana Bagley. LOC: Heber City.

Knife Party for Kiaserman (Psycho Boy Prods.). DIR: Trevor Leathem. CAST: Wayne Douglass, Bryan Draper, Jake Harper. LOC: Logan.

The Light Express (Willwood Prods.). DIR: Pamela Lockwood. CAST: Josh Francis, Tina Francis, Elijah Ford. LOC: Salt Lake City (Studio TEN05).

Love Everlasting (Wheelie Films). DIR: Rob Diamond. CAST: Emily Procter, Christie Burke, Lucky Blue Smith. LOC: Utah.

Minor (Paradise Pictures, Canada). DIR: Sam Catalfamo. CAST: Elissa Mielke, Alana DeVito, Elliott Jones. LOC: Monument Valley. OL: Toronto, Niagara Falls, Canada; Los Angeles, Malibu, CA; Alamogordo, White Sands, NM; Las Vegas, Hoover Dam, NV; Nashville, Memphis, TN.

On the Horizon (Y-US Prods., Canada/ France). DIR: Pascal Payant. CAST: Jessica Morris, Jade Harlow, Tyler Johnson. LOC: Utah. OL: Texas, France.

Punk's Dead: SLC Punk 2 (Liberty Spikes Prods.). DIR: James Merendino. CAST: Machine Gun Kelly, Devon Sawa, Hannah Marks. LOC: Salt Lake City.

Riot (Mainstay Prods.). DIR: John Lyde. CAST: Matthew Reese, Dolph Lundgren, Danielle C. Ryan. LOC: Salt Lake City.

Saturday's Warrior (Azevedo Studios). DIR: Michael Buster. CAST: Jacob Buster, Baileyy Michelle Johnson, Monica Moore Smith. LOC: Midvale, Ogden, Orem, Salt Lake City.

The Search for Simon (Gothic Manor, UK). DIR: Martin Gooch. CAST: Millie Reeves, Sophie Aldred, Julian Batista. LOC: Utah. OL: London, England; Bornholm, Denmark.

Secondhand Hearts (HI Integrated Prods.). DIR: Austin Everett. CAST: Ben Isaacs, Mallory Corinne, Allie Rae Treharne. LOC: Utah. OL: Kyoto, Japan.

Slender (Parking Garage Pictures). DIR: Joel Petrie. CAST: Joel Petrie, Dan Shovaers, Mili Parks. LOC: Salt Lake City.

Sonita (TAG/TRAUM Filmproduktion, Germany). DIR: Rokhsaareh Ghaem Maghami. CAST: Sonita Alizadeh, Latifa Alizadeh, Fadia Alizadeh. LOC: Utah. OL: San Francisco, CA; Tehran, Iran; Herat, Kabul, Afghanistan.

Touched With Fire (40 Acres & a Mule Filmworks). DIR: Paul Dalio. CAST: Katie Holmes, Luke Kirby, Christine Lahti. LOC: Utah. OL: New York, NY.

Vengeance (ITN Pictures). DIR: Gil Medina. CAST: Danny Trejo, 50 Cent, Houston Alexander. LOC: Salt Lake City. OL: Hollywood, Los Angeles CA.

Waffle Street (6 Foot Films). DIR: Eshom Nelms, Ian Nelms. CAST: James Lafferty, Danny Glover, Julie Gonzalo. LOC: Lehi (diner), Salt Lake City.

We All Fall Down (Arrowstorm Entertainment). DIR: Kurt Knight. CAST: David Phillip Fishman, Cardiff Gerhardt, Stephanie Guzman. LOC: Utah.

West of Her (Corner Piece Prods.). DIR: Ethan Warren. CAST: Ryan Caraway, Kelsey Slepser, Halli Herzog. LOC: Monument Valley. OL: Arizona, Colorado, Illinois, South Dakota, Tennessee, Wyoming.

Zen Dog (Future Park). DIR: Rick Darge. CAST: Kyle Gallner, Adam Herschman, Celia Diane. LOC: Salt Lake City. OL: California, Colorado, Illinois, Iowa, Michigan, Nebraska, New York, Pennsylvania.

Television:

12 Gifts of Christmas (Mayor Entertainment/ Hallmark Channel). DIR: Peter Sullivan. CAST: Katrina Law, Aaron O'Connell, Donna Mills. LOC: Provo (ice staking rink), Salt Lake City.

Hot Bot (Netflix). DIR: Michael Polish. CAST: Zach Pearlman, Doug Haley, Cynthia Kirchner. LOC: Salt Lake City; OL: Los Angeles, CA.

Ice Sharks (Syfy). DIR: Emile Edwin Smith. CAST: Edward DeRuiter, Jenna Parker, Kawi Lyman. LOC: Utah.

My Summer Prince (Mayor Entertainment/ Hallmark Channel). DIR: Peter Sullivan. CAST: Taylor Cole, Jack Turner, Lauren Holly. LOC: Park City.

Proper Manors (Ten Spoke Prods.). Various episodes. LOC: Ogden.

Westworld (Bad Robot/Jerry Weintraub Prods./HBO). Series. CAST: Evan Rachel Wood, Jeffrey Wright, Ed Harris. LOC: Dead Horse Point State Park, Moab, Monument Valley. OL: Kayenta, Monument Valley, AZ; Fillmore & Western Railroad, Newhall, Santa Clarita, Saugus, Simi Valley, Vasquez Rocks, CA.

You Again (DoYouSee Prods.). Series. CAST: Andrea Danee Peterson, Zachari Michael Reynolds, Troy Taylor. LOC: Salt Lake City.

You May Now Kill the Bride (Narrator Entertainment/Lifetime Television). DIR: Kohl Glass. CAST: Tammin Sursok, Ashley Newbrough, Ricky Myers. LOC: Salt Lake City.

2017:

6 Below: Miracle on the Mountain (Dune Entertainment/Sony). DIR: Scott Waugh. CAST: Josh Hartnett, Mira Sorvino, Sarah Dumont. LOC: Utah.

An Hour Behind (Silver Peak Prods./ SunWorld Pictures). DIR: Brian Brough. CAST: Emily Rose, Barry Watson, Casey Elliott. LOC: Provo, Pleasant Grove.

Before Your Time (Community Film Project). DIR: Lucas James McGraw. CAST: Landon Kasten, Roni D. Nybo, Erin Black. LOC: Bountiful, Centerville, Farmington, Kaysville, Layton.

Bigfoot at Millcreek (Whitley Entertainment). DIR: Devin Hansen. CAST: Devin Hansen, Mark Blockovich, Sheila Orey Sorensen. LOC: Millcreek Township, Salt Lake County, Wasatch National Forest.

Brigsby Bear (3311 Prods./Sony Pictures). DIR: Dave McCary. CAST: Kyle Mooney, Mark Hamill, Jorge Lendeborg, Jr. LOC: Salt Lake City.

Cataract Gold (Paul Kiener Prods.). DIR: Paul Kiener. CAST: Bryan Hanna, Morgan James, Dale Shane. LOC: Cataract Canyon, Glen Canyon Nat'l Recreation

Area, Utah; Borrego Springs, Indio, CA.
Monolith (Sky Italia). DIR: Ivan Silvestrini. CAST: Katrina Bowden, Katherine Kelly Lang, Brandon W. Jones. LOC: Utah.
My Brother Was a Time Traveler (Main Dog Prods./Purdie Dist.). DIR: Jake Van Wagoner. CAST: Maclain Nelson, Jake Van Wagoner, Clare Neiderpruem. LOC: Mt. Pleasant.
The Jade Pendant (Lotus Entertainment). DIR: Po-Chi Leong. CAST: Godfrey Gao, Clara Lee, Tzi Ma. LOC: Utah.
The Last Days of Billy the Kid (Forbesfilm/ITN). DIR: Christopher Forbes. CAST: William Adams, Jezibell Anat, Daniel Brahim. LOC: Utah. OL: Augusta, GA; Love Valley, NC; Brunson, SC; Flint Hills, KS.
The Space Between Us (STX Entertainment). DIR: Peter Chelsom. CAST: Gary Oldman, Asa Butterfield, Carla Gugino. LOC: Utah. OL: Albuquerque, NM (Albuquerque Convention Center, Highland High School, Central New Mexico Community College); Las Vegas, NV.
The Stray (Universal Home Entertainment). DIR: Mitch Davis. CAST: Michael Cassidy, Sarah Lancaster, Connor Corum. LOC: Utah.
Tim Timmerman: Hope of America (VidAngel Studios). DIR: Cameron Sawyer. CAST: Andrew Caldwell, Stephanie Drapeau, Monica Moore Smith. LOC: Sandy (Alta High School).
Under the Bed (Appian Way). DIR: Daniel Myrick. CAST: Hannah New, Beverly D'Angelo, Alexis Krause. LOC: Salt Lake City.
We Love You, Sally Carmichael (GoFilms/KOAN). DIR: Christopher Gorham. CAST: Christopher Gorham, Elizabeth Tulloch, Felicia Day. LOC: Heber; Provo: Pioneer Books.
Wind River (Acacia Filmed Entertainment). DIR: Taylor Sheridan. CAST: Kelsey Asbille, Jeremy Renner, Julia Jones. LOC: Summit & Wasatch Counties (mountain scenes), Coalville (county courthouse), Snowbird (Hidden Peak). OL: Wind River Indian Reservation, Lander, Fremont County, WY.
Television:
Andie Mack (Disney Channel). Series. CREATOR: Terri Minsky. CAST: Peyton Elizabeth Lee, Joshua Rush, Sofia Wylie. LOC: Salt Lake City (Wasatch Jr. High).
Chameleon Shadow (Amazon.com). DIR: Samuel Mills. CAST: Claudia Bethers, Louis Burkhardt, Kristin Caron. LOC: Salt Lake City.
Deidra & Laney Rob a Train (General Population/Netflix). DIR: Sydney Freeland. CAST: Ashleigh Murray, Rachel Crow, Lance Gray. LOC: Ogden, Orem, Park City, Salt Lake City (Judge Memorial Catholic High School).
Enchanted Christmas (Mission Pictures Int'l/Hallmark Channel). DIR: Terry Cunningham. CAST: Alexa PenaVega, Carlos PenaVega, Rene Rivera. LOC: Midway (Zermatt Resort).
The Landlord (Imoto Prods./Lifetime Network). DIR: Daniel Ringey. CAST: Ted McGinley, Molly McCook, Jack Turner. LOC: Salt Lake City.
Love at First Glance (Crown Media Prods./Hallmark Channel). DIR: Kevin Connor. CAST: Amy Smart, Adrian Grenier, Jonathan Bennett. LOC: Salt Lake City.
Sharing Christmas (Mayor Entertainment/Hallmark Channel). DIR: Peter Sullivan. CAST: Ellen Hollman, Bobby Campo, Cynthia Gibb. LOC: Salt Lake City (Trolley Square).
Switched for Christmas (Cartel Pictures/Hallmark Channel). DIR: Lee Friedlander. CAST: Candace Cameron Bure, Elon Bailey, Mark Deklin. LOC: Salt Lake City (Temple Square, Kim's Chop & Oyster House).

2018:

The Actor (Avanoir Films). DIR: Bijan Daryani. CAST: Bijan Daryani, Kaye Tuckerman, Harry Aspinwall. LOC: Grantsville (Salt Flats). OL: California, Illinois, Nevada, New York.
All About Books—The Movie (Caps Media Ventura). DIR: Joseph Bagley. CAST: John Alarid, Joseph Bagley, Karen Bagley. LOC: Virgin. OL: California; Africa: Zimbabwe.
Bigfoot at Millcreek 2: Dead End (Whitley Entertainment). DIR: Devin Hansen. CAST: Mark Blockovich, Yvonne D. Bennett, Cindy Manwill. LOC: Riverton, Salt Lake City.
Dead Trigger (Aldamisa Entertainment). DIR: Mike Cuff, Scott Windhauser. CAST: Dolph Lundgren, Autumn Resser, Romeo Miller. LOC: St. George (opening scene). OL: Cancun, Mexico.
Fear Level (Inglewood Films). DIR: J.D. Allen. CAST: Jaylon Allen, Jshaun Allen, McKenzie Arviso. LOC: Salt Lake City.
The Good Journey (Silver Hills Pictures). DIR: Tom Whitus. CAST: Nathan Todaro, Jeff Prater, Meredith Frankie Crutcher. LOC: Moab, Cedar City. OL: California, Colorado, Illinois, Kansas, Kentucky.
Hello I Love You (Otay Prods.). DIR: Spanky Dustin Ward. CAST: Ben Jarvis, Kabrina Miller, Weston Roberts. LOC: Salt Lake City.
Hereditary (PalmStar Media/A24). DIR: Ari Aster. CAST: Alex Wolff, Gabriel Byrne, Toni Collette. LOC: Salt Lake City, Sandy, Park City: Utah Film Studios.
I Don't Speak English (Do It Now Pictures). DIR: Jorge Ramirez Rivera. CAST: Nathan Smith Jones, Jorge Cervera, Jr., Leslie Garza. LOC: Salt Lake City. OL: Arizona, California.
In Emma's Footsteps (Foundation Films). DIR: Brittany Wiscombe. CAST: Shona Moyer, Anne Sward, Liz Christensen. LOC: Salt Lake City: This is the Place Pioneer Village.
The Infection (Lowder Entertainment). DIR: Keros Lowder. CAST: Cam Findley, Kyle Fotheringham, Cherie Julander. LOC: Salt Lake City.
In Memory Of (Wicked Pixel Pictures). DIR: Eric Stanze. CAST: Jackie Kelly, Jason Christ, Adam Ahlbrandt. LOC: Bluff, Moab. OL: Arizona Missouri, New Mexico, Oklahoma, Texas.
In Searching (Heart-Beat Prods.). DIR: Kush Mudy. CAST: Jake Borelli, Jacob Grodnik, Aley Underwood. LOC: Park City.
The Invisible Man (Homeward Pictures/Universal Home Entertainment). DIR: Rocky Brunswork. LOC: Park City: Deer Valley Resort; Midway.
Jane and Emma (Excel Entertainment). DIR: Chantelle Squires. CAST: Danielle Deadwyler, Emily Goss, Brad Schmidt. LOC: Salt Lake City. OL: Illinois: Nauvoo.
Juarez 2045 (Abrupt Films). DIR: Chris Le. CAST: Danny Trejo, Alexander P. Heartman, Brad Schmidt. LOC: Salt Lake City.
Little Women (Main Dog Prods.). DIR: Clare Neiderpruem. CAST: Sarah Davenport, Lea Thompson, Allie Jennings. LOC: Salt Lake City.
Metal Edge Assassin Team: A Double Shot of Whiskey (NRV Media). DIR: Daniel Jesse. CAST: Tracy Dickinson, Jamie Garzarelli, Daniel Jesse. LOC: Salt Lake City.
Not Cinderella's Type (Silver Peak Prods.). DIR: Brian Brough. CAST: Paris Warner, Tim Flynn, Tanner Gillman. LOC: Utah.
Nuuvu Thopu Raa (United Films). DIR: Harinath Babu B. CAST: Sudhakar Komakula, Nirosha, Nitya Shetty. LOC: Salt Lake City. OL: Hyderabad, India.
The Original Play (James Play) DIR: Glen David Miller, Alix Maria Taulbee. CAST: C. Thomas Howell, Greg Duke, Alex Maria

Taulbee. LOC: Salt Lake City. OL: California.
Thrasher Road (Betwixtnbetween Films). DIR: Samantha Davidson Green. CAST: Allison Brown, Christian Kohn, Joe Rogers. LOC: Monticello. OL: Arizona, California, Colorado, Kansas, Mississippi, Missouri, New York, Tennessee, Vermont.
Time Freak (QC Entertainment). DIR: Andrew Bowler. CAST: Asa Butterfield, Sophie Turner, Skyler Gisando. LOC: Salt Lake City: University of Utah.
Trash on Mars (Nyasa Films Int'l). DIR: Benjamin Tucek. CAST: Petra Nesvactlova, Halka Trasnakova, Tereza Tresnakova. LOC: Hanksville.
Trek: The Movie (Purdie Distribution). DIR: Alan Peterson. CAST: Austin R. Grant, Joel Bishop, Stefania Barr. LOC: Centerville, Erda, Lakepoint, Moab (Colorado River), Porterville.
Unexpected Race (Wolf Prods. UT). DIR: Stephen Groo. CAST: James Alexander, Micah Dahl Anderson, Brandon Arnold. LOC: Provo. OL: California.
West of Her (Corner Piece Prods.). DIR: Ethan Warren. CAST: Ryan Caraway, Kelsey Slepser, Halli Herzog. LOC: Monument Valley. OL: Chicago, IL; Grand Canyon Nat'l Park, Kayenta, Phoenix, AZ; Midland, Mitchell, SD; Guernsey, WY; Leadville, CO; Memphis, TN.
Zen Dog (Future Park). DIR: Rick Darge. CAST: Kyle Gallner, Adam Herschman, Celia Diane. LOC: Salt Lake City. OL: Los Angeles, San Francisco, Sausalito, CA; Reno, NV; Denver, CO; Omaha, NE; New York, NY; Chicago, IL; Dubuque, IO; Pittsburgh, PA; Detroit, MI.

Television:

Christmas Made to Order (Production Media Films). Movie. DIR: Sam Irvin. CAST: Alexa PenaVega, Jonathan Bennett, Joe Marie Payton. LOC: Salt Lake City.
Christmas Wonderland (Production Media Films). Movie. DIR: Sean Olson. DIR: Emily Osment, Ryan Rottam, Kelly Hu. LOC: Layton: Layton High School; Salt Lake City: Hope Gallery and Museum of Fine Art; Bountiful: Whisperwood & Co. Crafts. OL: Pennsylvania.
Jingle Belle (Production Media Films). Movie. DIR: Peter Sullivan. CAST: Tatyana Ali, Cornelius Smith, Jr., Loretta Devine. LOC: Brigham City.
My Christmas Inn (Production Media Films). Movie. DIR: Peter Sullivan. CAST: Tia Mowry-Hardrict, Rob Mayes, Jackee Harry. LOC: Salt Lake City.
Westworld (Bad Robot). Series. CREATOR: Lisa Joy. CAST: Thandiwe Newton, Jeffrey Wright, Ed Harris. EPISODES: 10. Aired April 22 through June 24. LOC: Kanab, Coral Pink Sand Dunes State Park; Moab, Dead Horse Point State Park; Monument Valley. OL: Southern California.
Yellowstone (Linson Entertainment/101 Studios/Paramount Network). Series. Season 1. CREATORS: John Linson & Taylor Sheridan. CAST: Kevin Costner, Luke Grimes, Kelly Reilly, Wes Bentley. EPISODES: 9. Aired June 20 through August 22. LOC: Park City: Utah Film Studios; Oakley: Thousand Peaks Ranch; Kamas, Salt Lake City, Grantsville, Ogden, Uinta National Forest. OL: Montana: Chief Joseph Ranch, Darby.

2019:

1 Versus 100 (Infinite Spiral) DIR: Bruno Straus. CAST: Anna McClean, Nancy Nezbit, Charlo Bocchicchio. LOC: Salt Lake City, Park City.
4K Killer (Hawk VS Truck Prods.). DIR: Channing Lowe. CAST: Trisha Adams, Cate Allen, Rosalie Bertrand. LOC: Utah.
6 Underground (Skydance Media). DIR: Michael Bay. CAST: Ryan Reynolds, Melanie Laurent, Manuel Garcia-Rulfo. LOC: Glen Canyon (opening plane flight)
Aspen 1989 for the 31st Century Part 1 (Hollywood Global Studios). DIR: Emile Razpopov. CAST: Mickey Hiatt, Claud Rush, Richard Rust. LOC: Bryce Canyon National Park. OL: California, Colorado.
Aspen 1989 for the 31st Century Part II (Hollywood Global Studios). DIR: Emile Razpopov. CAST: Mickey Hiatt, Dessie Markovsky, Emile Razpopov. LOC: Bryce Canyon National Park. OL: California, Colorado.
Burying Yasmeen (Ambulatin' Entertainment). DIR: Phillip Clark Davis. CAST: Mike Langer, Elena Tovar, Jason Lott. LOC: Utah. OL: California.
The Christmas Cabin (Quantum Arc Media). DIR: Dustin J. Robinson. CAST: Petton McDavitt, Chad Michael Collins, Gina St. John. LOC: St. George. OL: California, Nevada.
The Directive (Future of Film Prods.). DIR: Alexander Raye Pimentel. CAST: Kyle Abraham, Paul Askedall, Hashim Gari. LOC: Cisco.
The Fighting Preacher (Remember Films). DIR: T.C. Christensen. CAST: David McConnell, Charly Boon, Kenna Dawn. LOC: Utah. OL: Palmyra, NY.
The Interviews (NICH Entertainment). DIR: Will Taylor. CAST: Daphne Ballanger, Gordy Ewell, Lane Ross. LOC: Salt Lake City.
The Last Bell . . . The First of Many (Wolfwind Prods.). DIR: Ray Goldrup. CAST: Jim Goldrup, Jeff Greenwalt, Tom Goldrup. LOC: Salt Lake City, Lehi City.
Links of Life (1Divided Films). DIR: Marie-Helene Roux. CAST: Marie Bunel, Rene Heger, Catherine Samie. LOC: Devil's Garden, Arches National Park. OL: Paris, France.
Love, Inheritance and Lunch (Hallmark Channel). DIR: Clare Neiderpruem. CAST: Erin Cahill, Trevor Donovan, Gregory Harrison. LOC: Provo, Heber City.
Matchmaker Christmas (Silver Peak Prods.). DIR: Brian Brough. CAST: Emily Rose, Corey Sevier, Melanie Nelson. LOC: Lindon: Wadley Farms.
Midsommar (A24). DIR: Ari Aster. CAST: Florence Pugh, Jack Reynor, Vilhelm Blomgren. LOC: Utah.
Nuuvu Thopu Raa (United Films/Whacked Out Media). DIR: Harinath Babu B. CAST: Sudhakar Komakula, Nirosha, Nitya Shetty. LOC: Salt Lake City. OL: Hyderabad, Telangana, India.
On the Corner of Ego and Desire (Indie Film Hustle). DIR: Alex Ferrari. CAST: Rob Alecia, Richard Botto, Adam Bowman. LOC: Park City: Sundance Film Festival.
Out of Liberty (Three Coin Prods.) DIR: Garrett Batty. CAST: Care Allen, Corbin Allred, Larry Bagby. LOC: American Fork: The Haunted Forest.
Prescription for Love (Candelight Media Group). DIR: Brian Brough. CAST: Jillian Murray, Trevor Donovan, Jillian Joy. LOC: Lehi: Thanksgiving Point; Provo: The Shops at Riverwoods.
Snatchers (MAKE GOOD Content). DIR: Stephen Cedars, Benji Kleinman. CAST: Mary Nepi, Gabrielle Elyse, J.J. Nolan. LOC: Utah; OL: Albuquerque, NM.
Stalker DIR: Devin K. Hansen. CAST: Stefania Barr, Yvonne Bennett, Som Sengphachanh. LOC: Salt Lake City, Midvale, South Jordan, Riverton.
Twice the Dream (S&S Prods.). DIR: Savannah Ostler. CAST: Monica Moore Smith, Mason D. Davis, Adrian R'Mante. LOC: Utah.
The Utah Cabin Murders (North Bank Entertainment). DIR: Andrew Jones.

CAST: Lee McQueen, Derek Nelson, Tiffany Ceri. LOC: Oakley. OL: Wales, UK.

Valley of the Gods (Royal Road Entertainment). DIR: Lech Majewski. CAST: Josh Hartnett, John Malcovich, Berenice Marlohe. LOC: Salt Lake City; OL: throughout Europe.

What a Show Show (David Brothers). DIR: David Brothers. CAST: Cate Allen, Patrick de Freitas, Ivonna Earnest. LOC: Salt Lake City.

Television:

Check Inn to Christmas (Hybrid). Movie. D: Sam Irvin. CAST: Rachel Boston, Wes Brown, Richard Karn. LOC: Ogden. OL: California: Los Angeles.

Christmas Hotel (Hybrid/Lifetime Television). Movie. DIR: Tatyana Ali. CAST: Tatyana Ali, Sean Patrick Thomas, Sheryl Lee Ralph. LOC: Salt Lake City: Peery Hotel; Midway.

High School Musical: The Musical: The Series: The Special (Chorus Boy/ Disney+). Series. DIR: Clayton Cogswell. CAST: Joshua Bassett, Corbin Bleu, Matt Cornett. LOC: Salt Lake City.

High School Musical: The Musical: The Series: The Holiday Special (Chorus Boy/Disney+). Series. DIR: Tim Federle. CAST: Olivia Rodrigo, Joshua Bassett, Matt Cornett. LOC: Salt Lake City.

High School Musical: The Musical: The Series (Bell the Cat/Disney Channel). Series. CREATOR: Tim Federle. Season 1. 10 episodes. Aired November 8, 2019 through January 10, 2020. CAST: Olivia Rodrigo, Joshua Bassett, Matt Cornett. LOC: Salt Lake City: East High School.

Resilience and the Lost Gems (Area of Effect). Movie. DIR: Brian Finn. CAST: Kiara Finn, Brian Finn, Don Shanks. LOC: Castle Dale, San Rafael Swell, Skull Valley.

The Road Home for Christmas (Hybrid). Movie. DIR: Peter Sullivan. CAST: Maria Sokoloff, Rob Mayes, Marie Osmond. LOC: Salt Lake City, Farmington.

Staging Christmas (Production Media Films/Showtime). Movie. DIR: Eitan Almagor. CAST: Soleil Moon Frye, George Stults, Jaleel White. LOC: Ogden.

Timeless Love (Candlelight Prods.) Movie. DIR: Brian Brough. CAST: Rachel Scarsten, Brian Daughtery, Jill Adler. LOC: American Fork; Wadley Farms, Lindon; Aspenwood Manor, Provo; Utah Valley Hospital, Provo; Utah Valley University, Orem.

Yellowstone (Linson Entertainment/101 Studios/Paramount Network). Series. Season 2. CREATORS: John Linson &Taylor Sheridan. Series. CAST: Kevin Costner, Luke Grimes, Kelly Reilly, Wes Bentley. CAST: Kevin Costner, Luke Grimes, Kelly Reilly, Wes Bentley. EPISODES: 10. Aired June 19 through August 28. LOC: Park City: Utah Film Studios; Oakley: Thousand Peaks Ranch; Kamas; Grantsville; Salt Lake City; Ogden; Uinta National Forest. OL: Montana: Chief Joseph Ranch, Darby.

2020:

The 13th Cross (Space Titanium Prods.). DIR: Joseph DeGoyler. CAST: Eric Wood, Chelsea Jurkiewicz, Melanie Browning. LOC: Provo.

Black Beauty (Bolt Pictures/Disney). DIR: Ashley Avis. CAST: Kate Winslet, MacKenzie Foy, Iain Glen. LOC: Utah. OL: South Africa.

The Christmas Bow (Hallmark Movie & Mysteries). DIR: Clare Neiderpruem. CAST: Lucia Micarelli, Michael Rady, James Saito. LOC: Provo; Pleasant Grove: Evermore Park.

The Christmas Project Reunion (Infinity Rising). DIR: Brad Johnson. CAST: Corbin Bernsen, Daniel Baldwin, Brian Bosworth. LOC: Utah Valley.

City of Salt (Zepstone Media). DIR: Alicia Oberle Farmer, John D. Farmer. CAST: Charla Bocchicchio, Kayli Brummer, Wren Barnes. LOC: Salt Lake City.

Echo Boomers (Speakeasy). DIR: Seth Savoy. CAST: Michael Shannon, Patrick Schwarzenegger, Lesley Ann Warren. LOC: Salt Lake City. OL: Los Angeles, Chicago.

High School Musical: The Musical: The Holiday Special (Chorus Boy). DIR: Tim Federle. CAST: Olivia Rodrigo, Joshua Bassett, Matt Cornett. LOC: Salt Lake City.

Into the Soul (Stone Chapel Films). DIR: Scott Lambson. CAST: Ayden Tyler Hatch, McKenna Flory, Jack Karl. LOC: Utah.

Joe Bell (Argent Pictures). DIR: Reinaldo Marcus Green. CAST: Mark Wahlberg, Reid Miller, Gary Sinese. LOC: Salt Lake City.

The Killing of Two Lovers (Back 40 Pictures). DIR: Robert Machoian. CAST: Clayne Crawford, Sepideh Moafi, Chris Coy. LOC: Kanosh.

My Heart Can't Beat Until You Tell It To (Dualist). DIR: Jonathan Cuartas. CAST: Patrick Fugit, Ingrid Sophie Schram, Owen Campbell. LOC: Salt Lake City.

Married and Loving It! (New Ogden Cinema). DIR: Ryan McDonald. CAST: Michael Solarez, Nicole Finney, Demetrius Daniels. LOC: Ogden.

My Summer in the Chair (Amazon Prime Video). DIR: Nic Hale. CAST: Tucker Johnson, Aiden Kane, Robyn Lefler. LOC: Lehi.

The Night Clerk (Convergent Media). DIR: Michael Cristofer. CAST: Tye Sheridan, Ana de Armas, Helen Hunt. LOC: Tooele, Draper; Salt Lake City: Vape Ave & Smoke Shop; Provo: Provo Towne Center Mall.

Nine Days (30WEST). DIR: Edson Oda. CAST: Winston Duke, Zazie Beets, Bill Skarsgard. LOC: Salt Lake City: Abravanel Hall, Knolls Recreation Area, Saltair, West High School. OL: Sao Paolo, Brazil.

Phobic (Pale Moon Entertainment). DIR: Bryce Clark. CAST: Ernie Lively, Jacque Gray, Heather Beers. LOC: Salt Lake City.

A Reason (NICH Entertainment). DIR: Will Taylor. CAST: Ryan Patrick. LOC: Salt Lake City. LOC: Salt Lake City.

Shred of Decency DIR: Dan Fowlks. CAST: Stephen Harr, Charly Gledhill, Coby Oram. LOC: Pine Valley.

Simmer (Vibe Pictures). DIR: Nic Rush, Stephan van de Graaf. CAST: Marsuvio Sanchez, Richard Keep, Eliana Sua. LOC: Salt Lake City.

Ten Deaths of Hamlet (Controversial Entertainment). DIR: Ryan Davy. CAST: Antonio Lexerot, Barrett Ogden, Taylor Prue. LOC: Provo.

They Live Inside Us (Witching Season Films). DIR: Michael Ballif. CAST: James Morris, Hailey Nebeker, Stevie Dust. LOC: Nephi: The Booth House.

The Truth About Us (Make it Matter Pictures). DIR: Jason White. CAST: Pamela Beheshti, Marilee Crockett, Kate Heward. LOC: Ogden. OL: Ecola State Park, OR.

The Wolf of Snow Hollow (Orion Classics). DIR: Jim Cummings. DIR: Jim Cummings, Riki Lundhome, Robert Forster. LOC: Salt Lake City, Coalville, Echo, Solitude Ski Resort.

Television:

The Christmas Edition (Hybrid). Movie. DIR: Peter Sullivan. CAST: Carly Hughes, Rob Mays, Marie Osmond. LOC: Huntsville Astronomic & Lunar Observatory, Huntsville.

Christmas Tree Lane (Hallmark Movies & Mysteries). Movie. DIR: Steven R. Monroe. CAST: Alicia Witt, Andrew Walker, Shannon Engemann. LOC: Provo, Payson.

A Crafty Christmas Romance (Silver Peak Prods.). Movie. DIR: Brian Brough. CAST: Nicoloa Posener, Brad Johnson,

Benny Grames. LOC: Provo: The Shops at Riverwoods, Moon's Rare Books; Payson: Payson High School, Eli's Old Fashioned Ice Cream; Mapleton.

Dashing in December (The Ninth House). Movie. DIR: Jake Helgren. CAST: Peter Porte, Juan Pablo Di Pace, Andie MacDowell. LOC: Salt Lake City, Heber, Midway.

Yellowstone (Linson Entertainment/101 Studios/Paramount Network). Series. Season 3. CREATORS: John Linson & Taylor Sheridan. CAST: Kevin Costner, Luke Grimes, Kelly Reilly, Wes Bentley. EPISODES: 10. Aired June 21 to August 23, 2020. LOC: Park City: Utah Film Studios; Oakley: Thousand Peaks Ranch; Kamas; Grantsville; Salt Lake City; Ogden; Uinta National Forest.

2021:

The Abstergo Tapes (Yoldasi Films). DIR: Evann Kascinde. CAST: Chills, Aaron Faberbach, Gabriel Feberbach. LOC: Salt Lake City.

Avocado Toast (Good Coyote Films). DIR: Tyler Farr. CAST: Justin Ray, Joe Burns, Mikayla Iverson. LOC: Utah.

Bookworm and the Beast (Candlelight Media Group). DIR: Brandon Ho. CAST: Nicole Posoner, Jake Stormoen, Jill Adler. LOC: Utah.

The Canyonlands (Sadieland Films). DIR: Brendan Devane. CAST: Steph Barklay, Marqus Bobesich, Wayne Charles Baker. LOC: Moab.

Covid Release (Yellow Brick Studio). DIR: Eric Nemoto. CAST: Rebecca Lea McCarthy, T.C. Smith, James Roberts. LOC: Salt Lake City. OL: Georgia, Hawaii.

Even in Dreams (S&S Prods.). DIR: Savannah Ostler. CAST: Alison Arngrim, Monica Moore Smith, Savannah Ostler. LOC: Utah.

Faith, Hope, Love (Group 6 Films). DIR: Michael Flynn. CAST: Mason D. Davis, Alex Diaz, Kelsi Elana. LOC: Provo: Sundance Resort.

Miracle Valley (Sestero Pictures). DIR: Greg Sestero. CAST: Angela Mariano, Rick Edwards, Greg Sestero. LOC: Miracle Valley Canyon, Lake Powell. OL: Arizona.

Mistletoe Mixup (Mistletoe Mixup). DIR: Andrew Lawrence. CAST: Danielle C. Ryan, Joey Lawrence, Matthew Lawrence. LOC: Midway: Kringle's Christmas Shop, Midway Bakery on Main, Café Galleria; Heber City: Holiday Lanes; Daniel.

Never Seen Again (LeMonds Pictures). DIR: Devin K. Hansen. CAST: Kayli Brummer, Cystal Harris, Michele Willis. LOC: Utah.

The Parker Sessions (New Western Film Co.). DIR: Stephen Simmons. CAST: Rachel Sean, Danny James, Gil Wheatley. LOC: Salt Lake City.

Pleasant Grove (Pancreas Prods.). DIR: Harrison Koford. CAST: Naomi Winders, Harrison Koford, Kimille Cherie. LOC: Provo, Vineyard, Orem.

Project Alderaan (Vimeo). DIR: Will Terry, Tristen Tharp. CAST: Enoch Marshall, Chad Grady Saunders, Ryan Saunders. LOC: Salt Lake City. OL: Idaho: Idaho Falls.

Queen Pins (AGC Studios). DIR: Aron Gaudet, Gita Pullapilly. CAST: Kristen Bell, Lidia Porto, Joel McHale. LOC: Salt Lake City. OL: Arizona, California, Nevada, Washington, DC.

Stop and Go (Soro Films). DIR: Mallory Everton, Stephen Meek. CAST: Whitney Call, Mallory Everton, Julia Jolley. LOC: Utah.

Sweet Pecan Summer (Hallmark Prods.). DIR: Dustin Rikert. CAST: Christine Ko, Wes Brown, Lauren Tom. LOC: Salt Lake City, Riverton, Hurricane.

Television:

The Chosen (Loaves & Fishes Prods./Angel Studios). Series. CREATOR: Dallas Jenkins. CAST: Jonathan Roumie, Paras Patel, Elizabeth Tabish. EPISODES: 8. Aired April 4 to July 11, 2021. LOC: Goshen: The Church of Jesus Christ of Latter-day Saints Motion Picture Studio South (Jerusalem set and surrounding property). OL: Midlothian & Weatherford, TX.

High School Musical: The Musical: The Series (Bell the Cat/Disney Channel). Series. CREATOR: Tim Federle. Season 2. EPISODES: 12. Aired from May 14 to July 30, 2021. CAST: Olivia Rodrigo, Joshua Bassett, Matt Cornett. LOC: Salt Lake City: East High School.

Hot Chocolate Holiday (Silver Peak Prods.). Movie. DIR: Brian Brough. CAST: Aubrey Reynolds, Jonny Swenson, Kelsie Elena. LOC: Provo: The Shops at Riverwoods.

Lights, Camera, Romance (Silver Peaks Prods.). Movie. DIR: Brian Brough. CAST: Monica Moore Smith, Dan Fowlks, Mikayla Iverson. LOC: Provo: The Shops at Riverwoods, The Mighty Baker, Malawai's Pizza, Faktory, Bohme, Provo Marriott Hotel; Pleasant Grove: Water Garden Cinemas.

Love Lost and Found (Mainstay Prods./Candlelight Media Group). Movie. DIR: John Lyde. CAST: Trevor Donovan, Danielle C. Ryan, Melanie Stone. LOC: Utah.

Quarantine for Two (Tier 2 Media/Candlelight Media Group). Movie. DIR: Kels Goodman. CAST: Mason D. Davis, Ana Katia, Whitney Palmer. LOC: Orem.

Sister Swap: Christmas in the City (Crown Media Prods.). Movie. DIR: Sean McNamara. CAST: Ashley Williams, Kevin Nealon, Keith D. Robinson. LOC: Salt Lake City. OL: Vancouver, British Columbia, Canada.

Sister Swap: A Hometown Holiday (Hallmark Channel). Movie. DIR: Sean McNamara. CAST: Kimberly Williams-Paisley, Mark Deklin, Susan Yeagley. LOC: Salt Lake City. OL: Vancouver, British Columbia, Canada.

2022:

The Boy in the Tiny House and the Monster Who Lived Next Door (Housefire). DIR: Keith Ariaz. CAST: Caleb Hafen, Andre Alvarez, Jade Ariaz. LOC: Logan: Mountaincrest. OL: Los Angeles, CA; Fort Collins, CO.

Breaking Through (Beijing Hengyuan Entertainment). DIR: Fang Fang Wang. CAST: Meiqi Meng, Yu Xia, Kuishan Pei. LOC: Salt Lake City (Olympic Games). OL: Nagano, Japan; Heilongjiang, China.

The Chess Game (NICH Entertainment). DIR: Will Taylor. CAST: Gordy Ewell. LOC: Salt Lake City.

Cryo (Burgundie Pictures). DIR: Barrett Burgin. CAST: Jyllian Petrie, Emily Marie Palmer, Mason D. Davis. LOC: Provo.

Curse of the Crom: The Legend of Halloween (Firespire Prods./Premiere Entertainment Group). DIR: Rob York. CAST: Chelsea Jurkiewicz, Tanner Gillman, Colin Cunningham. LOC: Utah.

Falling for Christmas (Motion Picture Corp. of America). DIR: Janeen Damian. CAST: Lindsay Cohan, Chord Overstreet, George Young. LOC: Salt Lake City. Park City: Stein Erickson Lodge, North Star Lodge (interiors). West Jordan.

Halloween Ends (Bloomhouse Prods.). DIR: Jamie Lee Curtis, Andi Matichak, James Jude Courtney. LOC: Salt Lake City. OL: Savannah, Georgia (primary location).

Haul Out the Holly (Basset Hound Prods.). DIR: David Wulf. CAST: Lacey Chabert, Wes Brown, Stephen Tobolowsky. LOC: Salt Lake City: Cottonwood Heights.

Hunting Ava Bravo (MediaPro Studio). DIR: Gary Aurbach. CAST: Kate del Castillo, Marc

Blucas, Halem Medina. LOC: Park City.

Love in the Limelight (Crown Media Prods.). DIR: Ron Oliver. CAST: Alexa PenaVega, Carlos PenaVega, Ivonne Coll. LOC: Salt Lake City.

Lucy and Whitney (Kino Park Films). DIR: Parker Gehring. CAST: Naomi Winders, Sadie Veach, Susan Walker Gehring. LOC: Provo (interiors). OL: Washington.

Mr. Earth (Stone Chapel Films). DIR: Scott Lambson. CAST: Chandler Holloway, McKenna Flory, Kiera Saunders. LOC: Utah.

Murder at the Hive (Comedy Sandbox). DIR: JR Timothy. CAST: Bryson Alejandro, Brittany Breed, Adam Broud. LOC: Provo: The Hive Collaborative.

Other Monsters (Dirtfoot Films). DIR: Ben Lanoha. CAST: Alexander Holden, Chloe Farnworth, Kris Park. LOC: Salt Lake City.

Provo DIR: Emma Thatcher. CAST: Owais Ahmed, Pam Asen, Michael Brackney. LOC: Provo. OL: Illinois, Iowa, Nebraska, Wyoming.

Sherlock: The Musical (Chamber Media). DIR: Dallyn Vail Bayles, Stefan van de Graaff. CAST: Conlon Bonner, Kaden Caldwell, Paul Cartwright. LOC: American Fork: Chamber Media Studios.

Sick (Blumhouse Prods.) DIR: John Hyams. CAST: Gideon Aldon, Bethlehem Million, Dylan Sprayberry. LOC: Salt Lake City, Ogden, Weber State University.

Strong Enough (Kaleidoscope Pictures/ Gravitas Ventures). DIR: John Foss. CAST: Ashley Jerue, Demetrius Grosse, Jake Stormoen. LOC: Utah.

Television:

1923 (101 Studios/Paramount Network). Series. CREATOR: Taylor Sheridan. DIR: Ben Richardson. CAST: Helen Mirren, Harrison Ford, Brandon Sklenar. Season 1 Episode 2, "Nature's Empty Throne." LOC: Park City: Utah Film Studios (leopard hunt).

Beauty and the Billionaire (Silver Peak Prods./Candlelight Media Group). Movie. DIR: Brian Brough. CAST: Sashleigha Hightower, Chris Reid, Tanner Gillman. LOC:

The Chosen (Loaves & Fishes Prods./ Angel Studios). Series. CREATOR: Dallas Jenkins. CAST: Jonathan Roumie, Shahar Isaac, Paras Patel, Elizabeth Tabish. EPISODES: 8. LOC: Goshen: The Church of Jesus Christ of Latter-day Saints Motion Picture Studio South (Jerusalem exterior set and surrounding property). OL: Midlothian & Weatherford, TX.

High School Musical: The Musical: The Series. (Bell The Cat/Disney Channel). Series. CREATOR: Tim Federle. Season 4. EPISODES: 7. Aired August 2023. CAST: Joshua Bassett, Sofia Wylie, Dara Renee. LOC: Salt Lake City: East High School.

A Cozy Christmas Inn (Hybrid). Movie. DIR: Peter Sullivan. CAST: Jodi Sweetin, David O'Donnell, Vivica A. Fox. LOC: Huntsville Astronomic & Lunar Observatory.

Destined at Christmas (Silver Peak Prods.). Movie. DIR: Brittany Wiscombe. CAST: Shae Robins, Casey Elliott, Eve Elliott. LOC: Orem: University Place, Al's Sporting Goods; Provo: The Shops at Riverwoods; Springville: Springville Museum of Art; Rocky Ridge: Quality Craft Wood Work; Ogden: Ogden's George S. Eccles Dinosaur Park.

Destined at Christmas 2 (Silver Peak Prods.). Movie. DIR: Brittany Wiscombe. CAST: Shae Robins, Casey Elliott, Eve Elliott. LOC: Orem; Ogden: Ogden's George S. Eccles Dinosaur Park.

Haul Out the Holly (Basset Hound Prods./Hallmark Channel). Movie. DIR: Andy Sandberg. CAST: Lacey Chabert, Wes Brown, Stephen Tobolowsky. LOC: Cottonwood Heights.

The Holiday Stocking (Hallmark Entertainment). Movie. DIR: Roger M. Bobb. CAST: Nadine Ellis, Tamala Jones, B.J. Britt. LOC: Salt Lake City.

Love's Portrait (Silver Peak Prods./ Candlelight Media Group). Movie. DIR: John Lyde. CAST: Aubrey Reynolds, Richard McWilliams, Kathryn McKiernan. LOC: Utah.

2023:

April is Missing DIR: Eamonn Larsen. CAST: Liza Schoell, Melinda Yeaman, Syd Schoell. LOC: Provo, Salt Lake City.

Best Christmas Ever (Motion Picture Corporation of America). DIR: Mary Lambert. CAST: Heather Graham, Jason Biggs, Brandy Norwood. LOC: Payson.

Condor's Nest (MBG Films). DIR: Phil Blattenberger. CAST: Michael Ironside, Arnold Vosloo, Jackson Rathbone. LOC: Green River. OL: North Carolina, Peru, Texas.

The Death of Sisyphus (For Our Entertainment). DIR: Matthew Wade. CAST: James McKinney, Jason Sullivan, Matt Wade. LOC: Salt Lake City.

Devil's Men (COMv/KOAN). DIR: Dave Bresnahan, Weston Childers. CAST: Casey Elliott, Caleb Hafen, Dustin Harding. LOC: Utah. OL: Oklahoma.

The Dreaded Ballerinas DIR: Dallas Salyers. CAST: Keene Danza, Ethan McLain, Dylan Gilbert. LOC: Salt Lake City, South Jordan. OL: Kentucky.

The Graduates (Pinky Promise). DIR: Hannah Peterson. CAST: Musa Aden, Nicholas Anderson, Kaci Arena. LOC:

Grandpa's Crazy (Faranabrak). DIR: K. Danor Gerald. CAST: Mason D. Davis, Renny Grames, Dave Bresnahan. LOC: Tooele, Riverton, American Fork.

The Last Page (Rob Diamond Films/ Bridgestone Multimedia). DIR: Rob Diamond. CAST: Tara Berrett, Andrew Biasotti, Madison Bills. LOC: Utah.

Little Brother (Made by Limbo). DIR: Sheridan O'Donnell. CAST: Kevin Bransford, Daniel Diemer, Polly Draper. LOC: Arches National Park. OL: Idaho, New Mexico.

Scratchy, Cage and Tumbleweed (Faemearh). DIR: Chase Ramsey. CAST: Chase Ramsey, Joe Balanza, Colt Brown. LOC: Utah.

The Seeding (Unbranded Pictures/XYZ Films). DIR: Barnaby Clay. CAST: Scott Haze, Kate Lyn Sheil, Alex Montaldo. LOC: Kanab.

Television:

The Chosen (Loaves & Fishes Prods./ Angel Studios). Series. CREATOR: Dallas Jenkins. CAST: Jonathan Roumie, Shahar Isaac, Paras Patel, Elizabeth Tabish. EPISODES: 8. Aired December 11, 2022 to February 7, 2023. LOC: Goshen: The Church of Jesus Christ of Latter-day Saints Motion Picture Studio South (Jerusalem set and surrounding property). OL: Midlothian & Weatherford, TX.

Love in Zion National: A National Park Romance (Johnson Production Group). Movie. DIR: Sam Irvin. CAST: Cindy Busby, David Gridley, Raquel Gardner. LOC: Zion National Park.

PHOTO CREDITS

Bega Metzner: 307
Bette Larsen Stanton: 166
Bonnie Chamberlain Cutler/BYU Special Collections: 118 bottom
Bonnie Riding: 180 top; 185
BYU Special Collections: 1–3; 8; 11; 14–15; 18–19; 34–37; 40–41; 43–46; 50; 54–59; 60–61; 65; 71 right; 72–77; 80–83; 86 background; 87; 89–91; 93–95; 97 top; 98–99; 102–11; 117 top right; 119 bottom; 120 right; 122 bottom; 128; 129 top; 131; 133 top right, bottom left, and bottom right; 134; 136 bottom left; 137; 141–44; 147; 150; 154; 158 top; 160 left; 161–63; 167–69; 172; 173 top; 175–76; 178; 182–83; 186–87; 189–90; 192; 193 top right; 196–97; 200–203; 208–10; 212 top; 213 bottom; 214–15; 217; 219; 225; 228–30; 231 bottom; 232 bottom; 234 left; 235–36; 237 top right; 238–39; 242; 243 top; 246; 248–50; 252–53; 256 top; 259–61; 269–70; 273; 274
Carlo Gaberscek: 97 bottom left
Chris Hicks: 204–205; 213 top; 220 middle; 221; 243; 267; 268 top; 271
Cindi Pierce/Moab to Monument Valley Movie Museum: 256 bottom; 257; 260 bottom
Deseret News: 193 top left; 194 bottom; 195; 220 bottom; 224; 258; 262–63; 268 bottom; 272 top left and right; 299
Elizabeth Miller: 281
Ellen Schiess: 283; 284; 286; 287; 288; 289
George Eastman House: 63
George Schenck: 170
Harold Russell/J. L. Crawford: 62–64
Howard Pearson Papers/BYU Special Collections: 12; 227 top; 237 bottom left and bottom right; 265
J. L. Crawford: 32; 39
Jack Adams/BYU Special Collections: 184; 194 top; 199
Jackie Rife/BYU Special Collections: 160 right; 177
James D'Arc Collection: 300
Jean Adams Crosby/BYU Special Collections: 115–16; 120 left; 125; 133 top left
Kanab City Library: 114
Kanab Heritage Museum: 1; 121; 135 bottom left and right; 173 bottom; 179; 180 bottom; 181
Louise Parry Thomas: 20–23; 24–25; 28; 30–31
Marc Wanamaker/Bison Archives: 6; 10; 127; 158 bottom left and right
Marshall Moore: 276; 277 top and bottom; 279; 280; 285 top and bottom
Marvin Adams/BYU Special Collections: 100
Mary Gae Evans: 49 left
Moab to Monument Valley Movie Museum: 234 right
Morris Everett: 33; 42; 63; 117 bottom; 119 top; 145 bottom
Packy Smith: 96; 117 top left
Robert Johannes/BYU Special Collections: 217; 218
Rupert Ruesch/BYU Special Collections: 79
Scott Boyter: 188
Shafkat Anowar, *Deseret News*, 298
Taylor-Skewes Collection: 4; 226–27 bottom; 231 top; 233
Fred Hayes/©Territory Pictures, Inc: 303
Richard Foreman, Jr./©Territory Pictures, Inc: 8; 274–275; 305; 306
© 2023 The Chosen, Inc.: 290; 291; 293; 294 top and bottom
Twentieth Century-Fox: 5; 29; 48–49 right; 69–71; 112–113; 123 bottom; 124; 129 bottom; 130 bottom; 132; 135 top; 136 top and bottom right; 138–39; 148; 151; 152; 211; 222–23; 240–41; 244–46; 247
USC Cinematic Arts Library: 157; 159
Utah Film Studios: 302
Utah State Historical Society: 146; 155; 193 bottom
Zane Grey Papers/BYU Special Collections: 207
Zion National Park Museum: 26; 71 left

INDEX

JAMES V. D'ARC, PH.D., was born and raised in Glendale, California, where his fascination with classic films and interest in the film industry began. Earning degrees in history and motion picture history at Brigham Young University, he taught film courses there for 30 years while also serving, for 41 years, as curator of the BYU Motion Picture Archive at the university's L. Tom Perry Special Collections. D'Arc founded the BYU Film Music Archive, for which he produced a series of original motion picture soundtrack CDs, largely from the original recordings in the collection of famed composer Max Steiner that he acquired for BYU. He was also responsible for obtaining BYU's collections of correspondence, films, and memorabilia from Hollywood luminaries that include directors Cecil B. DeMille, Howard Hawks, Merian C. Cooper, and Henry Koster. D'Arc also programmed and hosted the BYU Motion Picture Archive Film Series for 18 years before his retirement in 2017.

WALT DISNEY PRODUCTIONS The APPLE DUMPLING GANG RIDES AGAIN
"HARRY IN YOUR POCKET!"
THE GIRL IN BLACK STOCKINGS
DE CARLO
TIMBUKTU
GEORGE STEVENS
THE GREATEST STORY EVER TOLD
ROBERT REDFORD
"JEREMIAH JOHNSON"
EPIC FRONTIER DRAMA
JOHN WAYNE
JOANNE DRU
JOHN AGAR
BEN JOHNSON
HARRY CAREY JR.
"SHE WORE A YELLOW RIBBON"
TECHNICOLOR
JOHN FORD
DOWN MILE AFTER TREACHEROUS MILE OF CHURNING RIVER FURY...
THROUGH A GAUNTLET OF INDIAN TERROR THEY FLED!
SMOKE SIGNAL
TECHNICOLOR
DANA ANDREWS PIPER LAURIE
REX REASON WILLIAM TALMAN
FRANK SINATRA DEAN MARTIN
PETER LAWFORD SAMMY DAVIS JR. JOEY BISHOP
SERGEANTS 3
One Will Die Tonight!
High Society Dames For Hire!
THE GIRL IN BLACK STOCKINGS
LEX BARKER ANNE BANCROFT MAMIE VAN DOREN RON RANDELL
JOHN FORD'S
My Darling Clementine
HENRY FONDA LINDA DARNELL VICTOR MATURE
WALTER BRENNAN
TIM HOLT
CATHY DOWNS
JOHN FORD
SAMUEL G. ENGEL
WALT DISNEY'S TEN WHO DARED
TECHNICOLOR
DASHING THIEVES OF BAGDAD...
riding out of the magic and splendor of
Arabian Nights
TECHNICOLOR
JON HALL MARIA MONTEZ SABU
An all NEW motion picture event—inspired by the novel "AIRPORT" by Arthur Hailey.
AIRPORT 1975
THE BLACK RAIDERS OUT OF THEIR FAR-FLUNG HIDEAWAYS!
ELLIOTT
A CHAPTER PLAY
"THE ELECTRIC HORSEMAN"
Tim HOLT
The FARGO KID
RAY WHITLEY
EMMETT LYNN
JANE DRUMMOND
He led the Apache Nation's wild revolt against Geronimo's pillaging hordes!
TAZA, SON OF COCHISE
TECHNICOLOR
ROCK HUDSON BARBARA RUSH

THUNDER in the VALLEY
TECHNICOLOR
LON McCALLISTER · EDMUND GWENN · PEGGY ANN GARNER
LOUIS KING
ROBERT BASSLER
20th CENTURY FOX
WHEN AMERICA'S FRONTIER FORT BECAME AN APACHE MASSACRE-GROUND!
FORT BOWIE
HOWARD HUGHES
JOHN WAYNE SUSAN HAYWARD
THE CONQUEROR
PONY EXPRES
Color by TECHNICOLOR
CHARLTON HESTON
RHONDA FLEMING
JAN STERLING
FORREST TUCKER
JOEL McCREA
VERONICA LAKE
DONALD CRISP
DON DeFORE
RAMROD
PRESTON FOSTER
ARLEEN WHELAN
CHARLIE RUGGLES
Will James'
SMOKY
Technicolor
FRED MacMURRAY
ANNE BAXTER
BURL IVES
LOUIS KING
ROBERT BASSLER
20th
STRANGE EXPERIENCE
ATTEMPTED MURDER
STAGECOACH
A WALTER WANGER Production · Directed by JOHN FORD
CLAIRE TREVOR · JOHN WAYNE
FRANK SINATRA DEAN MARTIN
PETER LAWFORD SAMMY DAVIS JR. JOEY BISHOP
SERGEANTS
EPIC FRONTIER DRAMA
John Ford's New and Finest Picture of the Fighting Cavalry!
JOHN WAYNE
JOANNE DRU
JOHN AGAR
BEN JOHNSON
HARRY CAREY, JR.
SHE WORE A YELLOW RIBBON
TECHNICOLOR
JOHN FORD
SULLIVAN
O'KEEFE
FREEMAN
JURADO
DRAGOON WELLS MASSACRE
CINEMASCOPE
THE DAY A THOUSAND DEVILS ROARED OUT OF AN APACHE HELL...
TROOPER HOOK
McCREA
STANWYCK
GREEN GRASS OF WYOMING
20th
THE DALTON GIRLS
ZANE GREY'S The VANISHING PIONEER
JACK HOLT
WILLIAM POWELL
FRED KOHLER
a Paramount Picture
GERONIMO
THE GIRL IN BLACK STOCKINGS
GLENN FORD · INGER STEVENS
HAMILTON
PETERSEN
A TIME FOR KILLING
The BIG CAT
TECHNICOLOR
FURY AT FURNACE CREEK
VICTOR MATURE
COLEEN GRAY · GLENN LANGAN · REGINALD GARDINER
BRUCE HUMBERSTONE
20th
FRED KOHLMAR
JOEL McCREA
VERONICA LAKE
DONALD CRISP
DON DeFORE
RAMROD
PRESTON FOSTER
ARLEEN WHELAN
CHARLIE RUGGLES